OLDER ADULTS
WITH DEVELOPMENTAL
DISABILITIES

This book is printed on recycled paper.

OLDER ADULTS WITH DEVELOPMENTAL DISABILITIES

OPTIMIZING CHOICE AND CHANGE

Edited by

Evelyn Sutton, M.A.
Institute for Life-Span Development and Gerontology
The University of Akron
Ohio

Alan R. Factor, Ph.D.
Illinois University Affiliated
  Program in Developmental
  Disabilities
College of Associated Health
  Professions
The University of Illinois at
  Chicago

Tamar Heller, Ph.D.
Illinois University Affiliated
  Program in Developmental
  Disabilities
College of Associated Health
  Professions
The University of Illinois at
  Chicago

Barbara A. Hawkins, Re.D.
School of Health, Physical
  Education and Recreation
Institute for the Study of
  Developmental Disabilities
Indiana University
  Bloomington

Gary B. Seltzer, Ph.D.
School of Social Work
  and
Program on Aging
  and Developmental
  Disabilities
Waisman Center
The University of
  Wisconsin—Madison

·P A U L·H·
BROOKES
PUBLISHING Cº

Baltimore • London • Toronto • Sydney

Paul H. Brookes Publishing Co.
P.O. Box 10624
Baltimore, Maryland 21285-0624

Copyright © 1993 by Paul H. Brookes Publishing Co., Inc.
All rights reserved.

Typeset by Brushwood Graphics, Inc., Baltimore, Maryland.
Manufactured in the United States of America by
Maple Press, York, Pennsylvania.

Library of Congress Cataloging-in-Publication Data
Older adults with developmental disabilities : optimizing choice and
    change / edited by Evelyn Sutton . . . [et al.].
        p.   cm.
    Includes bibliographical references and index.
    ISBN 1-55766-120-0
    1. Mentally handicapped aged—United States.   2. Mentally
handicapped aged—Services for—United States.   I. Sutton,
Evelyn.
HV3009.5.A3504   1993
362.1'968–dc20   92-47442
                                                          CIP

(British Library Cataloguing-in-Publication data are available from
the British Library.)

CONTENTS

CONTRIBUTORS

The researchers, consultants, administrators, and consumers who contributed to this volume are associates in the Rehabilitation Research and Training Center (RRTC) Consortium on Aging and Developmental Disabilities.

The Editors

Evelyn Sutton, M.A., Senior Fellow and Adjunct Professor, Institute for Life-Span Development and Gerontology, The University of Akron, 159 Carroll Hall, Akron, Ohio 44325-5007. Mrs. Sutton teaches courses in gerontology, with special interests in women's and family issues. Since 1982, she has also focused intensively on aging and developmental disabilities, conducting training events throughout Ohio and nearby states. Her recent research has centered on issues of later-life planning, choice, and "retirement" options for older adults with developmental disabilities. Mrs. Sutton is the co-author, with Dr. Marion Stroud, of *Expanding Options for Older Adults with Developmental disabilities: A Practical Guide to Achieving Community Access.* She writes and edits the international newsletter, *A/DDvantage,* for the RRTC Consortium.

Alan R. Factor, Ph.D., Research Assistant Professor, Illinois University Affiliated Program in Developmental Disabilities, College of Associated Health Professions, The University of Illinois at Chicago, 1640 West Roosevelt Road, Chicago, Illinois 60608. Dr. Factor has conducted policy research and program evaluations of community-based support services for frail older adults and other persons with disabilities, including Illinois' needs assessment of older adults with developmental disabilities. A major area of Dr. Factor's research has been later-life planning and residential transitions for older adults with lifelong disabilities. He has been a consultant to the New York State Office of Mental Retardation and Developmental Disabilities, the Illinois Department on Aging's Community Care Program, and the City of Chicago Department on Aging and Disability. Dr. Factor has lectured widely on policy and program development affecting services for older adults with developmental disabilities and has co-authored several articles on later-life planning and residential transitions.

Barbara A. Hawkins, Re.D., Research Faculty, Program on Aging and Developmental Disabilities, Institute for the Study of Developmental Disabilities, Indiana University, 2853 East 10th Street, Bloomington, Indiana 47408-2601. Dr. Hawkins is Associate Professor of Health, Physical Education and Recreation, and Research Director of the Program on Aging and Developmental Disabilities affiliated with the Institute for the Study of Developmental Disabilities, University Affiliated Program. Her professional expertise includes life-span development in persons with developmental disabilities with a focus on leisure behavior. She is Principal Investigator of several grants in the area of aging and developmental disabilities and has completed a curriculum development grant awarded by the Administration on Aging (United States Department of Health and Human Services). Dr. Hawkins has authored over 35 publications and is a frequent lecturer at state, national, and international meetings.

Tamar Heller, Ph.D., Associate Professor, Illinois University Affiliated Program in Developmental Disabilities, College of Associated Health Professions, The University of Illinois at Chicago, 1640 West Roosevelt Road, Chicago, Illinois 60608. Dr. Heller teaches Community Health Sciences in the School of Public Health and is Director of the Family Studies and Services program at the Illinois University Affiliated Program in Developmental Disabilities at The University of Illinois at Chicago. She has published widely on caregiving, residential transition, and later-life planning issues for families of adults with developmental disabilities. Dr. Heller directs a family support program encompassing a diagnostic clinic, family support services, staff training/technical assistance, and family research.

Gary B. Seltzer, Ph.D., Associate Professor, School of Social Work; Chair, Ph.D. Program in Social Welfare; Director, Clinic on Aging and Developmental Disabilities, Waisman Center, The University of Wisconsin—Madison, 1500 Highland Avenue, Madison, Wisconsin 53705. Dr. Seltzer has developed an interdisciplinary program on aging and developmental disabilities that is affiliated with the Section of Geriatrics and Gerontology of The University of Wisconsin—Madison Hospital and Clinics, Waisman Center University Affiliated Program, and disciplinary departments of the university. He and his colleagues in the program on aging and developmental disabilities have instituted a clinical training program that focuses on health care and functional assessment. They are developing research protocols to study age-related changes in persons with cerebral palsy and persons with other developmental disabilities. Dr. Seltzer and colleagues have published a number of articles on family issues related to aging and developmental disabilities.

The Chapter Authors

Marilyn Adlin, M.D., Medical Director, Program on Aging and Developmental Disabilities, Waisman Center, The University of Wisconsin—Madison, 1500 Highland Avenue, Madison, Wisconsin 53705. Dr. Adlin is also Assistant Professor in the Department of Medicine, Section of Geriatrics and Gerontology at The University of Wisconsin—Madison. She was a major presenter at the Boston Roundtable on Aging and Developmental Disabilities and has numerous presentations and publications to her credit.

Deborah J. Anderson, Ph.D., Minnesota University Affiliated Program on Developmental Disabilities, The University of Minnesota, 104 Pattee Hall, 150 Pillsbury Drive, S.E., Minneapolis, Minnesota 55455. Dr. Anderson is Associate Professor in the Department of Psychology and in the Paracollege at St. Olaf College in Northfield, Minnesota. She is also a senior research assistant at The University of Minnesota's Institute on Community Integration of the University Affiliated Program on Developmental Disabilities, where she has directed projects on aging and developmental disabilities since 1985. Her publications include articles and reports about policy and other issues affecting older adults with developmental disabilities.

Maureen Arcand, 2610 Myrtle Street, Madison, Wisconsin 53704. Ms. Arcand has spent her life as a community organizer and advocate in Dale County, Wisconsin, serving on nonprofit boards and city, state, and county advisory groups, including 6 years on the Dale County Board of Mental Retardation/Developmental Disabilities. After having completed 9 years as Advocacy Specialist at a local agency, Access to Independence, Ms. Arcand is currently moving into a career as a trainer in issues arising from the Americans with Disabilities Act.

Audrey Begun, M.S.W., Ph.D., Assistant Professor, School of Social Welfare, The University of Wisconsin—Milwaukee, P.O. Box 786, Milwaukee, Wisconsin 53201. Dr. Begun has published numerous articles on sibling relationships in families with a member with developmental disabilities.

Arthur Campbell, 515 South 18th Street, Apt. 122, Louisville, Kentucky 40203. Mr. Campbell is a disability activist and organizer and has been very involved in the self-advocacy movement in Kentucky, with a key role in developing a statewide disability coalition, Kentuckians Together. He is a member of many local, state, and national committees and boards. He speaks and writes on self-advocacy issues, a career that takes him to many parts of the United States.

Marci Chaikin, M.S.W., Project Coordinator-Pioneering Access for People with Mental Retardation, The Arc Hamilton County, 1821 Summit Road, Suite G-30, Cincinnati, Ohio 45237. Ms. Chaikin has worked extensively with adults with mental retardation and developmental disabilities on residential and self-advocacy issues.

Susan J. Eklund, Ph.D., Byron Root Professor in Aging and Professor of Counseling and Educational Psychology, Center on Aging and Aged, Indiana University, 910 State Road, 46 By-Pass, Bloomington, Indiana 47405. Dr. Eklund has done post-doctoral work at the Center for Aging and Human Development at Duke University. Her areas of professional expertise include adult development and aging, life-span development, school psychology, and issues of aging and developmental disabilities. She has authored numerous publications in these areas and has served as consultant to a variety of service agencies.

Pamela Imm-Thomas, B.A., Project Assistant, American Indian Studies Program, The University of Wisconson—Madison, Room 336, 1450 Linden Drive, Madison, Wisconsin 53706. Ms. Thomas is a graduate student in the Department of Sociology. As an undergraduate, she majored in Afro-American studies and sociology, with a concentration in analysis and research. She has had direct experience working with the Native American Indian community in Madison, Wisconsin, as tutor/consultant for the Title V Indian Education Program.

Dianne Koehler, President, People First of Hamilton County, P.O. Box 2004, Cincinnati, Ohio 45201-2004. Ms. Koehler is a board member of The Arc Hamilton County. She lives independently in Cincinnati and volunteers on a wide range of community committees. She has made numerous presentations on self-advocacy and leadership development of people with mental retardation and developmental disabilities.

Mariellen Laucht Kuehn, Ph.D., Associate Director, University Affiliated Program (UAP) on Aging and Developmental Disabilities, Waisman Center, The University of Wisconsin—Madison, 1500 Highland Avenue, Madison, Wisconsin 53705. Dr. Kuehn is Co-Chair of the multicultural Advisory Committee to the Federal Administration on Developmental Disabilities. She edited a four-part monograph series on the recruitment and retention of UAP trainees who are members of a minority group.

Phyllis Kultgen, Ph.D., Director, Program on Aging and Developmental Disabilities, Institute for the Study of Developmental Disabilities, Indiana University, 2853 East 10th Street, Bloomington, Indiana 47405. Dr. Kultgen is a social gerontologist with an interest in special populations of older adults. She has written a variety of training materials and directed numerous training, research, and demonstration projects in the area of aging and developmental disabilities.

Charlene M. Luchterhand, M.S.S.W., Clinical Service and Research Coordinator, Waisman Center, The University of Wisconsin—Madison, Room 389, 1500 Highland Avenue, Madison, Wisconsin 53705.

Randy Magan, Ph.D., Assistant Professor, School of Social Work, Columbia University, 622 West 113th Street, New York, New York 10025. Dr. Magan currently teaches courses on the foundations of social work practice. His professional interests include direct practice, social group work, crisis intervention, domestic violence, and family adaptation to members acting out. Dr. Magan's current projects include the development of a role play test to assess parenting skills, extending his recent research focusing on group work interventions for parents of children with aggressive behaviors.

Melton C. Martinson, Ph.D., Executive Director, Interdisciplinary Human Development Institute (IHDI), The University of Kentucky, Room 330, MIND Building, Lexington, Kentucky 40506-0051. The IHDI is a major, comprehensive institute providing interdisciplinary training, research, technical assistance, and service demonstration. Dr. Martinson has contributed to comprehensive interagency service development at local, state, regional, and national levels for over 30 years. His expertise in early intervention and programs for school-age children has led to many publications and major consultant responsibilities over the years.

William L. Martz, M.D., Professor Emeritus, School of Medicine, Indiana University, c/o 216 West Tilden, Brownsburg, Indiana 46112. Dr. Martz is former Director of the Indiana University Center on Aging and Aged. He continues private practice as a geriatrician with the Marion County General Hospital and the Indiana Masonic Home Hospital. His specialties are cardiology, pharmacology, and geriatric medicine. He has published widely in medical journals.

Lisa S. Schwartz Park, Ph.D., Management Consultant, Metropolitan Life Insurance Company, Southfield, Michigan, 28296 Raleigh Crescent, Chesterfield, Michigan 48051. Dr. Park received her doctoral degree in the field of Industrial/Gerontological Psychology. Her interests include issues regarding the older worker (training and retraining, retirement, mid- and later-life career change) and the older worker with developmental disabilities.

Esther Lee Pederson, M.Ed., University Affiliated Program, Cincinnati Center for Developmental Disorders (CCDD), 3300 Elland Avenue, Cincinnati, Ohio 45229. Ms. Pederson is the Coordinator of Adult and Outreach Services at the University Affiliated CCDD. Her interests are in the areas of empowerment (parents and people with disabilities), leadership development of people with disabilities, interagency networking and partnerships, aging, and issues affecting the community inclusion of adults with disabilities.

Barbara Polister, M.S., Project Coordinator, Institute on Community Integration Minnesota University Affiliated Program on Developmental Disabilities, The University of Minnesota, 207 Pattee Hall, 150 Pillsbury Drive, S.E., Minneapolis, Minnesota 55455. Ms. Polister is the parent of an adult daughter with autism. She is Vice President of the Board of Directors of Merrick Companies, Inc., provider of day program services for people with developmental disabilities. She has co-authored and reviewed a variety of publications and services as a member of Minnesota's Department of Human Services Review Committee, which specifically addresses state regulations covering the use of aversive and deprivation programming for people with developmental disabilities.

Robert Rominger, M.Ed., Research Associate, Institute for the Study of Developmental Disabilities, Program on Aging and Disabilities, Indiana University, 2853 East 10th Street, Bloomington, Indiana 47405. Mr. Rominger is a doctoral candidate in counseling psychology at Indiana University. Since 1988, he has specialized in training-related activities and evaluation of demonstration projects in the Program on Aging and Developmental Disabilities, part of the Indiana University Affiliated Program. His primary research interest at this time is family measurement, the topic of his doctoral thesis. Mr. Rominger is also a member of the *Adult Residential Care Journal* editorial board.

Harvey L. Sterns, Ph.D., Professor of Psychology, Director, Institute for Life-Span Development and Gerontology, The University of Akron, 179 Simmons Hall, Akron, Ohio 44325-4307. Dr. Sterns is a Fellow of the Gerontological Society of America, the American Psychological Association, and the Ohio Academy of Science. He is also a research professor of Gerontology in Community Health Science at the Northeastern Ohio Universities' College of Medicine. His research activities and numerous publications concern work on a range of topics, including age-related changes in perception, motor function, intelligence and problem-solving, adult education, and industrial gerontology. Dr. Sterns has served as an expert witness in age discrimination cases and as a consultant to many national, state, and local organizations concerned with issues of aging.

James A. Stone, M.S., Project Director, Interdisciplinary Human Development Institute, The University of Kentucky, Room 330, MIND Building, Lexington, Kentucky 40506-0051. Special interest and research in housing and transportation issues are the focus of training manuals, reports, and other materials developed by Mr. Stone, and he serves on numerous state committees and boards. He is Chair-Elect of the Southeast Region of the American Association on Mental Retardation and is currently editor of its newsletter, *Outreach Seven*. Mr. Stone also serves on the editorial board of the *Adult Residential Care Journal*.

FOREWORD

The aging of older adults with developmental disabilities is a growing issue in many nations, particularly those that are anticipating significant increase in the numbers of older persons within their general populations. In the past, issues concerning older persons with developmental disabilities were masked by reduced life expectancy, the invisibility of those in hospitals or institutions, or lifetime and often hidden care within large families. With changing contemporary demographics—particularly the aging of the post-World War II birth group; overall improved population health status due to better health care, nutrition, and housing; and greater longevity of persons with developmental disabilities born in the middle part of this century—many nations are experiencing new concerns. Whereas, historically, concerns were focused upon children and then work-age adults, these changing demographics and trends are now shaping expectations of a lengthier and more challenging third age and fourth age.[1]

Across the world, changing demographics show that the number of older persons in each nation's population is increasing and will continue to increase. For example, in many western nations, currently one out of every eight or nine persons is older. Within the next 20–30 years expectations are that this number will be one out of every four or five. Obviously, these changes in demographics will create varying demands on health and social services planners, administrators, clinicians, researchers, and service providers involved with both developmental disabilities and old-age services.

In many countries, responses that address these changing population characteristics have led to partnerships between gerontologists and other senior services workers and persons working in the field of developmental disabilities. Such partnerships and, more important, innovative crossdisciplinary approaches, have led to cooperative research efforts, ventures at cross training workers in both fields, cooperative program development, and targeted education campaigns that enlighten the public about the needs of older adults with lifelong disabilities. Examples of crossdisciplinary interests include the research done on Alzheimer's disease and Down syndrome, methods for successful utilization of general aging network services by persons with developmental disabilities, and provision of supports to aging families.

However, partnership approaches are but one type of service response. Others include third- and fourth-age programs and other modifications in generic practices to bet-

---

[1]The terms "third age" and "fourth age" (Lazlett, 1991) refer to those later-life stages that follow earlier years during which an individual is developing independence and maturity, while becoming increasingly absorbed in familial and social responsibility. The concept was first developed in Europe and has been applied widely in Great Britain and Canada. Individuals of the third age remain productive, seeking new roles and experiences, applying themselves to new learning, broadened experience, and even second and third careers. Entry into the third age is a personal occurrence beginning at a point chosen by the individual and has little to do with calendar, biological, or social age. Fourth age individuals are seen as less independent, more frail, and increasingly less motivated and capable of societal participation or individual achievement.

ter accommodate persons with developmental disabilities who are growing older. Depending on the construct of each nation's services for aging adults in general, and for adults with developmental disabilities in particular, many service challenges are being handled idiosyncratically. However, notwithstanding international differences, there are common service problems that are faced by older adults with developmental disabilities and their families. These include the general lack of availability of broad-based senior/ pensioner services, differential levels of supports for multi-generation aging families, and a void in the recognition of third-age program and retirement possibilities.

In many instances, state, regional, and federal efforts are directed at addressing third-age concerns, whether they are formal group programs or simply natural supports. Others are directed at fourth-age problems usually associated with frailty or senility and involve extended care needs, medical services, in-home aid, and other old-age supports. In those instances where there is recognition of viable third-age needs and the social system can accommodate targeted activities, many of these efforts are directed toward inclusive activities. In other instances, national or local efforts are a response to the needs of the aging segment of a population without much focus on strategies (e.g., random situations that result from aging in place) and often reflect a simple continuation of the types of services provided to younger persons with developmental disabilities. Interestingly, a dilemma among nonindustrialized nations (and among some industrialized nations as well) is that, although integration is highly regarded and is seen as more beneficial in helping people live ordinary lives, segregated services may be qualitatively better than anything available to age peers in the general population. Thus, many workers are placed in a peculiar quandary. Although commitment to integration and survivorship is valued, the possibilities this provides for living ordinary lives are few or of questionable quality. The choice presented is between integration with a possibility of diminished quality of life, or segregation in specialist services with enhanced survivorship.

Many old age–related programs have evolved from the participants aging in place. These often remain for the most part specialist or segregated efforts that provide solely for older adults with developmental disabilities. The nature of these programs may be no different from that of programs for younger persons or may be somewhat augmented with other activities due to the participants' changing needs related to their advancing age. The segregation remains for a variety of reasons—programmatic inertia, lack of funds, professional territoriality or elitism, or bureaucratic obstacles to innovation. This segregation is not necessary; the challenge is for innovators to propose and effect changes that offer participants a wider range of options and opportunities.

In other instances, we are witnessing specific organized inclusive strategies that are designed to aid older adults with retirement or otherwise shift the programmatic focus from second- to third-age activities. They include a variety of initiatives that may be age-specific or age-inclusive, including *retirement assistance ventures* (which aid, on an individualized basis, with the task of retiring, using leisure time and community amenities, and gaining access to generic community pensioner resources); *pull-out programs* (which draw two or more groups of people, some with disabilities and some without, some of the same age, some of varied ages, together for a common purpose during a set time); *senior friend/companion ventures* (which involve a senior friend or companion helping someone with a disability to use the common senior/pensioner services or generic community amenities); and *senior/pensioner center ventures* (which aid an older person with developmental disabilities in using a neighborhood or community senior/pensioner services center). We are also witnessing a variety of age-specific inclusive services that include *social model site programs* (which provide a day service composed of activities and supervision for aging adults with developmental disabilities and others with late-life disabilities or impairments [often persons with dementia]) and *health model site programs* (which provide a specialized day service composed of activities and supervision for more frail aging adults with special physical or mental needs under the direction of a physician).

Many of these efforts are organized around providing a service or program related to the needs or wants of older adults. Thus, they also function within an age-specific assumption of what programming for older adults means. For example, current practice in the United States (as in other industrialized nations) is to use the developmental model for younger persons with developmental disabilities as the basis for programming. Under this model, learning is viewed as probable, sequential, and continuous, with an invariable striving to promote ever greater independence and self-direction capacities. In the third age, and even more in the fourth age, some of these underlying beliefs become less tenable. In many situations, a different foundation is taking hold. For example, for older adults, competition is not as important as it was with younger persons, and vocational competence and personal independence are not important goals in most programmatic activities. For older adults, different values come into play—due partly to physiological and partly to social role expectations—and, thus, there is a shift in the emphasis of the construct of third-age programs or activities to an underlying assumption that their efforts should be designed more to promote productive and/or successful aging and place greater reliance upon interdependence.

Retirement and other third-age services as processes are greatly determined by a nation's social and health policies. Where national policies support the transition from worklife to third-age activities, public benefits may be forthcoming. Where policies do not support this transition, generally, no efforts are made to produce a different care system. Thus, such transitioning mechanisms only now are becoming issues in the field of developmental disabilities. Among them are debates about enabling contributory pensioning, old-age benefit pensioning, and retirement transitioning and milestones, and debates about whether social benefits that continue to focus on disability should be maintained or social benefits that shift to a new focus on old age should be obtained. In addition, notwithstanding the nature of any nation's old-age policies (or lack of policies), many nations are faced with the realities of aging parents continuing to provide lifetime care and supervision of their now gradually aging offspring well into the offspring's old age. Certainly, in nations with sophisticated service systems that provide supports to families, targeting assistance programs for aging parents is gaining attention. In other nations, most parents and the extended family continue to live as always. These third-age issues are beginning to gain more attention as service providers look to areas that need systemic supports.

Given social and health policy uncertainties, expectations are that public policies related to fourth-age services need attention. Many of these services, however, often are a reflection of a continuation of institutional practices for younger (second-age) persons with developmental disabilities. A question common to both areas of service is whether to use specialized nursing or extended care facilities. How to maintain extended care facilities that specialize in services to persons with developmental disabilities is a question that has raised many concerns and often is at the root of many debates about old-age services. Social gerontologists say that traditional extended care among the general population of older adults is encountering challenge and undergoing change, with advocates and planners proposing a greater emphasis on home care and other supports. The question may be asked whether to expect the same type of supports for fourth-age persons with developmental disabilities. The rationale for extended care facilities is that persons need a secluded, nurturing environment when they no longer can care for themselves or when their informal support system collapses. When people with developmental disabilities are already in some type of accommodation operated or overseen by a disability agency, this rationale for admission to an extended care facility may not hold. However, many agency accommodations have not yet evolved to support aging adults, which places these individuals in jeopardy of being considered for transfer to extended care facilities. Thus, there is a need for the evolution of care models for aging adults that preclude institutionalization and that recognize the value of aging in place. Such care models must incorporate training of personnel; adaptation for physical accessibility; provision of social, health, and other supports; and continued involvement in activities that engage and challenge to maintain intellectual abilities and promote mental health.

During the 1980s, research about the growing number of older adults with developmental disabilities was comparatively limited, although, staff/family training materials and reports of demonstration projects were produced and widely disseminated. The aging of persons with Down syndrome is the most explored aspect of gerontological research in the population of persons with developmental disabilities. Issues of premature aging and the Alzheimer–Down syndrome connection have driven this research. It can be argued, however, that insights into aging in general are being sought, rather than new knowledge specific to those with developmental disabilities.

The researchers, consultants, administrators, and consumers whose work makes up the content of this book provide a unique contribution to the body of knowledge about adults with developmental disabilities who are living into the third age. Their research sheds new light, raises critical issues, and offers guidance to planners and policymakers as well as service providers in effecting the most appropriate services. They present new and reliable information about a range of age-related physical changes, social status, leisure and living arrangement options, alternatives to work, and the dynamics of important later-life transitions. Their development and testing of new assessment instruments designed specifically for older adults with developmental disabilities should lead to further research and, in time, a clearer understanding of this emerging population.

The empowerment of people with developmental disabilities is also highlighted in the research and experience reported in this volume. This, too, is a unique and progressive contribution. While empowerment and self-advocacy have always been an integral part of generic senior services, only since the mid-1980s has this philosophy begun to flourish within the community of people with developmental disabilities.

Although work since the mid-1980s in the area of aging and developmental disabilities has contributed significantly to our knowledge and awareness, and this text certainly works toward that effort, there are still many challenges that lie before us. As workers, researchers, public policymakers, clinicians, and primary and secondary consumers, we are challenged to examine the transitions from second-age services and look at what third-age options are viable within the sociopolitical climates of our nations. We are further challenged to examine the facets of aging (in all its forms) and how these may change among successive generations of older persons, including those with histories of segregated care and those not impoverished by lifelong institutionalization, and we are challenged to examine practices of third- and fourth-age services, programs, and activities and offer solutions to problems on how to improve the quality of life and enable older adults to truly live successful, included lives. Toward that end, this book offers both a start in some areas and a continuing contribution in others.

Matthew P. Janicki, Ph.D.
Director for Aging Services
New York State Office
of Mental Retardation and Developmental Disabilities
Albany, New York

REFERENCE

Lazlett, P. (1991). *A fresh map of life: The emergence of the third age.* Cambridge, MA: Harvard University Press.

PREFACE

In 1988, a group of researchers from seven universities in six states came together to respond to a call from Washington for an expansion of the existing knowledge base concerning people with developmental disabilities living into middle and late adulthood. This book represents their first response to that call. The call came from the National Institute on Disability and Rehabilitation Research (NIDRR) in the United States Department of Education, and those who answered were The University of Akron, The University of Cincinnati, The University of Illinois at Chicago, Indiana University, The University of Kentucky, The University of Minnesota, and The University of Wisconsin—Madison.

Each researcher in his own way and on her own ground had been pursuing a piece of the picture. Separately they had investigated issues of health, housing, and community inclusion. Some had begun the task of training specialists who could deliver the most effective services to older adults with developmental disabilities. Others had studied the impact upon families resulting from the aging of their adult children with disabilities. All had been motivated by the knowledge that new technology had produced a general extension of life and that people with developmental disabilities were part of the growing population of older adults. They were also well aware that, although concern for this group of people was growing, there was a long way to go. The knowledge base did indeed need to be expanded. Awareness and concern among planners, service professionals, service providers, educators, people with disabilities, and their families, needed to be strengthened and focused upon the special needs of a relatively neglected population.

As their work began, these researchers organized themselves into the Rehabilitation Research and Training Center (RRTC) Consortium on Aging and Developmental Disabilities under the administrative wing of the Cincinnati Center for Developmental Disorders. A mission statement and a statement of shared values (see p. xxiii) were developed to guide their work. Among their first actions was the inclusion of consumer representatives from each state. These "representative participants" (as they later identified themselves) have shared in the decision-making and direction of the Consortium and have ensured the relevance and applicability of its research.

During the first 3 years, Consortium researchers, with the guidance of their Coordinating Council and state advisory groups, conducted nine projects contributing directly to the expansion of the existing knowledge base and providing resources for services to older adults with developmental disabilities and their families. In the 2-year period that followed, they built upon this work with an applied research model centering on retirement education and an investigation of case management practices. Extensive dissemination of research results also characterized this time frame. This book presents results of the Consortium researchers' first 3 years of work.

Issues of physical and cognitive well-being are the focus of Section I. Here, in Chapter 1, Eklund and Martz report on work conducted at Indiana University establishing

age-related markers that define a need for intervention. This longitudinal study differ-
entiates characteristics and changes found in persons with Down syndrome and persons
with other forms of mental retardation. In addition to the significant findings reported,
the authors describe and evaluate their assessment instruments, offer a few thoughts for
specific intervention, and suggest uses for the assessment battery to individualize planning and predict needed assistance as age increases.

In Chapter 2, Anderson compares results of the National Nursing Home Survey
completed in the mid-1980s and a 1990–1991 study of older adults with mental retardation
in community settings. The Center for Residential Community Services (CRCS) at The
University of Minnesota was the source of information for the latter study, and the University Affiliated Program for Developmental Disorders provided the nursing home data.
Her findings raise many questions about placement and treatment of adults with mental
retardation within nursing home settings and underline several areas in which community
services appear to be more appropriate.

In Chapter 3, Adlin presents a clear and comprehensive account of age-related
changes in older adults with mild or moderate retardation, and follows this with a discussion of differences, in which Down syndrome and cerebral palsy are given special attention. Families and providers of program and residential services for people with developmental disabilities will find this section very practical as they begin to recognize the
possibility of age-related change in those for whom they care.

Completing Section I, Anderson, in Chapter 4, continues her analysis with a
focus on use of psychotropic medication. Together with Polister, she analyzes and compares findings from four types of residential facility: foster home, group home, large
private facilities, and state-operated facilities. Results suggest an overall overuse of psychotropic medications, which may not come as a surprise to the reader. The associated
variables, however, add a significant dimension to our understanding of an important
health issue.

Section II examines a broad range of critical concerns. In Chapter 5, Anderson reports changes in social behavior, relationships, and inclusion that occurred over time
among older people with mental retardation living in different kinds of residential settings. Striking differences are found when results from the various settings are compared. The current focus on community inclusion characterizing services to older adults
with developmental disabilities will be enlightened by this research.

Sutton, Sterns, and Park further explore current lifestyles of this population in
Chapter 6. Results of a survey conducted in the state of Ohio are reported by these researchers at The University of Akron, who also conducted interviews with 59 older
adults. Gaps in the service system emerge from these findings, which should guide future planning and program delivery.

The effects of residential transitions in midlife and later life are the focus of research
reported by Heller and Factor at The University of Illinois at Chicago in Chapter 7. Theirs
is one of very few studies that highlight a need for participation by family members, including the person with developmental disabilities in decision-making regarding future
residence and lifestyle.

A study by Seltzer and his colleagues at The University of Wisconsin—Madison
centers upon the consistency and quality of family relationships when adult children with
disabilities live outside the family home. In Chapter 8, Seltzer, Begun, Magan, and Luchterhand show that the conclusions of this study support the view that placement out of the

home does not mean placement out of the family. Although limited by the nature of the private setting under investigation, this research contributes a new dimension to our understanding of families in later life.

Hawkins of Indiana University, in Chapter 9, summarizes findings of her research to inform the reader that older adults with various kinds of mental retardation including those with Down syndrome have a low level of life satisfaction that is significantly related to low levels of leisure participation. Her thoughtful discussion raises some important questions about the need for retirement and leisure education in preparation for later-life transitions.

In Chapter 10, Seltzer makes a unique contribution to the limited research about adult development and mental retardation, particularly in midlife. After examining the fit or nonfit between existing theories and knowledge of the individual with mental retardation drawn from empirical studies and clinical observation, Seltzer presents a conceptual model illustrating midlife psychological adjustment experienced by persons with developmental disabilities.

Section III comprises Chapters 11, 12, and 13 by Martinson and Stone of The University of Kentucky addressing small-scale (three or fewer) community living options for older adults with developmental disabilities. In light of the strong trend toward deinstitutionalization, their findings, based on a national survey, are especially timely. Funding streams often overlooked are presented along with models of interagency planning and best practices in service delivery.

Section IV is devoted to a variety of service trends affecting older adults with developmental disabilities. The relatively new concept of cross training among agencies of the aging and developmental disabilities services systems is described in Chapter 14 by Kultgen and Rominger. Their research-based discussion points to the importance of trainee preferences and recognition of differences from one service agency to another and across job levels.

Systemic change is the focus of Chapter 15 in which Factor reports upon existing model policies and programs identified in a national survey. Collaborative initiatives involving the aging and developmental disabilities services systems and other policies driving service delivery are discussed. Recommendations for further policy development emerge from this research.

Of special note is Chapter 16, which offers the reader unusual insight into the thoughts and feelings of several individuals with disabilities who are Consortium members. Their account of leadership experiences extends the meaning of community integration to purposeful inclusion and citizenship. Pederson and Chaikin, who co-authored the chapter with Dianne Koehler, Arthur Campbell, and Maureen Arcand, representative participants, offer guidelines that work as professionals facilitate the empowerment process.

In Chapter 17, Kuehn and Imm-Thomas apply their unique expertise in an overview of demographic changes and service utilization affecting ethnic and racial minorities among older adults with developmental disabilities. This chapter, like all others, includes a thorough literature review, which adds a defining perspective to the research findings presented by the 26 chapter authors.

The appendix by Pederson further describes the development of the Consortium from scattered beginnings into a dynamic and strongly focused entity. As a collaborative enterprise, the RRTC Consortium on Aging and Developmental Disabilities has had many rewards for its members. Crossing disciplines, sharing expertise, and pursuing a common concern has broadened each individual's knowledge and understanding. The partnership of researchers, other professionals, and consumers in a united purpose has deepened the commitment of all and motivated them to work together in a continuing effort to meet ongoing challenges as the post–World War II generation of people with disabilities becomes a larger segment of the growing aging American population.

It is our hope that the results of our individual and collective efforts will improve the lives of people with developmental disabilities and their families and influence those who plan, make policy, and design and provide service.

Evelyn Sutton

THE CONSORTIUM

The Rehabilitation Research and Training Center (RRTC) Consortium on Aging and Developmental Disabilities was funded in 1988 by the National Institute on Disability and Rehabilitation Research in the United States Department of Education, for the purpose of expanding the existing knowledge base concerning adults with developmental disabilities living into middle and late adulthood.

Mission Statement

The ultimate purpose of this Consortium is to **improve the quality of life** and **integration in the community** for older persons with mental retardation and other developmental disabilities.

Goals of the Consortium

- To develop a rehabilitation research and training center that will establish a national data base and study state-of-the-art methodologies of service and training as such
- To serve as a national resource for researchers, planners, service providers, and consumers on information regarding persons who have mental retardation and other developmental disabilities

Statement of Shared Values

The RRTC is committed to ensuring that older persons with developmental disabilities attain the full dimension of life through research and in its application. Also, inherent in the RRTC's activities are the following shared commitments and values reflecting a positive vision for the lives of older persons with disabilities:

- Older persons with mental retardation and other developmental disabilities can live successfully with appropriate supports in and as a part of the community.
- Older persons with mental retardation and other developmental disabilities can make positive contributions in their own personal lives and to the lives of their families and to their communities.
- Older persons with mental retardation and other developmental disabilities can benefit from enduring relationships with other people, including family members and community members without disabilities.
- Older persons with mental retardation and other developmental disabilities must have access to services that promote choices and contribute to full citizenship.
- Services and supports for older persons with mental retardation and other developmental disabilities must be responsive to their changing needs and those of their families.

- Services and supports for older persons with mental retardation and other developmental disabilities must be individualized so as to be responsive to cultural and ethnic differences, economic resources, personal abilities and needs and individual life circumstances.
- Public policy needs to stimulate opportunities for older persons with mental retardation and other developmental disabilities to lead productive and integrated lives through sustained involvement.

Language

The RRTC Consortium on Aging and Developmental Disabilities requests that ALL products not use the terms "mentally retarded," "developmentally disabled," and so forth, as nouns. The preference is people first language, that is, such phrases as "people with mental retardation," "people with developmental disabilities."

ACKNOWLEDGMENTS

Had it not been for the National Institute on Disability and Rehabilitation Research (NIDRR) in the United States Department of Education, this book would not have been written. The editors and their colleagues in the Rehabilitation Research and Training Center (RRTC) Consortium on Aging and Developmental Disabilities gratefully acknowledge the support of that agency and its concern for individuals with lifelong disabilities who are among aging Americans.

The editors also appreciate the generous assistance of their institutions: the University Affiliated Programs for Developmental Disabilities at The University of Cincinnati, The University of Illinois at Chicago, Indiana University, The University of Kentucky, The University of Minnesota, and the Institute for Life-Span Development and Gerontology at The University of Akron.

We thank the leaders of the RRTC Consortium, Jack Rubinstein, M.D., Director, and Ruth Roberts, Ph.D., Co-Director, for their guidance and encouragement. Our gratitude extends further to the 32 members of the RRTC Consortium Coordinating Council, including representative participants as well as researchers and other professionals from our affiliated states. Their commitment to the mission of the Consortium has shaped the outcomes of our combined effort and inspired our work in achieving this contribution to research and practice directed toward enhancing the lives of older adults with developmental disabilities.

The patient guidance of the staff of Paul H. Brookes Publishing Company, and in particular, Melissa Behm and Natalie Tyler, has been invaluable as we have worked together to make this book a reality. Able technical assistance generously given by Jan Myers and Joanne Stafford is also gratefully acknowledged.

It takes many minds and hands to bring together the diverse components of a text such as this, and the editors join in expressing their deep appreciation to all who have contributed to this accomplishment.

I

HEALTH AND MEDICAL ISSUES

Barbara A. Hawkins

While life expectancy for adults with developmental disabilities continues to improve, the consequences of aging as they affect health status and health care are of growing concern to these individuals, their families, caregivers, and service providers. For older adults in general, much is known about the physical, mental, emotional, and social changes associated with aging. However, a greater amount of information about these changes in individuals with mental retardation and other developmental disabilities continues to emerge. Globally researchers are pursuing expansion of the knowledge base about disease, functional competence, health status, and other health-related phenomena in these individuals. Maintaining health and functional status is clearly central to enhancing the inclusion, independence, and productivity of adults with developmental disabilities as they grow older.

This section provides background for interpreting the aging process as it occurs in adults with developmental disabilities. The authors present information on age-related change, an overview of normal aging versus disease states, an examination of the health status of different population groups based on residential status, and a review of the use of psychotropic medications among older adults. These chapters come together to form the basis for a general understanding of the aging process as it affects the health and day-to-day functioning of adults with developmental disabilities.

1

1

Maintaining Optimal Functioning

Susan J. Eklund and William L. Martz

Aging is a complex process involving change across a number of functional domains and bodily systems. There is increasing literature on age-related change in the population as a whole. This information serves to provide a sense of what is normal (or at least normative) aging in the general population. The physical, mental, and social changes that are associated with aging have been well documented for people without disabilities (see Shock et al., 1984). Little is known, however, about the same dimensions of aging in persons with developmental disabilities.

The purpose of this chapter is to describe a study using an assessment battery that was assembled for the purpose of allowing the description and documentation of age-related change in persons with mental retardation.[1] There has been no generally accepted yardstick for interpreting the aging process as the adult with developmental disabilities traverses the life span. The battery described here includes a physical assessment and a cognitive assessment. It was based on a bio-psycho-social model of aging and is described in more detail in Hawkins, Eklund, and Martz (1991). Such a battery should be useful as a screening tool to assist in decision-making about interventions needed when various mental and physical capabilities change. Some of these changes can be remediated or compensated for with assistive devices (e.g., glasses for presbyopia or

[1]This book was written before the American Association on Mental Retardation adopted a new definition of mental retardation in May 1992. This new definition no longer recognizes the four designations of mental retardation: mild, moderate, severe, and profound (except regarding diagnosis only). Rather than using this former approach of categorizing people, now AAMR focuses its definition on support needs of individuals and categorizes those needs.

hearing aids for presbycusis), while others require modifications in life activities. Such a battery is also useful in assessing outcomes of interventions designed to slow effects of aging and to maintain optimal functioning. The battery
is described along with results of a study in which it was used with two groups of
older adults with mental retardation. Members of one group had been diagnosed
with Down syndrome. Those in the other group had mental disabilities from
etiologies other than Down syndrome. Findings are interpreted in terms of their
potential implications for better understanding of persons with mental retardation as they age and for more age-appropriate programming.

ASSESSMENT BATTERY

Physical Assessment

The physical assessment battery consists of a number of tests of physical performance that have been found to be valid markers of biological aging in the general aging population. Use of objective physical performance measures can
improve the assessment of physical functioning when compared to the use of
self-report measures, especially when used with individuals who have some
cognitive impairment (Guralnick, Branch, Cummings, & Curb, 1989). The measures included height, weight, resting heart rate, systolic and diastolic blood
pressure, anthropometric percentage body fat, grip strength, vital capacity, reaction time (simple and choice), hand-eye coordination, hand-tapping (simple
and two-point), vibratory threshold (right thumb and right big toe), near and far
vision, audiometric assessment, and trunk flexibility. Detailed instructions and
descriptions of equipment used for each of these measures are available in
Hawkins et al. (1991).

   Full discussion of research on physical aspects of aging is beyond the scope
of this chapter. The reader is referred to sources such as Dean (1988),
Schneider and Rowe (1990), Shock (1981), and Shock et al. (1984) for discussion
of physical changes with age and their measurement in people without disabilities. References supporting specific measures included in the physical battery
are presented in Table 1.1.

Cognitive Assessment

While there is still some controversy over the extent to which cognitive function
declines with age, there is ample evidence in the gerontological literature that
there are changes in intellectual performance with age. On the one hand, typical
findings of cross-sectional studies comparing different age groups show a pattern of lower scores on full scale IQ scores in groups older than 30, with a tendency for performance abilities to decline earlier than verbal abilities. Longitudinal studies following the same people over time, on the other hand, tend to
show much stability in overall IQ scores until the late 60s, with gradual decline
thereafter. More detailed studies looking at component cognitive abilities find

Table 1.1. Measures of physical function and supporting studies

Physical functions	Supporting research
Height, weight, resting heart rate, systolic BP, percentage body fat	Borkan, 1980; Dean, 1988; Furukawa et al., 1975; Hollingsworth, Hashizume, and Jablon, 1966
Grip strength	Borkan, 1980; Furukawa et al., 1975; Hollingsworth, Hashizume, and Jablon, 1966; Mints, Dubina, and Lysenyk, 1984; Shock, 1981
Vital capacity	Borkan, 1980; Hollingsworth, Hashizume, and Jablon, 1966; Kannel and Hubert, 1982; Ludwig and Masoro, 1983
Reaction time	Hollingsworth, Hashizume, and Jablon, 1966; Salthouse, 1982
Hand-eye coordination	Ludwig and Masoro, 1983
Hand-tapping	Borkan, 1980
Vibratory threshold	Hollingsworth, Hashizume, and Jablon, 1966; Mints, Dubina, and Lysenyk, 1984
Vision	Corso, 1982; Ludwig and Masoro, 1983; Shock, 1981
Hearing	Corso, 1982; Ludwig and Masoro, 1983; Shock, 1981
Flexibility	Dean, 1988; Furukawa et al., 1975

earlier and more rapid decline in some abilities than in others (Perlmutter & Hall, 1985).

Horn and Cattell (Cattell, 1963; Horn, 1972, 1976, 1985, 1988; Horn & Cattell, 1966) proposed a theory of intelligence that distinguishes between crystallized and fluid abilities. Crystallized abilities represent a person's breadth and depth of accumulated knowledge about a culture. Fluid abilities involve a broad ability to reason when faced with new tasks that require one to discover the essential relations of a task for the first time. When studies of intellectual performance and aging are divided into crystallized and fluid abilities, performance in fluid abilities is found to decline with age, while crystallized abilities continue to show improvement until quite late in life (Horn, 1970).

A large body of research has focused on these and other age differences in adult cognitive functioning since the 1960s (cf. Arenberg & Robertson-Tchabo, 1977; Botwinick, 1977; Craik, 1977; Labouvie-Vief, 1985; Perlmutter, 1986, 1988). This work has resulted in a view of cognitive aging that supports some decline in cognitive processes with aging, particularly in the fluid or performance abilities, but less than was supported earlier. There is also evidence that decline in fluid abilities may be reversed through relatively simple and short-term educational interventions (Baltes & Willis, 1983; Willis, Blieszner, & Baltes, 1981). All of the studies discussed thus far have involved cognitive aging in subjects who do not have mental retardation.

The classic study on growth and decline of individuals with mental retardation was performed by Fisher and Zeaman in 1970. The findings of this semilongitudinal study were that the mental ages (MA) of persons with mental retardation were seen to increase in linear fashion from ages 2 to 16 years. Persons with higher mental functioning continued to grow in MA for longer periods of their life, at least into their late 30s. After age 60, MA for all levels of mental retardation showed a tendency to decline. Between the ages of 16 and 60, IQ was seen to be relatively stable.

In an earlier study, Bell and Zubek (1960) found that retest scores on the Wechsler-Bellevue (Form I) Full Scale (Wechsler, 1939) held up well between the ages of 20 and 45 in people who were institutionalized, but declined thereafter. Scores on the Verbal Scale (crystallized) also held up well between the ages of 20 and 45, but Performance Scale scores (fluid) declined gradually from the 20s to the 50s. In a 1976 study, Goodman looked at Verbal, Performance, and Full Scale IQ from either WISC (the Wechsler Intelligence Scale for Children [Wechsler, 1949]) or WAIS (the Wechsler Adult Intelligence Scale [Wechsler, 1955]) in 402 individuals ranging in age from 11 to 44 years who had received routine test administrations at two different times. Full Scale IQ did not decrease with age over this age range, although there were decrements in Performance abilities. Another study of institution residents using archival Stanford-Binet (1937) results found that from ages 6 to 60 all curves showed initial high growth rates and later decline (Silverstein, 1979).

Hewitt, Fenner, and Torpy (1986) drew upon an extensive data bank at a group of institutions in England. They studied records of 148 residents ages 65–88 years with a mean length of institutionalization of 54.8 years. Cross-sectional analyses of MA scores from the Stanford-Binet (Terman & Merrill, 1937) revealed an apparent increase in MA between ages 35 and 60 years, followed by a decrease thereafter. Longitudinal analyses showed small but significant gains in MA followed by a decline, commencing on the average at 65.8 years. Average MA in this study was about 5 years. Neither people with profound mental retardation nor those with Down syndrome were included due to decreased life expectancy.

These studies of age-related change in intelligence in individuals with mental retardation, mostly those who were institutionalized, have shown a pattern of some stability of intelligence scores until the 60s, with decline thereafter. Studies that have reported separate verbal (crystallized) and performance (fluid) results have found earlier and more rapid decline in performance. While these findings tend to parallel the findings in the general aging population, they have been predominantly post-hoc evaluations of archival data on institutionalized samples that have not included significant numbers of persons with Down syndrome.

Other studies have looked specifically at individuals with Down syndrome and found a somewhat different pattern of cognitive aging in this subgroup. The lessened life expectancy of persons with Down syndrome has long been documented, although life expectancy in this group has increased dramatically since the 1970s (Thase, 1982). Along with shorter life spans, persons with DS have been assumed to experience accelerated aging and earlier decline in intelligence. Actual evidence regarding such declines has not always been consistent, however.

On the one hand, Wisniewski, Howe, Williams, and Wisniewski (1978) found cognitive changes after age 35 in persons with Down syndrome. Changes included loss of vocabulary, recent memory loss, impaired short-term visual retention, difficulty in object identification, and loss of interest in surroundings. Fenner, Hewitt, and Torpy (1987), on the other hand, found in their study of persons with Down syndrome, ages 19–40 years, that for those over 35, intellectual deterioration had occurred in less than one third. There was an increase in MA on the Stanford-Binet for those in their 20s and 30s, followed by a decline. The 45- to 49-year-old group showed the greatest decline. These findings agreed with those of Hewitt and Jancar (1986) and Dalton and Crapper (1984), who found that significant intellectual deterioration does not begin until late in the 40s in persons with Down syndrome, and that it occurs in less than 50% of these individuals. Zigman, Schupf, Lubin, and Silverman (1987) found clear age-related deficits in those individuals with Down syndrome who were over age 50. In younger age groups, individuals with Down syndrome did not differ from other people with mental disabilities in the control group, but in groups over age 50, the performance of the group with Down syndrome was worse.

A few studies of specific cognitive abilities in older persons with mental retardation should be noted. Dalton and Crapper (1977) and Dalton, Crapper, and Schlotterer (1974) found evidence of memory loss in a group of persons with Down syndrome ages 44–58 years that was similar to the pattern in people with Alzheimer's disease. In following a group with Down syndrome ages 39–58 over a 3-year period, they found that 4 of the 11 participants deteriorated to the point where they could no longer learn a simple discrimination task. In addition, individuals with Down syndrome have been shown to have increased deficits with age in auditory processing and auditory memory (McDade & Adler, 1980). Young and Kramer (1991) reported a decline with age in ability to comprehend spoken language but not in verbal skills. Eisner (1983) reported that visual memory deficits were more prominent in older than younger persons with Down syndrome.

Among the studies discussed here, there is diversity of method, instrumentation, and analysis technique. Nevertheless, a picture does emerge of differences between the population with Down syndrome and those who have mental retardation from other causes. Among persons with Down syndrome, onset of age-related cognitive decline appears to have occurred in the 30s to 50s, while in the groups with mental retardation from causes other than Down syndrome there appears to be little decline until 50.

Cognitive Assessment Instrument

After consideration of the foregoing studies, the instrument chosen for assessment of cognitive function was the Woodcock-Johnson (Woodcock & Mather, 1989) Tests of Cognitive Ability-Revised (WJ-R), plus the Digit Span and Digit Symbol subtests from the WAIS. The WJ-R was chosen for its theoretical base, that is, the Horn-Cattell (Horn & Cattell, 1966) theory of fluid and crystallized intelligence (Woodcock, 1990). It was standardized on a large sample of people ranging in age from early childhood to 90 years. Reliability for most subtests is in the .80s or .90s. The WJ-R was thought to be particularly appropriate for use in the longitudinal study of adults with mental retardation because of its wide age range. It also provides the ability to look at a number of different components of intellectual functioning. The Wechsler subscales of Digit Span and Digit Symbol were chosen because they have been demonstrated to be sensitive to age-related change in the general aging population (Perlmutter & Nyquist, 1989).

The WJ-R Cognitive Standard Battery consists of seven subtests, each representing an area of cognitive ability. These include Memory for Names (long-term retrieval), Memory for Sentences (short-term memory and attention), Visual Matching (processing speed), Incomplete Words (auditory processing), Visual Closure (visual processing), Picture Vocabulary (comprehension—knowledge or crystallized ability), and Analysis—Synthesis (reasoning or fluid ability).

Assessment of Activities of Daily Living

Concerning older adults without mental retardation, there is now extensive literature on the assessment of how well the individual functions in his or her environment (Gallo, Reichel, & Anderson, 1988). "The items generally agreed on as comprising functional assessment are divided into the activities of daily living (ADL) and the instrumental activities of daily living (IADL)" (Gallo et al., 1988, p. 65). Measures of ADL were originally developed to differentiate functioning at the severe end of the spectrum of disability in older adults and are considered to be the most fundamental for independent living. Other more complex activities needed to function outside the home have been assessed in IADL scales.

For the assessment of activities of daily living, the Katz Index of ADL was selected and modified to include two items relating to ambulation on a flat surface and climbing stairs (Katz, Ford, Moskowitz, Jackson, & Jaffee, 1963). The Katz is one of the most widely used and carefully studied ADL assessment instruments. The measure consists of a three-tiered rating scale for each of the ADL functions: bathing, dressing, going to the toilet, transfer (from bed to chair), continence, feeding, and ambulation. The scale reflects three levels of ability in the individual for each activity, ranging from independent to semi-independent to dependent.

Instrumental Activities of Daily Living

For measuring IADL, items from several existing scales were selected, primarily the Philadelphia Geriatric Center Scale of IADL (Lawton, 1972) and the AAMR Adaptive Behavior Scale (Meyers, Nihira, & Zetlin, 1979; Nihira, Foster, Shellhaas, & Leland, 1974). The purpose of collecting data using an IADL measure was to describe the ability of the study participants to deal with their external environments. The IADL concept includes a range of activities that are more demanding and complex than those of personal self-care, which are included in the ADL measures (Gallo et al., 1988). The IADL measures, like those of the ADL, readily translate into services; that is, knowledge of an individual's ability to perform IADL tasks provides direct information about what services or supports the person might need.

The IADL items were intended to reflect levels of both age-appropriateness and active, engaged lifestyle. The modified instrument covers 11 areas of functioning: 1) travel around town; 2) use of telephone; 3) shopping; 4) food preparation; 5) housekeeping, such as room cleaning and laundry; 6) taking medications; 7) handling finances; 8) work habits; 9) communication; 10) self-direction, such as initiation, passivity, attention, and persistence; and 11) socialization, such as awareness and interaction with others.

Stress Index

In addition to the ADL and IADL measures, a Stress Index was administered concerning the occurrence within the past year of nine stress-provoking events for each individual studied. The events involved: 1) going to the hospital due to illness, 2) having a friend or relative go to the hospital or die, 3) experiencing a residential change, 4) having a friend or relative move far away, 5) taking a new job, 6) having money problems, or 7) having any other problems individually specified by participants. The Stress Index was designed to assess significant events in the individual's life or social milieu that potentially had a bearing on health or functional status.

PARTICIPANTS

Assessments were carried out with 128 participants over a 2-year period. The group with Down syndrome consisted of 64 individuals who ranged in age from 32 to 56. There were 32 males and 32 females, with females in their 30s, 40s, and 50s and males in their 30s and 40s only. The group without Down syndrome included 64 individuals who ranged in age from 52 to 79; half were males and half females. All the individuals were participants in a 3-year study of bio-psycho-social decline in adults with mental retardation that was conducted in Indiana (Hawkins et al., 1991). The majority (87%) lived either with their parents or in group homes. The remaining 13% lived in other residential arrangements, including independent living facilities, semi-independent facilities, nursing homes, or foster care.

RESULTS AND DISCUSSION

Physical Functioning

Correlations with age for each of the physical variables were calculated separately for the group with Down syndrome and the group without Down syndrome. The variables interacted with age differently in the two groups, perhaps because of the different age ranges involved. (Participants with Down syndrome ranged from 30s to 50s; those without Down syndrome ranged from 50s to 70s.) Grip strength was negatively related to age in both groups, as was vital capacity as measured by peak expiratory flow rate (PEF). The PEF measure was significantly correlated with age in the older group without Down syndrome at the .01 level, but just missed significance for the younger group with Down syndrome at the .05 level. Other significant age relationships for the group with Down syndrome included: higher diastolic blood pressure with age, poorer two-point tapping and hand-eye coordination, less trunk flexibility, and poorer auditory acuity at 6,000 Hz. In general, these findings would be consistent with the hypothesis about earlier aging for Down syndrome etiology than for other etiologies for mental retardation.

Sex Differences in the Group with Down Syndrome Data for the two times of testing, approximately 1 year apart, were analyzed both cross-sectionally and longitudinally. Data on the group with Down syndrome were analyzed separately for males and females because representation of both sexes did not exist in all age brackets. (No males with Down syndrome in their 50s were studied because they could not be found in the area.)

For males with Down syndrome, the only significant effect for age was on the two-point tapping test in which the younger group (30s) performed better than the older group (40s). Time of testing effects (from the first time they were tested to the second time, 1 year later) were present for the following variables: diastolic blood pressure, which was higher in Year 2; vibratory threshold in the big toe, which was higher in Year 2; flexibility, which was poorer in Year 2; far vision, which was poorer in Year 2; reaction time, which was slower in Year 2; and auditory acuity at 6,000 Hz, which was poorer in Year 2.

For females with Down syndrome, the only significant effect for age was on hand-eye coordination, in which there were also effects for time of testing and age by time interaction. The younger groups (30s and 40s) performed better than the oldest (50s). Performance was better for all groups in Year 2, with the best performance being for females in their 40s. This effect may have been due to participants becoming more familiar with requirements of the task by the second time of testing. Percentage of body fat declined significantly from Year 1 to Year 2. Vital capacity as measured by PEF was better in Year 2. Flexibility was poorer in Year 2. Far vision was poorer in Year 2. Auditory acuity at all Hz levels was better in Year 2. Diastolic blood pressure increased from Year 1 to Year 2 but just missed significance at the .05 level. All of these changes are consistent with phenomena of age-related decline except for improved vital capacity and hearing indices.

Other Major Findings   For the group with Down syndrome findings included a significant weight gain for males between Year 1 and Year 2. For resting heart rate, there was an increase from Year 1 to Year 2. Systolic blood pressure was higher in Year 2 due primarily to increases in the males in their 70s. Diastolic pressure was higher in Year 2. Percentage body fat was higher in females overall, but it was lower in Year 2 than in Year 1. Grip strength was less for females. The PEF measure of vital capacity was higher for males, higher for the 60s age group, and higher in Year 2.

The most improvement in vital capacity was shown by males in their 50s. For hand-eye coordination, there was a sex by age interaction, with poorest performance by males in their 50s. Two-point tapping performance declined from Year 1 to Year 2. Vibratory threshold in the thumb was highest (worst) for males, higher for older age groups, and highest of all for males in their 70s. Vibratory threshold measured in the big toe followed the same pattern as that for the thumb. Flexibility of the trunk was significantly poorer for males than females. Far vision declined between Year 1 and Year 2, as did auditory acuity at 2,000 Hz and 4,000 Hz.

Overall, blood pressure and resting heart rates were within normal limits for both groups studied. Systolic blood pressure increased with age just as it does in the general aging population (Asmussen, Fruensgaard, & Norgaard, 1975). It should be noted that blood pressure readings were lower in the group with Down syndrome, especially in the females, than in the general population at comparable ages (Hollingsworth, Hashizume, & Jablon, 1966). Resting heart rate showed no relationship to age in either group, although previous research has found a decrease in heart rate with age in people without mental retardation (Asmussen et al., 1975).

Body fat percentages were higher for females than males, which is consistent with the general population findings. Males with Down syndrome were in the above normal to very high fat range, while females with Down syndrome were at the high end of normal. Males and females without Down syndrome were in the low to average fat range. Body fat decreased from Year 1 to Year 2 for all females, both with and without Down syndrome, while weight remained stable or increased slightly. Such a finding could indicate better physical conditioning with an increase in heavier muscle tissue due to increased exercise, but we have not confirmed this interpretation.

Effect of Participant Involvement   The measures of blood pressure, resting heart rate, and percentage of body fat are objective measures not related to degree of participant understanding, cooperation, and motivation. All of the other measures of physical variables were strongly influenced by participant cooperation. Participants varied in their ability to understand directions and in their motivation to provide maximal performance. The vital capacity measures depended upon the participants' ability and willingness to blow into the spirometer as hard and as fast as they could. The vibratory threshold tasks required that the participants respond the instant they felt the vibratory stimulus in the thumb or big toe. Often it appeared that participants were waiting to be really sure that they felt it before they responded, thus providing higher threshold readings. This slowness in responding may have been due to a type of cautiousness in responding seen in older people in general or may have been an accurate representation of the slower reaction time seen in persons with mental retardation, especially those with Down syndrome.

Numerous problems were encountered with auditory assessments. Problems related to conveying the notion of responding as soon as they heard the tone. There were large standard deviations associated with all hearing assessments; therefore, caution should be used in their interpretation. Similar problems were encountered with some participants concerning reaction time and choice reaction time tasks. It was difficult to be sure that they were responding as quickly as they could or that they understood that speed was important. Great care was taken by the examiner to try to ensure communication. Given these caveats, results were generally in line with expectations based on the literature on the general aging population.

Grip strength values were in the low average range, better for males than females, and better for those without Down syndrome than for those with Down syndrome. In the group with Down syndrome and the group without Down syndrome, the younger participants had better grip strength. In the general population, grip strength is known to be different between the sexes and to decline with age (Hollingsworth et al., 1966). Vital capacity measures revealed the usual sex differences, with males having higher capacity. There was a trend toward lower capacity for older participants, which reflected a pattern that is consonant with age-related decline.

Reaction time and choice reaction time, which have been shown in studies with the general population to increase consistently with age, showed no age-related effects whatsoever in this study. All reaction time results were considerably slower than results from the general aging population at comparable ages, usually by a factor of two or three times. These results are in agreement with a large body of literature on reaction time deficits in people with mental disabilities (Baumeister & Kellas, 1968).

On the tapping measures, the only significant finding for age was for the males with Down syndrome; the younger males performed better than the older males. Tapping performance otherwise was unremarkable except that the group with Down syndrome did not perform as well on the crossover tapping (two-point tapping) as the group without Down syndrome in spite of the younger ages of the group with Down syndrome. Hand-eye coordination scores were poor for both groups and showed no consistent relationship with age. The trunk flexibility measure showed consistent sex differences similar to those in the general population, with males less flexible than females at all ages. The group with Down syndrome had better flexibility than the group without Down syndrome. Both male and female participants with Down syndrome had declines in flexibility from Year 1 to Year 2.

In the vision and hearing assessments, near vision was not related to age. Far vision was significantly correlated with age, and there were significant declines in ability to see at a distance from Year 1 to Year 2 for both groups. This finding is in accord with findings on the general aging population (Corso, 1971), but onset was earlier in the group with Down syndrome. Finally, the auditory assessments were too unreliable to warrant interpretation. A consistent finding in the general aging population is one of decreased sensitivity to high pitched tones with age (Corso, 1971), but present results did not consistently confirm that finding.

Application of Physical Assessment Instruments   The purpose in using this battery of physical measures with the participants of this study was to find a way to assess functional capacity and how that capacity changes over time. Such a battery would be useful as a screening tool to assist in decision-making about interventions needed when various physical capacities change. The battery would also be useful in assessing outcomes of interventions. Furthermore, a physical assessment battery that was noninvasive and relatively simple to administer in the field could be used to gather descriptive information on aging people with mental retardation that could serve as a baseline for future longitudinal follow ups as they continue to age. Based on current findings, the measures of weight, percentage of body fat, systolic and diastolic blood pressure, grip strength, vital capacity, vibratory threshold, far vision, and trunk flexibility appear to have the most promise for these purposes. Auditory acuity, an important age-related factor, should be assessed by an audiologist with special training in assessing persons with mental retardation and under more ideal conditions than are generally available in field-testing sites. All of the other recommended measures can be administered by a nonmedically trained examiner with brief training on these specific procedures.

Cognitive Functioning

Cross-sectional analyses were conducted for each year of the study, and longitudinal analyses were conducted to compare Year 1 with Year 2. From preliminary analyses it was evident that there were sex differences as well as differences between the group with Down syndrome and the group without Down syndrome. In Figure 1.2 (Figure 1.1 provides a key to Figures 1.2–1.5) cross-sectional results for male participants with Down syndrome in Year 1 are presented. Figure 1.3 presents cross-sectional results for females with Down syndrome in Year 1. Again it should be noted that there were female participants with Down syndrome in the age range 50–59, but no males with Down syndrome in that age range.

All scores for males with Down syndrome in their 40s were lower than those for males with Down syndrome in their 30s (Figure 1.2). All scores for females with Down syndrome in their 40s were higher than for those in their 30s (Figure 1.2). Females with Down syndrome in their 50s revealed a mixed pattern, showing better performance compared to those in the same group in their 30s and 40s on some subtests and lower performance on others.

For the group without Down syndrome, sex differences were not quite so strong. For males there was a pattern of equal or higher performance for those in their 60s when compared with those in their 50s. On two of the seven subtests, there was a lower performance for those in their 70s when compared with those in their 60s (Figure 1.4). For females in the group without Down syndrome those in their 60s performed better than those in their 50s on every subtest. More remarkable, however, is the fact that those in their 70s performed better than those in their 60s on four of the seven subtests (Figure 1.5).

Results for the Wechsler Digit Span Forward (Wechsler, 1955) showed a similar pattern, with peak performance for males with Down syndrome in their 30s and peak performance for females with Down syndrome in their 40s. Digit Span Backward (Wechsler, 1955) was not productive in that all participants performed so poorly that no meaningful patterns emerged. For Digit Symbol (Wechsler, 1955), females were highest in their 40s and males highest in their 30s. For participants without Down syndrome, gender difference patterns were less clear. More of the females showed peak performance in the 70s group, however, while more of the males had peak performance in the 60s group.

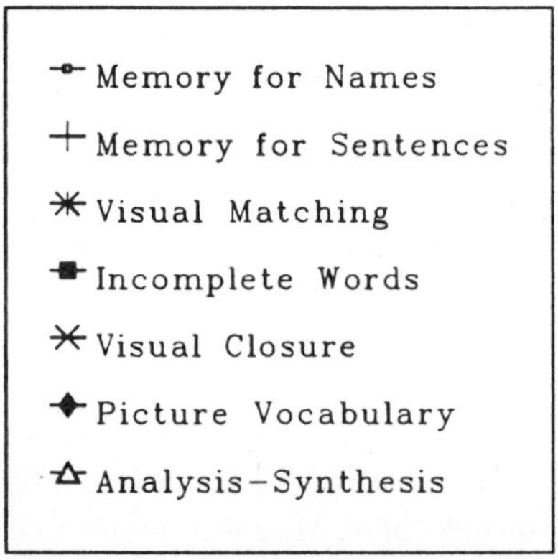

Figure 1.1.   Key for Figures 1.2–1.5.

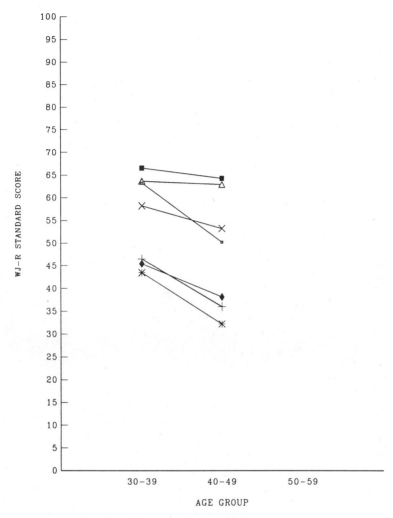

Figure 1.2.   Cross-sectional gradients of scores for WJ-R for males with Down syndrome in Year 1.

Generally, these cross-sectional results present a picture of sex differences in both groups, although much more pronounced in the group with Down syndrome, with males showing lower performance a decade sooner than females. Results for Year 2 analyses were quite similar (Hawkins et al., 1991). To what extent these differences are due to cohort (age group) effects is not known. Similar results have appeared in another study on persons without mental retardation done by Gur et al., 1991.

Longitudinal comparisons of the Year 1 and Year 2 results using MANOVA for the males with Down syndrome yielded a significant effect for cohort only for the Memory for Names subtest. Highest performance was found in the younger

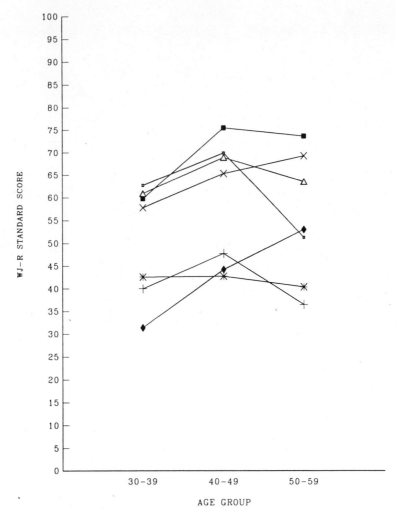

Figure 1.3. Cross-sectional gradients of scores for WJ-R for females with Down syndrome in Year 1.

group on this variable. There was a time of testing effect for Memory for Sentences and for Broad Cognitive Score. On Memory for Sentences, improvement was shown for both age groups from Year 1 to Year 2. For the Broad Cognitive Total Score, small but significant gains were found for both age groups.

For females with Down syndrome, the MANOVA analysis (Cohen & Cohen, 1983) included three age groups (30s, 40s, and 50s) and two times of testing. For the females with Down syndrome, significant age differences were found for Memory for Names, Picture Vocabulary, and Analysis–Synthesis. Highest per-

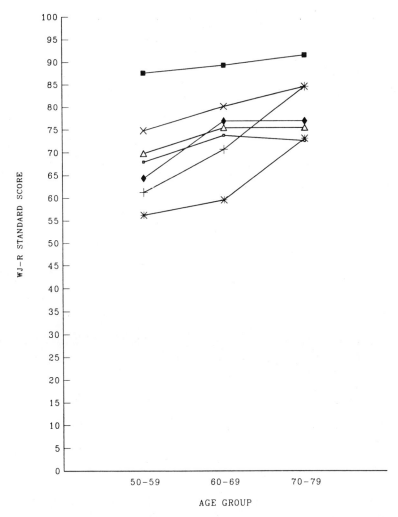

Figure 1.4. Cross-sectional gradients of scores for WJ-R for males without Down syndrome in Year 1.

formance on Memory for Names was for the 40s group. On Picture Vocabulary there was a linear relationship with age, with highest performance for the 50s group. For Analysis–Synthesis, the picture was more complex, with highest performance averaged across both years appearing in the 50s group. For the Year 1 and Year 2 comparison, there was a significant difference on Incomplete Words and Digit Span Forward. Incomplete Word scores increased for the 30s group and also for the 50s group. Digit Span Forward increased from Year 1 to Year 2 for all three age groups.

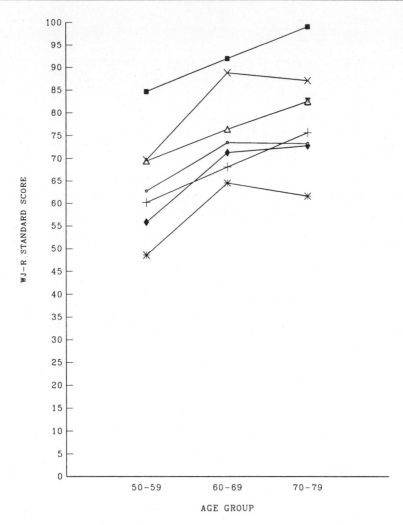

Figure 1.5. Cross-sectional gradients of scores for WJ-R for females without Down syndrome in Year 1.

Findings for Participants without Down Syndrome Analyses for the group without Down syndrome included both sexes in the same design. There were no males in their 50s. The procedure used was MANOVA to compare Year 1 with Year 2 data by sex by age group. Age differences were found on the three subtests—Memory for Names, Picture Vocabulary, Analysis–Synthesis—and on Broad Cognitive Total Score. For Memory for Names, the youngest group (50s) performed significantly lower than either of the other age groups. On Analysis–Synthesis the oldest group (70s) performed best, then the

60s group, and finally the 50s. For Broad Cognitive Total Score, the pattern was the same as for Analysis–Synthesis, showing a linear positive relationship with age. For Picture Vocabulary, the picture was more complex. The youngest age group performed more poorly than the older groups. Time of testing was also significant, with overall scores higher at Year 1 than Year 2. This result was primarily accounted for by decline in performance by males in their 70s and 60s. Females of all age groups increased their scores from Year 1 to Year 2 on Picture Vocabulary. There were a number of other interaction effects, but they are not of major interest here.

The purpose of the 2-year comparisons was to begin to lay the base for a more extended longitudinal study to follow these participants over a more sub-stantial period of time and to track their increases or declines in performance as they age. It was not anticipated that findings over a 2-year period would be of major import. Changes from Year 1 to Year 2, even when statistically significant, were small and probably not of great practical significance except in the case of the oldest (70s) males without Down syndrome, who did show significant and meaningful decline on several subtests. The participants with Down syndrome showed improvement in some subtests and no declines from Year 1 to Year 2. Had there been any male participants with Down syndrome in their 50s, decline comparable to that of the males without Down syndrome in their 70s might have been seen, but, unfortunately, this group was missing. Inability to recruit males with Down syndrome in their 50s may speak to the increased vulnerability of this group. For participants without Down syndrome, the small number of males in their 70s showed significant decline. The overall picture in this 1-year interval was one of stability except for the decline in the oldest males. Findings for the group without Down syndrome tended to parallel the literature on the general aging population, with stability until the late 60s or early 70s (Schaie & Strother, 1968). For the group with Down syndrome, cross-sectional results were com-patible with a picture of earlier onset of decline (40s for males, 50s for females).

The evidence of earlier decline in males (although decline here was in-ferred from cross-sectional evidence of age differences and not actual within-subject change over time) may be tentatively compared to findings (Gur et al., 1991) of earlier brain deterioration in males than in females. A report stated that a study of males and females without mental retardation, ages 18–80, found that deterioration in the brain, especially on the left side, which controls language and verbal abilities, is two to three times faster in men. The data "suggest that women are less vulnerable to age-related changes in mental abilities, whereas men are particularly susceptible to aging effects on left hemispheric functions" (p. 2845). These findings involved magnetic resonance research (MRI) on only 34 men and 35 women and have yet to be replicated but might possibly shed light on the present findings.

Efficacy of Instruments Used   The Woodcock-Johnson-Revised Cogni-tive Standard Battery (WJ-R) (Woodcock & Mather, 1989) appears to be a useful instrument for assessing and tracking cognitive functioning over time in a group of adults with mental retardation because of its wide age range of standardization and its theoretical base. The original intention of analyzing changes in fluid versus crystallized abilities, however, did not prove viable for several reasons. First, the test developers warn against interpretation of any of the separate factors on the test on the basis of less than two subtests per factor, and only one was used. Second, the subtest that loads most heavily on fluid ability is Analysis–Synthesis. Although participants' standard scores for these two groups appear to be relatively high compared with some of their other scores, it was possible for them to receive standard scores as high as 65 with raw scores of 0. Thus, these scores are spuriously high and not useful for looking at change in fluid ability. It is recommended that, in the future, the Early Developmental version of the WJ-R, which drops Visual Matching and Analysis–Synthesis, be employed with this population. Furthermore, if performance on specific factors is of interest, two measures of each of the five factors on the Early Developmental battery should be used. If only the Broad Cognitive Score is of interest, the five-subtest Early Developmental battery has been found to correlate .96 with the full Standard Battery in the adult range (Woodcock & Mather, 1989).

The Wechsler items for Digit Span memory, although found useful in prior research with the general aging population, were not useful in the present study because scores were universally so low and showed so little variability (Craik, 1977). Digit Symbol was highly correlated with Visual Memory from the WJ-R and did not seem to add anything of significance. In future research with this sample these measures will be dropped.

When turning to the consideration of usefulness for program planning, WJ-R findings are subject to most of the criticisms of intelligence testing in general. The test authors appear to "assume that more information about cognitive processing will contribute positively to improved interventions," according to Reschly (1990, p. 264). Witt and Gresham (1985) describe this same issue with respect to the WISC-R and other intelligence batteries. "For a test to have treatment validity, it must lead to better treatments, i.e., better educational programs, teaching strategies, etc." (p. 1717). Ysseldyke (1990) has assessed the "'goodness of fit' of the WJ-R to the Horn-Cattell . . . model of intelligence. . . . I am convinced that the test is a good fit to the model" (p. 268), he said. Furthermore, he stated that the WJ-R represents a significant milestone in the applied measurement of intellectual abilities. "The manner in which theory and prior research were used in the development of the WJ-R . . . should serve as a model for future research and development in the fields of applied psychometrics and psychoeducational assessment" (p. 268), he said. What we now need to resolve the question of treatment validity of the WJ-R is aptitude-treatment interaction (ATI) research on implications of subtest patterns for treatment (Reschly, 1990; Woodcock, 1990; Ysseldyke, 1990). Until such research is available, however, the WJ-R appears to be at least as satisfactory for the assessment of cognitive functioning in persons with mental retardation as the more commonly used Wechsler and Binet instruments.

Daily Life Functioning and Stress

Results from the modified Katz Index of Activities of Daily Living showed that, in most of the areas assessed, persons in this study were completely independent, with a higher than anticipated incidence of bladder and bowel accidents (20%) being the only exception. More than 10% across the two samples also needed help with bathing and with stair climbing. From Year 1 to Year 2 there were only minor shifts, with the patterns remaining much the same as in Year 1. No remarkable differences between the group with Down syndrome and the group without Down syndrome were observed.

Assessment of Instrumental Activities of Daily Living (IADL) provided information about those instrumental activities that participants had the greatest difficulty carrying out independently. Most of the participants needed some assistance in most areas of functioning. For example, 20% could not use the telephone, and over 50% could not use money correctly. Initiative is an area in which help is needed; 52% of the group would engage in activities only if assigned or directed to do so. Under the area of persistence, 43% were rated as needing constant encouragement to complete a task.

The Stress Index was intended to provide insight into the degree of stress experienced by the aging adults in this study. During Year 1 and Year 2, only 15.2% and 18.8% of the subjects had not experienced at least one stressful event during the previous year. In Year 1, 63.5% of the group had experienced two or more major events that were stressful, and in Year 2, the comparable figure was 61.2%. (See Table 1.2.) The particular events experienced by the participants are presented in Table 1.3 along with the percentages of participants experiencing each event based on the total group (those with Down syndrome and without Down syndrome combined).

A review of the findings from the ADL, IADL, and Stress Index measures provides useful information regarding the overall functional skills for aging adults with mental retardation, with or without Down syndrome. In general, both groups were high functioning or independent in terms of basic activities of daily living, for example, bathing, dressing, toileting, transferring, continence, feeding, and ambulation. Findings from the modified IADL scale, however, indicate the need for assistance with the instrumental activities of daily living, for

Table 1.2. Number of stressful events experienced by percentage of participants

	Number of stressful events					
	0	1	2	3	4	5
Year 1	15.2	21.2	24.2	24.2	7.6	7.5
Year 2	18.8	20.0	32.9	17.6	5.9	4.8

Table 1.3.   Percentage of participants experiencing various stressful events in past year

Event	Year 1	Year 2
A. Going to the hospital because he or she was sick	35.9	30.5
B. Having a friend or relative go to the hospital or die	51.6	48.8
C. Moving	18.3	9.6
D. Having a friend or relative move far away	21.0	17.1
E. Having a new roommate or house supervisor	55.6	34.9
F. Losing a job or retiring	11.3	11.8
G. Taking a new job	8.3	11.8
H. Having money problems	8.1	13.3
I. Having any other problems	15.8	20.7

example, traveling around the community, using the telephone, shopping, preparing meals, work skills, using money, medications, and speech articulation. In each of the aforementioned areas, a high percentage of the total sample (between 70% and 80%) needed some assistance. Those instrumental areas in which a lower percentage of the sample needed assistance (40%–50%) included: room cleaning, attentiveness, and socialization, including awareness of and interaction with others.

The potential value of using the modified Katz Index of ADL in combination with the modified IADL scale is that they are quick and easy to administer while providing information of direct application in daily care planning. Once an individual begins to decline in basic ADL, the level of independence clearly alters, thus suggesting that additional care and assistance are needed. The IADL scale provides direction in terms of daily instrumental skill areas that will need support of focused interventions that are designed to regain or promote independence. The main utility of these scales seems to be in tracking individuals from year to year in their ability to perform basic daily functions. Each function in which an individual loses independence has implications for intervention/care planning. Some of the participants in the study already needed help with continence, bathing, and stair climbing. As they continue to age it is predictable that they will require greater assistance. Both the ADL and IADL scales provide a simple method of monitoring performance over time.

The value of the Stress Index in this battery is that it serves as a reminder of the experience of events in an older person's life that can generate stress. Based on the concept that stress is additive, such an index can alert careproviders to the need for stress-reducing activities and emotional support. For older adults with mental retardation who may sometimes be seen as sheltered from the stresses common to most adults, the Stress Index demonstrates that they experience many of the same changes and losses common to other older adults. The most commonly experienced event in Year 1 was having a new roommate or housekeeper, followed closely by having a friend or relative go to the hospital. During Year 1, both events had been experienced by more than

50% of the sample within the past year. For Year 2, the hospitalization of a friend or relative was the most common stressful event; it was experienced by 48.8% of the sample.

SUMMARY AND IMPLICATIONS

The research described here was undertaken based upon a concern with maintaining optimal functioning in persons with developmental disabilities as they age. The first step was the development of an assessment battery that would provide a yardstick for measuring levels of functioning and be sensitive to changes in functional status. Since aging is a complex process involving biological, psychological, and social changes, an assessment battery based on a bio-psycho-social model of aging was assembled (Hawkins et al., 1991). Potential utility of the battery for maintenance of function lies in its ability to pinpoint areas of change in an individual over time.

For example, in the physical assessment area, if increased percentage of body fat and increased systolic blood pressure are seen between Time 1 and Time 2 of measurement, this finding has implications for the need for a regular exercise program that has the potential to ameliorate both the amount of body fat and the blood pressure increase. In the cognitive area, if short-term memory begins to decline, techniques to help maintain function in this area can be used; among these are: memory exercises, use of mnemonics to assist in remembering (including such simple techniques as the old "string around the finger"), more repetitions of material to be remembered, and more reminders from others.

The IADL assessment provides information about maintenance of skills for dealing with one's environment from day to day. If skills for housekeeping begin to deteriorate, the physical battery can be helpful with respect to clues that may explain why. If flexibility is less than it used to be, then bending and stooping required for some household tasks may simply be more difficult than previously. Stretching exercises may help with flexibility to some extent, but emphasis on different household chores not requiring flexibility may be necessary. Another possibility may relate decline in housekeeping skills to memory loss. The individual may be having difficulty remembering what tasks are supposed to be done and may need frequent reminders.

The ADL measure can be useful in making decisions about the need for out-of-home care when function can no longer be maintained without a great deal of assistance. Some gerontological literature has suggested that if help is needed in more than two ADLs, nursing home placement may be needed (Kane & Kane, 1981). While such decisions rarely are that clear, the ADL scale can serve as a monitoring and tracking device in late life to alert care planners to changes in status. Some changes in basic ADLs are also subject to remediation, as exemplified by behavioral intervention programs for incontinence.

The Stress Index is a useful device for reminding care planners and persons with developmental disabilities themselves how many life changes they may be experiencing as they grow older. Such changes are known to produce stress and may help to explain changes in functional status in biological and/or psychological areas. Stress reduction techniques, ranging from physical activity to emotional support, may be needed to help people with developmental disabilities cope with multiple changes, including losses, in their lives.

Finally, the battery described here may be useful for the evaluation of programming for older adults with developmental disabilities. Tracking about once a year with the complete battery, or with those parts that reflect areas of concern for a particular individual, will provide a measure of outcome for some aspects of programming. It is important to keep in mind, however, that for older adults with developmental disabilities, as for the general older population, maintaining levels of performance or slowing rates of decline are valid goals of active programming. It is not necessary to have gains in performance for older age groups to show positive outcomes of programming. While gains may be possible for some individuals in some areas until quite late in life, it is not realistic to demand that they be shown by all individuals across all areas of functioning. Maintenance of functional levels for as long as possible is a worthy goal for all people in late life.

REFERENCES

Arenberg, D., & Robertson-Tchabo, E.A. (1977). Learning and aging. In J.E. Birren & K.W. Schaie (Eds.), *Handbook of the psychology of aging* (pp. 421–449). New York: Van Nostrand Reinhold.

Asmussen, E., Fruensgaard, K., & Norgaard, S. (1975). A follow-up longitudinal study of selected physiologic functions in former physical education students—After forty years. *Journal of the American Geriatric Society, 23,* 442–450.

Baltes, P.B., & Willis, S.L. (1983). Enhancement of intellectual functioning in old age: Penn State's Adult Development and Enrichment Project (ADEPT). In F.I.M. Craik & S.E. Trehub (Eds.), *Aging and cognitive processes* (pp. 353–389). New York: Plenum.

Baumeister, A.A., & Kellas, G. (1968). Reaction time and mental retardation. In N.R. Ellis (Ed.), *International review of research in mental retardation: Vol. 3* (pp. 290–331). New York: Academic Press.

Bell, A., & Zubek, J.P. (1960). The effect of age on the intellectual performance of mental defectives. *Journal of Gerontology, 15*(3), 285–295.

Borkan, G. (1980). Assessment of biological aging using a profile of physical parameters. *Journal of Gerontology, 55,* 177–184.

Botwinick, J. (1977). Intellectual abilities. In J.E. Birren & K.W. Schaie (Eds.), *Handbook of the psychology of aging* (pp. 580–603). New York: Van Nostrand Reinhold.

Cattell, R.B. (1963). Theory for fluid and crystallized intelligence: A critical experiment. *Journal of Educational Psychology, 54,* 1–22.

Corso, J.F. (1971). Sensory processes and age effects in normal adults. *Journal of Gerontology, 26,* 90–105.

Corso, J.F. (1982). Auditory clinical markers of aging. In M.E. Reff & E.L. Schneider

(Eds.), *Biological markers of aging*. Bethesda, MD: United States Department of Health and Human Services, National Institutes of Health, PHS #82-2221.

Craik, F.I.M. (1977). Age differences in human memory. In J.E. Birren & K.W. Schaie (Eds.), *Handbook of the psychology of aging* (pp. 384–420). New York: Van Nostrand Reinhold.

Dalton, A.J., & Crapper, D.R. (1977). Down's Syndrome and aging of the brain. In P. Mittler (Ed.), *Research to practice in mental retardation: Biomedical aspects* (Vol. III). Baltimore: University Park Press.

Dalton, A.J., & Crapper, D.R. (1984). Incidence of memory deterioration in aging persons with Down's Syndrome. In J.M. Berg (Ed.), *Perspectives and progress in mental retardation, Vol II: Biomedical aspects* (pp. 55–62). Baltimore: University Park Press.

Dalton, A.J., Crapper, D.R., & Schlotterer, G.R. (1974). Alzheimer's disease in Down's Syndrome: Visual retention deficits. *Cortex, 10,* 366–377.

Dean, W. (1988). *Biological aging measurement: Clinical application.* Thousand Oaks, CA: Center for Bio-Gerontology.

Eisner, D.A. (1983). Down's Syndrome and aging: Is senile dementia inevitable? *Psychological Reports, 52,* 119–124.

Fenner, M.E., Hewitt, K.E., & Torpy, D.M. (1987). Down's Syndrome: Intellectual and behavioral functioning during adulthood. *Journal of Mental Deficiency Research, 31,* 241–249.

Fisher, M.A., & Zeaman, D. (1970). Growth and decline of retardate intelligence. *International Review of Research in Mental Retardation, 4,* 151–191.

Furukawa, T., Inoue, M., Kajiya, F., Takasugi, A., Fukui, S., Takeda, H., & Abe, H. (1975). Assessment of biological age by multiple regression analysis. *Journal of Gerontology, 30,* 422–434.

Gallo, J.J., Reichel, W., & Andersen, L. (1988). *Handbook of geriatric assessment.* Rockville, MD: Aspen Publishers.

Goodman, J.F. (1976). Aging and IQ change in institutionalized mentally retarded. *Psychological Reports, 39,* 999–1006.

Gur, R.C., Mozley, P.D., Resnick, S.M., Gottlieb, G.L., Kohn, M., Zimmerman, R., Herman, G., Atlas, S., Grossman, R., Berretta, D., Erwin, R., & Gur, R.E. (1991). Gender differences in age effect on brain atrophy measured by magnetic resonance imaging. *Proceedings of the National Academy of Sciences, 88,* 2845–2849.

Guralnick, J., Branch, L.G., Cummings, S.R., & Curb, J.D. (1989). Physical performance measures in aging research. *Journal of Gerontology, 44*(5), M141–146.

Hawkins, B.A., Eklund, S.J., & Martz, B.L. (1991). *Detection of decline in aging adults with developmental disabilities.* Cincinnati: Research and Training Center Consortium on Aging and Developmental Disabilities.

Hewitt, K.E., Fenner, M.E., & Torpy, D. (1986). Cognitive and behavioral profiles of the elderly mentally handicapped. *Journal of Mental Deficiency Research, 30,* 217–225.

Hewitt, K.E., & Jancar, J. (1986). Psychological and clinical aspects of aging in Down's Syndrome. In J.M. Berg (Ed.), *Science and service in mental retardation* (pp. 370–379). London: Methuen.

Hollingsworth, J.W., Hashizume, A., & Jablon, S. (1966). Correlations between tests of aging in Hiroshima subjects—An attempt to define "Physiologic Age." *Yale Journal of Biology and Medicine, 38,* 11–26.

Horn, J.L. (1970). Organization of data on life-span development of human abilities. In L.R. Goulet & P.B. Baltes (Eds.), *Life-span developmental psychology: Research and theory.* New York: Academic Press.

Horn, J.L. (1972). State, trait and change dimensions of intelligence. *British Journal of Educational Psychology, 42,* 159–185.

Horn, J.L. (1976). Human abilities: A review of research and theory in the early 1970's. *Annual Review of Psychology, 27,* 437–485.

Horn, J.L. (1985). Remodeling old models of intelligence. In B.B. Wolman (Ed.), *Handbook of intelligence* (pp. 267–300). New York: John Wiley & Sons.

Horn, J.L. (1988). Cognitive diversity: A framework for learning. In P.L. Ackerman, R.J. Sternberg, & R. Glaser (Eds.), *Learning and individual differences.* New York: W.H. Freeman.

Horn, J.L., & Cattell, R.B. (1966). Refinement and test of the theory of fluid and crystallized intelligence. *Journal of Educational Psychology, 57,* 253–270.

Kane, R.A., & Kane, R.L. (1981). *Assessing the elderly.* Lexington, MA: D.C. Heath.

Kannel, W.B., & Hubert, H. (1982). Vital capacity as a biomarker of aging. In M.E. Reff & E.L. Schneider (Eds.), *Biological markers of aging.* Bethesda, MD: United States Department of Health and Human Services, National Institutes of Health, PHS #82-2221.

Katz, S., Ford, B.S., Moskowitz, R.W., Jackson, B.A., & Jaffee, M.W. (1963). Studies of illness in the aged. The Index of ADL: A standardized measure of biological and psychosocial function. *Journal of the American Medical Association, 185,* 94ff.

Labouvie-Vief, G. (1985). Intelligence and cognition. In J.E. Birren & K.W. Schaie (Eds.), *Handbook of the psychology of aging* (pp. 500–530). New York: Van Nostrand Reinhold.

Lawton, M.P. (1972). Assessing the competence of older people. In D. Kent, R. Kastenbaum, & S. Sherwood (Eds.), *Research planning and action for the elderly.* New York: Behavioral Publications.

Ludwig, F.C., & Masaro, E.J. (1983). The biological measure of age. *Experimental Aging Research, 9,* 219–220.

McDade, H.L., & Adler, S. (1980). Down's Syndrome and short-term memory impairment: A storage or retrieval deficit? *American Journal of Mental Deficiency, 84,* 561–567.

Meyers, C.E., Nihira, K., & Zetlin, A. (1979). The measurement of adaptive behavior. In N.R. Ellis (Ed.), *Handbook of mental deficiency: Psychological theory and research—* (2nd ed., pp. 431–481). Hillsdale, NJ: Lawrence Erlbaum Associates.

Mints, A.Y., Dubina, T.L., Lysenyk, P.V., & Zhuk, E.V. (1984). Defining the biological age of an individual and an appraisal of the degree of aging. *Physiologichiski Zhurnal, 30,* 39–45.

Nihira, K., Foster, R., Shellhaas, M., & Leland, H. (1974). *AAMD Adaptive Behavior Scale.* Washington, DC: American Association on Mental Deficiency.

Perlmutter, M. (1986). A life-span view of memory. In P.B. Baltes, D.L. Featherman, & R.M. Lerner (Eds.), *Life span development and behavior, Vol. 7* (pp. 272–308). Hillsdale, NJ: Lawrence Erlbaum Associates.

Perlmutter, M. (1988). Cognitive potential throughout life. In J.E. Birren & V. Bengston (Eds.), *Emergent theories of aging* (pp. 247–268). New York: Springer-Verlag.

Perlmutter, M., & Hall, E. (1985). *Adult development and aging.* New York: John Wiley & Sons.

Perlmutter, M., & Nyquist, L. (1989). Relationships between self-reported physical and mental health and intelligence performances across adulthood. *Journal of Gerontology, 44,* 145–155.

Reschly, D.J. (1990). Found: Our intelligences: What do they mean? *Journal of Psychoeducational Assessment, 8,* 259–267.

Salthouse, T. (1982). Psychomotor indices of physiological age. In M.E. Reff & E.L. Schneider (Eds.), *Biological markers of aging.* Bethesda, MD: United States Department of Health and Human Services, National Institutes of Health, PHS #82-2221.

Schaie, K.W., & Strother, C.R. (1968). A cross-sequential study of age changes in cognitive behavior. *Psychological Bulletin, 70,* 671–680.

Schneider, E.L., & Rowe, J.W. (Eds.). (1990). *Handbook of the biology of aging* (3rd ed.). San Diego: Academic Press.

Shock, N.W. (1981). Indices of functional age. In D. Shanon, N.W. Shock, & M. Marois (Eds.), *Aging: A challenge to science and society, Vol. 1, Biology* (pp. 270–286). New York: Oxford University Press.

Shock N.W., Greulich, R.C., Costa, P.T., Andres, R., Lakatta, E.G., Arenberg, D., & Tobin, J.D. (1984). *Normal human aging: The Baltimore longitudinal study of aging.* Washington, DC: NIH Publication No. 84-2450, Superintendent of Public Documents, United States Government Printing Office.

Silverstein, A.B. (1979). Mental growth from six to sixty in an institutionalized mentally retarded sample. *Psychological Reports, 45,* 643–646.

Terman, L.M., & Merrill, M. (1937). *Measuring intelligence.* Boston: Houghton Mifflin.

Thase, M.E. (1982). Longevity and morbidity in Down's Syndrome. *Journal of Mental Deficiency Research, 26,* 177–192.

Wechsler, D. (1939). *Measurement of adult intelligence.* Baltimore: Williams & Wilkins.

Wechsler, D. (1949). *Wechsler intelligence scale for children.* New York: Psychological Corporation.

Wechsler, D. (1955). *Wechsler Adult Intelligence Scale.* New York: Psychological Corporation.

Willis, S.L., Blieszner, R., & Baltes, P.B. (1981). Intellectual training research in aging: Modification of performance on the fluid ability of figural relations. *Journal of Educational Psychology, 73,* 41–50.

Wisniewski, K., Howe, J., Williams, D.G., & Wisniewski, H.M. (1978). Precocious aging and dementia in patients with Down's Syndrome. *Biological Psychiatry, 13*(5), 619–627.

Witt, J.C., & Gresham, F.M. (1985). Review of the Wechsler Intelligence Scales for Children-Revised. In J. Mitchell (Ed.), *Ninth mental measurements yearbook* (pp. 1716–1719). Lincoln, NE: Buros Institute.

Woodcock, R.W. (1990). Theoretical foundations of the WJ-R measures of cognitive ability. *Journal of Psychoeducational Assessment, 8,* 231–258.

Woodcock, R.W., & Johnson, M.B. (1989). WJ-R Tests of Cognitive Ability-Standard and Supplemental Batteries: Examiner's manual. In R.W. Woodcock & M.B. Johnson. *Woodcock-Johnson Psycho-Educational Battery Revised.* Allen, TX: DLM Teaching Resources.

Young, E.C., & Kramer, B.M. (1991). Characteristics of age-related language decline in adults with Down Syndrome. *Mental Retardation, 29*(2), 75–79.

Ysseldyke, J.E. (1990). Goodness of fit of the Woodcock-Johnson Psychoeducational Battery-Revised to the Horn-Cattell Gf-Gc Theory. *Journal of Psychoeducational Assessment, 8,* 268–275.

Zigman, W.B., Schupf, N., Lubin, R.A., & Silverman, W.P. (1987). Premature regression of adults with Down Syndrome. *American Journal of Mental Deficiency, 92*(2), 161–168.

2

Health Issues

Deborah J. Anderson

The unprecedented rate of increase in numbers of older adults in general has been paralleled among older adults with developmental disabilities (DD) (Di-Gioranini, 1978; Chadwick & Lubin, 1982 [cited in Janicki, Ackerman, & Jacobson, 1985]; Jacobson, Sutton, & Janicki, 1985). This demographic trend, coupled with the depopulation of state institutions and the Omnibus Budget Reconciliation Act of 1987 (OBRA, Public Law 100-203) mandating diversion of people with developmental disabilities from nursing homes, threatens to overwhelm an already burdened system of care. This chapter examines, through two separate studies, the health status of older adults with mental retardation living in nursing homes and of those living in residential facilities licensed by mental retardation and developmental disabilities (MR/DD) agencies. The health conditions and care received by people living in different types of facilities are compared, in part, to determine: 1) the extent of their need for medically intensive care, 2) whether community-based alternatives are capable of meeting the need for residential services, and 3) whether current levels of care are appropriate.

DEMOGRAPHIC TRENDS

It is estimated that people 65 and older make up approximately 12% of all people with developmental disabilities, similar to the population of people without developmental disabilities. People with mental retardation are increasingly likely to survive into the older age ranges, even though their average life expectancy remains less than that of the general population (Eyman, Grossman, Tarjan, & Miller, 1987). This increase is thought to be due to a number of factors, among them improvements in health care and social services programs, including residential services, which in turn have led to prevention of morbidity and to later mortality (Janicki, Ackerman, & Jacobson, 1985). Death rates for people with developmental disabilities in institutional settings have declined from 19.4 per 1,000 average daily residents in 1970 to 13.2 per 1,000 in 1986. This is true despite the increase in the proportions of people who are older and/or have profound mental retardation (White, Lakin, Hill, Wright, & Bruininks, 1987). Mortality rates are approaching those for the general population, with the exception of people with Down syndrome or those with the most serious disabilities, (Carter & Jancar, 1983; Janicki, 1986). Women, people who are ambulatory and/or have mild levels of mental retardation, and those who have remained in the community have the greatest life expectancy (Walz, Harper, & Wilson, 1986).

Prevalence

In 1985, Jacobson et al. estimated that there were between 200,000 and 500,000 older adults with developmental disabilities in the United States, and that their numbers are expected to double in the next 40 years. Janicki et al. (1985) estimated that between 10.0% and 13.3% of all persons with developmental disabilities are 65 and older. Walz et al. (1986) estimated, based on averages obtained in large area studies conducted in New York, California, and Australia, that persons ages 65 and older represented approximately 12% of all persons with developmental disabilities *receiving formal services*. In actual numbers this is a total of about 196,000 older individuals. Lakin, Hill, and Anderson (1991) estimated that over 22,000 people with developmental disabilities in nursing homes were 55 years of age and older, and that up to 75% could benefit from movement to facilities operated for people with mental retardation.

Numbers in Nursing Homes

The primary placement for adults with developmental disabilities over 65 years of age traditionally has been the nursing home (Lakin, 1985; Lakin et al., 1991). In 1985, it was estimated that over half (58%) of adults 63 and older living in some type of residential setting were in nursing homes, with the remainder being fairly evenly divided among community residential facilities and public facilities owned, operated, and/or licensed by state developmental disabilities agencies (Anderson, Lakin, Bruininks, & Hill, 1987). If we include all persons *considered to have a diagnosis of mental retardation* over the age of 62, then approximately 88% were living in nursing homes or state institutions at that time. The OBRA-mandated review of nursing home placements of people with developmental disabilities is expected to exert significant pressure upon the existing system of residential care to absorb sizeable numbers of persons currently living in nursing homes. In addition, the increased emphasis on family caregiving since the 1980s has resulted in unknown numbers of people with developmental disabilities living in the community with aging parents who are, or soon will be, facing placement decisions.

The demographic and placement trends, coupled with the relative paucity of knowledge about older adults with developmental disabilities compared with knowledge about children and adolescents, underscore the need for more specific knowledge upon which to base efforts to plan for this population. One of the issues that becomes critical is health status. This includes the specific nature of health conditions, the types and extent of medical and related care received in different settings, the issues faced by careproviders in caring for this population when health care needs exist, and the capabilities of the residential services system to address these issues.

STUDIES EXAMINED

Findings about health issues from a longitudinal study of older adults with mental retardation living in residential facilities licensed by MR/DD agencies conducted at the Center for Residential and Community Services (CRCS) at the University of Minnesota (Anderson et al., 1987) were examined. This study provided a national database about the characteristics of older adults with mental retardation in residential facilities, which had previously been unavailable. The national character of the database was important, since states vary widely in their practices, including the extent of their use of different community-based and institutional options. A follow-up study was conducted with the original sample of 370 persons in 1990–1991 to determine whether changes had occurred over time in residents' characteristics and/or in practices. Information was obtained about residents still living in their initial residences, as well as about residents who had transferred or died in the 4- to 5-year interim. In addition, analyses of the National Nursing Home Survey (NNHS) of 1985 were conducted to determine how older adults with mental retardation might have differed in health from their peers without disabilities who also resided in nursing homes.

National Nursing Home Survey

The National Nursing Home Survey, conducted by the National Center on Health Statistics (NCHS) in 1977 and 1985 (National Center for Health Statistics, 1979, 1986), is the major source for national statistics on the numbers and characteristics of persons with mental retardation and related conditions in nursing homes. NNHS surveys were completed by staff members, usually nurses.

The NNHS employs a weighted sample to estimate the actual numbers of persons residing in nursing homes. The actual number of persons with primary diagnoses of mental retardation in the 1985 NNHS was 177, including 59 ages 65 and older and 43 ages 55–64. These numbers are used to project the total estimated population, which is nearly 300 times the actual sample size. Weighted estimates were used for reporting percentages, and unweighted actual samples were used for calculating statistical results.

Comparisons were made between persons with primary diagnoses of mental retardation, people with secondary diagnoses of mental retardation, and people without mental retardation. Separate analyses were performed on the sample of persons with cerebral palsy and epilepsy who did not have additional diagnoses of mental retardation. Among persons with primary mental retardation, age-related changes were examined.

The analyses focused upon persons ages 65 and older with primary diagnoses of mental retardation. The restriction to primary diagnoses of mental retardation (or another developmental disability with an additional mental retardation diagnosis) minimized confounding of results by conditions related to aging and conditions acquired beyond the first 21 years. Evidence of confounding conditions was sufficiently ample to warrant this exclusion. In addition to the estimated 49,757 people with primary diagnoses in the 1985 NNHS, there were an additional 33,280 people who were considered to have the condition of mental retardation, that is, secondary diagnoses of mental retardation, even though they had primary diagnoses other than mental retardation or another developmental disability. Focusing on persons ages 65 and older permitted comparisons between similar-age groups in the CRCS Residential Survey and the NNHS.

Comparison with CRCS Sample

The CRCS sample of 370 older persons with mental retardation living in facilities operated and/or licensed by state developmental disabilities agencies (Anderson et al., 1987) studied during the same time period provided detailed information on a comparison group of persons of this age living outside the nursing home environment. Even though these data are not entirely comparable, due to differences in wording and data collection methodologies, they provide an approximate picture of some of the similarities and differences between older adults with mental retardation in nursing homes and those in residential facilities licensed by MR/DD agencies.

Results

People without mental retardation (all ages combined) made up 94.4% of the total estimated nursing home population in 1985, people with primary mental retardation made up 3.3%, and those with secondary mental retardation an additional 2.2%. A total of 21% of persons with primary diagnoses of mental retardation also were diagnosed as having a psychotic disorder, as were 14% of persons without mental retardation and 28% of persons with secondary diagnoses of mental retardation.

The vast majority (93%) of persons in nursing homes at that time were 60 years of age or older. However, only 48% of persons with primary diagnoses of mental retardation were 60 or older, as were 71% of persons with secondary diagnoses of mental retardation.

There were no statistically significant differences due to age in any demographic variables, including age, marital status, children, race/ethnic origin, and location. An estimated 11% of all persons with primary diagnoses of mental retardation were hospitalized in a general, short-term hospital just prior to their entry into the present nursing home. Among those persons, the longest stays involved those under the age of 40. The numbers of persons 65 and older who had been hospitalized since entering the nursing home, however, were greater than for their younger cohorts.

Differences due to age in admitting conditions were found only for injuries or poisoning, and Down syndrome, which was more prevalent among those under age 40 (27% compared with 18% of persons 40–54, and 6%–8% of persons 55–64 and 65 and older). There were no *reported* cases of Alzheimer's disease or other dementia on admission among persons with primary diagnoses of mental retardation. Age-related differences in current conditions were slight in most areas. Diabetes occurred most frequently among those 65 and older, as did heart disease and stroke.

Residents 65 and Older with and without Mental Retardation

This study found more women 65 years of age and older in the nursing home population without mental retardation. About nine out of 10 had married, compared with about one in 10 among those with primary mental retardation, and 68% of the older residents without mental retardation had children, compared with 4% of those with primary mental retardation. People age 65 and older with primary diagnoses of mental retardation were more likely than people of this age group without mental retardation to be residing in nonmetropolitan area nursing homes. Among those living outside of a formal residential facility, significantly more older people without mental retardation lived alone than did those with primary diagnoses of mental retardation. Among those living in a formal residential facility prior to admission to a nursing home, there were significant differences as well, with the vast majority (70%) of persons without mental retardation residing in a general or short-term hospital (excluding psychiatric units), suggesting serious medical involvement, in contrast with only 13% of those with primary diagnoses of mental retardation. An estimated 5,230 individuals with primary diagnoses of mental retardation in this age range had lived in informal settings, including 4,021 estimated to have lived with their families.

Persons with primary diagnoses of mental retardation ages 65 and older typically had less health impairment than their same-age peers without mental retardation in the nursing home. (See Table 2.1.) The former had a significantly lower prevalence of mental illness of an organic nature. Also, on admission there were fewer diagnoses of Parkinson's disease, heart disease or other circulatory system disorders, respiratory disorders, arthritis, and nonspecific disorders. They were more likely to have had epilepsy and other nervous system disor-

Table 2.1. Admitting conditions of persons 65 and older in nursing homes

Admitting condition	65+ without mental retardation %	Primary mental retardation %	Other diagnoses of mental retardation %	Chi-square
Infectious/ parasitic	1.5	1.6	2.3	.96
Cancer	5.5		3.6	3.44
Diabetes	11.8	6.1	18.7	3.15
Endocrine/ metabolic	7.5	11.9	6.0	.14
Anemia	4.3		6.5	2.90
Other blood disorders	.3			.41
Organic psychosis	6.2		5.6	4.10
Other psychoses	7.9	1.3	7.1	3.26
Neurosis	1.8	2.7		1.40
Brain damage	17.2	6.4	28.9	10.97[b]
Mental retardation		86.6	28.0	3199.26[c]
Sexual/drug disorder	4.6	1.1	4.7	1.22
Alzheimer's	4.9			6.97[a]
Parkinson's	4.5	1.5	11.5	10.92[b]
Multiple sclerosis	.3			.50
Epilepsy	.4	10.9	3.0	138.37[c]
Glaucoma	2.3	4.3	1.2	2.34
Cataracts	2.6	1.9	9.5	9.00[a]
Blind	1.1	1.5		1.02
Hearing	1.7	1.8	4.9	6.39[a]
CNS impairment	10.3	20.4	13.6	6.50[a]
Hypertensive	15.5	10.1	11.8	1.65
Heart	56.5	24.4	51.1	28.79[c]
Respiratory	10.3	2.3	5.6	6.84[a]
Digestive	11.0	5.4	14.3	2.27
Genitourinary	8.8	4.5	10.1	1.08
Skin problems	3.5	6.5	5.6	2.33
Arthritis	18.4	2.3	12.9	10.97[b]
Osteoporosis	3.3		3.2	2.07
Musculo- skeletal	6.8	5.9	6.7	.00
Down syndrome	.4	7.6		90.04[c]

(continued)

Table 2.1.   (*continued*)

Admitting condition	65+ without mental retardation %	Primary mental retardation %	Other diagnoses of mental retardation %	Chi-square
Perinatal				
Senility	3.9			5.39
Nonspecific	11.4	6.5	16.6	2.81
Fractures	8.5	2.3	3.9	5.46
Other injury/ poisoning	2.0			2.77

$^a p < .05$.
$^b p < .01$.
$^c p < .001$.
CNS = Central nervous system.

ders. There were no differences in the prevalence of diabetes, endocrine disorders, digestive disorders, genitourinary disorders, or psychosis. The findings about their health conditions at the time of the survey were similar.

Adaptive behaviors are somewhat difficult to assess, since the only indicator of limitation on the NNHS is the respondent's (typically a nurse or other staff member) judgment regarding the individual's need for assistance, which may be confounded with institutional practices. In most areas of self-care, there were no statistically significant differences between groups, although persons without mental retardation were slightly more likely to require assistance in toileting than their counterparts with mental retardation. In the area of mobility, considerably fewer persons with mental retardation required assistance in most tasks.

Older persons without mental retardation were more likely than persons with a primary diagnosis of mental retardation to have received physical therapy, but the reverse was true for recreational therapy, speech and hearing therapy, and mental health evaluation or treatment by a physician. However, the overall level of these services was low. Between 2% and 18% of the nursing home population ages 65 and older with mental retardation received one of these services.

Residents of Nursing Homes versus Facilities Licensed by MR/DD Agencies

Preliminary comparisons were made of selected chronic conditions among persons 65 and older with mental retardation living in nursing homes and persons 63 and older living in facilities licensed by MR/DD agencies. Statistical comparisons were not performed due to the fact that these findings are from different data sets. However, it is notable that the prevalence of these disorders (e.g., diabetes, glaucoma or cataracts, Parkinson's disease, high blood pressure, respiratory disorders, and arthritis) among nursing home residents with primary diagnoses of mental retardation was similar to or lower than the prevalence reported for persons in community residential facilities licensed by MR/DD agencies. Such agencies included foster care, group homes, and large private facilities.

In the NNHS of 1985, respondents (nurses and other staff) indicated whether the individual had a condition influencing overall health status, whereas the CRCS survey requested information about limitations due to health-related conditions. Hence, they are not entirely equivalent, and differences in interpretation of the two questions are unknown. However, it is interesting that very few (4%) persons with mental retardation in nursing homes were reported to have conditions that influenced their health status, which was lower than the incidence in group homes, large private facilities, and state institutions.

Other Factors Influencing Placement

As the study progressed, it seemed to the researchers that other factors might have influenced decisions to place many older persons with developmental disabilities in nursing homes. To test this hypothesis, comparisons were made between persons living in foster care, group homes, large private facilities, state institutions, and nursing homes on a number of psychological and other conditions thought possibly to affect their placement. No statistical tests were performed. However, it appears that there was no greater prevalence of chemical dependency, severe mental illness, depression, anxiety and other neurotic disorders, epilepsy, or Down syndrome among nursing home residents than among residents of facilities operated by developmental disabilities agencies.

Furthermore, comparisons of persons 65 and older in nursing homes found no differences between older persons without mental retardation and older persons with a primary diagnosis of mental retardation in alcohol or drug abuse or in personality/character disorders. (See Table 2.2.) In contrast, older persons without retardation had a markedly higher prevalence of senile dementia/chronic and organic brain syndrome, depression, and anxiety disorders. The only condition in which persons with a primary diagnosis of mental retardation had a higher prevalence was schizophrenia, reported for 10% of the former compared with 3% of the latter. Nevertheless, 32% of older adults without mental retardation were rated as having excellent or good mental health, compared with only 17% of persons with primary diagnoses of mental retardation, who were most likely to be rated as having fair mental health (52%). These data suggest that persons with mental retardation may be viewed as having poorer mental health than is actually the case.

The level of services received in nursing homes by residents with mental retardation is far below the service level of their counterparts in MR/DD licensed facilities (Anderson et al., 1987). Among persons ages 63 and older in facilities licensed by MR/DD agencies, 12% in all but foster care received physical therapy whereas 2% received this service in nursing homes. Between 14%

Table 2.2. Mental health and related conditions among persons 65 and older in nursing homes

Condition	65+ without mental retardation %	Primary mental retardation %	Other diagnoses of mental retardation %	Chi-square
Alcohol abuse	2.1		2.4	1.40
Drug abuse	.8			1.10
Senile/ organic brain damage	47.5	13.9	51.4	25.22[c]
Depression	13.5	2.9	22.9	9.29[b]
Schizophrenia	3.2	9.6	7.2	8.40[a]
Other psychoses	2.2	1.1	5.9	3.26
Anxiety disorder	13.0	6.8	26.2	12.00[b]
Personality/ character disorder	10.0	8.5	18.5	4.44
Other mental disorder	.5			.53
No mental disorder	36.6	3.3	2.3	64.84[c]

[a] $p < .05$.
[b] $p < .01$.
[c] $p < .001$.

and 29%, depending on facility type, saw a psychologist. None was reported to have seen a psychologist in the nursing home survey. Between 50% and 69% had contact with a social worker over a month's time, depending upon facility type. In the nursing home survey only 16% had such contact; thus, a much higher level of service appears to exist in MR/DD licensed facilities.

Discussion

These findings raise a number of questions. First, there is a question concerning the accuracy of diagnosis. It appears likely that the secondary diagnoses of mental retardation are overreported in nursing homes, and that these include an unknown melange of genuine diagnoses of mental retardation as well as later life disabilities such as senile dementia, mental illness, brain injuries, and other organic or neurological conditions that may affect mental functioning, but that are not mental retardation. In addition, there are questions about underreporting of other conditions among persons with primary diagnoses of mental retardation in nursing homes. For example, only 5% of persons with primary diagnoses of mental retardation were noted as having arthritis at the time of the NNHS survey. However, on the CRCS survey, between 18% and 26% were noted as having this condition, which is similar to the 20% of older persons without mental retardation in nursing homes who are said to have this condition. General population surveys of persons ages 65–74 living in the community (National Center for Health Statistics, 1986) suggest that this is one of the most prevalent conditions among this age group. Similarly, the use of corrective eyeglasses among persons with primary diagnoses of mental retardation ages 65 and older was surprisingly low, with only 32% reportedly needing them, compared with twice this number in the nursing home population without mental retardation at the same age. The levels of severe visual problems were only slightly higher among the former group, and the difference is not sufficient to explain much of the remaining differences in use of glasses. It is possible that sufficient attention may not have been paid to some health and visual problems of persons with mental retardation, although the data are not detailed enough to explain this fully.

Second, the data suggest that there may be a public relations problem with persons with mental retardation who live in nursing homes. In particular, they seem to be viewed as having poorer mental health than appears to be the case, given their markedly lower rates of dementia, anxiety, and depression compared with older people in general in nursing homes. The incidence of schizophrenia, while higher among the former (10% versus 3% among the latter), is nevertheless relatively infrequent, contrasted with the small numbers of people with developmental disabilities considered to have good mental health (only 17%).

Third, it appears to be not necessarily true that most of the people ages 65 and older with primary diagnoses of mental retardation are in need of medically intensive services. These analyses suggest that this group is in better physical condition than their peers without mental retardation. Although it is possible that they may also have health problems that warrant care, the findings about health conditions both on admission and at the time of the survey strongly suggest that the population of persons in nursing homes with primary diagnoses of mental retardation is substantially different from persons without mental retardation, in ways that generally suggest a lower level of chronic disease and fewer health problems. This contention is supported by the relatively small percentage of persons with mental retardation residing in general or short-term hospitals prior to their nursing home placement. In contrast, the percentage for the general aging population in nursing homes is much higher. The substantial number of older persons without mental retardation having diagnoses of senile dementia, compared with relatively few *with* mental retardation having this diagnosis, further supports the contention that many in the latter group may be inappropriately placed. The findings about urban/rural differences in nursing homes for the two groups suggest that convenience, or availability, may be driving some of the placements of older people with mental retardation, rather than suitability. Nursing homes are likely to be one of the few resources available for long-term care for aging people with mental retardation in nonurban areas.

Fourth, older adults with mental retardation in nursing homes do not appear to be receiving the same level of care as their counterparts in facilities licensed by MR/DD agencies. It appears that they receive few health-related services. The general level of care received by persons with mental retardation in nursing homes is considerably lower than that received by their same-age peers in facilities licensed by MR/DD agencies. This situation has not changed since the earlier National Nursing Home Survey done in 1977 (Lakin et al., 1991). Thus, need for specialized medical services does not appear to be a major factor in nursing home placement.

Fifth, a critical policy issue, which is only partially addressed by the findings, concerns the reasons for placement in nursing homes instead of community residential facilities licensed by MR/DD agencies. There appears to be considerable overlap between persons in nursing homes who have developmental disabilities and persons in the same age range in facilities licensed by MR/DD agencies. The CRCS survey, for example, found few differences in level of retardation of functional skills among persons in foster care, group homes, and large residential facilities, although persons in state institutions were found to have more severe disabilities. When viewed together, the findings suggest that residential placement of older persons with mental retardation probably is based on factors other than the residents' characteristics and needs. One of these factors apparently is geographic location, with persons who have mental retardation being represented disproportionately in nonurban area nursing homes. The opportunity for placement in smaller, community-based settings requires proactive planning for this age group to be ensured an appropriate array of smaller, less restrictive residential alternatives. This is particularly true for rural areas, which tend to have relatively few group homes and relatively more state hospitals and foster care than urban areas. In the absence of such planning, implementation of OBRA-87 in the spirit in which it was originally intended may be viewed as unlikely.

LONGITUDINAL STUDY OF
OLDER ADULTS WITH MENTAL RETARDATION

Method

The original study of older adults with mental retardation was conducted at the CRCS, University of Minnesota, from 1985 to 1986. A prior study, conducted by the CRCS in 1982, had obtained basic information about all residential facilities owned, operated, and/or licensed by MR/DD agencies. The information covered included the numbers of residents in various age ranges (Hauber, Bruininks, Hill, Lakin, & White, 1984). Using this sample of facilities, a 10% sample of facilities with one or more persons over the age of 62 was selected. This sample included residents of foster care, small group homes, large private facilities, and

public institutions. The facility-based sampling procedure was conducted to ensure adequate representation of persons in the smaller, community-based facilities. Information was obtained by means of mail surveys, followed by telephone
interview supplements, for careproviders identified by facility contacts as being
the direct care persons who best knew the residents. In facilities with two or
more persons of this age group, two older individuals were selected randomly
for study; otherwise one person per facility was studied. A total of 235 facilities,
or 10.2% of the total sample of facilities with one or more older persons, and 370
individuals were studied. Most of those studied were between 63 and 74 years
of age, with an average of 70 years.

The original sample was studied again from 1990 to 1991 as a research
effort of the Rehabilitation Research and Training Center Consortium on Aging
and Developmental Disabilities in Akron, Ohio. The purpose was to examine
age-related changes as well as changes resulting from increasing awareness of
the needs, rights, and even the existence of this group of people. At the time of
the original study (1985–1986), there were few programs specifically for this
age group. Planning for this age group was minimal, as was training for staff
members. Aging and MR/DD agencies had little contact with one another, and
stereotypes about older people with disabilities were commonly expressed.
The most frequent residential placement for older adults with mental retardation was a nursing home, and the next most frequent a state hospital. Little was
known about these older persons. By 1990, there were significantly more
efforts, including research centering on older people, OBRA-87 had been enacted, and programs and activities were in existence to accommodate the special
needs of these people.

The follow-up sample consisted of 213 residents, 126 of whom were living
in their original (Year 1) residence. Of the remaining 87, about two thirds had
transferred to another facility, and one third had died.

Procedure

A variety of attempts were made to contact direct care providers who had participated in the original study, including sending letters to participating facilities
explaining the follow-up study, reviewing the original study, and offering to send
another summary of findings. Post cards were enclosed indicating the options to
consent, request additional information, and/or refuse. Information was requested on the current status (e.g., transferred, deceased) of the residents respondents initially studied. Callbacks asking that an appropriate respondent be
selected were made to nonrespondents and to facilities in which the initial careprovider had left. In some cases, three mailings of questionnaires per careprovider were made, with additional callbacks as needed. Careproviders of residents still living in the residence in which the survey had initially been
conducted were given three instruments: 1) a Resident Questionnaire, 2) an
Inventory for Client Assessment and Planning (ICAP), and 3) a Careprovider

Questionnaire. Careproviders of persons who were no longer living in their initial residence were given the Transfer/Death Survey and the Careprovider Questionnaire.

The Resident and Careprovider Questionnaires contained many questions from the initial study to determine whether changes had occurred in the interim; included were questions on health conditions and services received to address these conditions. Open-ended questions probed the issues of supports needed to enhance care for the resident, and methods by which facilities were coping with health problems requiring medical care, including any ways in which facilities had been able to maintain individuals with these problems in the community.

Careproviders of persons who were no longer living in their original residence were given a very brief version of the Resident Questionnaire and also received the Transfer/Death Survey, which focused upon health issues, adaptive behavior, and residential movement. Most of the questions were common to both the original survey and the follow-up Resident Questionnaire for purposes of comparison.

Analysis

All questions asked in the follow-up period were compared by facility type. All questions asked in both time periods were compared for original (Year 1) and current (Year 2) responses among the sample of participants common to both time periods living in their original residential facilities. The sample common to the two time periods was smaller than the full follow-up sample due to missing data in one of the two time periods. Questions asked in the Transfer/Death Survey were compared with responses to these same questions in the follow-up period (Year 2).

Results

Chronic Health Problems   In the follow-up period (1990–1991), there were few facility-linked differences in chronic health problems, a finding similar to that of the initial study period (1985–1986). Among persons still living in their original residences, the most common chronic health problems were, as in the original study, high blood pressure, which was indicated for one fourth to one half of residents, depending upon facility type; arthritis, cited for 24%–42% of residents; heart disease, noted for 18%–30% of residents; and glaucoma/ cataracts, indicated for 11%–47% of residents. (See Table 2.3.) These disorders are consistent with the top three health problems within this age group in general: 1) arthritis, 2) heart disease, and 3) high blood pressure. Alzheimer's disease was infrequently reported (between 0 and 5%). Residents of state institutions had a higher incidence of blood disorders, muscle atrophy, and glaucoma/ cataracts, and foster care residents were most frequently cited as having Parkinson's disease. All foster care and state institution residents had at least one

Table 2.3. Chronic health problems by facility type: Residents in initial residence at Time 2

Condition	Foster %	Group %	Large private %	State %	Chi-square
Cancer	0	11	3	0	7.44
Diabetes	12	8	14	16	1.35
PKU/thyroid	0	9	0	5	7.29
Obesity/mal-nutrition	0	6	5	21	6.67
Blood problems	0	2	8	26	12.20[b]
Glaucoma/cat-aracts	12	26	11	47	10.80[a]
Parkinson's	12	0	0	0	8.22[a]
MS/neurologi-cal disorder	0	4	5	16	4.90
Stroke	6	6	3	10	1.42
Atherosclerosis	18	6	3	10	3.96
Heart disease	18	19	30	26	1.83
High blood pressure	47	24	24	32	3.45
Respiratory problems	6	15	8	10	5.66
Allergies	6	4	3	16	3.66
Ulcers	6	0	0	0	4.06
Gum/mouth disease	0	6	11	10	3.65
Liver/kidney/ gall bladder/ prostate problems	18	6	5	26	7.30
Colostomy	0	0	0	0	
Women's diseases	0	2	0	10	5.64
Skin problems	6	19	8	26	5.20
Arthritis	24	30	30	43	1.55
Back problems	0	8	8	16	4.10
Muscle atrophy	0	0	8	26	16.86[c]
Congenital disorders	6	2	5	5	1.14
Brain damage	0	2	3	16	6.38
Current injury/ poisoning	0	2	0	0	1.74
Alzheimer's	0	0	3	5	3.51
No disease	0	13	5	0	7.91[a]

$N = 126$, df = 3.

[a]$p < .05$.

[b]$p < .01$.

[c]$p < .001$.

chronic disease, but 13% of group home and 5% of large private facility residents had none. The findings are similar for all residents, including those in their original residences as well as residents who had transferred or died.

Differences between Years 1 and 2 were slight for chronic disease in people still in their original residences, with the exceptions of heart disease, which had increased from 14% to 24%, and arthritis, which had increased from 21% to 33% during this time period. Comparisons of residents who had transferred or died with residents in their original residences found, somewhat paradoxically, a higher incidence of skin problems, thyroid disorders, muscle atrophy, and arthritis among people still in their original residences than among people who had transferred or died. In addition, 7% of the former but 19% of the latter reportedly had no chronic diseases. These findings, which are the reverse of what might have been expected, suggest underreporting of information about people who had transferred or died. Such a conclusion is also substantiated by the fact that the reported incidence of arthritis among those currently in their residences (31%) more closely approximates the prevalence of arthritis among older people living in the community than the 17% reported for people who had transferred or died.

Medical Care   Foster care residents received the least medical care, with nearly two thirds receiving care less than once a month, followed by group home residents. (See Figure 2.1.) Few residents of large private facilities or state institutions received care this infrequently, typically receiving daily or 24-hour care. Residents who had transferred or died and those in their original residences were similar in the amount of medical care received. Most residents (between 88% and 95%) were taking at least one medication, either prescribed or over-the-counter, for a health or mental health condition in the sample common to both time periods. Twenty-five percent were not taking drugs in

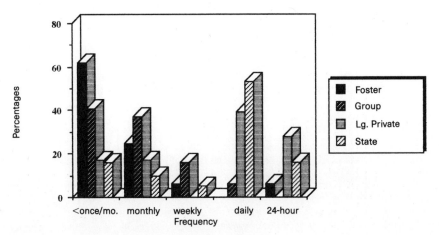

Figure 2.1.   Medical care received, by facility type.

the original survey, compared with 12% in the follow-up period (Chi-square [N = 120(1)] = 10.32, $p < .01$).

Careproviders indicated that the majority of foster care residents had no limitations due to health problems. (See Figure 2.2.) Few foster care and group home providers indicated many or significant health-related limitations for the residents in their homes, and only one third of state facility providers indicated this level of limitation. (Differences failed to reach statistical significance.) There were no differences in medical limitations between residents who had transferred or died and those in their original residences. Comparisons of all residents surveyed in Year 2 (including current residents and those who had transferred or died) by facility type found a significant difference between facilities in the direction indicated above (59% of foster care, 42% of group homes, 20% of large private facilities, and 27% of state facilities reported that the residents had no health-related limitations [Chi-square (N = 173 [6]) = 20.67, $p < .01$]).

Group home residents were least likely to have seen a nurse within the past month (62% versus 82%–90% in other facilities) and most likely to say that none of the residents had seen any professionals in the past month (17% versus none in foster care and 3%–5% of other residents). Between 34% and 58% saw a nutritionist, 24%–58% a psychologist, and 0–13% a speech therapist. Residents in state hospitals were more likely to have seen an occupational therapist (32% versus 8%–27%) and a physical therapist (42% versus 11%–24%). The professional most frequently seen overall was a social worker (57%–81%). There were no differences between Years 1 and 2 in medical and related services received. The average number of hours of nursing care residents received declined from about 26 hours to less than 5 hours in the previous month, about one fifth the earlier level ($\pm$ [40] = 3.81, $p < .001$). In the follow-up study,

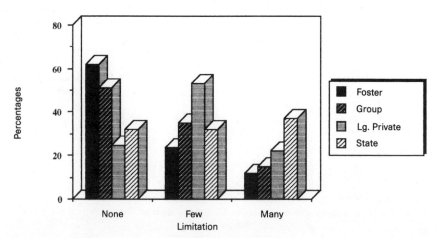

Figure 2.2.   Effect of health problems on daily activities.

additional needs for support were infrequent; between 9% and 14% of staff indicated that residents needed more support from nursing, nutritional, physical therapy, psychological, and social work services.

About one in five residents had been hospitalized in the past year (between 19% and 25%), the majority being hospitalized only once (71% overall). A minority of providers indicated that they had encountered problems in finding or obtaining appropriate medical services for the resident (14% overall). The most commonly cited problem, among those having problems, was that reimbursement rates were too low, so medical professionals would not accept the resident.

Respondents generally indicated that they had noticed changes in the resident related to the aging process, which is not surprising given the advanced age of these residents. They averaged 74.5 years if still in their residence, 73.8 years if they had transferred to another facility, and, among those who had died during the time period, a projected 76.8 years had they lived. In the follow-up study, one of the most frequent responses regarding age-related changes was that the resident had less energy or stamina. Physical/health changes were noted by 19%, which typically related to general health decline or problems in mobility. Skill changes were noted by 13% and cognitive changes by 6% of respondents.

To a lesser extent, careproviders noted that residents' service/support needs had changed because they were growing older, particularly in large private facilities (42%–70%). In addition to age, between 30% and 37% of community residential facility staff noted other factors that had influenced residents' support/service needs either positively or negatively in the past 4 years. Most of these responses indicated that health status and family contact had declined, or that there had been a change in the residential or day program.

Careproviders of people who had transferred or died were much more likely to mention that medical supports would have been useful in working with the resident than careproviders of people still living in their original residences. These responses, as well as responses to other health-related questions, suggest that, although routine health care did not seem to be problematical for most, there often was little planning or capability for handling short-lived emergencies. In addition, mobility limitations seemed to be difficult for many residences to manage.

Adaptive Behavior Adaptive behavior is discussed because needs for assistance with adaptive behavior are often addressed by placement in medically intensive settings. Also, discussing adaptive behavior provides a baseline for evaluating care needs. Substantial differences were noted in adaptive behavior skills by facility type. Residents of state institutions were reported as being far less independent than residents of other facilities in most behaviors measured. Differences among other facility types were relatively small, with residents of large private facilities being somewhat less independent in both mobility and self-care skills than residents of foster or group homes. (See Table 2.4.) Very

Table 2.4.   Percentage independent in self-care and mobility skills of residents in original
residences at Time 2

Skill	Foster %	Group %	Large private %	State %	Chi-square
Getting in/out of bed	100	94	81	47	29.41[c]
Standing alone	100	94	76	47	28.90[c]
Walking on level surface 10 feet	88	92	73	42	25.16[b]
Climbing stairs	88	83	57	21	37.60[c]
Eating	88	96	81	58	20.04[a]
Dressing	76	87	70	47	21.49[c]
Toileting	82	91	78	53	33.44[c]
Bathing/showering	47	60	38	21	35.58[c]

$N = 126$, df $= 3$.
[a] $p < .05$.
[b] $p < .01$.
[c] $p < .001$.

slight differences were observed between foster care and group home residents. Few residents of community-based facilities were unable to do the basic
skills at any level. There were no differences among residents who had transferred or died and residents still in their original residences on adaptive behaviors. However, the average level of adaptive behavior declined slightly among
residents living in the original facility in both time periods in all areas of adaptive
behavior except dressing.

Discussion

Health status findings should be interpreted with caution because of an apparent
tendency to underreport certain conditions. This was particularly true of residents no longer residing in the facility, whose conditions might have been more
difficult to recall. Certain conditions, however, seem to be underreported due to
inattention to the issue. For example, a very low rate of eyeglass use was reported in both time periods for older state institution residents. Reported rates
of heart disease, high blood pressure, and arthritis appear to be lower than rates
reported for older people in general living in the community at the time of the
original CRCS survey and the NNHS of 1985 (National Center for Health Statistics, 1986). Comparisons with national studies of older people without developmental disabilities may be helpful in anticipating likely areas of needed attention,
normal age-linked decline, and areas in which the absence of reported disability
may suggest poor detection.

The medical care received by residents was similar to that noted in the original survey, with larger facilities typically providing daily or 24-hour care and foster care homes having the least medically intensive care. This appears to be due to institutional policy and to some extent to greater medical need on the part of individual residents.

Foster care residents had the fewest medical limitations due to health problems, and large private and state facility residents the most, but even in state facility residents, the majority, or about two thirds of residents, had few or no limitations. Thus, as in the first time period, this group seems to be functioning at a reasonable level despite their advancing age.

The high frequency of visits by nurses, psychologists, and social workers to residents living in MR/DD facilities in the follow-up period contrasts sharply with the very low level of these services received by older people with mental retardation in nursing homes. However, the precipitous decline for residents of MR/DD facilities in the average number of hours they are served may reflect service more targeted to needs and less to institutional practice, or it may be a spurious finding attributable to the relatively small number of respondents' reporting hours. This issue requires further study to clarify the reasons for these changes. It appears that foster care residents received a higher level of service than they did 4 years earlier, when they fell behind all other residents in services as well as service hours reported.

Hospitalization rates were similar to rates in the initial study, but more changes in residents related to the aging process were noted, and service and support needs were perceived by careproviders to have increased due to the aging process. The general pattern was for greater health care and assistance needs, and declines in energy. The majority of residents, however, were still able to perform most if not all activities of daily living independently, with the exception of residents in state institutions.

Planning for health emergencies, which need not be long-term nor the signal for changes in residential status, typically is lacking. Without such planning, older people who experience such emergencies run the risk of nursing home placement due to the facility's inability to handle people with limited or no ambulation; provide extra staffing on a temporary basis; and/or handle the other aspects of medical care, such as transportation to the physician. In other cases, people needing more intensive medical care may not receive such care due to difficulties in gaining access to the system. It appears that a substantial number of people currently living in institutional settings, including nursing homes and state facilities, are not sufficiently in need of medical services to warrant their being removed from the community. Without concerted planning, however, they are unlikely to enjoy the benefits of community living, and, without flexibility within the system to respond to occasional medical needs, their tenure in the community may be jeopardized.

REFERENCES

Anderson, D.J., Lakin, K.C., Bruininks, R.H., & Hill, B.K. (1987). *A national study of residential and support services for elderly persons with mental retardation.* Minneapolis: University of Minnesota.

Carter, G., & Jancar, J. (1983). Mortality in the mentally handicapped: A fifty year survey at the Stoke Park group of hospitals (1930–1980). *Journal of Mental Deficiency Research, 27*(2), 143–156.

DiGiovanini, L. (1978). The elderly retarded: A little known group. *The Gerontologist, 18*(3), 262–266.

Eyman, R., Grossman, H., Tarjan, G., & Miller, C. (1987). *Life expectancy and mental retardation: A longitudinal study in a state residential facility.* Washington, DC: American Association on Mental Deficiency.

Hauber, F.A., Bruininks, R.A., Hill, B.K., Lakin, K.C., & White, C.A. (1984). *1982 census of residential facilities for mentally retarded people.* Minneapolis: University of Minnesota, Department of Educational Psychology.

Jacobson, J.W., Sutton, M.S., & Janicki, M.P. (1985). Demography and characteristics of aging and aged mentally retarded persons. In M.P. Janicki & H.M. Wisniewski (Eds.), *Aging and developmental disabilities: Issues and approaches* (pp. 115–142). Baltimore: Paul H. Brookes Publishing Co.

Janicki, M. P. (1986). Some comments on aging and a need for research. *Annals of the New York Academy of Sciences, 477*, 261–264.

Janicki, M.P., Ackerman, L., & Jacobson, J.W. (1985). State developmental disabilities/aging plans and planning for an older developmentally disabled population. *Mental Retardation, 23*(6), 297–301.

Lakin, K.C. (1985). *Estimated mentally retarded population in nursing homes according to the National Nursing Home Survey of 1977* (Brief No. 26). Minneapolis: University of Minnesota, Department of Educational Psychology.

Lakin, K.C., Hill, B.K., & Anderson, D.J. (1991). Persons with mental retardation in nursing homes in 1977 and 1985: A comparison of findings from the 1977 and 1985 National Nursing Home Survey. *Mental Retardation, 29*(1), 25–33.

National Center for Health Statistics. (1979). *The National Nursing Home Survey: 1977 Summary for the United States.* Washington, DC: United States Department of Health, Education, and Welfare.

National Center for Health Statistics. (1986). Prevalence of selected chronic conditions, United States, 1979–1981. *Vital and Health Statistics*, Series 10, No. 155, DHHS Publ. No. (PHS) 86–1583. Public Health Services. Washington, DC: United States Government Printing Office.

Walz, T., Harper, D., & Wilson, J. (1986). The aging developmentally disabled person: A review. *The Gerontologist, 26*(6), 622–629.

White, C.C., Lakin, K.C., Hill, B.K., Wright, E.A., & Bruininks, R.H. (1987). *Persons with mental retardation in state-operated residential facilities: Year ending June 30, 1986 with longitudinal trends from 1950 to 1986.* Minneapolis: University of Minnesota, Department of Educational Psychology.

3

Health Care Issues

Marilyn Adlin

A major issue concerning health in aging adults is the question of what can be considered normal aging as opposed to disease. Many of the original studies on aging were cross-sectional in design and compared groups of younger individuals with groups of older individuals (Andres & Tobin, 1977; Rowe, Andres, Tobin, Norris, & Shock, 1976). From these data there arose the theory that all organ systems in the human body demonstrate a gradual decline beginning in early adulthood. Later longitudinal studies have begun to call this long-held assumption into question (Svanborg, Bergstrom, & Mellstrom, 1982).

In these studies, changes in persons followed longitudinally have been found to be much less striking and generally have been found not to occur until after the age of 70. Many conditions that have been attributed to normal aging may in fact result from specific diseases, environmental factors, or deconditioning due to disuse. When a group of 90-year-old institutionalized volunteers participated in an 8-week, high intensity weight training program, strength was shown to increase an average of 174%, and functional mobility improved (Fiatarone et al., 1990). While further studies on aging are needed, caution is necessary in attributing any observed declines to old age. Potentially reversible and treatable conditions frequently occur in aging adults.

FACTORS AFFECTING AGING

Increased life expectancy has led to an increase in the size of the population of older adults with developmental disabilities. With more people living longer comes the expectation of an increased prevalence of some of the same age-related health problems that are seen in the general aging population, including

49

vision and hearing losses, heart disease, cancer, and cerebrovascular disease. The challenge in providing health care for older adults with developmental disabilities can be in properly diagnosing and treating some of these common conditions. Communication impairments and cognitive deficits frequently impede self-reporting of symptoms. Careproviders may be unfamiliar with people's health histories due to frequent residential moves or staff turnover. Family members may be unavailable or uninvolved.

In addition, some types of disabilities have unique aging trends associated with them. To a certain extent, aging in persons with developmental disabilities will be determined by the etiology of the disability (i.e., toxic, metabolic, prenatal or postnatal infection, genetic). Environmental history and lifestyle issues such as diet, exercise, smoking or alcohol use; work; and recreational activities, will also affect the aging process. Patterns of medication usage and medication history can influence physical aging as well.

POLYPHARMACY

Many older adults with developmental disabilities take multiple medications and may have taken a variety of medications during a good part of their lives. With age the body becomes more sensitive to the effects of medication because of alterations in drug metabolism (Everitt & Avorn, 1986). Furthermore, the onset of age-related disease states may require the addition of new medications that have the potential to interact with prescription and nonprescription medications already in use. Older adults with developmental disabilities are at very high risk for complications associated with polypharmacy due to the nature of the types of medications they are frequently prescribed.

Medications are metabolized, or broken down, on the body by a variety of mechanisms in the body. Renal function is known to decline with age, leading to reduced clearance of some medications by the kidneys. This can result in higher blood levels and longer duration of action of some medications. The liver is also responsible for the metabolism of many medications. Some pathways for the breakdown of medications in the liver are more affected by aging than others. This can be an important factor in choosing a medication. For example, certain benzodiazepines (a class of medications used to treat anxiety and sleep disorders) are better tolerated because they can be metabolized more rapidly, while other benzodiazepines can cause prolonged sedation due to a retarded degradation process.

Another important factor in drug metabolism in older adults is the decline in lean body mass with age. This results in a higher proportion of fat in the body of older individuals. Many medications prescribed for persons with developmental disabilities, such as phenothiazines and psychotropic medications, are fat soluble and will be more widely distributed in the body with age, leading to a longer half-life and increased effect from the same dosage. Side effects not previously seen can occur in clients if dosages are not adjusted downward or discontinued completely as an individual ages.

Concerning managing seizure disorders, Dilantin (phenytoin) is a medication commonly prescribed for persons with developmental disabilities. This medication has a high potential to interact with many other prescribed medications because it is highly protein bound. This means that only a portion of the medication is in the active or free state. When other medications are taken with Dilantin, they may compete with it for the protein binding sites. This may cause an increase in the amount of free medication and an enhanced pharmacological effect. Medication levels are not always accurate as they usually measure total medication (protein bound and free), not just the amount of active (free) medication. Chronic disease associated with aging or poor nutrition can cause a lowering of the amount of serum protein and also lead to an increase in the amount of circulating active medication in an older person.

The potential for medication interactions and the risk for adverse reactions from prescribed medications increase with age. Medication use in older adults with developmental disabilities needs to be reviewed frequently. Dosages need to be readjusted when indicated, and medications should be eliminated in the absence of proven need and efficacy.

PHYSICAL AGING

In the general aging population, there is more variability both within the individual and between individuals than among younger persons. Older individuals with developmental disabilities probably encompass an even greater heterogeneity than is found in the general aging population. It is difficult, therefore, to discuss physical aging in persons with developmental disabilities in general terms. Every older person needs to be evaluated individually in the context of his or her unique history and special concerns. For the purpose of discussion, aging characteristics among five groups will be addressed, keeping in mind that there is a great deal of overlap between these groups. They include other adults with:

1. Mild to moderate mental retardation
2. Severe and profound mental retardation
3. Epilepsy
4. Down syndrome
5. Cerebral palsy

Mild to Moderate Mental Retardation

Older adults with mild to moderate mental retardation have a life expectancy that closely corresponds to that of the general aging population (Eyman, Grossman, Tarjan, & Miller, 1987). They will experience many of the same age-related changes that their peers experience. Frequently, however, diagnosis and treatment are delayed or ignored. The presentation of illness can vary from that seen in the general population. Diseases may present with unusual or challenging behaviors or with unexplained loss of adaptive skills. Functional declines and behavioral changes are symptoms of an underlying change in health status and deserve a comprehensive evaluation.

Sensory Losses Loss of vision and hearing can lead to functional declines, social isolation, and depression. Older adults with mild to moderate mental retardation rarely are able to report changes in sensory input and may be unaware or unable to comprehend how these losses are affecting their ability to interact with their environment. For this reason, regular screening is important for timely intervention. This can help prevent loss of functional skills and avert unnecessary residential moves.

Vision The prevalence of cataracts in the general aging population is 46% at ages 75–85 (Kini et al., 1978). While the prevalence of cataracts in older persons with developmental disabilities is not known, until further data are available, the assumption will be that similar prevalence rates exist. In persons with MR, it may be advantageous to perform cataract removal early, before declining function impairs the ability to cooperate during the required postoperative care. When cataract surgery is not indicated, visual function may be enhanced by soft lighting and reduced glare in the environment. Other causes of visual loss in aging adults include glaucoma, macular degeneration, and diabetic retinopathy.

Hearing Sensorineural hearing loss associated with aging (presbycusis) affects 60% of persons over the age of 65 in the United States. Older persons with mental retardation have been found to have a greater prevalence of hearing loss compared with younger persons with mental retardation (Janicki & Jacobson, 1986; Janicki & MacEachron, 1984). This type of hearing loss usually causes a decline in the ability to hear high frequencies. The result is difficulty hearing when background noise is present or if a speaker talks too quickly. Hearing aids can be helpful; however, if they cannot be tolerated, functional hearing still can be improved by environmental alteration. Minimizing background noise, facing the person spoken to, speaking to the better ear (for asymmetric hearing loss), and speaking slowly with good articulation, for example, all will improve comprehension. Generally when older persons have difficulty discriminating sounds, shouting only increases distortion and is not effective. If hearing loss is detected early, communication can be augmented for persons with mental retardation through the use of sign language or a communication picture book. Another common cause of hearing loss is cerumen impaction.

Cardiovascular Disease The prevalence of heart disease among persons with developmental disabilities currently is not known. Some individuals actually may have fewer risk factors because certain lifestyle choices such as smoking, drinking, and overeating may have been limited by lack of access. If exercise tolerance is noted to decline, further investigation into possible cardiovascular disease is indicated.

Confusion   Confusion is a common presenting symptom among older persons with mental retardation. Many conditions can present in this manner. If the confusion is of recent onset, over a few hours or days, possible causes include an acute illness such as an infection, dehydration, heart failure, or a metabolic disorder (e.g., high or low blood sugar, abnormal blood sodium). Many medications can also be responsible for an acute confusional state. If the confusion has occurred over a longer period of time, perhaps months or years, dementia may be present. Generally, in cases of dementia, the level of alertness is normal, whereas in an acute confusional state, also known as delirium, the level of alertness fluctuates, and the person may be drowsy or sleepy at times. Depression can also present as confusion. When depression is present, progression of the confusion can be rapid, and social and functional skills may be lost early. Sometimes in the case of depression, the time of onset can be fairly closely identified and associated with a particular life event.

Immobility   Mobility can be impaired by a variety of conditions associated with aging. These include arthritis, fractures, foot problems, stroke, cardiovascular disease, lung disease, and depression. Regardless of the cause, immobility can result in complications such as osteoporosis and increased risk for fractures, pressure sores, contractures, pneumonia, incontinence, and constipation and fecal impaction. Marked cardiovascular deconditioning and muscular atrophy can occur during even short periods of bedrest. Moderate regular exercise is essential for maintaining mobility in older adults with mental retardation. Even when physical limitations such as arthritis develop, muscle strengthening can play an important role in protecting joints. In addition, exercise can improve strength and balance, thereby reducing the risk of falls. Physical therapists are an excellent resource for planning appropriate exercise programs when physical impairments exist. Bedrest should be avoided if at all possible; if unavoidable, bed and chair exercises need to be encouraged in order to prevent deconditioning and the resulting loss of functional skills.

Constipation   Many persons with developmental disabilities have distended, poorly functioning bowels due to years of poor toileting habits. Frequently they have lifelong histories of constipation. Aging for most people leads to a decline in bowel motility which predisposes older individuals to developing problems with constipation. Persons who are both old and have developmental disabilities, then, are at much greater risk for severe problems from constipation. Aging adults and careproviders may be unaware of the severity of the problem due to infrequent direct observation and recording of bowel habits in persons who do not require assistance with toileting. Constipation can be responsible for physical, behavioral, and functional decline, especially in the area of bowel and urinary continence.

In addition, many medications can contribute to the development of con-stipation. These include antidepressant medications, antipsychotic medica-tions, and anticholinergic medications such as antihistamines found in allergy or cold pills. Benadryl is a frequently prescribed drug that is highly anticholinergic.

Urinary Incontinence   When persons with mental retardation develop urinary incontinence, it is frequently seen as a behavioral problem or a sign that they are experiencing expected functional declines because of growing old. Uri-nary incontinence is not a part of normal aging and usually has a treatable cause. Urinary incontinence can be divided into four types.

Urge Incontinence   Many people as they age develop an increased blad-der tone, which may cause urge incontinence. In this condition the bladder has a tendency to be hyperactive, or contract frequently. This causes the inability to hold urine for any length of time, and, therefore, frequent voiding of small amounts occurs. Many times a person may be aware of the need to void but unable to reach the bathroom in time. This type of incontinence can be treated with medication and bladder training programs.

Stress Incontinence   Stress incontinence usually occurs in women who experience a relaxation of the pelvic floor muscles due to age-related decrease in estrogen. Incontinence in this case usually is worse with coughing or laughing and is not a problem at night when a person is lying down. It can be treated with medication.

Overflow Incontinence   Overflow incontinence occurs when there is an obstruction of the flow of urine from the bladder. In men this is commonly caused by enlargement of the prostate gland and can be treated both medically and surgically. In women this can occur from constipation causing pressure on the bladder or from a pelvic tumor.

Hypotonic Bladder   Hypotonic bladder often is referred to as a neuro-genic bladder. Incontinence occurs because the bladder is unable to contract and empty effectively. Usually this is due to a neurologic insult such as a stroke. It can be more difficult to treat, although, some medication can be helpful, and bladder retraining sometimes is beneficial.

Urinary incontinence is a commonly occurring problem with age. It de-serves careful evaluation to determine the cause and the proper treatment.

Severe and Profound Mental Retardation

Persons with mental retardation in the severe to profound range experience a shortened life expectancy. Frequently they have additional chronic medical problems such as scoliosis, dislocated hips, respiratory disease, and chronic otitis media (McDonald, 1985). In addition, they are more likely to have vision and hearing deficits not associated with age alone. This is an extremely high risk group, very challenging to diagnose and treat. Community placement does seem to improve life expectancy, and there is some indication that community medical resources can meet their additional needs (Minihan & Dean, 1990). Expanded home care availability is needed in order to help maintain these individuals in the community as they age.

Epilepsy

Persons with lifelong histories of use of anti-seizure medications are at increased risk for osteoporosis and could experience a higher risk of fractures as they grow older. Maintaining adequate calcium and vitamin D intake is important to assist in reducing this risk. In addition, exercise probably is beneficial in decreasing bone loss and preventing injury from falls.

Down Syndrome

Improved Life Expectancy of People with Down Syndrome Life expectancy for persons with Down syndrome has increased dramatically since the 1940s. In 1949, Penrose reported the life expectancy for persons with Down syndrome to be 9 years. In 1963, Collmann and Stoller reported the life expectancy to be 18.3 years. Today the life expectancy is approximately 55 years (Eyman, Call, & White, 1989; Eyman, Grossman, Tarjan, & Miller, 1987).

The primary reasons for this increase in life expectancy are improvements in health care and decreased rates of institutionalization. Previously, deaths among people with Down syndrome were attributed to respiratory and other types of infectious disease, malignancy (i.e., childhood acute leukemia), and congenital heart disease (Fryers, 1986). The discovery and improved availability of antibiotics in the 1940s helped to reduce death due to infection. In addition, deinstitutionalization reduced exposure to potentially lethal infections (Eyman & Widaman, 1987; Nelson & Crocker, 1978). Since 1960, surgical expertise has been available increasingly to correct congenital heart abnormalities that are present in 40% of infants born with Down syndrome. Today the primary causes of death in persons with Down syndrome are stroke, dementia, and infection. Further increases in life expectancy can be expected (Thase, 1982).

Alzheimer's Disease Approximately 40% of persons with Down syndrome develop the dementia symptoms associated with Alzheimer's disease. The average age of onset of Alzheimer's disease symptoms in individuals with Down syndrome is 53–55 years. Autopsy studies have shown that the neuropathological changes associated with Alzheimer's disease in the general population (i.e., neurofibrillary plaques and tangles) occur in 100% of Down syndrome cases studied beginning at the age of 40 (Barcikowska, Silverman, Zigman, Kozlowski, Kujawa, Rudelli, Wisniewski, 1989). It is not clear why some individuals with Down syndrome appear to be resistant to developing dementia in spite of these cellular changes in the brain (Wisniewski & Rabe, 1986). There are reported cases of some individuals with Down syndrome living to the age of 85 without developing signs of dementia.

Duration of Alzheimer's dementia has been reported to be 3.5–10.5 years from diagnosis until death in persons with Down syndrome (Dalton &

Wisniewski, 1990). This represents a more rapid progression than in people without Down syndrome who have Alzheimer's disease. Diagnosis can be difficult due to the current lack of adequate assessment instruments for lower functioning persons with mental retardation, and the floor effect of standardized cognitive tests. Higher functioning persons with Down syndrome will present with some of the same signs of Alzheimer's disease seen in the general aging population. These include memory loss, temporal disorientation, and decreased verbal output (Evenhuis, 1990). Some of the reported early signs of dementia in lower functioning persons with Down syndrome include apathy, inattention, decreased social interaction, daytime sleepiness, gait deterioration, myoclonus, and seizures (Evenhuis, 1990). Due to the difficulties encountered with diagnosing early dementia in this population, these signs may actually represent a later stage of the disease, thus shortening the apparent duration of symptoms.

It is also possible that these symptoms may be incorrectly attributed to Alzheimer's disease. Other conditions can present with a very similar clinical picture. Sleep apnea and sensory losses (vision and/or hearing) may cause some of these same symptoms. Behavioral changes and functional declines also may be mistakenly attributed to Alzheimer's disease. Other causes of alterations in behavior include depression, an adjustment reaction to an environmental change, and poor capacity to express emotional states due to lack of education or due to prior institutionalization. Before observed changes in behavior or functioning are attributed to Alzheimer's disease, a complete evaluation should be undertaken by experienced individuals.

Among people with Down syndrome and dementia of the Alzheimer type, the incidence of seizures has been noted to be up to eight times higher as compared with that in people with dementia of the Alzheimer type who do not have Down syndrome (Evenhuis, 1990; Lai & Williams, 1989). Seizures occur in 5% of persons with Down syndrome who do not have dementia, while in those with Down syndrome and dementia of the Alzheimer type, seizures are present up to 85% of the time.

Hearing Loss Persons with Down syndrome are more likely than others to develop a problem with hearing as they grow older. Many individuals with Down syndrome acquire a conductive hearing loss in childhood due to a propensity for middle ear infections. In addition, persons with Down syndrome are prone to sensorineural hearing loss (presbycusis). This is the same type of hearing loss experienced by the general aging population and results in a loss in the ability to hear higher pitched sounds. This causes difficulty in distinguishing sounds, especially when background noise is present. Persons with Down syndrome can begin to develop this type of hearing loss in their 20s (Buchanan, 1990). For persons with this type of hearing loss it is best that speakers face them directly and articulate in a quiet setting.

Diagnosis of hearing loss in persons with developmental disabilities can be difficult. They generally are unable to indicate that they are experiencing this problem. Service providers and family members usually are unaware that this is a problem. Testing needs to be done by an audiologist who has experience in evaluating persons who have difficulty with testing.

Thyroid Disease Hypothyroidism occurs in 20%–30% of persons with Down syndrome (Baxter et al., 1975). Symptoms of hypothyroidism include lethargy, functional decline, confusion, constipation, dry skin and hair, fatigue, and depression. If untreated, hypothyroidism can lead to hallucinations and coma. Persons with Down syndrome should be tested annually for thyroid disease.

Immune System Persons with Down syndrome seem to experience a premature aging of the immune system (Levin, Nir, & Mogilner, 1975; Whittingham, Pitt, Shaema, & Mackay, 1977). Changes in the immune system seen in older individuals in the general population have been identified in persons with Down syndrome at a much earlier age (Rabinowe, Rubin, George, Adri, & Eisenbarth, 1989). Children with Down syndrome have higher rates of leukemia, but adult cancers, such as colon cancer, seem to occur at the same rates as in the general population. Breast and cervical cancer may occur less commonly.

Sleep Apnea Obstructive sleep apnea has been reported in both children and adults with Down syndrome (Hultchrantz & Svanholm, 1991; Marcus, Keens, Bautista, von Pechmann, & Ward, 1991; Telakivi, Partinen, Salmi, Leinonen, & Harkonen, 1987). Predisposing factors among those with Down syndrome include: abnormally small upper airway, increased secretions, obesity, generalized hypotonia causing a collapse of the airway during inspiration, tongue hypotonia, and adenoid and tonsilar enlargement caused by frequent infections. Symptoms include excessive daytime sedation, behavioral disturbances, failure to thrive, declining functional skills, and disrupted sleep pattern.

Sleep apnea can be present even when not clinically expected. Untreated, it can lead to heart and lung disease and congestive heart failure. In the general population, the prevalence of sleep apnea has been noted to increase with age. It was diagnosed in 60% of older adults complaining of sleeping difficulties (Roehrs, Zorick, Wittig, & Roth, 1985) and in 24% of older adults in a random sample (Ancoli-Israel, Kripke, & Mason, 1987). Because persons with Down syndrome have so many predisposing factors, an increase in the prevalence of obstructive sleep apnea among individuals with Down syndrome as they grow older can be expected. It is important that the potential for this be evaluated in any individual experiencing behavioral or functional changes.

Heart Disease Congenital heart disease occurs in 40% of persons with Down syndrome. Most cardiac lesions are now routinely corrected within the first year of life. Because cardiac surgery was not available until after 1960, persons who have had repairs have not yet reached old age. It is unclear whether this group will have special needs as they grow older. It is known that 30%–50% of adults with Down syndrome have mitral valve prolapse and 10%–15% have aortic regurgitation. These conditions are often asymptomatic, and an echocardiogram should be obtained if a murmur is noted.

Musculoskeletal Problems Individuals with Down syndrome often have problems with the musculoskeletal system, including decreased muscle tone, ligamentous laxity, atlanto-axial subluxation, hip subluxation, and scoliosis (Diamond, Lynne, & Sigman, 1981). All of these conditions can impair mobility and limit activities in later life. In addition, up to 90% of persons with Down syndrome have bunions, which can cause difficulties with ambulation due to pain and problems with balance.

Vision Approximately 50% of adults with Down syndrome develop cataracts (Hestnes, Sand, & Fostad, 1991). Visual impairment, especially when combined with the higher rates of hearing loss and dementia in this population, can interfere markedly with the ability to negotiate the environment and contribute to functional or behavioral declines. Whenever possible, cataracts should be removed early to prevent loss of skills.

Cerebral Palsy

How the aging process affects persons with cerebral palsy is not well studied. Older persons with cerebral palsy may have earlier age-specific mortality. The co-existence of cerebral palsy and mental retardation probably creates additional risk factors depending on the level of mental retardation (Janicki, 1989). When evaluating persons with cerebral palsy it is difficult to determine what is related to general aging, what is related to pathological aging, and what may be preventable secondary conditions. It appears that at least some persons with cerebral palsy experience increasing problems with mobility as they age. This may be due, at least in part, to pain syndromes from degenerative joint disease resulting from overuse of an irregular joint. In addition, persons with cerebral palsy may be at increased risk for osteoporosis due to limitations in mobility throughout life, inadequate calcium intake, and decreased sun exposure leading to low circulating levels of vitamin D. This may cause a predisposition to increased fracture rates at earlier ages than in the general population. Persons with cerebral palsy seem to experience increased difficulty with speech and ventilation as they grow older. Sensory losses may occur at a higher rate or cause increased disability. It appears that individuals with cerebral palsy are at risk for increased dependency with age.

EVALUATION

Perhaps the greatest limitation in evaluating the health status of aging persons with developmental disabilities is the difficulty in obtaining an accurate health history. The history is the most important component of the assessment (Besdine, 1988) and, when available, it alone can provide a diagnosis 80% of the time. Deficiencies in health-related information and poor documentation of current physical problems are common (Walz, Harper, & Wilson, 1986). This occurs when there have been frequent residential moves or staff changeovers, leaving few reporters with any past knowledge of health status and functioning. Even in situations in which consistent careproviders are present, reporting may be deficient due to poor observational skills. Family members and direct care staff often are unaware of the changes that can occur with age and do not know what to be looking for. Health professionals need to teach observational skills to careproviders and encourage good recording of health behaviors. Improved history taking can reduce the need for more costly and inconvenient testing.

REFERENCES

Ancoli-Israel, S., Kripke, D.F., & Mason, W. (1987). Characteristics of obstructive and central sleep apnea in the elderly: An interim report. *Biological Psychiatry, 22,* 741–750.

Andres, R., & Tobin, J.D. (1977). Endocrine systems. In C.E. Finch & L. Hayflick (Eds.), *Handbook of the biology of aging* (pp. 357–378). New York: Van Nostrand Reinhold.

Barcikowska, M., Silverman, W.P., Zigman, W.B., Kozlowski, P.B., Kujawa, M., Rudelli, R., & Wisniewski, H.M. (1989). Alzheimer-type neuropathology and clinical symptoms of dementia in mentally retarded people without Down syndrome. *American Journal on Mental Retardation, 93,* 551–557.

Baxter, R.G., Larkins, R.G., Martin, F.I., Heyma, P., Myles, L., & Ryan, L. (1975). Down syndrome and thyroid dysfunction in adults. *Lancet, ii,* 794–796.

Besdine, R.W. (1988). Clinical approaches to the elderly patient. In J.W. Rowe & R.W. Besdine (Eds.), *Geriatric medicine* (pp. 23–36). Boston: Little, Brown.

Buchanan, L.H. (1990). Early onset of presbycusis in Down syndrome. *Scandinavian Audiology, 19,* 103–110.

Collmann, R.D., & Stoller A. (1963). Data on mongolism in Victoria, Australia: Prevalence and life expectation. *Journal of Mental Deficiency Research, 7,* 60.

Dalton, A.J., & Wisniewski, H.M. (1990). Down's syndrome and the dementia of Alzheimer's disease. *International Review of Psychiatry, 2,* 43–52.

Diamond, L.S., Lynne, D., & Sigman, B. (1981). Orthopedic disorders in patients with Down syndrome. *Orthopedic Clinics of North America, 12,* 57–71.

Evenhuis, H.M. (1990). The natural history of dementia in Down's syndrome. *Archives of Neurology, 47,* 263–267.

Everitt, D.E., & Avorn, J. (1986). Drug prescribing for the elderly. *Archives of Internal Medicine, 146,* 2393–2396.

Eyman, R.K., Call, T.L., & White, J.F. (1989). Mortality of elderly mentally retarded persons in California. *Journal of Applied Gerontology, 8,* 203–215.

Eyman, R.K., Grossman, H.J., Tarjan, G., & Miller, C.R. (1987). *Life expectancy and mental retardation.* Washington, DC: American Association on Mental Retardation.

Eyman, R.K., & Widaman, K.F. (1987). Life-span development of institutionalized and community-based mentally retarded persons, revisited. *American Journal of Mental Deficiency, 91,* 559–569.

Fiatarone, M.A., Marks, E.C., Ryan, N.D., Meredith, C.N., Lipsitz, L.A., & Evans, W.J. (1990). High-intensity strength training in nonagenarians: Effects on skeletal muscle. *Journal of the American Medical Association, 263*(22), 3029–3034.

Fryers, T. (1986). Survival in Down's syndrome. *Journal of Mental Deficiency Research, 30,* 101–110.

Hestnes, A., Sand, T., & Fostad, K. (1991). Ocular findings in Down's syndrome. *Journal of Mental Deficiency Research, 31,* 31–99.

Hultchrantz, E., & Svanholm, H. (1991). Down syndrome and sleep apnea: A therapeutic challenge. *International Journal of Pediatric Otorhinolaryngology, 21,* 263–268.

Janicki, M.P. (1989). Aging, cerebral palsy, and older persons with mental retardation. *Australian and New Zealand Journal of Developmental Disabilities, 15,* 311–320.

Janicki, M.P., & Jacobson, J.W. (1986). Generational trends in sensory, physical, and behavioral abilities among older mentally retarded persons. *American Journal of Mental Deficiency, 90,* 490–500.

Janicki, M.P., & MacEachron, A.E. (1984). Residential, health, and social service needs of elderly developmentally disabled persons. *The Gerontologist, 24,* 128–137.

Kini, M.M., Liebowitz, H.M., Colton, T., Nickerson, M.A., Ganley, J., & Dawber, T.R. (1978). Prevalence of senile cataract, diabetic retinopathy, senile mascular degeneration, and open-angle glaucoma in the Framingham eye study. *American Journal of Ophthalmology, 85,* 28–34.

Lai, F., & Williams, R.S. (1989). A prospective study of Alzheimer disease in Down syndrome. *Archives of Neurology, 46,* 849–853.

Levin, S., Nir, E., & Mogilner, B.M. (1975). T-system immune-deficiency in Down's syndrome. *Pediatrics, 56,* 123–126.

Marcus, C.L., Keens, T.G., Bautista, D.B., von Pechmann, W.S., & Ward, S.L. (1991). Obstructive sleep apnea in children with down syndrome. *Pediatrics, 88,* 132–139.

McDonald, E.P. (1985). Medical needs of severely developmentally disabled persons residing in the community. *American Journal of Mental Deficiency, 90,* 171–176.

Minihan, P.M., & Dean, D.H. (1990). Meeting the health services needs of persons with mental retardation living in the community. *American Journal of Public Health, 80,* 1043–1048.

Nelson, R.P., & Crocker, A.C. (1978). The medical care of mentally retarded persons in public residential facilities. *New England Journal of Medicine, 299,* 1039.

Penrose, L.S. (1949). The incidence of mongolism in the general population. *Journal of Mental Science, 9,* 10.

Rabinowe, S.L., Rubin, I.L., George, K.L., Adri, M.N., & Eisenbarth, G.S. (1989). Trisomy 21 (Down's syndrome): Autoimmunity, aging and monoclonal antibody-defined T-cell abnormalities. *Journal of Autoimmunity, 2,* 25–30.

Roehrs, T., Zorick, F., Wittig, R., & Roth, T. (1985). Efficacy of a reduced triazolam dose in elderly insomniacs. *Neurobiology of Aging, 6,* 293–296.

Rowe, J.W., Andres, R., Tobin, J.D., Norris, A.H., & Shock, N.W. (1976). The effect of aging on creatinine clearance in man: A cross-sectional and longitudinal study. *Journal of Gerontology, 31,* 155–163.

Svanborg, A., Bergstrom, G., & Mellstrom, D. (1982). *Epidemiological studies on social and medical conditions of the elderly.* Copenhagen: World Health Organization.

Telakivi, T., Partinen, M., Salmi, T., Leinonen, L., & Harkonen, T. (1987). Nocturnal periodic breathing in adults with Down's syndrome. *Journal of Mental Deficiency Research, 31,* 31–39.

Thase, M.E. (1982). Longevity and mortality in Down's syndrome. *Journal of Mental Deficiency Research, 26,* 177–192.

Walz, T., Harper, D., & Wilson, J. (1986). The aging developmentally disabled person: A review. *The Gerontologist, 26,* 622–629.

Wisniewski, H.M., & Rabe, A. (1986). Discrepancy between Alzheimer-type neuropathology and dementia in people with Down syndrome. *Annals of the New York Academy of Science, 477,* 247–259.

Whittingham, S., Pitt, D.B., Shaema, D.L., & Mackay, I.R. (1977). Stress deficiency of the T-lymphocyte system exemplified by Down syndrome. *Lancet, i,* 163–166.

4

Psychotropic Medication Use Among Older Adults with Mental Retardation

Deborah J. Anderson and Barbara Polister

Estimates of the prevalence of use of psychotropic medications among people with mental retardation vary widely (Cohen & Sprague, 1977; Hill, Balow, & Bruininks, 1985; Jonas, 1980; Intagliata & Rinck, 1985; Knoll, 1987; Radinsky, 1984). Studies vary considerably in their sample composition, with various and, at times, unspecific mixes of ages, institutional and community-based samples, and conditions (e.g., epilepsy) that are included or excluded. In addition, the types of medications studied vary, as do the definitions of such terms as *psychoactive* and *psychotropic*. For example, some studies include antipsychotic medications, anticonvulsants, and medications prescribed to control the side effects of antipsychotic medications, antianxiety medications, antidepressants, stimulants, and sedatives/hypnotics. Others use some combination of the above or focus on subgroups among the larger categories. Psychoactive medications typically include all of the above, whereas psychotropic medications typically include mind-altering medications (i.e., antipsychotic medications, antianxiety medications, antidepressants, stimulants, and sedative/hypnotics) but often exclude anticonvulsants and medications used for controlling the Parkinson-like effects of antipsychotic medications. Some researchers, however, focus upon the intention of the prescriber, that is, the primary reason for which the medication was prescribed, rather than on the typical effects of the medication in defining terms such as *psychotropic*. To add to the confusion, antipsychotic medications are also described as neuroleptics and antianxiety medications as anxiolytics. At a minimum, researchers need to examine closely sample characteristics and categories of medications reviewed, in order to obtain meaningful comparisons of similar groups of people with similar medications.

ASPECTS OF RESEARCH

There is a paucity of research on the prevalence and effects of the use of psychotropic medications among people with developmental disabilities compared with the research available on such medications used among people without developmental disabilities. Among people with developmental disabilities, studies have dealt almost exclusively with children and young people, who may be expected to respond differently than older adults (Werry, 1988). Prior to 1980, many of these studies failed to meet minimum standards for methodology. In addition, other conditions may also affect the individual's response to medications (e.g., ambulation, medical conditions), and medication patterns may differ appreciably between people with severe disabilities, who often have multiple disabilities and complex medical needs, and those with milder disabilities who are ambulatory (Dura, Aman, & Mulick, 1988). People with severe disabilities also present unique methodological considerations, such as lack of adequate sample sizes, heterogeneity of participants, and participant attrition (Schroeder, 1988). Studies on topics other than medication use among persons with developmental disabilities typically have omitted any mention of whether or not participants were taking medications. Agran, Moore, and Martin's (1988) review of applied research journal articles, which focused on people with mental retardation over an 11-year period, found that only 3.4% (43 out of 1,175) indicated whether or not participants were taking psychotropic or anticonvulsant medications.

RESEARCH ON COMMUNITY SETTINGS LACKING

Only a handful of studies on medications have been conducted in community residential settings, the setting where more than 90% of persons with developmental disabilities are estimated to live (Aman & Singh, 1988). Although older people with developmental disabilities have been disproportionately placed in state facilities and nursing homes (Lakin, Hill, & Anderson, 1991), they are expected to move to community settings as a result of the continued depopulation of state institutions and the Omnibus Budget Reconciliation Act of 1987 (OBRA, Public Law 100-203) mandated diversion of inappropriate nursing home placements. The importance of the residential setting is illustrated by a study of 178 adults with mental retardation receiving services from a comprehensive community mental retardation agency. These persons were living in a variety of settings, including a 65-bed intermediate care facility for persons with mental retardation (ICF/MR), an apartment living program, single family homes, intermediate care facilities (ICF/nursing home), and a state hospital providing short-term services (Martin & Agran, 1985). The researchers found correlations between medication use and both the vocational and residential settings. As the vocational placement became more restrictive, medication use increased. (Half of this population in sheltered work were taking psychotropic or anticonvulsant medications, versus only 9% in nonsheltered employment.) Similarly, as the residential placement became more restrictive, medication use increased (33% living with their families, 60% in ICFs/MR, and 77% in ICFs were on medications).

PREVALENCE

The estimated prevalence of use of psychotropic medications varies from approximately 30% to 50% among residents of state institutions (Cohen & Sprague, 1977; Hill et al., 1985) and from 26% to 36% among community residents (Hill et al., 1985; Radinsky, 1984). Total psychoactive medication use among institutional residents with mental retardation has been found to vary from 50% to 70% (Hill et al., 1985; Jonas, 1980), and for adults in the community from 36% to 48% (Intagliata & Rinck, 1985; Radinsky, 1984).

Studies of the prevalence of use of psychotropic medications among older persons with developmental disabilities are rare in the literature, and those that are available report different findings. Intagliata and Rinck (1985) used statewide data on antipsychotic medication use in Missouri and found that antipsychotic medications were prescribed for 47% of older (60 years or more) community residents and for 50% of older institutional residents. Total psychoactive medication use prevalence was 68% for older community residents and 67% for older institutional residents in Missouri. Jacobson (1988) studied medication patterns among 35,000 people with mental retardation in community care and developmental disabilities centers in the state of New York. Among persons ages 65 and over, psychotropic medications were administered to only 14%, a figure that differs considerably from the findings of Intagliata and Rinck (1985). Harper, Wadsworth, and Michael (1989) reported in a sample of 87 older persons in congregate care and group home settings, a prevalence rate of 45% for psychotropic medications, and a rate of 38% for antipsychotics. However, the persons studied were relatively young, averaging 55 and 44 years of age in the congregate care settings and group homes respectively; it is not known whether the figures for antipsychotics are unduplicated, and the sample selection method is not reported, leaving it unclear as to whether it was a statewide sample or just selected settings. James (1986) reported the prevalence of use of antipsychotic medications to be 36% for older (60 years or more) residents of a British hospital ($N = 50$) studied over a 20-year period. The widely differing results in these few studies may reflect different sampling procedures and/or statewide and national differences. In sum, these results raise a number of questions about prevalence rates for older adults with developmental disabilities.

OVERUSE OF PSYCHOTROPIC MEDICATIONS

International comparisons of the prevalence of the use of antipsychotics for people with developmental disabilities indicated that they are used more sparingly in Europe, Scandinavia, Australia, and New Zealand than in the United States (Schroeder, 1988). In studies of facilities using well-designed medication evaluation techniques, researchers consistently found a reduction in the number of antipsychotic prescriptions and in polypharmacy, and lower average dosages (Schroeder, 1988). Bates, Smeltzer, and Arnoczky (1986), focusing upon psychoactive medications administered to people with mental retardation, used multidisciplinary teams to reexamine medication regimens. They concluded that between 39% and 55% of the medical regimens were inappropriate for the conditions diagnosed. Most of the medications were prescribed by nonpsychiatrists, even though diagnoses were made by psychiatrists.

DELETERIOUS EFFECTS OF PSYCHOTROPIC MEDICATIONS

Use of psychotropics is viewed by many as being problematic. Knoll (1987) reviewed research on psychotropic medications with people having severe developmental disabilities. He concluded that most people with severe developmental disabilities do not need to be on such medications, that widespread use is indicative of a programmatic emphasis on control, and that the use of psychotropics does not aid the inclusion of people with severe developmental disabilities in the community, since the side effects often interfere with the ability to develop skills, to work up to potential, and to relate well. Although Martin and Agran's (1985) study demonstrated only a correlational link between the restrictiveness of day and residential placements and the use of psychoactive medications, the findings are provocative. Sprague and Baxley (1978) raised some serious legal/ethical issues involved in the use of psychotropic medications for behavior management, since "persons having severe intellectual deficiencies are incapable of either exercising or protecting many of the legal rights . . . being *limited* or *incapable* of either assenting to or refusing treatment" (p. 93).

Psychotropic medications have side effects, some of which are long-term and irreversible. Tardive dyskinesia, a neurological disorder involving repetitive movements that often are irreversible, has been estimated to affect as many as 30% of the people with developmental disabilities who are using chronic antipsychotic medications (Golden, 1988). Richardson, Haugland, Pass, and Craig (1986) reported that tardive dyskinesia was associated with increasing age, sex (females are affected significantly more often than males), and the presence of metabolic disorders. Older adults are particularly affected for two reasons: 1) reduction in the ability to metabolize and eliminate pharmacological substances, and 2) the cumulative effect of lifetime dosage of psychotropic medications. Gowdy, Zarfas, and Phipps (1987) noted that the use of anti-Parkinson medications for anything other than short-term Parkinson-like side effects of neuroleptics is not advisable and may contribute to the formation of tardive dyskinesia. Tardive dyskinesia is difficult to diagnose in general and in people with disabilities in particular because high medication dosages mask the symptoms of this side effect, and many people with developmental disabilities display, for other reasons, some of the movements and symptoms associated with tardive dyskinesia. Given all of these factors, careful monitoring, judicious research, and precise evaluation of efficacy are particularly essential when the use of psychotropic medications is proposed for older adults with developmental disabilities.

AGE-RELATED DIFFERENCES IN RESPONSE TO MEDICATIONS

Older adults undergo a variety of physiological changes that influence the way they react to pharmacological substances, further complicating the use of psychotropic medications among them. An age-related decrease in serum albumin decreases the amount of the medication capable of binding with protein, which in turn increases the free fraction of drugs in the blood, the consequence of which is to increase the potential for toxic concentrations. The decrease in lean body mass and total body water associated with age produces a similar effect with water soluble medications. The increase in total body fat associated with aging decreases plasma concentrations of fat soluble medications, making larger dosages necessary. With age, the liver becomes less efficient in metabolizing medications, with the result that the effect of the medication in the body is prolonged for most psychotropic medications. In addition, renal clearance tends to decrease with age, so that certain medications that are excreted in the urine (e.g., lithium) tend to have prolonged half life among older adults. In most, although not all instances, the net effect is a more potent or longer lasting response to psychotropic medications (Aman, 1988).

AGE-RELATED DIFFERENCES IN PATTERNS OF MEDICATION USE

Medication patterns of older and younger people are also quite different, for example, the prevalence of use of psychotropic medications is lower among children with developmental disabilities than among adults with developmental disabilities (Aman, Field, & Bridgeman, 1985). Buck and Sprague (1989) studied Medicaid recipients with mental retardation in Illinois, 82% of whom were living in larger facilities with 16 beds or more. They found that middle age and older residents were significantly more likely to receive psychotropic medications than younger residents (46% of people 45–64 and 65 years of age versus 34% and 21% of individuals ages 30–44 and 18–29 years respectively). Among those receiving medications, 88% of the medications used were antipsychotic medications.

Other medications commonly used by these aging adults can alter the effects of psychotropic medications. For example, antacids can reduce the absorption of psychotropic medications. Polypharmacy is common among aging adults in general, as well as among aging adults with mental retardation. Anderson, Lakin, Bruininks, and Hill (1987) found that, among residents ages 63 and older with mental retardation living in residential facilities licensed by mental retardation/developmental disabilities (MR/DD) agencies, most were using medications. They also found that among those using medications, the average number of medications was 2.4. Gowdy et al. (1987) found that, in a community population, about half of the residents surveyed received two or more psychoactive medications daily. This study included anticonvulsants as psychoactive medications. Twenty-four percent of residents received nonredundant combinations (copharmacy), 94% of these regimens being judged as either uncertain or inappropriate by the authors.

SUMMARY

There is little research about use of psychotropic medications among older adults with developmental disabilities, and the few studies that exist report widely discrepant prevalence rates. Individual, residential, and day program characteristics appear to be related to use of psychotropic medications among younger adults with developmental disabilities, while the relationships among older adults with developmental disabilities are unclear. The appropriateness of use of psychotropic medications among older adults with developmental disabilities is virtually unknown.

The study described in the next section was designed to respond to these issues by presenting findings based on a national sample of facilities where older adults with developmental disabilities lived. It was hoped that a national sample would resolve some of the questions about the prevalence of use of psychotropic medications across states. In addition, a relatively large national sample provides the opportunity to determine whether different rates of psychotropic medication use are associated with different types of residential placements. Also, the questions raised by a number of separate studies about the relationships between various individual and facility-linked differences and psychotropic medication use are explored in this study. Questions about whether such individual characteristics as level of mental retardation, adaptive behavior skills, and presence of significant behavior problems are associated with use of psychotropic medications among older adults with developmental disabilities are addressed, as are the issues of whether day program participation, level of social activity, and community inclusion (e.g., acceptance by neighbors) are related to psychotropic medication use. Finally, this study addresses the extent to which antipsychotic medications, or antipsychotics, which have implications for long-term, frequently irreversible side effects, are being used for persons with diagnoses of psychosis in particular or whether they are being used more broadly as a medication for behavior control.

MINNESOTA NATIONAL STUDY

During 1985–1986, the Center for Residential Community Services (CRCS) at the University of Minnesota collected data on a national sample of older adults with mental retardation living in residential facilities owned, operated, and/or licensed by developmental disabilities agencies. A 10% sample of facilities with one or more persons over the age of 62 was selected, including foster care, group homes, large private facilities (with 16 or more residents), and state institutions. A facility-based sampling method was utilized in order to have adequate numbers of smaller residential facilities. Each facility had an equal chance of selection, regardless of size. One or, if present, two randomly selected aging residents were surveyed per facility. The final sample consisted of 370 residents in 235 facilities, who were an average age of 70 years old. Information about the residents was completed by direct careproviders who knew the residents well.

Instruments

Careproviders were requested to "list any drugs/medication [the] resident takes regularly." The information provided included the type of medication, dosage, frequency, and purpose. Responses were coded by type of medication, with reference to the intended purpose when necessary for certain health-related medications. Psychotropic medications included all mind-altering medications, including antipsychotics (neuroleptics), antianxiety medications (anxiolytics), antidepressants, antimanics, sedatives/hypnotics, and stimulants. Anticonvulsant medications were not included as psychotropic medications, since their primary purpose is not mood/personality alteration, but prevention of a specific medical condition (i.e., seizures). Detailed additional information about the residents, including a variety of questions concerning their health status and health treatment, functional limitations, level of mental retardation, and other characteristics was also obtained.

Analysis

Responses were analyzed by facility type (i.e., foster care, group home, large private facility, and state institution). In addition, residents of different facilities who were taking major tranquilizers (i.e., antipsychotics, or neuroleptics) or any type of psychotropic medication were compared with residents who were not taking such medications on a variety of demographic, health status, and other questions. The sampling method described above resulted in a disproportionately small sample of persons in state institutions, which predominate placement for older persons with developmental disabilities (Lakin et al., 1991), and a disproportionately large sample of persons in smaller, community-based facilities, in order to provide adequate sample sizes for all of the four facility types. The method used for estimating prevalence of medication use for the total sample involved weighting the values obtained for the facility subsamples with the formula below, with f, g, p, and s being the number of sample residents in foster care, group homes, large private facilities, and state facilities who were using the medications in question (i.e., neuroleptics or psychotropics), and F, G, P, and S being the total number of residents responding to this item ($N = 369$):

$$\text{Weighted Total Percentage} = \frac{.3727f + .3968g + 1.013p + 3.823s.}{F + G + P + S}$$

Results

A total of 109 persons out of 369 respondents were taking psychotropic medications, including antipsychotics (neuroleptics), minor tranquilizers, antidepressants, sedatives/hypnotics, or stimulants. Consistent with most medication studies, the majority of persons taking psychotropic medications were prescribed antipsychotic medications (74%, or a total of 81 persons). Weighted population estimates are that 27% of older adults with developmental disabilities are using psychotropic medications, and 19% are prescribed antipsychotics. Population estimates give a particularly heavy weighting to responses from residents of state institutions, since it is the most common residential placement licensed by state MR/DD agencies for older adults with developmental disabilities (Lakin et al., 1991).

Facility Differences   Residents living in foster care homes were least likely to be using antipsychotics, with only 10% of this sample reportedly using such medications. (See Figure 4.1.) Residents of state institutions had only slightly higher rates (12%), but the prevalence of antipsychotics among persons in group homes was more than twice as high as in state institutions (27%), exceeded only by persons in large private facilities (33%) (Chi-square [3, $N = 369$] $= 20.74$, $p < .001$). Similarly, foster care and state institution residents were least likely to be using any type of psychotropic medication. Only 21% were using psychotropic medications in this setting, whereas 30% of persons in group homes and 42% of persons in large private settings were taking at least one type of psychotropic medication (chi-square [3, $N = 369$] $= 11.55$, $p < .01$).

Demographic and Psychological Characteristics   In this study, sex and level of mental retardation were found to be unrelated to psychotropic medication use. People considered to have severe mental illness, which included schizophrenia, manic depression, and autism, were significantly more likely to be receiving antipsychotic and psychotropic medications than people who did not have diagnoses of severe mental illness. (See Figure 4.2.) However, the vast majority of persons receiving antipsychotics did not have diagnoses of severe mental illness. A total of 81 out of 370 persons surveyed in all facilities were taking some type of antipsychotic, but only 18 of those persons (22%) were diag-

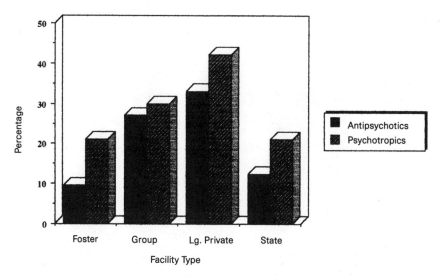

Figure 4.1.   Percentage using mind-altering medications, by facility type.

nosed as having severe mental illness. In addition, another 15 persons (8 of whom were living in foster care homes) reportedly had severe mental illness but were not receiving antipsychotics.

The picture was quite different, however, for persons diagnosed as having nonpsychotic disorders, such as depression, anxiety, mood disturbance, or other less severe mental health problems. Among those persons taking antipsychotics in the sample, slightly under half (46%) were diagnosed as having a nonpsychotic disorder; similar percentages were reported among persons taking psychotropic medications. Seeing a psychologist was unrelated to whether or not one was prescribed psychotropic medications.

Medical and Social Indicators   The patterns of medication use and medical limitations, the frequency of medical care received, and hospitalizations in the past year were unrelated to medication use, as were having Down syndrome, cerebral palsy, or another developmental disability. Verbal ability and activities of daily living, with the exception of bathing, were also unrelated to medication use. The relationship between use of medications and chronic medical conditions was unclear. Taking psychoactive medication was associated with a number of social indicators, however, including a lower frequency of day program involvement, fewer visits with friends, less likelihood of having friends without disabilities, more negative responses of neighbors, and less likelihood that the resident had ever visited a neighbor's home.

Behavior Problems   People taking antipsychotics were more likely to engage in self-injurious behaviors, uncooperative behaviors, and odd/stereotypic behaivors that were considered serious (extremely, very, or moderately

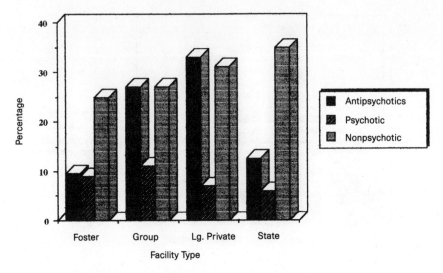

Figure 4.2.   Percentage using antipsychotic medications, by facility type.

serious) by careproviders than people not taking antipsychotics, according to their careproviders (7.4% versus 2.7%, 13.6% versus 4.8%, and 6.2% versus 2.7% respectively). The vast majority, however, did not engage in these behaviors: 75%–79% of people taking antipsychotics, depending upon the behavior, and 86%–92% of people not taking antipsychotics. Even among people taking antipsychotics, almost twice as many self-injurious and odd/stereotypic behaviors were considered to exist "not at all" or be only "slightly serious" as were considered "serious." (See Table 4.1.)

DISCUSSION

Numerous differences have been cited in the literature between adults and children in patterns of psychotropic medication use, in the use of other medications that may influence the response to psychotropic medications, in response to medications in general, and in the presence of other conditions that may influence response to medication. These differences suggest that it is extremely risky to generalize findings from children and adolescents with developmental disabilities to older adults with developmental disabilities and that it is particularly important to study older adults in their own right. The findings from the present study suggest a national prevalence rate of 27% for use of psychotropic medication, excluding seizure medication, and 19% for use of antipsychotic (neuroleptics) among older (age 63 and older) adults with developmental disabilities. The former is higher than the prevalence rate of 14% found in New York (Jacobson, 1988) but lower than the rates of 47%–50% found in Missouri (Intagliata & Rinck, 1985), with similar age groups. It may be more informative, how-

Table 4.1. Percentages of behaviors listed by antipsychotic medication use

| | Rating of seriousness | | | | | | |
Behavior	Extremely	Very	Moderately	Slightly	Not at all	No such behavior	Chi-square
Hurts self							
On antipsychotics[a]	0%	1.2%	6.2%	6.2%	7.4%	79.0%	12.74%[c]
Not on antipsychotics[b]	0%	.3%	2.4%	.7%	4.9%	91.7%	
Uncooperative							
On antipsychotics	0%	6.2%	7.4%	4.9%	6.2%	75.3%	14.36%[c]
Not on antipsychotics	1.7%	1.0%	2.1%	3.5%	5.6%	86.1%	
Odd/stereotyped							
On antipsychotics	2.5%	1.2%	2.5%	6.2%	9.9%	77.8%	14.50%[c]
Not on antipsychotics	.7%	.3%	1.7%	.7%	4.5%	92.0%	

[a]$N = 81$.
[b]$N = 2.88$.
[c]$p < .05$.

ever, to view prevalence rates by type of residential facility, since variations were considerable across the four types, and weighted population estimates do not reflect this. Residents of foster care homes and state institutions were the least likely to use either psychotropics or antipsychotics, large private facility residents being twice as likely as foster care and state institution residents to use psychotropics and approximately three times as likely to use antipsychotics. Although states may vary considerably in their practices with respect to psychotropic medications, prevalence rates are also likely to be affected by the state's reliance on particular types of residential care for older adults with developmental disabilities. At the time of this study, for example, New York State used foster care homes extensively for older adults with developmental disabilities, which may partially explain the low rate of use of psychotropic medications in this state.

Unlike some of the findings with younger populations, medical problems/limitations, adaptive and communicative behavior, and level of mental retardation generally were unrelated to the use of psychotropics among older adults with developmental disabilities. The reasons for this difference are unknown. One can speculate that the findings for younger people were a function of severe behavior problems associated with severe medical conditions, and that, for the most part, the older sample in the present study had less severe disabilities, so there may have been few with a compelling need for such pharmacologic treatment. It is also possible that medications are less associated with the individual's characteristics (i.e., are more random) if the person is older than if he or she is younger, because of the effect of ageism. An additional perspective, however, might be that there is no logical reason for which psychotropic medications *should* be related to any of these factors, since their purpose is not to remediate medical problems nor to enhance adaptive functioning.

The findings that: 1) people considered to have a psychosis or less severe mental health problem (i.e., a nonpsychotic disorder) were much more likely to use psychotropic medications, and 2) people with psychotic disorders were significantly more likely to be receiving antipsychotic medications than people without such diagnoses, suggest that there is some rationality to the distribution of psychotropic medications. However, the vast majority (78%) of people taking antipsychotic medications, which are designed to reduce or eliminate some of the major symptoms of psychoses, were not considered to have a psychosis. In addition, being prescribed a psychotropic and/or antipsychotic medication did not imply greater access to psychological services; people using such drugs were no more likely to see a psychologist than people who were not prescribed such medications. Finally, the diagnosis of a psychosis, by itself, did not necessarily imply that one should or would be receiving an antipsychotic medication. Nearly as many people with psychoses *were not* taking antipsychotics as *were* taking them.

In addition to mental health problems, however, there were other factors that were related to increased use of psychotropic medications. The severity of a few selected behavior problems was directly related to the use of psychotropic medications. People taking psychotropic medications were less likely to be in a day program of any type, were less likely to visit with friends, and received more negative reactions from neighbors. It is not known which came first, the negative reactions and noninvolvement or the psychotropic medications. Hence, it is possible that the medications were prescribed to reduce the behaviors that were resulting in these consequences (but that they did not entirely succeed) or that use of the medication adversely affected neighborhood involvement, friendship patterns, and even specialized and community-based activities. However, it is clear that these social indicators were stronger correlates with psychotropic and antipsychotic medication use than other factors identified for younger people with developmental disabilities. Certainly some of the known side effects of antipsychotic medications (e.g., sedation and tardive dyskinesia with its attendant grimaces and movements) would not be conducive to social inclusion.

In the findings as a whole, it is apparent that, although antipsychotics are being prescribed for some people who qualify as having psychoses, the majority of people receiving such medications do not have psychoses; rather, they have less serious mental health problems and/or behavior problems. In addition, social involvement and type of facility in which people live appear to be important factors in whether or not they receive such medications. The patterns of relationships associated with psychotropic medication use for older people differed considerably from those reported for younger people. However, among both older and younger people with developmental disabilities, antipsychotics appear to be widely used for purposes other than their intended purpose of controlling psychotic symptomatology.

REFERENCES

Agran, M., Moore, S., & Martin, J.E. (1988). Research in mental retardation: Underreporting of medication information. *Research in Developmental Disabilities, 9,* 351–357.

Aman, M.B. (1988, October). *Use and misuse of psychotropic drugs in elderly persons with mental retardation.* Paper presented at the annual meeting of the American Association of University Affiliated Programs for Persons with Developmental Disabilities, Denver.

Aman, M.G., Field, C.J., & Bridgeman, G.D. (1985). City-wide survey of drug patients among non-institutionalized mentally retarded persons. *Applied Research in Mental Retardation, 6,* 159–171.

Aman, M.G., & Singh, N.N. (1988). Patterns of drug use, methodological considerations, measurement techniques, and future trends. In M.G. Aman & N.N. Singh (Eds.), *Psychopharmacology of the developmental disabilities* (pp. 1–28). New York: Springer-Verlag.

Anderson, D.J., Lakin, K.C., Bruininks, R.H., & Hill, B.K. (1987). *A national study of residential and support services for elderly persons with mental retardation.* Minneapolis: University of Minnesota, Department of Educational Psychology.

Bates, W.J., Smeltzer, D.J., & Arnoczky, S.M. (1986). Appropriate and inappropriate use of psychotherapeutic medications for institutionalized mentally retarded persons. *American Journal of Mental Deficiency, 90*(4), 363–370.

Buck, J.A., & Sprague, R.L. (1989). Psychotropic medication of mentally retarded residents in community long-term care facilities. *American Journal of Mental Retardation, 93*(6).

Cohen, M.N., & Sprague, R.L. (1977, March). *Survey of drug usage in two midwestern institutions for the retarded.* Paper presented at the Gatlinburg Conference on Research in Mental Retardation, Gatlinburg, TN.

Dura, J.R., Aman, M.G., & Mulick, J.A. (1988). Medication use in an ICF-MR for nonambulatory severely and profoundly mentally retarded children. *Journal of the Multihandicapped Person, 1*(3), 155–160.

Golden, G.S. (1988). Tardive dyskinesia and developmental disabilities. In M.G. Aman & N.N. Singh (Eds.), *Psychopharmacology of the developmental disabilities* (pp. 197–215). New York: Springer-Verlag.

Gowdy, C.W., Zarfas, D.E., & Phipps, S. (1987). Audit of psychoactive drug prescriptions in group homes. *Mental Retardation, 25*(6), 331–334.

Harper, D.C., Wadsworth, J.S., & Michael, A.L. (1989). Psychotropic drug use in older developmentally disabled with behavioral difficulties. *Research in Developmental Disabilities, 10,* 53–60.

Hill, B.K., Balow, E.A., & Bruininks, R.H. (1985). A national study of prescribed drugs in institutions and community residential facilities for mentally retarded people. *Psychopharmacology Bulletin, 21,* 279–284.

Intagliata, J., & Rinck, C. (1985). Psychoactive drug use in public and community residential facilities for mentally retarded persons. *Psychopharmacology Bulletin, 21,* 268–278.

Jacobson, J.W. (1988). Problem behavior and psychiatric impairment within a developmentally disabled population. III: Psychotropic medication. *Research in Developmental Disabilities, 9,* 23–28.

James, D.H. (1986). Psychiatric and behavioral disorders amongst older severely mentally handicapped inpatients. *Journal of Mental Deficiency Research, 30,* 341–345.

Jonas, O. (1980). Pattern of drug prescribing in a residential center for the intellectually handicapped. *Australian Journal of Developmental Disabilities, 6,* 25–29.

Knoll, J. (1987). *Psychotropic medications and community integration: Implications for service providers.* Syracuse: Syracuse University, Community Integration Project, Center on Human Policy.

Lakin, K.C., Hill, B.K., & Anderson, D.J. (1991). Persons with mental retardation in nursing homes in 1977 and 1985: A comparison of findings from the 1977 and 1985 National Nursing Home Survey. *Mental Retardation, 29*(1), 25–33.

Martin, J.E., & Agran, M. (1985). Psychotropic and anticonvulsant drug use by mentally retarded adults across community, residential and vocational placements. *Applied Research in Mental Retardation, 6,* 33–49.

Radinsky, A.M. (1984). *A descriptive study of psychotropic and antiepileptic medication use with mentally retarded persons in three residential environments.* Unpublished doctoral dissertation, University of Pittsburgh.

Richardson, M.A., Haugland, G., Pass, R., & Craig, T.J. (1986). The prevalence of tardive dyskinesia in a mentally retarded population. *Psychopharmacology Bulletin, 22,* 243–249.

Schroeder, S.R. (1988). Neuroleptic medications for persons with developmental disabilities. In M.G. Aman & N.N. Singh (Eds.), *Psychopharmacology of the developmental disabilities* (pp. 82–100). New York: Springer-Verlag.

Sprague, R.L., & Baxley, G.B. (1978). Drugs for behavior management, with comment on some legal aspects. In J. Wortis (Ed.), *Mental retardation and developmental disabilities. An annual review* (pp. 92–129). New York: Brunner/Mazel.

Werry, J.S. (1988). Conclusions. In M.G. Aman & N.N. Singh (Eds.), *Psychopharmacology of the developmental disabilities* (pp. 239–245). New York: Springer-Verlag.

II

LIFESTYLES AND TRANSITIONS

Alan R. Factor

Older adults with developmental disabilities face the same fundamental later life concerns as older adults in general: changes in health and physical stamina, dealing with the loss of family and friends, and the prospect of retirement and its financial and leisure-time implications. Their growing numbers and increased community presence are creating new challenges for professionals as they respond to the later life needs of these older individuals and their families. This scenario is occurring in an ideological climate that fosters increased empowerment and self-advocacy and greater community inclusion for people of all ages with disabilities.

This section presents several key issues that professionals need to consider in facilitating later life transitions for older adults with developmental disabilities and their families. The chapters address a wide range of concerns examined through empirical research: the factors related to social and community inclusion, accomplishing a successful transition to retirement, older families' caregiving roles and needed supports, the relationship between leisure activities and life satisfaction, and the older individual's psychological adjustment to midlife. The collective recommendation that emerges calls for the service delivery system to actively involve older adults and their families in the choicemaking process and to develop the flexibility to support their unique needs and preferences.

5

Social Inclusion of Older Adults with Mental Retardation

Deborah J. Anderson

Researchers, parents, careproviders, and people with mental retardation, since the 1980s, have given much attention to issues of social inclusion. Lovett and Harris (1987) found considerable agreement between adults with mental retardation and the other adults with whom they had significant contact concerning the skills considered important for successful community living. Vocational and social skills were identified as more important than personal, academic, or leisure skills. Anderson, Lakin, Hill, and Chen (1992) found a modest relationship between living in community settings and social inclusion among people with developmental disabilities in many of the studies they reviewed (Bell, Schoenrock, & Bensberg, 1981; Dalgleish, 1983; Gollay, Freedman, Wyngaarden, & Kurtz, 1978; Hill, Rotegard, & Bruininks, 1984; Scheerenberger & Felsenthal, 1977). No studies, however, investigated the social inclusion of older adults with mental retardation, and, typically, the studies failed to compare different facility types or to control for differences in residential characteristics. A study by Eastwood and Fisher (1988), however, compared matched samples of people who were deinstitutionalized with people remaining in the institution setting and found community residents to have better community orientation, social interaction, leisure time, and vocational skills.

The study discussed in this chapter was part of a longitudinal study of a national sample of older adults with mental retardation. The study provided information about the extent of social inclusion, as well as basic descriptive information about activities of daily living (ADL) skills and other personal characteristics that might influence social inclusion. In addition, since there were many unanswered questions about the reasons for the prevalence of low levels of social inclusion, these data were analyzed further to determine whether differences in social inclusion across four facility types were due to the residents in these facilities having different characteristics, to facility-linked differences, or to other factors. It was expected that a number of individual resident characteristics (e.g., level of mental retardation, severe sensory impairments, inability to walk, incontinence, and serious challenging behaviors) as well as selected facility characteristics (e.g., type, size, urban/rural setting, per diem reimbursements, staff/resident ratio) might affect the level of social inclusion. These findings are summarized in this chapter since they provide a more complete and balanced picture of the multiple factors that might affect social inclusion than would focusing on one issue at a time.

During 1990–1991, the original sample of residents was studied again after a period of approximately 4–5 years. This provided an opportunity to determine whether the original findings were stable over time or changes had occurred that had affected the level of social inclusion of the study sample. Social inclusion was defined through a procedure developed by Copher (1988), using the following questionnaire items, as inclusion within four spheres of activity: 1) household integration, 2) recreation/leisure integration, 3) social relationships, and 4) community resource use. Specific indicators of each of these four types of social inclusion are described in the analysis section of this chapter.

ORIGINAL STUDY

During 1985–1986, the Center for Residential and Community Services (CRCS) at the University of Minnesota conducted a national study of people over the age of 62 with mental retardation. They were residents of facilities licensed by developmental disabilities agencies (Anderson, Lakin, Bruininks, & Hill, 1987). The sample was developed from a census of all residential facilities owned, operated, and/or licensed by developmental disabilities agencies conducted by the CRCS in 1982 (Hauber, Bruininks, Hill, Lakin, & White, 1984). The sample consisted of a 10% sample of all facilities known at that time to have residents with mental retardation ages 63 or older ($N = 235$). Facility types included foster care homes, small group homes, large (with 16 or more residents) private facilities, and state institutions. One or, if present, two older persons per facility were randomly selected for study, for a total of 370 residents. Respondents were identified by contacts at the facilities as careproviders who knew the residents well. A minimum of 6 months of working with the resident was required for participation. Respondents were initially contacted through a letter to introduce the study. This was followed by a telephone call to determine whether they were still eligible for inclusion in the study. The survey was then mailed to eligible respondents, and extensive follow-up by telephone was conducted to ensure an adequate response rate and to edit surveys and clarify questions. Residents were selected randomly within the facilities selected for study. Findings from this study were reanalyzed to develop statistical indicators of social inclusion among older people with mental retardation and to obtain comparisons among the four types of residential facilities included in the study.

Respondents were given a Resident Survey, a Careprovider Survey, and a Day Program Survey. The careproviders who knew the resident well completed the Resident Survey, which contained extensive questions about the resident's health, independent living skills (ADL), social/leisure skills, and more. The Careprovider Survey, containing questions about the training, experience, and attitudes of careproviders as well as some questions about the facility, was to be completed by the same direct careprovider. Directors of day programs in which the study sample was involved, which were external to the facility, were interviewed by telephone, primarily for the purpose of obtaining descriptive information about the program, including information about any special programs for older adults.

Social Inclusion Indices

A total of four indices of social inclusion were developed. Hierarchical multiple regression analyses were then performed, using these indices, in order to determine the relative contribution of various factors to social inclusion. These factors were: 1) resident characteristics expected to affect social inclusion, including level of mental retardation, age, severe visual limitations, severe hearing limitations, severe limits to ambulation, incontinence, and severe aggression toward others; 2) facility type; and 3) selected facility characteristics, including size and location.

The four indices of social inclusion were: 1) household inclusion, with scores ranging from 0 to 8 based on the number of tasks in which the individual participated (e.g., doing laundry, buying groceries, cleaning, taking out trash, lawn mowing, bed making, meal preparation, and washing dishes); 2) recreation/leisure inclusion, based on the number of activities in which the individual participated at least monthly (e.g., spectator events, senior centers/clubs, specialized recreation activities, use of parks, shopping, and eating out); 3) social relationships based on the number of family, friend, and neighbor interactions (e.g., having met neighbors, having been invited to neighbors' homes, having neighbors who responded as "friendly, warm or accepting," visiting friends [not staff or family] at least monthly, having regular social contact with people without disabilities other than family or friends, monthly visits from family, and not being abandoned by living family members); and 4) community resource use, based on the use of seven community resources at least monthly (i.e., grocery stores, department/discount/clothing stores, libraries, religious services, banks, senior citizen centers, and public transportation).

Each of the items within each of the four indices was dichotomously coded, with "1" indicating some degree of participation in the activity in question. The scores within each index were summed and then divided by the total number of items in the scale. The resulting index scores ranged from 0 to 1, representing the proportion of each scale's items scored in a favorable direction. A total community inclusion score was calculated as the sum of the four subscale (index) scores, following the basic procedure used by Copher (1988), who had applied similar items to a different sample.

Individual Characteristics and Facilities Indices

Resident characteristics that made up the individual characteristics index were: age, level of mental retardation (1 = borderline, 5 = profound), severe visual limitations (defined as having either great difficulty seeing even with glasses or having little or no vision), severe hearing limitations (defined as either having great difficulty hearing or having no usable hearing), severe limits to ambulation (inability to walk on a level surface for more than 10 feet or requiring assistance by another person), incontinence (defined as requiring physical assistance for toileting or being unable to perform this skill at all), and moderate to severe aggression toward others (defined as hurting other people to an extent judged by the careproviders as moderately, very, or extremely serious).

Facility characteristics that were used in these analyses were type of residence, size of residence, size of community, per diem resident costs, percentage of older residents, and resident to staff ratio at 7:30 P.M. This time period was selected because it was one in which both residents and staff typically are in the residence, so it would not be subject to as much variation as earlier times.

A series of multiple regression analyses were conducted for the purpose of understanding the contributions of individual resident characteristics, facility type, and facility characteristics in explaining social inclusion. Resident variables were first included in the equations, then facility type, and then all remaining facility variables. Facility variables such as size of residence, size of community, and per diem resident costs were entered after facility type because these vary considerably by facility type and, hence, would be strongly influenced by it. The study method selected: 1) allows one to understand the contribution of individual characteristics to social inclusion, controlling for facility type and other facility characteristics; 2) then allows one to understand how facility type, above and beyond individual characteristics, additionally contributes to social inclusion, and, finally; 3) allows one to understand whether the remaining variables, such as facility size, have any additional power to explain aspects of social inclusion that are unexplained by the other variables.

FOLLOW-UP STUDY

During 1990–1991, careproviders of residents studied in the initial sample were recontacted to the extent possible. Full surveys were given to careproviders working with people still living in the residences in which they had been living in the initial study. Abbreviated surveys were given to careproviders of people who had transferred to other residences or died during the interim. The final sample consisted of 213 residents, 126 of whom were still in their original residences and 87 of whom had transferred or died.

In the follow-up period, revised versions of the Resident and Careprovider surveys were administered for residents still in their original residences, as was the Inventory for Client Assessment and Planning (ICAP), an instrument that assesses adaptive behavior, challenging behaviors, and other areas. Revisions included combining questions from the Day Program and Resident Surveys, elimination of unproductive questions, and inclusion of some newer areas of emphasis affecting older people in residential settings. A very abbreviated version of the Resident Survey, consisting primarily of health questions, was given to careproviders who had worked with residents who had transferred or died during the interim, together with a full Careprovider Survey.

The types of issues studied that were felt to be significant to the issue of social inclusion in both time periods were repeated in the two surveys and, in some cases, expanded during the second time period. As in the initial study, responses were compared by facility type. The multiple regression analyses were not repeated because of extensive sample attrition. Comparisons were made of original (Time 1) and follow-up (Time 2) responses provided by careproviders about sample members still in their initial residences to determine whether changes had occurred over time.

RESULTS

Analysis of the data from Time 1 found that residents' personal characteristics explained 24% of the total social integration score. Level of mental retardation, age, and incontinence were particularly associated with less social inclusion. Residents with more severe levels of mental retardation studied in Time 1 had significantly lower social integration scores in every scale (i.e., household integration, leisure/recreation integration, social relationships, and community resource use). Residents' ages ranged from 63 to 90 years. Increasing age in this sample was associated with lower household and community inclusion, as well as total inclusion (across all four scales). Controlling for other resident characteristics, incontinent residents had lower scores in each scale.

Controlling for resident characteristics, type of facility explained an additional 11.5% of the variance in the total inclusion score. Group home residents had higher scores in household integration, recreation/leisure integration, and community resource use, but significantly lower scores in the area of social relationships when compared with residents of foster homes. Foster home residents were compared with residents of large private facilities and state institutions with similar characteristics. Large private facility residents scored lower in social relationships, and state institution residents had lower scores in social relationships and overall inclusion scales than residents in foster care, even when residents' personal characteristics were statistically controlled.

After controlling for both resident characteristics and type of facility, the only remaining variable that accounted for a significant degree of variance in social relationships was size of community. Residents of large communities engaged in more household activities, used more community resources, and participated in more recreation/leisure activities.

Both individual characteristics (adaptive behavior) and facility types were examined in the follow-up study period. It was expected that the relative contribution of these two factors would be similar to that found in Time 1 with a more extensive sample, that is, that individual differences in level of mental retardation and certain other areas would be highly influential but that facility type would also affect the level of social relationships, even among people with similar individual characteristics.

Social Relationships

Foster care residents excelled in social relationships of all types, with group home residents following, but residents of state institutions lagged far behind. There were marked facility differences in the extent to which residents knew their neighbors, with more than four out of five foster care and group home residents having met their neighbors, compared with about three out of five residents of large private facilities and only one in five residents of state facilities. (See Table 5.1.) Foster care and group home residents were much more likely than residents of state and large private facilities ever to have been invited into any neighbors' homes, with over half of foster care compared with only one in 10 state hospital residents having this invitation. Foster care providers reported the highest frequency of positive neighbor response to the resident, with three in four indicating positive responses, compared with about half of respondents in group homes and large private facilities and one sixth of residents in state institutions. Negative responses were reported only by foster care (12%) and group homes (8%). Notably, those reporting the most contact with neighbors also reported the most positive (and occasionally negative) responses from these neighbors.

An important part of residents' social experiences derives from friendships they form with other individuals who may or may not have disabilities. In Time 2, as in Time 1, there were a substantial number of residents who apparently had no friends outside of staff and/or family. When asked how often the resident visited with friends who were not staff or family, 13% of foster care respondents, about three in 10 group home and large private facility respondents, and two thirds of state institution respondents indicated "never." Facility differences were considerable and in the direction of other friendship patterns noted previously, concerning whether the resident had any regular social contact with anyone without disabilities (who was not staff or family), with most (82%) foster

Table 5.1. Extent of social integration listed by facility type

Event	Foster (%)	Group (%)	Large private (%)	State (%)	N	Chi-square
Has met neighbors	82	85	62	16	125	32.04[b]
Invited into neighbors' homes	59	48	22	10	125	16.89[b]
General neighbor response to resident was positive	75	55	51	17	116	10.22[a]
Has no friends (other than staff, family)	13	29	30	67	116	33.19[a]
Has nondisabled friend	82	57	49	16	124	18.35[b]
No living relatives	46	20	34	33	104	22.46[a]

Dft = T3 for all questions, which were recoded into dichotomous (yes/no) form.
[a]$p < .05$.
[b]$p < .001$.

care respondents answering affirmatively and slightly over half of group home, half of large private, and very few (16%) state institution staff so responding.

Foster care residents were least likely to have living relatives, nearly half reporting that they did not, compared with 20%–34% of residents of other facilities. Few from any facility type had relatives living within about a ½ hour drive, however. Among those with living relatives, about half of all but state institution residents visited with them several times a year or more often.

Comparisons of the two time periods among residents studied in both time periods still living in their initial place of residence found that residents were no more likely in Time 2 to have met their neighbors than in Time 1. However, there was an increase in the percentage who had been invited into a neighbor's home. The number of residents with no friends and with friends without disabilities was stable, as was the number of residents having no living relatives and those who had relatives whom they never visited because the relatives had abandoned them. Fifteen percent in each time period had no visiting relatives.

Residents living in smaller facilities were much more likely to participate in a wide variety of leisure activities than residents in larger facilities, with state institution residents being least involved. Residents differed significantly by facility type in the extent to which they participated in certain leisure activities, including attending movies and other spectator events, shopping, walking/exercising, going out to eat, and attending religious services. (See Table 5.2.) About half of community-based residents and one third of state institution residents "wrote letters, sewed, read or engaged in hobbies" in a typical month. Almost all "listened to music, watched TV or listened to the radio" (89%–95%). Group home residents were significantly more likely to attend "movies, concerts, plays or sports events," about four in five going to one or more of these

Table 5.2.   Participation in leisure activities listed by facility type

Activity	Foster %	Group %	Large private %	State %	Chi-square
Writing letters, sewing, reading, hobbies	59	53	49	32	3.34
TV, radio, records	94	94	89	95	1.00
Movies, concerts, sports events	59	83	65	42	12.32[b]
Senior citizen centers, clubs	29	24	27	16	1.20
MR/DD recreation activities	59	62	60	37	3.84
Shopping	88	89	62	42	20.21[c]
Bowling, fishing, other sports	59	49	30	26	7.39
Cards, games	47	49	46	47	.09
Walking, exercise	82	87	57	58	13.25[b]
Restaurant	88	87	68	63	8.16[a]
Ice cream shop/bar	82	76	49	58	9.73[a]
Religious services	76	76	62	37	10.06[a]

N = 126, df = 3.
[a]$p < .05$.
[b]$p < .01$.
[c]$p < .001$.

events at least monthly, followed by large private facility and foster care residents. State institution residents were least likely to attend, with about half the level of participation of group home residents.

Participant sports, such as bowling, were relatively common among foster care (59%) and group home (49%) residents. Twenty-six percent to 30% of other residents engaged in these sports. A similar pattern was seen in the frequency with which residents went for a walk or engaged in other physical exercise, although this type of exercise was more frequent overall. More than four in five residents in the smaller facilities engaged in this type of exercise, and over half of residents in the larger facilities did also. Card/game playing was engaged in by almost half of all residents. Monthly or more frequent attendance at senior citizen clubs or meetings was relatively uncommon (16% of state institution and between 24% and 29% of community residential facility residents), compared with attendance at leisure activities specifically for people with developmental disabilities (other than day programs), 59%–62% of community and 37% of state institution residents participating in the latter. Religious services were much more likely to be attended by residents of community-based facilities than by those living in state institutions, 62%–76% of the former compared with 37% of the latter attending at least once a month.

Residents of smaller facilities were most likely to go shopping, almost nine in 10 foster care and group home residents doing this at least monthly, compared with six in 10 residents of large private facilities and four in 10 state facility residents. Foster care and group home residents were most likely to go out to eat.

The only difference over the two time periods among residents studied at both times was in attendance at senior citizen centers, which increased significantly over the 4–5 year time span. Fifteen percent of residents attended in Time 1, compared with 25% in Time 2.

Despite a moderate level of activity among the smaller, community-based facilities, across facilities, activities were viewed as not being integrated with persons without disabilities. Spectator events, such as movies, were the most likely to be integrated. Between 11% and 29% of respondents indicated that the residents would like to engage in some activities that they had not engaged in, or would like to do more of some activities. Lack of money was the reason most often mentioned for nonparticipation, although lack of transportation, skills, or someone to accompany them were also mentioned.

Between 41% and 49% of residents of community facilities (all but state institution residents) took educational trips into the community. Residents infrequently volunteered or taught skills that they possessed to others in a day program or elsewhere. Between 0% and 9% engaged in either of these activities, depending upon facility type.

Community Resources

Group home and foster care residents were most likely to use a variety of community resources, and state institutions were the least likely. Another indicator of social/community inclusion is the use of generic community resources such as banks, grocery stores, and department stores. There were considerable differences among residents living in different facility types in the use of all community resources except senior citizen centers. (See Table 5.3.) About two thirds of residents in foster care and group homes, but only three in 10 residents of large private facilities and one in 10 residents of state facilities shopped at grocery stores. Residents in group homes and foster care were considerably more likely than residents in the larger facilities to go to shopping centers or department stores, 79% and 65% of the former respectively compared with 42% and 46% of the latter. Religious services were attended most by residents of foster care and group homes, about three fourths of them going to community religious services, compared with slightly over half of persons in large private facilities and only one quarter of state facility residents. Parks were used by three fourths of group home residents and used least by residents in foster care and state institutions. Restaurants were used by most (87%–88%) of foster care and group home residents, about two thirds of state facility residents, and less than half of residents of large private facilities. About half of the total group used banks. These were least used by state institution residents, only 5% of whom ever went to a bank. Libraries were not commonly used, but 38% of group home

Table 5.3. Use of community resources listed by facility type

Resource	Foster %	Group %	Large private %	State %	Chi-square
Grocery store	65	76	30	10	35.69[c]
Shopping center/dept., discount, clothing store	65	79	46	42	14.34[b]
Library	18	38	19	10	8.02[a]
Park	41	79	51	42	14.97[b]
Religious services	76	77	57	26	17.62[c]
Bank	24	49	22	5	17.44[c]
Senior citizen center	35	34	24	10	5.05
Restaurant	88	87	43	68	22.76[c]

$N = 126$, df $= 3$.
[a] $p < .05$.
[b] $p < .01$.
[c] $p < .001$.

residents, and 10%–19% of other residents availed themselves of library services. Senior citizen centers were used by about one third of foster care and group home residents, one fourth of residents of large private facilities, and 10% of state facility residents.

Comparisons of residents still in their original residences were made over the two time periods. It was revealed that visits to department stores and restaurants had declined, but visits to grocery stores had increased. (See Figure 5.1.)

Household Inclusion

Group home residents were the most likely to be involved in household chores, and, as in the other areas of social inclusion, residents of state institutions were by far the least likely to be so involved. Significant differences were found between residents of different types of facilities in the level of involvement in all household tasks studied. (See Table 5.4.) Group home residents were only slightly more likely than foster care residents to make their beds, buy groceries, and do other housekeeping activities. Both groups were more likely than large private facility residents and much more likely than state institution residents to do these chores. Mowing the lawn was a task reserved only for foster care (18%) and group home (8%) residents. In other home-related duties, however, group home residents clearly excelled over all others. Slightly over half of group home residents but only 21%–30% of other residents washed their own clothes. Half of group home residents, slightly over one quarter of foster care and large private facility residents, and 10% of state institution residents took out the

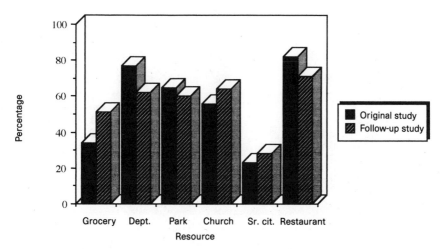

Figure 5.1. Percentage using community resources over time. (Dept. = department store, Sr. cit. = senior citizen center).

trash. Food preparation was done by two thirds of group home residents, but only 26%–38% of other residents. Nearly two thirds of group home residents washed dishes, compared with about four in 10 foster care residents, about two in 10 large private facility residents, and no state institution residents.

Over the two time periods, there were few major changes in household participation, but when changes occurred, they tended toward less involvement. House cleaning and washing dishes declined significantly over the two time periods. (See Figure 5.2.)

Table 5.4. Involvement in household chores listed by facility type

Chore	Foster %	Group %	Large private %	State %	Chi-square
Laundry	24	53	30	21	10.01[a]
Taking out the trash	29	51	27	10	13.01[b]
Vacuuming/cleaning	35	47	19	5	16.81[c]
Mowing the lawn	18	8	0	0	9.86[a]
Making the bed	76	83	60	37	15.67[b]
Preparing food/setting the table	29	68	38	26	16.30[c]
Washing dishes	41	64	22	0	37.56[c]
Buying groceries	24	30	5	0	17.67[c]

$N = 126$, df = 3.
[a]$p < .05$.
[b]$p < .01$.
[c]$p < .001$.

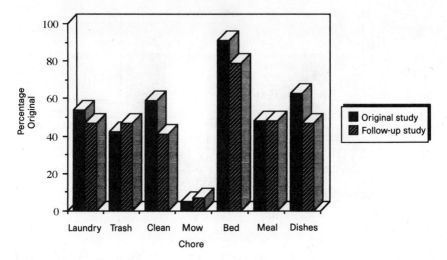

Figure 5.2.   Percentage involved in household chores over time.

Adaptive Behavior

Changes in adaptive behavior over the two time periods were examined, since certain adaptive behaviors such as walking or independent toileting were seen to be important factors in the overall level of social inclusion. Among the group of residents studied in both time periods, there were slight but significant changes in most areas of ADL, including getting in or out of bed, standing alone, walking, climbing stairs, eating, toileting, and bathing. Only dressing showed no change over the 4- to 5-year time period. All changes were in the direction of less independence, but changes were slight, even though statistically significant. (See Table 5.5.)

As in Time 1, there were marked, statistically significant differences between facility types in all areas of ADL. State institution residents were far less independent than residents of other facilities. Foster care and group home residents had similar proportions of residents who were completely independent in most areas. When differences occurred, the former were slightly less likely to be independent. More than four in five residents of these two smaller facility types were completely independent in all areas of ADL except bathing. (See Table 5.6.)

DISCUSSION

In this investigation of changes over time in persons over age 62 with mental retardation, comparisons of the different types of residential settings reveal striking differences among residents. Those in the smaller facilities (foster care and group homes, with less than 16 residents) were much more likely to experi-

Table 5.5. Average level of independence in self-care and mobility skills

Skill	Year 1 M	Year 2 M	N	t
Getting in/out of bed	3.79	3.65	126	2.29[a]
Standing alone	3.79	3.67	125	2.52[a]
Walking on level surface 10 feet	3.72	3.56	125	2.69[b]
Climbing stairs	3.50	3.29	126	2.70[b]
Eating	3.87	3.75	126	2.01[a]
Dressing	3.60	3.52	126	1.16
Toileting	3.75	3.62	124	2.40[a]
Bathing/showering	3.20	2.98	125	2.85[b]

4 = independent; 3 = requires reminders, prompts; 2 = requires physical assistance/assistive devices; 1 = cannot do at all.
[a]$p < .05$.
[b]$p < .01$.

ence social inclusion both within and outside of the residence in almost all areas examined. State institution residents were by far the least involved in most areas of social inclusion.

A few differences may be attributable to the fact that foster care and state institution residents were much more likely to be living in rural areas than residents of group homes and large private facilities. Hence, the opportunities for certain activities vary somewhat. Presumably, the lower level of involvement in outdoor activities, such as going to parks or to nature centers in the community, among foster care and state institution residents was associated with their more rural location, which tends to make parks less needed and perhaps less avail-

Table 5.6. Independence in self-care and mobility skills listed by facility type

Skill	Foster %	Group %	Large private %	State %	Chi-square
Getting in/out of bed	100	94	81	47	29.41[c]
Standing alone	100	94	76	47	28.90[c]
Walking on level surface 10 feet	88	92	73	42	25.16[b]
Climbing stairs	88	83	57	21	37.60[c]
Eating	88	96	81	58	20.04[a]
Dressing	76	87	70	47	31.49[c]
Toileting	82	91	78	53	33.44[c]
Bathing/showering	47	60	38	21	35.58[c]
Making bed	65	76	56	32	36.78[c]

$N = 126$, df = 9.
[a]$p < .05$.
[b]$p < .01$.
[c]$p < .001$.

able. Of greater relevance are the substantial differences in level of mental retardation and ADL skills among residents of the four facility types. In this study, state institutions clearly had the highest proportion of residents with severe and profound levels of mental retardation and the highest proportion of residents who were not fully independent in ADL skills. The factor most directly associated with the low levels of social inclusion of older adults in facilities for persons with mental retardation was level of mental retardation. Increased age and incontinence were also associated with lower levels of inclusion. These factors explain some of the substantial differences between state institution resident involvement and the involvement noted for residents of other facility types. It should be noted, however, that approximately half of state institution residents were independent in ADL skills other than climbing stairs and bathing, and that generally is a considerable figure.

In Time 1, even after taking into account statistical control for resident characteristics, state institutions and large private facilities offered a considerably less inclusive lifestyle than did foster care and group home facilities. This was true for each specific type of inclusion studied, as well as for overall levels of community inclusion. One might suspect that the typically self-contained, often physically isolated total institution is efficient for service delivery, but is not conducive to social inclusion, particularly outside of the institution.

Although there were some changes over time in adaptive behavior, the average level of independence was still quite high, and it is not clear that the relatively small changes in ADL skills are directly linked to the few changes seen in social inclusion areas. Overall, declines in social inclusion were small, and in some areas, they were in the reverse direction (e.g., more being invited into neighbors' homes more often, and greater use of grocery stores). The declines noted tended to be associated with tasks requiring more physical strength, such as household chores, and it is clear from a comparison of ADL skills and household participation that the practices of the facility itself are very important in influencing the degree of participation. Group homes, in particular, seem able to foster extensive participation in household tasks among residents who are only slightly more independent than their peers in all facilities except state institutions. Foster care and large private facilities, however, have a more modest level of involvement.

Declining expectations seem to affect older adults with mental retardation with less expected of them even when they may have higher levels of mental retardation and ADL skills than younger cohorts (Anderson et al., 1992). In both time periods, foster care appeared to be less oriented toward habilitation and training, but more attuned to typical family and community living. As such, it presents a good model for encouraging socialization with friends and within the neighborhood. However, residents of foster care homes could benefit from greater participation in household activities. Group homes appear to emphasize training in independence skills, and household integration, accordingly, was found to be high in those settings. Still, residents of group homes could benefit from staff giving more attention to building relationships with neighbors and other people without disabilities. Large private facility residents lagged somewhat in all of the areas of social inclusion, although residents of these facilities typically were considerably more included than residents of state institutions.

The substantial differences between facility types are particularly important in assessing and planning for the quality of life of older adults with mental retardation. Considering the fact that the majority of older people with mental retardation are in state institutions and nursing homes (Lakin, Hill, & Anderson, 1991), the important differences in life experiences associated with community versus institutional placement, and particularly smaller community placements, should not be ignored.

REFERENCES

Anderson, D., Lakin, K., Bruininks, R., & Hill, B. (1987). *A national study of residential and support services for elderly persons with mental retardation*. Minneapolis: University of Minnesota.

Anderson, D.J., Lakin, K.C., Hill, B.K., & Chen, T. (1992) Social integration of older persons with mental retardation in residential facilities. *American Journal of Mental Retardation, 96*(5), 488–501.

Bell, N.J., Schoenrock, C.J., & Bensberg, G.J. (1981). Change over time in the community: Findings of a longitudinal study. In R.H. Bruininks, C.E. Meyers, B.B. Sigford, & K.C. Lakin (Eds.), *Deinstitionalization and community adjustment of mentally retarded people* (pp. 195–206). Washington, DC: American Association on Mental Deficiency.

Copher, J.I. (1988). Integration into the life of the community of small community residential facilities for individuals with mental retardation. *Dissertation Abstracts International, 29/02-B,* 4062.

Dalgleish, M. (1983). Assessments of residential environments for mentally retarded adults in Britain. *Mental Retardation, 21,* 204–208.

Eastwood, E.A., & Fisher, G.A. (1988). Skills acquisition among matched samples of institutionalized and community-based persons with mental retardation. *American Journal of Mental Retardation 93,* 1, 75–83.

Gollay, E., Freedman, R., Wyngaarden, M., & Kurtz, N. (1978). *Coming back: The community experiences of deinstitutionalized mentally retarded people*. Cambridge: Abt.

Hauber, F.A., Bruininks, R.A., Hill, B.K., Lakin, K.C., & White, C.A. (1984). *1982 census of residential facilities for mentally retarded people*. Minneapolis: University of Minnesota, Department of Educational Psychology.

Hill, B.K., Rotegard, L.R., & Bruininks, R.H. (1984). Quality of life of mentally retarded people in residential care. *Social Work, 29*(3), 275–281.

Lakin, K.C., Hill, B.K., & Anderson, D.J. (1991). Persons with mental retardation in nursing homes in 1977 and 1985: A comparison of findings from the 1977 and 1985 National Nursing Home Surveys. *Mental Retardation, 29*(1), 25–33.

Lovett, D.L., & Harris, M.B. (1987). Identification of important community living skills for adults with mental retardation. *Rehabilitation Counseling Bulletin, 31*(1), 34–41.

Scheerenberger, R.C., & Felsenthal, D. (1977). Community settings for mentally retarded persons: Satisfaction and activities. *Mental Retardation, 15*(4), 3–7.

6

Realities of Retirement and Pre-Retirement Planning

Evelyn Sutton, Harvey L. Sterns, and Lisa S. Schwartz Park

The withdrawal of older workers from the labor force has caused major changes in American society during the twentieth century. There is a general consensus that people are entitled to some leisure at the end of their working years (Rix, 1990). The process of retirement involves the transition from filling a job role, a role performed for pay, to the role of a person not actively employed. Atchley (1988) has emphasized that retirement relates to jobs rather than to work. For example, people continue to work around their homes or in a volunteer capacity. In this sense, people never stop working; rather, they cease going to a place of employment. A job is a position of employment within the labor force, and it is from a job that a person retires.

Maxwell (1985) has stated that there are few events that occur over the life span that have the enormous ramifications of retirement. Perhaps this significance is due to the role of work in American society. Work not only provides an organizing force in daily activities but also helps to form the self-image. Thus, when employment ceases, readjustment in activities and the self-image must occur. Retirement creates many lifestyle changes for older adults.

The decision to retire is a personal one. Both the decision to retire and the consequences of retirement are as varied as the individuals considering this decision. The factors associated with the decision to retire are discussed in this chapter in terms of the population in general; some of the factors cited will also apply, in part, to the decisions of older persons with mental retardation/developmental disabilities (MR/DD). This chapter focuses on the retirement experience of older adults with developmental disabilities. It is intended to provide information as well as recommendations to planners, service providers, educators, and others who must consider the realities of an aging population.

FACTORS INVOLVED IN THE DECISION TO RETIRE

The effects of retirement are determined largely by an individual's specific life experiences (Sterns, Laier, & Dorsett, in press). Both individual and institutional or work-related factors can influence the decision to retire (Atchley, 1988; Robinson, Coberly, & Paul, 1985; Sterns, Matheson, & Schwartz, 1990). Retirement adjustment is influenced by the following factors: voluntary versus involuntary retirement, health, income, attitudes toward work and retirement, and pre-retirement preparation. These are discussed briefly below.

Voluntary versus Involuntary Retirement

Retirement may be different for people who *choose* to retire than for people whose retirement is involuntary. Each person views retirement differently. A poll conducted by the American Association of Retired Persons (1986) found that the closer workers come to their chosen retirement age, the more they want to continue to work. The poll also found that 40% of retired people would prefer to be at work. In addition, a 1982 Public Agenda national survey showed that a majority of adults over 65 would continue to work if opportunities were available to them (Bird, 1987). Reportedly, this majority enjoys working to the extent that they would continue to work for the rest of their lives even if they were financially secure. These expressed preferences for an ongoing work role probably do not apply so much to full-time work as to part-time and volunteer work. It appears that most older adults do not want to stop working completely but want to have a blend of work and leisure. When considering such issues, some workers entertain ideas of retiring from their first careers to begin second and sometimes third careers but postponing the final retirement.

Voluntary retirees are reported to have higher life satisfaction, income, health, and occupational status than retirees who had no choice in their retirement process (Howard, Marshall, Rechnitzer, Cunningham, & Donner, 1982; Kimmel, Price, & Walker, 1978). The latter, reportedly, have shown signs of poor adaptation (Markides, 1978; Peretti & Wilson, 1975). Issues of voluntary versus involuntary retirement constitute a significant contemporary issue for older adults with developmental disabilities.

Health, Income, Attitudes, and Preparation

Health is a pervasive influence that affects the experiences and decisions of older adults. The decision to retire is influenced significantly by health. Although not always the primary factor in the decision to retire, poor health is probably the most salient reason for poor adjustment to retirement (Sterns et al., in press). Healthy retirees have higher life satisfaction and an easier retirement transition than less healthy persons (Howard et al., 1982; Kimmel et al., 1978; Singleton, 1985).

Income has been found to be a significant predictor of retirement satisfaction (Dorfman, Kohout, & Heckert, 1985; Liebig, 1984; Riddick & Daniel, 1984). Although the loss of money may be an important factor in considering retirement, what may be more important to the retirement decision is the adequacy of one's income. Successful adaptation to retirement requires adequate financial resources.

Positive attitudes, a realistic appraisal of the retirement situation, and adequate preparation make adjustment to retirement easier. For example, a preference for early retirement exists among those individuals who have a desire for less work and have a positive image of retirement (Orbach, 1969).

People who plan for major life changes tend to be more successful in dealing with them. Similarly, people who prepare for retirement will be better able to adapt to the retirement process (Sterns et al., 1991). Personal characteristics influence the degree to which an individual is prepared for retirement. These include an adequate income, a sufficient number of resources and support systems, and a realistic outlook. Pre-retirement education and planning seminars offered by some corporations, businesses, and institutions assist the individual to make realistic plans.

SUCCESS AND SATISFACTION IN RETIREMENT

Numerous factors mediate post-retirement life satisfaction. Consistent with the predictors of retirement, subjective and financial indicators often emerge as significant predictors of retirement satisfaction (Barfield & Morgan, 1978; Bengston, Kassachau, & Ragan, 1976; Riddick, 1985).

The research findings concerning the effects of the retirement decision on post-retirement satisfaction are mixed. Research has found no significant change in life satisfaction with retirement. Many studies indicate that retirement makes little difference according to a number of measures of subjective reactions. Satisfaction in retirement appears to be related to such factors as family situation, job history, monetary resources, and health, rather than to the loss of employment itself (Atchley, 1988). Furthermore, no consistent gender differences appear to exist with regard to adjustment in retirement. Although research on women and retirement is limited, the results suggest that only a small proportion of retired women experience dissatisfaction with retirement, which is primarily related to health, financial, and social resources (George & Maddox, 1977; Szinovacz, 1983).

Retirement may be viewed, therefore, as a continuation of the life course and should be anticipated while one is still actively engaged in the workforce. As noted, numerous factors enter into the decision to retire. In addition, a realistic view of the consequences of retirement is crucial to preparation. Although these factors are pertinent to older adults in the general population, they also have relevance in the retirement decisions of older workers with developmental disabilities. These issues should be emphasized in training people who provide services to these workers.

RETIREMENT AND OLDER ADULTS WITH
MENTAL RETARDATION/DEVELOPMENTAL DISABILITIES

Parallels between the retirement lifestyles and pre-retirement planning experiences of the general population and people with developmental disabilities can be drawn. Researchers argue that whether or not an individual is perceived as retired will depend upon which definition of retirement is adopted.

Fields and Mitchell (1984) describe six frequently used definitions of retirement: 1) absence of participation in the labor force, 2) acceptance of social security benefits, 3) receipt of a private pension, 4) reduction in hours of work or pay per hour, 5) subjective evaluation by the individual as being retired, and 6) permanent withdrawal from a long-term job or career. Within a sociological framework, retirement can be conceptualized as an event, a process, a role, or even a phase of life (Atchley, 1976).

Some advocates for people with developmental disabilities appear to object to application of the retirement concept to this population (Blaney, 1991). They suggest, for example, that programming runs counter to the idea of retirement, that goals, objectives, and outcomes (which are set for individuals through agency plans) are just more manipulation of their lives at a time when a more relaxed and less structured approach should be applied. Others caution against the double jeopardy that may result when older individuals with developmental disabilities are included in activities for older adults where some older adults may already feel the effects of ageism (Wolfensberger, 1985).

Pragmatically, the MR/DD system as it exists indicates that alternative-to-work programming (retirement programs) is realistic and necessary. The use of time is a classic issue of immense importance to the general population and not unique to people with developmental disabilities. The trend is toward providing a wide range of work and leisure options for later life and giving individuals the information they need to make good choices.

Clearly, not all of the definitions cited by Fields and Mitchell (1984) are applicable to a retired adult with a developmental disability. Indeed, retirement for the older person with a developmental disability presents a picture different from that of the general population. While practices have varied from state to state, most people who have been included in the MR/DD services system have experienced structured work only since deinstitutionalization began in the 1970s. Prior to that time, many people worked in the institutions, primarily doing service or agricultural tasks related to functioning in the setting until peonage laws made this illegal (*Townsend v. Treadway*, 1973). For the people who never left home, employment was not common. Placement in sheltered workshops or, for a limited number, in supported employment, was one consequence of deinstitutionalization. Thus, work histories leading to a possible retirement for the current cohort of older persons with developmental disabilities are quite different from the work experiences of the general population. Older persons with developmental disabilities may even be viewed as part of the class of underemployed persons for whom retirement is inappropriate (Janicki, 1986). Thus, the authors have chosen to place the term "retirement" in quotation marks when it is used with reference to people with developmental disabilities, because it reflects a context that is different from traditional retirement in American society.

Currently, "retirement" age for persons with developmental disabilities is considered in some states to be 55–60. Ohio, for example, defines the "retirement" option as beginning at age 55 (Ohio Revised Code 5123:2-2-06). The use of an age marker probably is based on an assumption of more rapid age-related decline in people with developmental disabilities. Evidence for this assumption is lacking except, perhaps, for individuals with Down syndrome (Hawkins, Eklund, & Martz, 1992). While some workers in the general population do retire in their 50s or early 60s, the more common practice is to retire after age 65; however, a small number of people elect later retirement (Atchley, 1988).

Many individuals with developmental disabilities in the MR/DD system who have worked for any length of time find the workplace a major source of life satisfaction and express reluctance to leave it. One study found that people with developmental disabilities prefer structured time to leisure time that involves many unstructured hours (Stroud, Roberts, & Murphy, 1986). They realize that work is valued in American society. Their friendships and social interactions are centered in the workplace, and, perhaps most important, it is the source of discretionary funds.

The consequences of "retirement," thus, may be viewed differently by individuals with developmental disabilities than by nondisabled workers. The latter typically have thought about and planned for retirement and look forward to a change of pace. They may maintain some contact with the workplace, but, for the most part, a new series of experiences and/or even a change of career is initiated. By contrast, the typical "retiree" from a sheltered workshop may return to the workplace on a daily basis, but participate in alternative-to-work or retirement programming developed by a staff team (Herrera, 1984). Priorities and associated funding limitations will influence the service plan directly. Often missing are the preferences and opinions of the individual whose life is the focus of the plan, although inclusion of this input currently is being emphasized by many advocacy groups.

OHIO: AN OVERVIEW OF COUNTY PROGRAMS
FOR OLDER ADULTS WITH DEVELOPMENTAL DISABILITIES

The 1980s were a decade of raising awareness, model program development, and retraining for professionals and paraprofessionals who work with people with developmental disabilities. In Ohio, this effort entailed state-wide training of professionals and service providers from the aging and MR/DD services networks. This training occurred first in 1985 and 1986 under the sponsorship of the Ohio Developmental Disabilities Planning Council and the 12 area agencies on aging. At The University of Akron, faculty from departments of gerontology and special education developed and presented training for thousands of individuals during this period (Stroud & Sutton, 1988). Other major training initiatives occurred in New York, Maryland, Missouri, and Indiana. During this same period there were limited research data available on characteristics, life history, current life status, and activity preferences of the older population with developmental disabilities.

An investigation conducted at The University of Akron in 1990 (Sutton, Sterns, & Schwartz, 1990), described below, was based on the belief that in the early 1990s, the majority of older persons with developmental disabilities would have an option to "retire" from sheltered work, day training programs, or other employment. They also would have a choice of activities and pursuits representative of traditional retirement. It also was thought that some preparation for making the retirement decision and for the changes and unique experiences of later life would be provided for these people by way of individual counseling or small group education. In cases in which individuals had gone from a work role to a "retirement" role, the researchers wanted to know how their adjustment to and satisfaction with the new lifestyle was perceived by the individuals themselves and by those most closely associated with them.

Research Approach

A survey instrument that addressed all of the issues under investigation was developed. It was pilot tested with the superintendents of the 88 county boards of MR/DD in the State of Ohio, and/or other persons in Ohio counties who, by virtue of a position or a relationship to the older population with developmental disabilities, might appropriately speak for the county. Only older adults with developmental disabilities known to the formal MR/DD services system constituted the population of interest in the study.

The survey instrument was slightly revised to incorporate suggestions from 55 respondents (representing 47 counties), as well as input from the research team and its advisory group. The revision primarily consisted of eliminating some questions that seemed redundant or difficult for the respondents to interpret. The instrument then was redistributed with a particular focus on those counties that had not responded to the original (pilot) request for participation.

In addition to the survey, interviews were conducted with 59 older individuals with developmental disabilities who were "retired" or "semi-retired." The objective was to gain feedback that would add depth to the understanding of these individuals. An interviewer trained in communication strategies with persons who have developmental disabilities spent a considerable amount of time with the interviewees, their supervisors, and their careproviders prior to interview sessions to establish a strong rapport. Questions focused on the individual's feelings about reducing full-time work involvement and about his or her current daily routine. The interviews explored issues of friendship, time structuring, and income. Following each session, the interviewer evaluated the individual's feelings of satisfaction with the "retired" lifestyle and later compared these perceptions with a staff member who was most closely involved with the individual. The setting for these interviews was an Ohio county board of MR/DD.

Results

The final data set provided information from 63 of Ohio's 88 counties (72%). Included in the sample were all major urban areas, as well as a broad rural representation and cities of medium size. Seventy-one surveys were returned representing sites in the 63 counties with unduplicated information. Urban areas (e.g., Cincinnati and Columbus) submitted a composite report summarizing more than one site.

From these sites, information was obtained concerning 1,482 persons over age 55 with developmental disabilities. This number represents 15.3% of all the adults (over age 22) enrolled in county board programs at the time of surveying. Other researchers (Janicki & Wisniewski, 1985; Stroud et al., 1986) have found similar percentages of older adults within the population with developmental disabilities.

The number of individuals included in the study represented about 70% of those known to the MR/DD system in Ohio (Ohio Department of MR/DD, 1991). On a national basis, demographic information about this population is very limited, and researchers have experienced cross analysis difficulties based on the varying use of age cutoff figures, definitions of functional level, and other differences in practices across state and community lines.

Characteristics It was found that 47%, or almost one half, of those surveyed were engaged in full-time work, 33% were working part-time, and 41%

were involved in some form of work alternative programming, full-time or part-time. Twenty-five sites reported full-time retirement programs, and 32 indicated a part-time schedule of activities for older adults.

The survey indicated that 231 (16%) individuals in this study reported having *no* health problems. However, a variety of chronic health conditions were indicated with an incidence of less than one per person. Mobility problems were reported by 189 (13%) individuals, arthritis by 160 (11%) individuals, and heart disease by 132 (9%) persons. One hundred nineteen people (8%) were reported as having a seizure disorder. Only 16 individuals (1%) reportedly had a diagnosis of Alzheimer's disease, and 33 people (2%) had some form of dementia.

Retirement Activities Data on alternative-to-work ("retirement") activities were analyzed for only 57 sites operating such programs. Outings and trips (51 sites), crafts (39 sites), music (39 sites), and exercise (39 sites) were the activities most frequently offered. Mentioned, but less frequently, were dance (26 sites), health care education (19 sites), horticulture (17 sites), cooking (11 sites), and volunteer work (9 sites). Thirty-nine (68%) of the 57 sites indicated some use of generic services for older adults by 325 (54%) of the 595 older "retired" adults at those specific sites. Thirty-five (61%) of the sites conducted habilitation education classes.

Community-based adult day care was utilized by less than 9% (123 persons), although higher rates of day care utilization have been found in other states. Two hundred and eight persons (14%) were involved in programs sponsored by churches or other religious organizations.

Scheduling The information gathered in this study indicated some flexibility on the part of the service system in adjusting to the changing physical status of older persons. However, 28 (39%) of the 71 sites reported that they did *not* allow extra rest breaks. Thirteen sites serving 61 older adults permitted a later time for morning arrival at the site, and 14 sites reported that 45 persons had the opportunity to leave earlier.

Preparation for Retirement Pre-retirement classes were reported to occur at seven (12%) sites, and 21 (37%) sites reported some pre-retirement counseling. Twenty-seven sites (47%) reported no advance preparation for the lifestyle change. More than one third of the respondents (27 sites) indicated that the individual typically requested the change, and more than half reported that the client was involved in some choices during the transition. Declining health was cited most frequently as the major factor in the decision to "retire."

Pensions and choices in living arrangements, which are regarded as normal events in traditional retirement, seemed relatively unavailable to people with developmental disabilities. Twelve sites reported that some individuals had personal income as a result of family planning. Two reported a pension as a source of income. Most (47 sites) reported that individuals' retirement income was supplemental security income (SSI), which was not different from the "pre-retirement" situation and typically went to the room and board provider, with only a small allowance available to the individual.

Careproviders perceived the "retirees" to be well adjusted to their retirement status and to have high life satisfaction. However, these ratings were based only on subjective observation.

Discussion

Ohio provided important leadership in the 1980s in raising awareness about the changing needs and interests of older adults with developmental disabilities through mounting a number of training initiatives to prepare professionals as well as paraprofessionals for effective service delivery. A major demonstration project, Community Access, took place in Ohio from 1985 to 1988 (Roberts & Davis, 1988). Also, a major conference on issues in developmental disabilities and aging was convened in Akron, Ohio in 1988. The results of the study presented here did not support a total commitment across the state to issues of later life planning and innovative programming for aging people with developmental disabilities. Many counties (28%) failed to respond to the pilot and follow-up surveys. It was noted, however, that the number of counties that reported having alternative programs for older persons had increased significantly. An informal survey conducted in 1984 by The University of Akron researchers found only seven such programs in contrast to the 57 reported in the 1990 survey.

In this Ohio study, the older adults with developmental disabilities were reportedly in good health. Since the system can provide opportunities for continuing work into later life, either full-time or part-time, this may explain why so many of the 1,482 persons reported that they were still at work. It is also possible that the option of discontinuing or reducing work has not been available for all. Again, since two thirds of the sample (990 persons) were between the ages of 55 and 64, relative youth may be another factor to be considered.

The researchers found that work alternative programs for those who were either partly or fully "retired" did not reflect great variety or innovation. One exception was found in the utilization of generic services for older adults, including senior centers and nutrition sites. Sixty-eight percent (325) of the older "retirees" included in this study were involved to some degree in such community-based activities. Not all older persons who are developmentally disabled can be expected to participate appropriately in community-based activities, because of health problems, difficulties in mobility, lack of social skills development, or other conditions. The high level of community participation found in this study may be reflective of the relatively good health reported in this sample of people over age 55. It also may be related to the concerted efforts made by the Ohio Developmental Disabilities Planning Council, the Ohio Departments of MR/DD and Aging, The University of Akron, the Ohio Interagency Training Network, and others who pioneered the concept of community inclusion during the 1980s. Akron's project, Community Access, funded by the Joseph P. Kennedy, Jr. Foundation (1985–1988), which implemented the peer companion model, demonstrated the effectiveness of these efforts.

CONCLUSION

Retirement for the general population has become firmly established as a new stage in the life cycle of the average American. Although affected by fluctuations in the economy, most workers leave the workplace between the ages of 55 and 65 to pursue leisure activities, hobbies, or new career paths. Health, income, attitude, preparation, and the opportunity for choice all influence the decision to retire.

While some parallels may be drawn between the general population and people with developmental disabilities, many lifestyle differences are apparent. Limited research suggests that good health and a positive attitude characterize many adults with developmental disabilities and should enhance their later life activities. Loss of discretionary income, lack of preparation and information about options for leisure, and the relative unavailability of new experiences are limiting factors. Opportunities for phase-down, part-time, or continuation of full-time work are, however, more available to this population than to others, at least at present. Planners and service providers within the MR/DD system must recognize the later years and "retirement" as a new stage in the lives of the individuals they serve. Knowledge and imagination must be used in presenting options and opportunities. Above all, it is imperative that older adults with developmental disabilities participate in the decision to modify work schedules or give up active work roles entirely.

REFERENCES

American Association of Retired Persons. (1986). *Workers 45+: Today and tomorrow.* Washington, DC: American Association of Retired Persons.

Atchley, R. (1976). *The sociology of retirement.* Cambridge, MA: Schenkman.

Atchley, R. (1988). *Social forces and aging: An introduction to social gerontology.* Belmont, CA: Wadsworth.

Barfield, R.E., & Morgan, J.N. (1978). Trends in planned early retirement. *The Gerontologist, 18,* 13–18.

Bengston, V.L., Kassachau, P., & Ragan, D.L. (1976). The impact of social structure on aging individuals. In J.E. Birren & K.W. Schaie (Eds.), *Handbook of the psychology of aging* (pp. 327–353). New York: Van Nostrand Reinhold.

Bird, C.B. (1987). The shape of work to come. *Modern Maturity, 30*(3), 33–45.

Blaney, B. (1990). *Planning a vision: A resource handbook on aging and developmental disabilities.* Cambridge, MA: Human Services Research Institute.

Dorfman, L.T., Kohout, F.J., & Heckert, D.A. (1985). Retirement satisfaction in the rural elderly. *Research on Aging, 7*(4), 577–599.

Fields, G.S., & Mitchell, O.S. (1984). *Retirement, pensions, and social security.* Cambridge, MA: The MIT Press.

George, L.K., & Maddox, G.L. (1977). Subjective adaptation to loss of the work role: A longitudinal study. *Journal of Gerontology, 32,* 456–462.

Hawkins, B.A., Eklund, S., & Martz, B.L. (1992). *Detection of decline in aging adults with developmental disabilities* (Monograph). Cincinnati, OH: RRTC Consortium on Aging and Developmental Disabilities.

Herrera, P. (1984). *Innovative programming for the aging and aged.* Akron, OH: Exploration Press.

Howard, J.H., Marshall, J., Rechnitzer, P.A., Cunningham, D.A., & Donner, A. (1982). Adapting to retirement. *Journal of the American Geriatric Society, 30,* 488–500.

Janicki, M. P. (1986). *Growing old: Responding to the needs of older and elderly developmentally disabled persons.* Washington, DC: National Association of Developmental Disabilities Councils.

Janicki, M.P., & Wisniewski, H.M. (Eds.). (1985). *Aging and developmental disabilities: Issues and approaches.* Baltimore: Paul H. Brookes Publishing Co.

Kimmel, D.C., Price, K.F., & Walker, J.W. (1978). Retirement choice and retirement satisfaction. *Journal of Gerontology, 33,* 575–585.

Liebig, P.S. (1984). The three legged stool of retirement income. In H. Dennis (Ed.), *Retirement preparation: What retirement specialists need to know* (p. 43). Lexington, MA: Lexington Books.

Markides, K.S. (1978). Reasons for retirement and adaptation to retirement by elderly Mexican Americans. In E. P. Stanford (Ed.), *Retirement: Concepts and realities of ethnic minority elders* (pp. 83–90). San Diego: San Diego State University, University Center on Aging.

Maxwell, N. (1985). The retirement experience: Psychological and financial linkages to the labor market. *Social Science Quarterly, 66,* 22–23.

Ohio Department of MR/DD. (1991). *Statistical report of the Ohio Department of MR/DD.* Columbus: Author.

Orbach, H.L. (1969). *Trends in early retirement.* Ann Arbor: University of Michigan, Wayne State University Institute of Gerontology.

Peretti, P.O., & Wilson, C. (1975). Voluntary and involuntary retirement of aged males and their effect on emotional satisfaction, usefulness, self-image, emotional stability, and interpersonal relationships. *International Journal of Aging and Human Development, 6,* 131–138.

Riddick, C.C. (1985). Life satisfaction for older female homemakers, retirees, and workers. *Research on Aging, 7,* 383–393.

Riddick, C.C., & Daniel, S.N. (1984). The relative contribution of leisure activities and other factors to the mental health of older women. *Journal of Leisure Research, 16,* 136–148.

Rix, S.E. (1990). *Older workers: Choices and challenges.* Santa Barbara, CA: ABCC–LIO.

Roberts, R., & Davis, G. (1988). Expanding options for seniors with mental retardation. *Aging, 357,* 17–19.

Robinson, P.K., Coberly, S., & Paul, C. (1985). Work and retirement. In R.H. Binstock & E. Shanas (Eds.), *Handbook of aging and the social sciences* (2nd ed.)(pp. 503–527). New York: Van Nostrand Reinhold.

Singleton, J.F. (1985). Retirement: Its effects on the individual's activities. *Adaptation and Aging, 6,* 1–7.

Sterns, H.L., Laier, M.P., & Dorsett, J.G. (in press). Enhancing the work and retirement experience of older adults. In B. Bonder (Ed.), *Occupational performance in the elderly.* Philadelphia, PA: F. A. Davis.

Sterns, H.L., Matheson, N.S., & Schwartz, L.S. (1990). Work and retirement. In K.F. Ferraro (Ed.), *Gerontology: Perspectives and issues* (pp. 163-178). New York: Springer-Verlag.

Stroud, M., Roberts, R., & Murphy, M. (1986). Life status of elderly mentally retarded/

developmentally disabled persons in northeast Ohio. In J. Berg (Ed.), *Science and service in mental retardation* (pp. 317–327). London: Methuen.

Stroud, M., & Sutton, E. (1988). *Expanding options for older adults with developmental disabilities: A practical guide to achieving community access.* Baltimore: Paul H. Brookes Publishing Co.

Sutton, E., Sterns, H., & Schwartz, L. (1991). *"Retirement" for older persons with developmental disabilities: The realities* (Monograph). Cincinnati, OH: RRTC Consortium on Aging and Developmental Disabilities.

Szinovacz, M.E. (1983). Beyond the hearth: Older women and retirement. In E.W. Markson (Ed.), *Older women: Issues and prospects* (pp. 93–120). Lexington, MA: D. C. Heath.

Townsend v. Treadway, Civil No. 6500. D. Tenn., September 21, 1973.

Wolfensberger, W. (1985). An overview of social role valorization and some reflections on elderly mentally retarded persons. In M.P. Janicki & H.M. Wisniewski (Eds.), *Aging and developmental disabilities: Issues and approaches* (pp. 61–76). Baltimore: Paul H. Brookes Publishing Co.

7

Support Systems, Well-Being, and Placement Decision-Making Among Older Parents and Their Adult Children with Developmental Disabilities

Tamar Heller and Alan R. Factor

She's been with us all of our life, and we feel like she is our responsibility, and as long as the Lord gives us strength we will like to keep her in our home and take care of her.

I would like to find a place for my daughter soon; I want to be there to see that she is taken care of. I'll have peace of mind that she is in a good place.

Most families of persons with developmental disabilities provide lifelong family-based care for them. Although the incidence of out-of-home placement for their adult children increases as parents age, it is not the predominant residential arrangement for persons with developmental disabilities until their parents die or become disabled (Meyers, Borthwick, & Eyman, 1985). As expressed above, two major concerns faced by these families are whether they can continue providing care in their homes and what will happen to their relative when they can no longer provide care. As family caregivers of adults with developmental disabilities age, they face the dual strain of their own aging process and the aging of their relative who may outlive them.

Drawing upon the results of two studies conducted by the authors as part of the Rehabilitation Research and Training Center Consortium on Aging and Developmental Disabilities, this chapter examines the roles of informal and formal support resources and caregiving reciprocity between parents and their adult children with developmental disabilities and the effect on the well-being of both groups. It also examines how these factors affect the decision-making process regarding plans for future living arrangements, from the perspective of the parents and of their adult children with developmental disabilities. This chapter first reviews the findings of previous studies of family support resources and placement issues and then presents the results of the authors' two new studies.

PREVIOUS RESEARCH ON CAREGIVER
SUPPORTS, WELL-BEING, AND PLACEMENT DECISIONS

The most prominent theoretical framework of family stress applicable to families caring for a relative with mental retardation is the Double ABCX Model of Adjustment and Adaptation (McCubbin & Patterson, 1983). This model emphasizes that the difficult demands on a family can be mitigated by internal and external resources. Further expanding on this model, Cole (1986) has provided a theoretical framework for understanding the roles of family stressors and resources in influencing the decision to place a child with developmental disabilities out of the home. When stressors related to the child combine with other family stressors to produce a crisis, the family may cope by removing the stressors, including placing the child out of the home. Family resources and positive perceptions of the circumstances can buffer the impact of these stressors, allowing the family to cope while maintaining the relative in the family home.

Effects of Informal and Formal Support Resources

Many studies focusing on families of children with developmental disabilities have found positive effects of informal and formal support resources on the well-being of family members (e.g., Dunst, Trivette, & Cross 1986; Friedrich, Cohen, & Wilturner, 1987; Orr, Cameron, & Day, 1991; Waisbren, 1980) and on reducing out-of-home placement of children with developmental disabilities (German & Maisto, 1982; Sherman, 1988; Sherman & Cocozza, 1984). However, two studies have found that formal support was not significant to (Cole & Meyer, 1989) or only a moderate predictor of (Bromley & Blacher, 1991) parents' plans to seek placement in the future.

The few studies that have examined the impact of support resources on the caregiving burden and out-of-home placement requests of families of adults with developmental disabilities have produced mixed findings. On the one hand, in Seltzer and Krauss's (1989) study of 462 older mothers providing in-home care to adult children with mental retardation, informal social support rather than formal service support was related to perceived caregiving burden. Roccoforte (1991), on the other hand, found that among families of adults with developmental disabilities both informal support and degree of unmet formal service need were associated with family caregiving burden and stress. In a study of placement requests for adults with mental retardation, Black, Cohn, Smull, and Crites (1985) found that, as predicted by Cole's model, low service utilization was related to out-of-home placement requests. However, in Heller and Factor's (1991) study of families caring for a relative with developmental disabilities over age 30, formal service utilization had an opposite effect. Greater, rather than less, use of formal services was related to caregivers' preference for a residential program placement. Informal support was related to preference for family care.

Caregiving Reciprocity

In their earlier work on the types of future plans made by aging parents, Heller and Factor (1988) suggested that reciprocity in caregiving was a factor overlooked in explaining family well-being and future residential placement plans. Caregiving reciprocity refers to the instrumental and affective supports that parents and their adult child with developmental disabilities give to each other. Much has been written about the caregiving demands on parents caring for children with developmental disabilities (Turnbull, Summers, & Brotherson, 1986). Yet there is little known about the reciprocal caregiving provided by the adult children with disabilities to their parents. Parents in Heller and Factor's (1988) study reported that their adult children with developmental disabilities provided meaning to their lives. Twenty-one percent did chores for their parents, 36% contributed financially through their Supplemental Security Income, and 54% of parents reported that their adult children kept them from feeling lonely.

While there have been numerous studies focusing on the caregiving burden experienced by families of persons with developmental disabilities, few studies have examined the more positive aspects of caregiving, such as caregiving satisfaction. Seltzer and Krauss's (1989) research on older parents of persons with mental retardation has emphasized the positive caregiving appraisals expressed by many of these families. In the gerontological literature, Lawton, Moss, Kleban, Glicksman, and Roving (1991) have shown that caregiving burden and caregiving satisfaction are two different concepts with different determinants. They have conceptualized caregiving satisfaction as the realization that what one does or feels as a caregiver is a source of personal satisfaction. In a study of 244 adult child caregivers of older parents, Lawton et al. (1991) found that high levels of caregiving behavior (one aspect of caregiving reciprocity) resulted in both greater caregiving satisfaction and greater burden.

Placement Decision-Making Process and Plans

Despite the importance of making future living arrangement plans, there has been little research on family decision-making regarding these plans and on the preferences of caregivers and adults with developmental disabilities regarding available and desired options. Estimates of the percentage of families preferring future out-of-home residential placements (versus continued home placement with a family member) when they can no longer care for their relative with developmental disabilities have ranged from one half to two thirds of caregivers (Goodman, 1978; Heller & Factor, 1991; Roberto, 1988). Among families desiring continued home placement with a family member, the preferred family member was a sibling (Heller & Factor, 1988; Krauss, 1990).

Concrete planning for both types of placements (within or outside a family home) tends to be limited. It has long been noted that older caregivers often neglect to plan for their relative's long-term care, put it off for years, or give up in frustration (Gold, Dobrof, & Torian, 1987; Goodman, 1978; Heller & Factor, 1991; Roberto, 1988; Turnbull et al., 1986). Surprisingly, many families do not discuss future arrangements with siblings or other relatives who might eventually assume caregiving responsibilities (Heller & Factor, 1991; Kriger, 1975). Similarly, family caregivers frequently refrain from discussing future care preferences and options with their relative with disabilities (Gold et al., 1987; Goodman, 1978; Heller & Factor, 1988; Roberto, 1988).

Researchers also have paid scant attention to the future living arrangement preferences of persons with developmental disabilities, despite the growing recognition that planning must take into account the choices of persons with developmental disabilities and their perceived quality of life. Certainly, the growing self-advocacy movement among persons with disabilities and the current emphasis on person-centered planning requires greater understanding of individuals' preferences and choices.

DESCRIPTION OF THE REHABILITATION RESEARCH AND TRAINING CENTER STUDIES OF FAMILY WELL-BEING AND PLACEMENT DECISIONS

The two studies described in this chapter focused on future planning and residential transitions for adults with developmental disabilities (ages 30 and over) living with their aging parents. Study 1 was a 2½-year longitudinal study of support resources, caregiving burden, and placement desires of 62 parent caregivers in Illinois. Study 2 investigated the effects of caregiving reciprocity and other support resources on the well-being of 80 parents and their adult children with developmental disabilities living in Illinois, Indiana, and Ohio. It also examined how these factors determined the urgency of placing their adult children out of the home and the children's desire to move out of the home.

Description of Study 1: Support Resources and Changes in Caregiving Burden and Placement Desires

Most of the earlier studies of families of persons with developmental disabilities focused on caregiving concerns and placement issues at a single point in time. Because caregiving is an ongoing responsibility, examining parents' use of informal and formal resources over time provides a better understanding of their impact on caregivers. By using a longitudinal design, Study 1 was able to address the following questions:

1. To what extent do informal and formal support resources affect caregivers' perceived burden and their desire for out-of-home placement of their adult child with developmental disabilities?
2. Do family support resources, caregiving burden, and out-of-home placement preferences change as families age over a 2½-year period?
3. To what extent do changes in support resources affect changes in burden and placement desires over a 2½-year period?

This study was a 2½-year follow-up of an earlier study of 100 family caregivers of persons with developmental disabilities ages 30 and older living with them (Heller & Factor, 1991). The follow-up sample included 77 parent primary caregivers, of whom 77 responded at Time 2. Interviews addressed functioning level of the person with disabilities, caregiver's characteristics, support resources, caregiving burden, and future plans.

Support resources included informal support from the spouse, other relatives, and friends, and formal services for unmet needs. The informal support scale developed for this project assessed "the degree to which one could count on each of the three types of people to assist in six areas pertaining to the care of our disabled relative." The six areas were providing: 1) emotional support, 2) transportation, 3) daily respite, 4) extended respite for 1–2 weeks, 5) information on formal services, and 6) personal care. The study measured unmet formal service need by asking respondents whether or not they needed, but were not receiving in the last year, each of 17 listed existing operating services developed to assist families in caring for a relative with mental retardation.

Caregiving burden was defined as the degree of perceived strain experienced in caring for a relative with developmental disabilities. It reflected subjective rather than objective burden and consisted of statements reflecting the physical, socioemotional, financial, and time demand strains of caregiving.

The preference for out-of-home placement was measured. Taking this measure involved asking families what future living arrangement they expected for their relative when they could no longer care for him or her.

Description of Study 2:
Effects of Support Resources and Caregiving
Reciprocity on Family Well-Being and Placement Urgency

Study 2 examined the effects of caregiving reciprocity and other support resources on the well-being of both the parents and their adult children with developmental disabilities who were living with them. It also examined how these factors determine the urgency of placing the person with disabilities outside the family home. It is one of the rare studies that have examined the perspective both of the parents and of the person with developmental disabilities.

The sample included 80 persons with developmental disabilities ages 30 and over who were living with their parents in Illinois, Indiana, and Ohio. It was selected for a longitudinal study of residential transitions. Hence, service providers were asked to present families who were likely to request residential placements in the near future. A subsample of 43 persons with developmental disabilities who could be interviewed also was included. The parent surveys and interviews (completed by the parent who was the primary caregiver) addressed the parents' and their adult child's demographic characteristics, health, caregiving reciprocity, other support resources, well-being, and future planning.

Caregiving reciprocity included three variables: 1) support to parents, 2) support from parents, and 3) *parent caregiving time.* The "support to parent" scale referred to whether the adult child helped the parents in the following seven aspects: 1) helping them feel better when upset, 2) helping with personal care, 3) helping with chores, 4) helping financially, 5) keeping them from feeling lonely, 6) sharing enjoyable activities, and 7) giving useful advice and information. "Support from parent" referred to the degree that the parent helped the adult child in the seven support functions listed above. "Parent caregiving time" referred to the number of hours that the parent spent helping the child.

Other support resources included formal services for unmet needs and informal support. Unmet formal service need was measured with the same index used in the previous study. Informal support referred to the number of the seven support functions listed above that parents received from their spouse, other children (excluding the child with disabilities), other relatives, and friends.

The parents' well-being measures included morale (Philadelphia Geriatric Center Morale Scale—Lawton, 1975), caregiving burden, (Zarit Burden Inventory—Zarit, Reever, & Bach-peterson, 1980), and caregiving satisfaction using the caregiving satisfaction scale developed by Lawton et al. (1991). The placement urgency measure assessed the time frame in which parents watned placement out of the home to occur.

The measure of the adult child's well-being evaluated life satisfaction and community inclusion. Life satisfaction was measured by the Life Satisfaction Scale (Heal & Chadsay-Rusch, 1985). In order to increase the validity of the responses, pictures with five faces of varying expressions ranging from very happy to very sad were used to augment the interview question. The interviewees pointed to the picture that represented the degree of satisfaction they felt regarding each aspect of life satisfaction. The community inclusion measure noted the number of activities in which the person engaged in the last month, drawing upon a list of 10 types of community activities.

The future planning questions asked about the individual's moving preferences and about the decision-making process regarding future transitions. These questions assessed the desire to move by asking how happy the individual would feel about moving out of the present home.

FINDINGS FROM THE REHABILITATION RESEARCH AND TRAINING CENTER STUDIES OF FAMILY WELL-BEING AND PLACEMENT DECISIONS

Important Role of Support Resources

Both studies highlight the important role of support resources in improving the well-being of older parents of adult children with developmental disabilities and in helping famiilies maintain them in the family home. Key aspects of support resources include formal services for perceived unmet needs, the informal support network, and caregiving reciprocity between the parents and their children with developmental disabilities.

Unmet Formal Service Needs   In both studies, the number of perceived unmet formal service needs was a key variable influencing parental well-being. In Study 1, a high number of initial unmet formal service needs were associated with both higher caregiving burden and out-of-home placement preference at Time 1 and 2½ years later. Also, increases in unmet formal service needs over time were related to greater caregiving burden at Time 2. In Study 2, a high number of unmet formal service needs were associated with greater caregiving burden, less caregiving satisfaction, lower morale, and greater placement urgency. These findings indicate that parents' perceptions that they are not receiving needed services influence their ability and desire to maintain their aging relative in the family home. Hence, it appears that family support initiatives that provide for flexible, family-driven arrays of supports would have the greatest success in alleviating family stress and perceived need for out-of-home placement.

Although the parents in these studies were all known to the service system, generally, they used very few formal services, averaging 3.5 services utilized. Yet, they had a considerable number of unmet formal service needs (average of four services), particularly for services related to planning for the future. In both assessments the greatest unmet need was for information on residential programs. Other greatly unmet needs were for out-of-home respite, social recreational services, in-home respite, case management, information on guardianship, information on financial planning, and family counseling.

Interestingly, in Study 1, service utilization and unmet needs did not change significantly over time. Also, in the cross-sectional analyses older parents did not report using or needing more services than younger parents. It may be that age is related to greater need for some specific services and less need for other services. For example, Lutzer and Brubaker (1988), in a cross-sectional study of service needs, found that older parent caregivers (over age 56) had greater needs for out-of-home respite care than did younger parents but had fewer needs for a parent cooperative or for training.

Informal Support   As anticipated, Study 1 found that families who had extensive informal supports experienced less caregiving burden both initially and 2½ years later. During this time period, informal support was the only variable that decreased significantly over time. The significant decreases were in support from the spouse and other relatives. One of the obvious reasons for this was that five of the spouses had died during the 2½ years. Spouse support was negatively correlated with age, as older parents were more likely to be widowed. This finding suggests that, as caregivers age, formal support services that bolster their informal support networks may become increasingly important. In particular, greater emphasis is needed on supporting siblings, who are likely to assume greater responsibility for their brother or sister with developmental disabilities with age (Heller & Factor, 1988; Krauss, 1990; Seltzer, Begun, Magen, & Luchterhand, Chapter 8, this volume). Furthermore, the sibling's level of involvement with the relative who has developmental disabilities has been related to maternal well-being (Seltzer, Begun, Seltzer, & Krauss, 1991).

Caregiving Reciprocity   The present research indicates that caregiving reciprocity between these parents and their adult children with developmental disabilities is a key factor in predicting both groups' well-being. Parents who provided greater caregiving support to their adult child with disabilities experienced both greater caregiving satisfaction and greater caregiving burden, and their adult child was less included in the community. Greater support from the adult child to the parent related to lower parental caregiving burden.

The findings that parents' caregiving efforts are associated with both greater satisfaction and greater burden are similar to those found by Lawton et al. (1991) regarding family care of older adults. Caregiving satisfaction and caregiving burden appear to be different factors, rather than opposite ends of a continuum. Apparently, parents experience personal rewards for providing support to their adult child that they perceive as helpful. In fact, they report greater satisfaction when caring for a child who is more dependent on them for assistance with tasks requiring adaptive behavior skills (Heller & Factor, 1991). These findings attest to the importance of incorporating the positive aspects of caregiving in the conceptualization of life span family adaptation to having a member with developmental disabilities.

The fact that parents' high time commitment to caring for their adult child with disabilities was associated with their child's lesser inclusion in the community suggests that parents who have children with developmental disabilities living with them need to begin to loosen their child's dependence on them as they age. One parent echoed this point: "It's time for her to go on her own like other children when they grow up."

A cross-sectional study (Heller, 1993) examining family adaptation to a member with mental retardation throughout the life span found that, for most families, a decrease in parent involvement with their child with developmental disabilities occurs with age. This pattern closely mirrors findings in families without a member with mental retardation. These findings underscore the importance of understanding reciprocal caregiving roles and the key supportive roles that persons with disabilities and their parents can fill for each other.

The subsample of adult children interviewed were compared with their parents on their perception of the support each provided for the other. Generally, parents felt that they provided more support to their adult child than their child reported receiving, especially in regard to socioemotional support. Parents' perceptions were most similar regarding financial support, which was listed by about two thirds of the parents, and help with personal care, which was listed by over 84% of the parents. In regard to supports given by the child to the parents, the parents and the children were fairly similar in their reports of socioemotional supports given. However, the children were more likely to report helping their parents with instrumental tasks than the parents reported receiving.

The following comments describe caregiving reciprocity occurring in these families:

> Right now my son is more help to me than I am to him physically. Mentally, I still have to be always around him, be his pillar which he depends on.
> Taking care of her needs is time-consuming—but she is a pleasure to have around because she has a good sense of humor, is sharp-witted, and contributes greatly to our daily conversations.
> I do the laundry and help Dad rake the leaves.
> I take care of Mom and she takes care of me.

Assessing reciprocity from both viewpoints highlights the divergent perceptions of parents and their adult children with developmental disabilities regarding the support they provide each other. These divergent reports could exist because of unreliable reporting or forgetfulness regarding specific supports offered. However, it is also possible that children truly feel that their parents' support does not adequately meet their socio-emotional needs and that parents underreport instrumental supports received due to embarrassment about their own support needs.

Decision-Making Process and Plans

Parental Views Families participating in both studies reported having done very little planning for their adult children's living arrangements after the parents' death. In the longitudinal study, about one half of the families wanted a residential program placement eventually, and seven actually made a placement during the 2½ years. Of the 29 families who still wanted a residential placement and had not made one, over 40% had not yet discussed the matter with anyone, 28% were in the discussion stage, 10% were looking into residential programs, and 21% had placed their child on a waiting list.

When asked when they would like the change in living arrangements to occur, the majority of the caregivers in Study 1 (about two thirds at each time of inquiry) wanted it to occur after they died; about one third (both times) wanted it to occur within their lifetime; and only 3% in Time 1 and 7% in Time 2 wanted it to occur within the next year.

Despite being selected by agencies as potential candidates for placements, only one third of families in Study 2 families had made any arrangements for future placements. At least 20% of the families had not progressed past the discussion stage in planning for these placements. Generally, as in the Study 1 sample, most of these families did not want the placements to occur in the immediate future. In fact, only one quarter of the families wanted the placements to occur in the next year, and at least one third of the families wanted placements to occur only after the parents became sick or died. Heller and Factor (1988) have noted that families often do not plan for future living arrangements because of ambivalence, lack of appropriate residential options, fear of abuse and sexual permissiveness in residences, and long waiting lists. The apprehensiveness regarding future placements is described by one of the parents: "It breaks our heart to just think about placement as she loves her home so much; to think of her any other place is unthinkable."

For those families in both studies who wanted residential program placements, the main reason for wanting those placements was their desire to see their child adjust to living in a group home while they were still alive. Other reasons related to the parent's or the spouse's deteriorating health. Parents also felt that placement would help facilitate their child's increased independence.

The following comments from families interviewed illustrate their multiple reasons for wanting to make plans for present or future living arrangements:

> Since we are getting older, we would like our child placed in a residential program to help him adjust while we are still able. Several years ago, my spouse developed a heart condition. This really put our minds thinking more strongly about this.
>
> Susan has been our main concern in life in taking care of her, but our years of life are fast coming to the end for this, and other arrangements will have to be made. If one or the other should die, the decision would have to be made because as a team we can manage, but one alone will not be able to carry the load. I as a mother may go a little longer, but for Dad it would be impossible without a lot of help at home.
>
> I know he needs to be on his own, and I'd feel better if I was still here to see him settled and happy. He says he wants to have his own apartemtn. He enjoys his independence and is doing more talking and seeing his friends that have made the move.
>
> I would like to see him settled in a living facility before I pass on and be happy and independent. I have cared for him all these years so will continue until he gets in a living facility. He is on 3 or 4 lists.

A key to successful residential transition is preparatory planning and participative decision-making among family members, including the adult with developmental disabilities (Heller, 1988). Preparatory planning could include family discussions, visits to sites, and discussions with other families who have gone through similar experiences. Most of the families in Study 2 who had made concrete plans for placements ($n = 46$) did take steps to prepare the family. Over 80% of these families discussed these decisions with their adult child with developmental disabilities and their other children, and about half of these families visited residences with their child. About one third of the adult children spent time at the prospective residence. Nearly one half of the families discussed their decision with other parents who had placed their child out of the home. Often families who have gone through the experience of placement are in the best position to help allay families' anxieties regarding the transition.

The Views of Persons with Developmental Disabilities   This study is one of the first to examine the views of persons with developmental disabilities regarding their residential choices and quality of life. The major factor associated with their desire to move out of the home was their lower life satisfaction. Neither their level of functioning nor their caregiving reciprocity with their parents had a significant influence on their desire to move out of the family home. The majority of the adult children interviewed (63%) wanted to remain in the family home, often because of their fear of the alternatives and their desire to be near their parents. There was a fairly even split between those who felt happy about the prospect of moving and those who felt unhappy about it.

Individuals who wanted to move felt dissatisfied at home and desired greater independence. The following comments depict these feelings:

> I want to be my own boss, be free, free to stay out, shop more.
> I want to live where it is more quiet. The reason I want to move is to get away from my Mom and Dad; I'd like to be on my own. I want to move in with my sister, but moving somewhere by myself would be even better.

Others anticipated opportunities for better social relationships:

> I would like to move in with my best friend. I see that my parents are getting older; pretty soon they won't be able to take care of me anymore. I don't want to be alone.
> I'd very much like to move in with my sister. I'd have more privacy and time for myself.
> I want to move in with my girlfriend. I'm in love.

For the majority who wanted to remain in the family home, the major reasons were that they enjoyed the stability and care provided in the home by their parents:

> I want to stay with Mom. I take care of her and she takes care of me.

> The hard thing is leaving here . . . memories.

I like my home. My parents care about me.

I want to stay home; I don't want to be in a nursing home unless I am very old.

The majority of the individuals had discussed future living arrangements with others, primarily their parents. Nearly three quarters of those who had plans were pleased with them. Most of the individuals expecting residential placement in the near future had taken some preparatory steps and had been involved in the decision-making regarding the transition to some extent. Although most of these adults had discussed the prospective residences with parents and had visited prospective residences, few had discussed the transition with friends, other family members, or agency staff. Less than one half of these individuals had discussed potential roommates and possessions or visited prospective day programs or workshops.

Predictors of Placement Preferences and Actual Placement   Further research on placement issues must be longitudinal and examine factors that predict both placement preferences and actual placements. Also, there is a need for larger samples, including people who are currently not identified by the service network. The present research focused primarily on parents' and their adult children's desires for future out-of-home placement rather than actual placements. In Study 1, which had seven placements over the 2½ years, the number of placements was too small for statistical analyses. However, one striking difference between the families who made placements and those who did not was that 86% of the former group (versus 52% of the total sample) reported at Time 1 that they thought it would become more difficult to care for their child in the next 10 years. This suggests that planning for residential placements must take into consideration both the current and anticipated perceived burden families experience.

Blacher (1986) has noted that placement can be conceptualized as a process rather than a single act. The tendency to make a placement may begin with occasional thoughts and progress through decision-making, to active searching, to actual placement. In a 3-year study of child placements, she found that once plarents took active steps to explore placement, the probability of placement was high. In the research reported in this chapter all but one of the families who eventually placed their children had reported desiring out-of-home placements during the Time 1 interview. Three of the seven persons who moved into a residential program had been on a waiting list at Time 1, although only one moved into the waiting list residence. In the present study the high relationship between Time 1 placement preference and Time 2 placement preference and the fact that nearly all the families who did place their adult children reported wanting placement in the first interview 2½ years earlier corroborates Blacher's findings.

POLICY IMPLICATIONS

This study suggests the need for both family support programs serving families of adults with mental retardation living with them and the development of residential options for those needing them when families can no longer provide care in the home. For families who continue to provide home care to an adult member with developmental disabilities, support programs designed to enhance their caregiving capacities are needed. A survey of family support programs nationwide indicated that, as of fiscal year 1988, 42 states had discrete MR/DD agency–based family support initiatives (either cash subsidy, respite, or other family support) (Fujiura, Garza, & Braddock, 1990). However, at least eight of these states limited the family support initiative to families of children, while four other states limited only their financial assistance programs to families of children.

A key finding in both studies presented here is that parents who experience high caregiving burden reported a greater need for placement of their adult children with developmental disabilities. This points to the necessity of providing family support programs that alleviate family burden to those most at risk. This would include directing programs toward families with greater unmet needs and to those parents providing a high level of caregiving support to their children with developmental disabilities. Other factors that research has highlighted as increasing risk for caregiving burden and out-of-home placement have included lesser adaptive behavior skills and more maladaptive behaviors in the persons with developmental disabilities, and caregivers' older age and poor health (Heller & Factor, 1991; Seltzer & Krauss, 1989; Sherman & Cocozza, 1984).

For families requiring placements out of the family home, there is a need for other alternatives. Often families approach the service system for emergency placement after the illness or death of a family caregiver (Janicki, Otis, Puccio, Retting, & Jacobson, 1985). In such cases, families face long waiting lists and few acceptable options. An Association for Retarded Citizens study in 45 states indicated that over 63,000 persons were estimated to be waiting for MR/DD residential services (Davis, 1987). Furthermore, many of the 135,000 residents of large MR/DD facilities and 50,000 nursing home residents with mental retardation are slated to move into smaller residential alternatives (Fujiura et al., 1990). Clearly, the service system needs to plan for the future residential service needs of the older adult with developmental disabilities.

This research indicates the need for greater participation of family members, including the person with developmental disabilities, in decision-making regarding future placement. Although in families anticipating placements in the near future persons with developmental disabilities tend to discuss these plans with their parents, there is a need for greater encouragement of more discussion with a wider spectrum of family, friends, and service providers. Also, there is a need for greater consideration of the views of persons with disabilities regarding their choices of future roommates, possessions, and day programs. Although most of the persons with developmental disabilities interviewed experienced anxiety talking about the time when parents could no longer provide care for them, they had thought about it before and had definite ideas about where and with whom they would like to live someday.

This research has delineated a method of individually assessing the residential preferences and the life satisfaction of persons with developmental disabilities. Certainly, there is a need for further refinement of instruments and techniques that could better illuminate the feelings and desires of persons with developmental disabilities and that could facilitate their involvement in their own life planning.

REFERENCES

Blacher, J. (1986). *Placement of severely handicapped children: Correlates and consequences* (Grant No. HD21324). Washington, DC: National Institute of Child Health and Human Development.

Black, M., Cohn, J., Smull, M., & Crites, L. (1985). Individual and family factors associated with risk of institutionalization of mentally retarded adults. *American Journal of Mental Deficiency, 90,* 271–276.

Bromley, B.E., & Blacher, J. (1991). Parental reasons for out-of-home placement of children with severe handicaps. *Mental Retardation, 29,* 275–280.

Bruininks, R.H., Hill, B.K., Weatherman, R.F., & Woodcock, R.W. (1986). *Inventory for client and agency planning.* Allen, TX: DLM Teaching Resources.

Cole, D.A. (1986). Out-of-home child placement and family adaptation: A theoretical framework. *American Journal of Mental Deficiency, 91,* 226–236.

Cole, D.A., & Meyer, L.H. (1989). Impact of needs and resources on family plans to seek out-of-home placement. *American Journal on Mental Retardation, 93,* 380–387.

Davis, S. (1987). *A national status report on waiting lists of people with mental retardation for community services.* Arlington, TX: Association for Retarded Children.

Dunst, C.J., Trivette, C.M., & Cross, A.H. (1986). Mediating influences of social support: Personal, family, and child outcomes. *American Journal of Mental Deficiency, 90,* 403–417.

Friedrich, W.N., Cohen, D.S., & Wilturner, L.S. (1987). Family relations and marital quality when a handicapped child is present. *Psychological Reports, 61,* 911–919.

Fujiura, G.T., Garza, J., & Braddock, D. (1990). *National survey of family support services in developmental disabilities.* Chicago: University of Illinois at Chicago.

German, M.L., & Maisto, A.A. (1982). The relationship of perceived family support system to the institutional placement of mentally retarded children. *Education and Training of the Mentally Retarded, 17,* 17–23.

Gold, M., Dobrof, R., & Torian, L. (1987, March). *Parents of the adult developmentally disabled.* Final report presented to the United Hospital Trust Fund, New York.

Goodman, D.M. (1978). Parenting an adult mentally retarded offspring. *Smith College Studies in Social Work, 94,* 259–271.

Heal, L.V., & Chadsey-Rusch, J. (1985). The Lifestyle Satisfaction Scale (LSS): Assessing individuals' satisfaction with residence, community setting, and associated services. *Applied Research in Mental Retardation, 6,* 475–490.

Heller, T. (1988). Transitioning: Coming in and going out of community residences. In M.P. Janicki, M.W. Krauss, & M.M. Seltzer (Eds.), *Community residences for persons with developmental disabilities: Here to stay* (pp. 149–158). Baltimore: Paul H. Brookes Publishing Co.

Heller, T. (1993). Self-efficacy coping, active involvement, and caregiver well-being throughout the life course among families of persons with mental retardation. In A.P. Turnbull, J.M. Patterson, S.K. Behr, D.L. Murphy, J.G. Marquis, & M.J. Blue-Banning (Eds.), *Cognitive coping, families, and disability* (pp. 195–206). Baltimore: Paul H. Brookes Publishing Co.

Heller, T., & Factor, A. (1988). *Transition plan for older developmentally disabled persons residing in the natural home with family caregivers.* Public Policy Monograph Series. Chicago: University of Illinois at Chicago.

Heller, T., & Factor, A. (1991). Permanency planning for adults with mental retardation living with family caregivers. *American Journal on Mental Retardation, 96,* 163–176.

Janicki, M.P., Otis, M.R., Puccio, P.S., Retting, J.S., & Jacobson, J.W. (1985). Service needs among older developmentally disabled persons. In M.P. Janicki & H.M. Wisniewski (Eds.), *Aging and developmental disabilities: Inssues and approaches* (pp. 289–304). Baltimore: Paul H. Brookes Publishing Co.

Krauss, M.W. (1990). *Later life placement: Precipitating factor and family profiles.* Paper presented at the 114th annual meeting of the American Association on Mental Retardation, Atlanta.

Kriger, S. (1975). *Lifestyles of aging retardates living in community settings in Ohio.* Columbus: Psychologia Metrika.

Lawton, P.M. (1975). The Philadelphia Geriatric Center Morale Scale: A revision. *Journal of Gerontology, 30,* 85–89.

Lawton, P.M., Moss, M., Kleban, M.H., Glicksman, A., & Roving, M. (1991). A two-factor model of caregiving appraisal and psychological well-being. *Journal of Gerontology: Psychological Sciences, 46,* 181–189.

Lutzer, V.D., & Brubaker, T.H. (1988). Differential respite needs of aging parents of individuals with mental retardation. *Mental Retardation, 26,* 13–15.

McCubbin, H.I., & Patterson, J. (1983). Family stress adaptation to crises: A double ABCX model of family behavior. In H.I. McCubbin, M. Sussman, & J. Patterson (Eds.), *Social stresses and the family: Advances and developments in family stress theory and research* (pp. 7–37). New York: Haworth Press.

Meyers, C.E., Borthwick, S.A., & Eyman, R. (1985). Place of residence by age, ethnicity, and level of retardation of the mentally retarded/developmentally disabled population of California. *American Journal of Mental Deficiency, 90,* 266–270.

Orr, R.R., Cameron, S.J., & Day, D.M. (1991). Coping with stress in families with children who have mental retardation: An evaluation of the double ABCX model. *American Journal on Mental Retardation, 95,* 444–450.

Roberto, K.A. (1988). *Caring for aging developmentally disabled adults: Perspectives and needs of older parents.* Final report presented to the Colorado Developmental Disabilities Planning Council, Greeley, CO.

Roccoforte, J.A. (1991). *Stress, financial burden and coping resources in families providing home care for adults with developmental disabilities.* Unpublished master's thesis, University of Illinois at Chicago.

Seltzer, G., Begun, A.L., Seltzer, M.M., & Krauss, M.W. (1991). The impacts of siblings in the lives of adults with mental retardation and their aging mothers. *Family Relations, 40,* 310–317.

Seltzer, M.M., & Krauss, M.W. (1989). Aging parents with mentally retarded children: Family risk factors and sources of support. *American Journal on Mental Retardation, 94,* 303–312.

Sherman, B. (1988). Predictors of the decision to place developmentally disabled family members in residential care. *American Journal on Mental Deficiency, 92,* 344–351.

Sherman, B.R., & Cocozza, J.J. (1984). Stress in families of the developmentally disabled: A literature review of factors affecting the decision to seek out-of-home placements. *Family Relations, 33,* 95–103.

Turnbull, A.P., Summers, J.A., & Brotherson, M.J. (1986). Family life cycle: Theoretical and empirical implications and future directions for families with mentally retarded members. In J.J. Gallagher & P.M. Vietze (Eds.), *Families of handicapped persons: Research programs, and policy issues* (pp. 45–66). Baltimore: Paul H. Brookes Publishing Co.

Waisbren, S. (1980). Parent reactions after the birth of a developmentally disabled child. *American Journal of Mental Deficiency, 34,* 345–351.

Zarit, S., Reever, K., & Bach-Peterson, J. (1980). Relatives of the impaired elderly: Correlates of feelings of burden. *The Gerontologist, 20,* 649–655.

8

Social Supports and Expectations of Family Involvement after Out-of-Home Placement

Gary B. Seltzer, Audrey Begun, Randy Magan, and Charlene M. Luchterhand

Little research has been conducted on family involvement following out-of-home placement of individuals with developmental disabilities (Baker & Blacher, 1988). This issue is neglected even though family involvement has been shown in past research to be correlated with residential and employment success for a relative with developmental disabilities (Schalock & Lilley, 1986). While their children live at home, parents are instrumentally involved with them, acting as advocates, overseeing educational or vocational instruction, providing financial support, and encouraging social and recreational activities (Harris & McHale, 1989). Although parents may alter the type of support they provide after out-of-home placement, many remain committed to their adult children in ways that enhance the quality of their adult children's lives (Close & Halpern, 1988). In fact, parenting is a lifelong commitment, both for persons with and without developmental disabilities (Rossi, 1980). Yet, very little is known about the specific types of activities and supports parents provide after they have placed their adult children with developmental disabilities out of the home. Moreover, even less is known about what parents expect from their other children in regard to providing support to the child with developmental disabilities, particularly after their own involvement is curtailed by health problems or death.

This chapter addresses the issue of family involvement when a member with developmental disabilities lives outside of the parental home. It begins with a review of the literature on family involvement as it relates to social supports, sibling relationships, and planning for the future of family members with developmental disabilities. It then reports the results of a study of family involvement that was conducted by the authors with funding from the Rehabilitation Research and Training Center Consortium on Aging and Developmental Disabilities. This study differs from most studies that have investigated the issue of family involvement in out-of-home placement in that most of the prior studies examined family involvement by measuring only the frequency of visits and mail and telephone contacts made between parents, siblings, and their family members with developmental disabilities (Hill, Rotegard, & Bruininks, 1984; Intagliata, Willer, & Wicks, 1981; Lei, Nihira, Sheehy, & Meyers, 1981). This study reports findings on visitation and other contact but also examines the reciprocal nature of contact, specifically the types of affective as well as instrumental supports that are exchanged among family members after out-of-home placement. Furthermore, since persons with developmental disabilities frequently require assistance with decision-making, measuring family involvement takes into account the extent to which parents expect siblings, other family members, and professionals to be involved as decision-makers in specific aspects of their adult childrens' lives. The chapter concludes with a discussion of the implications and generalizability of the findings.

REVIEW OF THE LITERATURE

Social Supports and Family Involvement

Generally, very little is known about the social supports of adults with developmental disabilities (Seltzer, 1985). Until the late 1980s, research that studied out-of-home placements found that persons with developmental disabilities had to rely primarily on friends and staff for social support rather than family members (Baker & Blacher, 1988). Observational studies in group homes found that group home characteristics were better predictors of social behavior than were individual behaviors (Landesman-Dwyer, Berkson, & Romer, 1979; Landesman-Dwyer, Sackett, & Kleinman, 1980). Generally, there was more social interaction in large group homes than in small ones. Intensity of affiliation patterns, however, did not relate to the size of the group home. Of particular concern from this research and other similar research is the finding that there is significantly less social behavior among older residents in comparison to younger ones (Heller, Berkson, & Romer, 1981). Unfortunately, also, staff interact relatively little with group home residents; Landesman (1988) estimated that staff spent only about 10% of their time on the job engaging in some form of social exchange.

Older age may be a time of increasing isolation for persons with developmental disabilities because their social support networks are unlikely to include children or spouses. Nevertheless, some older adults with developmental disabilities do have contact with friends, acquaintances, professionals, paraprofessionals, coworkers, employers, and many others. In most cases, their family networks consist of siblings, aging parents, and perhaps nieces and nephews. Krauss and Erickson (1988) compared the social support networks of persons who lived with their parents and those who lived in out-of-home placements. They found that persons with developmental disabilities who lived with their parents had a smaller network of supports, which consisted primarily of family members. This finding is consistent with a later study that found that, although the networks of persons who lived at home were reasonably large and active, they consisted primarily of family members (Krauss, Seltzer, & Goodman, 1992). In addition, these authors found that there were very few paid professionals (7%) included in the support networks of their participants who lived with their parents, a finding that contrasts with that of other studies of adults with developmental disabilities living out of the home (e.g., Kennedy, Horner, & Newton, 1990; Krauss & Erickson, 1988). Unfortunately, close friends seem to be absent from the social support networks of persons with developmental disabilities whether they live with their parents (Krauss & Erickson, 1988; Krauss et al., 1992) or in the community (Clegg & Standen, 1991; Gollay, Freedman, Wyngaarden, & Kurtz, 1978; Halpern, Close, & Nelson, 1986).

Research on people without disabilities indicates that parents and their children have a high level of reciprocal involvement throughout the life span, well beyond the years during which they live together (Cicirelli, 1989). This is true also for siblings. The gerontological literature is replete with studies suggesting that informal supports from adult children help maintain the quality of life for aging parents (Seltzer, 1985), but only since the late 1980s has this literature found that many aging parents also provide considerable support and care for their middle aged children (Greenberg & Becker, 1988). Increasingly, there is an appreciation that social supports are complex networks in which there are reciprocal exchanges of affective and instrumental support intergenerationally. The older generation provides assistance as well as receiving it from the younger generation. The parent–child, child–parent, and sibling relationships in adulthood represent critical components of an individual's social support network (Avioli, 1989; Barnett, Kibria, Baruch, & Pleck, 1991; Bedford, 1989; Fine & Norris, 1989; Gold, 1989; Spitze & Logan, 1990).

Heller and Factor (1988) noted that reciprocity of support has been overlooked in families with a member with developmental disabilities. Their research suggested that family well-being is related to the reciprocity of affective and instrumental supports between parents and their adult children with developmental disabilities.

As family systems theory would predict (Carter & McGoldrick, 1980), the receipt of social supports by an adult with developmental disabilities has implications for other family members. Parents are affected by the support that their adult child with developmental disabilities receives from siblings and other family members. For example, it has been found that mothers of children with developmental disabilities who live with them have better psychological well-being when there is a high level of involvement among all of their adult children (Seltzer, Begun, Seltzer, & Krauss, 1991). Within a family system then, social support networks extend well beyond the parent–child dyad.

Sibling Relationships

This section reviews one aspect of family involvement, sibling relationships. Sibling relationships was chosen for review because, generally, it is absent or at least not highlighted in the very few reviews of the literature that exist on family involvement. (See Blacher & Baker, 1992 for a thorough review of the issues and literature on family involvement after out-of-home placement.) Generally, these reviews refer to parent and/or family involvement and do not look at the unique contributions made by sibling relationships in these families who have adult children with developmental disabilities living in residential facilities out of the parents' or siblings' home. This section explores the unique contribution that siblings may be making in the lives of their brothers and sisters with developmental disabilities.

As noted earlier, among adults without disabilities, the exchange of emotional support is commong among siblings (Gold, 1989; Springer & Brubaker, 1984). As a general developmental pattern, siblings interact less during early adulthood than in earlier years of co-residence but once again increase interaction during middle and old age (Bedford, 1989). Among some siblings, later-life relationships are shaped by longstanding conflicts, dependencies, or rivalries; the lifelong patterns of attachment and affectional bonds, among others, dictate the qualities of later-life relationships (Cicirelli, 1988). These siblings indicate that their feelings of closeness originated in childhood, and as adults they share memories of their early closeness, as well as internalized shared values, goals, and interests. Thus, they are able to maintain a sense of continuity in spite of physical separation during adulthood. The commitment to adult sibling relationships is also influenced by expectations regarding family bonds, which have, in turn, been shaped by the family's social class, religion, culture, and ethnicity (Cicirelli, 1988).

The nature of sibling relationships for adults with developmental disabilities has emerged as a focus for research since the mid 1980s (Seltzer et al., 1991; Zetlin, 1986). This research is based not only upon the relationships among adult siblings in general, but also upon the body of knowledge concerning sibling relationships that involve individuals with developmental disabilities (e.g., Crnic & Leconte, 1986; Lobato, 1983; McHale & Gamble, 1989).

Some studies suggest that the emotional impact of having grown up with a brother or sister with disabilities influences the pattern of relationships among siblings (Lobato, 1990; San Martino & Newman, 1974; Stoneman, Brody, Davis, Crapps, & Malone, 1991; Wilson, Blacher, & Baker, 1989). Some conditions thought to affect sibling relationships negatively include: the increased amount of time, energy, and care that parents may give to the child with developmental disabilities; the likelihood of siblings assuming caregiving responsibilities; negative reactions from their peer groups; and anxiety or guilt related to the cause (real or imagined) of the sibling's disabilities (Begun, 1989).

Other differences in sibling relationships may relate directly to the nature of interactions that take place between the siblings. Zetlin (1986) investigated the emotional quality of the relationships between 35 adults with mental retardation and their siblings. She identified patterns of relating that ranged from high sibling involvement to no involvement. Siblings without mental retardation provided more support, both emotional and instrumental, than they received, regardless of the relationship pattern. This result is contrasted with the pattern of balanced reciprocity that typically develops between siblings when neither has a disability. In addition, Zetlin found that individuals with mental retardation had hierarchical (rather than equal) relationships and were strongly dependent emotionally upon their brothers and sisters. Begun (1989) researched the qualitative aspects of relationships between adolescent and adult females and their siblings with mental retardation. Consistent with past research, she found disproportionate reciprocity in these sibling pairs such that the one with the developmental disability gave less than he or she received.

Another factor in the balance of reciprocity in sibling relationships is the age of the other family members. As family members age, family composition changes. Accompanying these changes is often a revision or redefinition of roles and functions within the family such that who provides what type of support may change. As parents age, they have concerns about the future role that others may take in relation to their son or daughter with developmental disabilities; however, it is not clear what events may spur families into the actual planning process (Heller & Factor, 1991) or to what extent siblings are involved in future planning. Research findings do suggest that the majority of mothers whose children with developmental disabilities live with them expect their other children to take responsibility for overseeing the future care of their brothers or sisters (Krauss, 1992).

REHABILITATION RESEARCH AND
TRAINING CENTER CONSORTIUM ON AGING AND
DEVELOPMENTAL DISABILITIES STUDY ON FAMILY INVOLVEMENT

Participants

Families participating in the Rehabilitation Research and Training Center Consortium on Aging and Developmental Disabilities Study were recruited from a list of residents of a large, multi-site, not-for-profit residential facility. In order to maintain confidentiality, social workers from the facility contacted 403 families of adult children living at one of the sites. Families were sent packets that contained a letter requesting that they sign and return an informed consent form acknowledging their willingness to participate in the study. The packet also contained another stamped envelope, and parents were requested to select the sibling they perceived as most involved with their adult child with developmental disabilities and to address and send the envelope to that sibling. A family was included only if they sent the enclosed letter to one of their adult children. Families in which parents were deceased but a sibling was available to participate were included.

A total of 403 packets were sent and 204 families responded (51%). Of those who responded, 44 families were excluded because of incomplete data; another 34 were excluded because, as the data collection process continued, they decided to drop out, or they were ineligible because they did not fit the study inclusion criteria. A total of 126 families completed the data collection process. For 103 of the families, data were available from both a parent and a sibling; for 23 families, data were available from a sibling only. In total, data were collected from 103 parents and 126 siblings (no more than one of each per family).

The participants with developmental disabilities ranged in age from 18 to 56 years (M = 29.31 years). The proportion of men and women was not quite equal (56% and 44% respectively). According to agency records, 42% of the residents had mild mental retardation, 23% moderate mental retardation, and 35% severe or profound mental retardation. Each participant had lived in the facility for a minimum of 1 year; the mean length of time in this facility was 12 years, while the mean length of time in all out-of-home placements was 15 years.

The parent participants were most often mothers (n = 97 mothers, 93% of the parents). From families with both parents available, the study solicited mothers' responses in order to parallel earlier research in the area. The mean age of the parents was 60. Sixty-three percent of the parents reported their religion as Catholic, reflecting the sectarian nature of the facility. Thirty percent were Protestant, 2% Jewish, and 5% other. In general, parents' educational levels were high (mean = 15 years). A considerable number of the parents worked outside of the home at least part time (40% of the males and 47% of the females). The parents reported a mean annual family income of $50,747. This high income reflects a middle-class group, many of whom were paying for this private residential program without assistance. The majority of parents no longer had any children living with them (74%), although 26% still had at least one child living with them. Twenty-one percent of the parents lived 50 miles or fewer away from their children's residential facility, 45% lived between 50 and 200 miles away, while 34% lived more than 200 miles away.

Ideally, all of the siblings from a family would be the target of this study in exploring family support. However, given the limited resources available, it was decided to include only one sibling per family. Past research traditionally has utilized selection criteria based upon birth order, age spacing, and/or gender (e.g., Begun, 1989; Zetlin, 1986). However, because family dynamics differ, it was decided not to force families into using uniform, predetermined criteria for selecting a sibling to participate in the study. Instead, parents were asked to identify the one child who was "most involved" with the sibling with mental retardation.

The average family had three siblings, one of whom was designated as the most involved. In 66% of the families, the most involved sibling was a sister, while in 34% it was a brother. The mean age of the most involved siblings was 32 years. The most involved siblings were older than the residents in 66% of the families and younger in 34% of the families. The age span between most involved and resident siblings ranged from 0 (twins) to 22 years ($M = 6$ years). Siblings tended to live farther away than their parents from their brothers and sisters, with 45% living more than 200 miles away, 34% living between 51 and 200 miles away, and 20% living 50 miles away or fewer.

Procedures

The parent data were collected in two forms: a mailed questionnaire and a telephone interview. The telephone interviews ranged from 45 minutes to 1½ hours long. Sibling data were collected by mailed questionnaire only. It is estimated that the mailed questionnaires required 1 hour for completion. Data relevant to this chapter included: family demographics; residential placement history; parents' physical health status; visitation and other contacts; family members' involvement in present and future planning; and the support system of the adult with developmental disabilities. Physical health status questions were based upon the OARS Multidimensional Functional Assessment Questionnaire (Part A) (Fillenbaum, 1988). Questions about contacts with other family members included scales designed to assess how often parents and siblings had in-person, telephone, and mail contact with their family members with developmental disabilities. An additional section of 15 questions, written by the investigators, measured how often parents and siblings engaged in various activities with the residents (e.g., shopping, vacationing, discussing their welfare).

Questions about planning also were written by the investigators. Thirteen items asked about past planning processes and who had been involved. Twenty-two items asked about the process by which plans were being made for the residents' living situations, daytime programs, health needs, relationship and companionship needs, recreation and leisure, and financial management. For each item, the parents responded by listing the first name and relationship of each person who had been or who would be involved. Parents rated each person's level of involvement on a 4-point Likert scale from "not at all involved" to "very much involved." The most involved siblings were asked the questions about future planning, but only in terms of their own involvement. The siblings were also asked to rate their satisfaction with the future plans. Parents and siblings were asked about their discussions of future planning with each other.

The support system of the family members with developmental disabilities was described by both the parents and the most involved siblings using the Norbeck Social Support Questionnaire (Norbeck, Lindsey, & Carrieri, 1981). The participants first identified each of the people significant in these resident family members' lives. Each person was identified by first name and by relationship to the family member (e.g., friend, careprovider, relative, clergy). The participants then rated each person on each of several network items. The investigators wrote additional items in order to investigate the reciprocity of the relationships. For example, the original Norbeck Social Support Questionnaire asked, "How much does this person make you feel loved?"; an added item asked, "How much do you make this person feel loved?" As a result, there were a total of 10 questions about each person in the network. A final item was also added which asked the participants about the residents' overall satisfaction with their relationships to the people listed.

Results

Table 8.1 lists the types of visits and other contacts that occurred annually between parents, most involved siblings, and their family members with developmental disabilities. The mean number of visits per year by parents to their adult children's residential programs was 8.77, and by the most involved siblings, 5.54. Parental contact by telephone or mail was reported to occur an average of 44.21 times per year. Sibling mail and telephone contact were considerably less frequent but still occurred an average of 15.95 times per year.

Table 8.2 lists the frequency and type of activities that siblings and parents shared with their family members with developmental disabilities. When together, parents and most involved siblings spent time engaged in instrumental tasks like shopping and in recreational/affective events with their resident family

Table 8.1. Visiting and other contact by parents and the most involved siblings with their relatives with developmental disabilities (DD) on a yearly basis

Type of contact		Parent	Most involved sibling
Relative visited residence of child with DD	Mean	8.77	5.54
	SD	9.48	8.11
Child with DD visited home—not overnight	Mean	3.33	2.90
	SD	4.95	5.89
Child with DD visited home and spent night	Mean	6.39	2.34
	SD	7.65	5.64
Child with DD visited home of friend or relative	Mean	3.74	2.36
	SD	2.83	3.35
Telephone or mail contact	Mean	44.21	15.95
	SD	14.33	17.89

Table 8.2.   Types of activities engaged in by parents and the most involved siblings on a yearly basis with their relatives with developmental disabilities

Types of activities[a]		Parent	Most involved sibling
Going to a restaurant	Mean	7.46	3.54
	SD	7.88	4.14
Going shopping for personal care items, clothing, etc.	Mean	4.70	2.98
	SD	3.46	3.03
Going to a recreational activity	Mean	4.18	2.24
	SD	4.08	2.51
Going on vacation	Mean	1.51	.54
	SD	1.03	.89
Going to a private doctor or clinic	Mean	2.54	.45
	SD	3.47	.88
Helping to decorate a residence	Mean	1.38	.46
	SD	1.85	.83

[a]From Instrumental Task and Activities Scale.

members. Parents and the most involved siblings together appeared to share a great deal of time engaged in a number of varied activities with their relatives with developmental disabilities.

Another objective of the study was to describe the characteristics of social support systems of adults with mental retardation who are living out of the home. Table 8.3 lists the types of support that parents and siblings listed as being exchanged with their family members with mental retardation. The sup-

Table 8.3.   Reciprocity of social support with adults who have developmental disabilities

Type of support		Parent rating			Sibling rating		
		N	X	t	N	X	t
Love	Receive	95	4.36	1.32	113	4.30	.55
	Give	95	4.28		113	4.26	
Respected/admired	Receive	94	4.23	2.33[a]	111	4.04	1.81
	Give	94	4.07		111	3.90	p = .074
Confide	Receive	91	2.37	−5.03[b]	109	2.46	−8.17[b]
	Give	91	2.88		109	3.13	
Support actions/ thoughts	Receive	89	3.72	2.13[a]	107	3.81	1.96
	Give	89	3.50		107	3.61	p = .052
Need money/ place to stay	Receive	90	3.68	11.70[b]	110	3.90	17.44[b]
	Give	90	1.85		110	1.83	
Total received		97	3.68	6.55[b]	117	3.71	5.85[b]
Total given		97	3.34		117	3.33	

[a]p < .05.
[b]p < .001.

port domains included: 1) making each other feel loved or liked, 2) making each other feel respected or admired, 3) confiding in each other, 4) supporting the actions and thoughts of each other, and 5) providing money and/or a place to stay if needed.

Table 8.3 displays the results of the t-tests that examined the extent of reciprocity in the support systems of the adults with developmental disabilities as rated by parents and most involved siblings. The t-tests indicate, for a given type of support, whether the levels of support received by the persons with developmental disabilities from their networks (as rated by the parents or siblings) were different from those given by the persons with developmental disabilities to the support network members (as rated by the parents or siblings). In all of the support domains except "confiding," parents rated their adult children receiving significantly more than they gave. Siblings also rated their brothers or sisters with mental retardation to be less able to give support than receive it in all domains except "confiding." Two other domains, "supporting actions and thoughts" and "feeling respected or admired," although not significant at the < .05 level, have values that are very close to that level.

There were no significant differences between parent ratings and sibling ratings within each domain. That is, parents and siblings rated their resident family members' support reciprocity similarly. Since parents and siblings responded to the measure of social support independently, this finding suggests that parents and siblings tend to perceive their resident family members' support networks similarly.

The investigators also were interested in the extent to which parents included their children without developmental disabilities in the social support networks of their adult children with developmental disabilities. Parents reported that siblings accounted for 26% of the network members for their adult children with developmental disabilities; 50% of all available siblings provided social support to their brothers and sisters with developmental disabilities.

Another way of investigating the support available to adults with developmental disabilities is to examine the extent to which siblings, parents, and others are involved in making decisions about the resident family member's life, in the present and future, in critical areas such as health and financial management. Table 8.4 presents data from parents on the degree of involvement in present and future planning of three categories of network members: family members who are not siblings, siblings, and professionals. The category of "family members who are not siblings" include the other parent and extended family such as brothers-in-law and sisters-in-law.

The data in Table 8.4 indicate that parents expected siblings to become much more involved in decision-making processes in the future than they were in the present. Across families, an average of 19% of the network of present decision-makers were siblings. For the future, parents envisioned that 69% of the network of planners would be siblings. The parent ratings of increased sib-

Table 8.4. Formal supports and family involvement in present and future decision-making for adults with developmental disabilities

Areas of involvement	Present		Future		
	X	n	X	n	t
Sibling					
Residence	2.88	32	3.59	96	2.89[a]
Daytime programs	1.70	35	2.72	97	5.71[b]
Health	2.35	37	3.56	97	6.15[b]
Recreation/leisure	2.38	37	2.82	97	2.82[a]
Relationship/companionship	2.40	37	2.92	97	4.80[b]
Managing finances	1.72	36	3.34	97	8.85[b]
Family not sibling					
Residence	3.62	80	3.52	29	.23
Daytime programs	2.34	84	2.37	30	2.00[a]
Health	3.48	87	3.04	30	−.20
Recreation/leisure	2.75	87	2.69	30	.01
Relationship/companionship	2.78	87	2.79	30	.49
Managing finances	3.33	85	3.08	29	−.24
Professional supports					
Residence	3.49	69	3.76	61	1.75
Daytime programs	3.69	74	3.77	63	1.25
Health	3.38	74	3.79	63	3.93[b]
Recreation/leisure	3.36	73	3.67	62	2.78[a]
Relationship/companionship	3.30	76	3.54	63	1.60
Managing finances	3.11	75	3.44	63	2.48[a]

[a]$p < .05$.
[b]$p < .001$.

ling involvement are statistically significant (using t-tests) in all six areas of planning: residential arrangements, daytime programming, health, recreation and leisure, relationship and companionship, and financial management.

The number of families reporting individuals from the formal support system as network members changes very little from the present to the future. In three areas of planning—residential programs, daytime programs, and relationships—parents' ratings indicate that they expected no change in the level of involvement of persons from the formal support system. However, in three other planning areas—health, recreation and leisure, and managing finances— there are statistically significant increases in the level of involvement expected from individuals in the formal support system.

When current conditions required increased involvement from siblings, parents perceived them to be more involved in the decision-making process. Specifically, parental age, health status variables, and the percentage of siblings who were present planners were intercorrelated. Older parents were more likely to have siblings function as present planners than were younger parents ($r = .40$,

$p < .01$). Similarly, parents were more likely to list siblings as present planners when the parents were in poorer health ($r = .23$, $p < .05$); when they had physical problems that stood in the way of their activities ($r = .26$, $p < .01$); and when they were too sick to carry out their usual activities ($r = .28$, $p < .01$).

Discussion of Family Involvement

Contact   The purpose of this study was to examine family involvement when a member with developmental disabilities lives out of the home. The study has produced a number of specific findings. First, it seems to confirm the Baker and Blacher (in press) suggestion that "placement out of the home need not mean placement out of the family." It appears that some families remain very actively involved with their family members even after placement in a private residential facility. Parents and siblings visit their family members with developmental disabilities frequently and take them shopping, to recreational activities, and home for vacations. They have frequent contact by telephone and by mail. The following comments from parents and siblings highlight the type and quality of family involvement:

> Every three weeks I drive my mother down to pick up my brother for a weekend visit at home. I also drive him back on Sunday. I drive them to church every time he's home.

> I feel I help my sister by *listening* to her talk about her program and all the activities she's involved with or any of the unhappy things that might be troubling her.

> I transport him to and from events when he's on vacation at home (several times a year). My son is pretty independent and doesn't want a lot of help. He's very protective of his room, so I would never help him decorate unless he asked, and he hasn't.

One of the differences between this sample and others used to study family involvement is that this sample is drawn from a private residential facility, and often families themselves were paying for all or some of the costs of the residential placement. This circumstance and the higher socio-economic status of these families limit the generalizability of the finding that families maintain a very active profile in the lives of their members with developmental disabilities. This finding contrasts with that of others (e. g., Conroy & Feinstein, 1985; Hill et al., 1984; Intagliata et al., 1981; Lei et al., 1981) who have studied family contact in publicly supported residential facilities and found the amount of contact to be considerably less. In fact, after reviewing the findings of these studies, Baker and Blacher (1988) concluded that the statistics suggest that the majority of residents from these publicly supported residential programs are virtually isolated from their families.

Since family contact is such an important component of the social support networks for persons with developmental disabilities, the implications of this discrepancy between publicly supported residential facilities and the privately supported facility from which the findings are drawn in the present study should be explored. Specifically, one wonders whether there is a sense of connectedness, even privilege, that develops when one perceives that he or she is purchasing these out-of-home services. In that vein, family members may feel more comfortable approaching staff to make arrangements for vacations and telephone contacts as well as asserting some control over decisions related to health and social needs of their resident family members. One might hope that empowerment through family involvement would not be motivated by economic involvement; however, there are empirical findings suggesting that requiring a token payment or a refundable deposit increases the level of participation in group intervention situations and in other therapeutic programs (Rose, 1989). A similar dynamic may be operating in relation to these out-of-home programs. Families may feel that because they are paying, they are going to remain active consumers.

Family payment may also influence staff behavior. That is, the messages coming from staff may be more inviting of family participation when there is an economic incentive. Staff may be more committed to listen and involve family members when they know that their employment is somewhat connected to keeping these families involved in the program.

On the one hand, these economic considerations may be troubling. On the other hand, they may suggest that families need to have more control over the "method of payment" for programs. Payment need not come directly from the family's income; rather, it might come under the family's control through a state or federal subsidy or some other type of voucher system.

In addition, staff may perceive family payment for care as an expression of caring and commitment. Obviously, there are many other ways that families can be encouraged by staff to express their caring and commitment to their family members with developmental disabilities. In this regard, the work of Baker and Blacher (1988) and Blacher and Baker (1992) is extremely helpful. These investigators have prepared a thorough and thoughtful outline of ways that service providers can enhance family involvement in community residential programs. Their outline gives specific suggestions for helping families remain involved during transitions into and out of community programs; for facilitating, and thereby increasing, family visitation; and for increasing family involvement in the decision-making process.

Social Support   A second finding from this study is that family members provide a significant amount of social support, even when the support is not fully reciprocated by the family member with developmental disabilities. However, while support is not evenly reciprocated by adults with developmental disabilities, these individuals do make their parents and siblings feel loved:

> George personifies unconditional love. It is great being his best friend and knowing how much he loves and respects me. He's fun and honest to a fault. He is a constant challenge.

> The joy she has brought to her family and friends through her unconditional love and concern for everyone, awareness and empathy you and your family develop for persons with disabilities, patience, understanding, acceptance, selflessness—all qualities learned through this experience.

These comments illustrate the depth of feeling that family members have for their members whom they have placed out of the home, but from whom they have not separated. Data on social supports from the present study suggest that there are strong bonds of attachment that remain in family systems after placement.

Reciprocity of social supports may be more complicated than is conveyed by the findings of this study, which are limited because they represent only the perceptions of the parents and siblings and not the perceptions of family members with developmental disabilities. In one of the few studies to include this voice, Heller and Factor (chap. 7, this volume) found that their sample of adult children with developmental disabilities reported that they received less socio-emotional support than their parents perceived giving and that they gave more instrumental help than their parents reported receiving. Although this sample of adult children differs from the present sample in that they were living with their parents, the discrepancy in perceptions about reciprocity of social supports suggests that the participants in the present study might also have had a different perception in regard to how much support they perceived receiving and giving.

Siblings   The findings of the present study suggest that parents expected that in the future the family would retain responsibility for overseeing the well-being of their sons and daughters with developmental disabilities even though they did not live with the family. It seems that in both families who had placed their relative out of the home and those who said they wanted to do so, siblings in particular were expected to assume greater responsibility for meeting the long-term needs of their brothers and sisters with developmental disabilities (see Heller & Factor, chap. 7, this volume). Parents expected that siblings would play a much more active, instrumental role in the support of their brothers and sisters in the future than in the present. The following comments are illustrative:

> He will have a trust fund; siblings will take care of this.

> Future plans are that [brother] will be financial manager and guardian. Other siblings will help out. Shifts will probably occur as the years go by.

> We expect that she will be in good hands in the future. Her brother has excellent judgment and will make decisions that are in her best interest. He truly loves and cares for her.

A longitudinal study is needed to determine the extent to which these future plans materialize. Without this research, the extent to which siblings assume the decision-making responsibility expected of them by their parents and the extent to which they do become the next generation of careproviders will not be known.

Given the out-of-home placement of the family members with developmental disabilities, it is not surprising that individuals in the formal support system were also rated as very involved in decisions and made up a significant proportion of the planning networks. Parents foresaw increased involvement of formal support system staff in health, recreation and leisure, and managing finances. It is clear that in the future parents would expect their adult children with developmental disabilities to remain in their current residential program, as the following comments illustrate:

> My husband and I both agree his needs will be best met at [name of program]—a place that has become home. . . . He will continue to get the structure he needs in [name of program]'s "community," not restricted and yet structured to give him freedom.

> My plan is for him to stay at [name of program]. I have sent him there because I am worried about where he will go when I am no longer around. He's happy there.

It is concluded that parents in this study, who had placed their adult children with developmental disabilities out of the home, expected family involvement to continue throughout the parents' lifetimes and into the next generation. This study is limited by the nature of the private setting and by the economic means of the parents. There remains a need to investigate family involvement in other types of residential settings.

REFERENCES

Avioli, P.S. (1989). The social support functions of siblings in later life: A theoretical model. *American Behavioral Scientist, 33*(1), 45–57.

Baker, B.L., & Blacher, J. (1988). Family involvement with community residential programs. In M.P. Janicki, M.W. Krauss, & M.M. Seltzer (Eds.), *Community residences for persons with developmental disabilities: Here to stay* (pp. 173–188). Baltimore: Paul H. Brookes Publishing Co.

Baker, B.L., & Blacher, J. (in press). Out-of-home placement for children with mental retardation: Dimensions of family involvement. *American Journal on Mental Retardation.*

Barnett, R.C., Kibria, N., Baruch, G.K., & Pleck, J.H. (1991). Adult daughter-parent relationships and their associations with daughters' subjective well-being and psychological distress. *Journal of Marriage and the Family, 53,* 29–42.

Blacher, J., & Baker, B.L. (1992). Toward meaningful family involvement in out-of-home placement settings. *Mental Retardation, 30,* 35–43.

Bedford, V. (1989). Understanding the value of siblings in old age: A proposed model. *American Behavioral Scientist, 33*(1), 33–44.

Begun, A. (1989). Sibling relationships involving developmentally disabled people. *American Journal of Mental Retardation, 93*(5), 566–574.

Carter, E.A., & McGoldrick, M. (Eds.). (1980). *The family life cycle: A framework for family therapy.* New York: Gardner Press.

Cicirelli, V.C. (1988). Interpersonal relationships among elderly siblings. In M.D. Kahn & K.G. Lewis (Eds.), *Siblings in therapy: Life span and clinical issues* (pp. 435–456). New York: W.W. Norton.

Cicirelli, V.C. (1989). Helping relationships in later life: A reexamination. In J.A. Mancini (Ed.), *Aging parents and adult children* (pp. 167–179). Lexington, MA: Lexington Books.

Clegg, J.A., & Standen, P.J. (1991). Friendship among adults who have developmental disabilities. *American Journal on Mental Retardation, 95*, 663–671.

Close, D.W., & Halpern, A.S. (1988). Transitions to supported living. In M.P. Janicki, M.W. Krauss, & M.M. Seltzer (Eds.), *Community residences for persons with developmental disabilities: Here to stay* (pp. 159–171). Baltimore: Paul H. Brookes Publishing Co.

Conroy, J.M., & Feinstein, C.S. (1985). *Attitudes of the families of CARCU. Thorne class members.* Interim report number 2. Connecticut Applied Research Project. Philadelphia: Conroy P. Feinstein Associates.

Crnic, K.A., & Leconte, J. (1986). Understanding sibling needs and influences. In R.R. Fewell & P.F. Vadasy (Eds.), *Families of handicapped children: Needs and supports across the life span* (pp. 75–98). Austin: PRO-ED.

Fillenbaum, G.G. (1988). *Multidimensional functional assessment of older adults: The Duke Older American Resources and Services Procedures.* Hillsdale, NJ: Lawrence Erlbaum Associates.

Fine, M., & Norris, J.E. (1989). Intergenerational relations and family therapy research: What we can learn from other disciplines. *Family Process, 28*, 301–315.

Gold, D.T. (1989). Generational solidarity: Conceptual antecedents and consequences. *American Behavioral Scientist, 33*(1), 19–32.

Gollay, E., Freedman, R., Wyngaarden, M., & Kurtz, N.R. (1978). *Coming back: The community experiences of deinstitutionalized mentally retarded people.* Cambridge, MA: Abt.

Greenberg, J., & Becker, M. (1988). Aging parents as family resources. *The Gerontologist, 28*, 786–791.

Halpern, A.S., Close, D.W., & Nelson, D.J. (1986). *On my own: The impact of semi-independent living programs for adults with mental retardation.* Baltimore: Paul H. Brookes Publishing Co.

Harris, V.S., & McHale, S.M. (1989). Family life problems, daily caregiving activities, and the psychological well-being of mothers of mentally retarded children. *American Journal on Mental Retardation, 94*, 231–239.

Heller, T., Berkson, G., & Romer, D. (1981). Social ecology of supervised communal facilities for mentally disabled adults: VI. Initial social adaptation. *American Journal on Mental Deficiency, 86*, 43–49.

Heller, T., & Factor, A. (1988). *Transition plan for older developmentally disabled persons residing in the natural home with family caregivers* (Public Policy Monograph Series). Chicago: University of Illinois at Chicago.

Heller, T., & Factor, A. (1991). Permanency planning for adults with mental retardation living with family caregivers. *American Journal on Mental Retardation, 96*, 163–176.

Hill, B.K., Rotegard, L.L., & Bruininks, R.H. (1984). The quality of life of mentally retarded people in residential care. *Social Work, 29*, 275–280.

Intagliata, J., Willer, B., & Wicks, N. (1981). Factors related to the quality of community adjustment in family care homes. In R.H. Bruininks, C.E. Meyers, B.B. Sigford, & K.C. Lakin (Eds.), *Deinstitutionalization and community adjustment of mentally retarded people* (Monograph No. 4, pp. 217–230). Washington, DC: American Association on Mental Deficiency.

Kennedy, C.H., Horner, R.H., & Newton, J.S. (1990). The social networks and activity patterns of adults with severe disabilities: A correlational analysis. *Journal of The Association for Persons with Severe Handicaps, 15,* 86–90.

Krauss, M.W. (1992). *Placement is no panacea: Relation between long-term care plans and the well-being of mothers of adults with mental retardation.* Paper presented at the 25th Annual Gatlinburg Conference on Research and Theory in Mental Retardation and Developmental Disabilities. Gatlinburg, TN.

Krauss, M.W., & Erickson, M.E. (1988). Informal support networks among aging mentally retarded persons: Results from a pilot study. *Mental Retardation, 26,* 197–201.

Krauss, M.W., Seltzer, M.M., & Goodman, S.J. (1992). Social support networks of adults with retardation who live at home. *American Journal on Mental Retardation, 96,* 432–441.

Landesman, S. (1988). Preventing "institutionalization" in the community. In M.P. Janicki, M.W. Krauss, & M.M. Seltzer (Eds.), *Community residences for persons with developmental disabilities: Here to stay* (pp. 105–116). Baltimore: Paul H. Brookes Publishing Co.

Landesman-Dwyer, S., Berkson, G., & Romer, D. (1979). Affiliation and friendship of mentally retarded residents in group homes. *American Journal of Mental Deficiency, 83,* 571–580.

Landesman-Dwyer, S., Sackett, G.P., & Kleinman, J.S. (1980). Relationship of size to resident and staff behavior in small community residences. *American Journal of Mental Deficiency, 85,* 6–17.

Lei, T., Nihira, L., Sheehy, N., & Meyers, C.E. (1981). A study of small family care for mentally retarded people. In R.H. Bruininks, C.E. Meyers, B.B. Sigford, & K.C. Lakin (Eds.), *Deinstitutionalization and community adjustment of mentally retarded people* (Monograph No. 4, pp. 265–281). Washington, DC: American Association on Mental Deficiency.

Lobato, D.J. (1983). Siblings of handicapped children: A review. *Journal of Autism and Developmental Disabilities, 13,* 347–364.

Lobato, D.J. (1990). *Brothers, sisters, and special needs: Information and activities for helping young siblings of children with chronic illnesses and developmental disabilities.* Baltimore: Paul H. Brookes Publishing Co.

McHale, S.M., & Gamble, W.C. (1989). Sibling relationships of children with disabled and nondisabled brothers and sisters. *Developmental Psychology, 25,* 421–429.

Meyers, C.E., Borthwick, S.A., & Eyman, R.K. (1985). Place of residence by age, ethnicity and level of retardation of the MR/DD population of California. *American Journal of Mental Deficiency, 90,* 266–270.

Norbeck, J.S., Lindsey, A.M., & Carrieri, V.L. (1981). The development of an instrument to measure social support. *Nursing Research, 30*(5), 264–269.

Rose, S.D. (1989). *Working with adults in groups.* San Francisco: Jossey-Bass.

Rossi, A.S. (1980). Aging and parenthood in the middle years. In P.B. Baltes & O.G. Brim (Eds.), *Life span development and behavior* (Vol. 3, pp. 138–205). New York: Academic Press.

San Martino, M.S., & Newman, M.B. (1974). Siblings of retarded children: A population at risk. *Child Psychiatry and Human Development, 16,* 168–177.

Schalock, R.L., & Lilley, M.A. (1986). Placement from community-based mental retardation programs: How well do clients do after 8 to 10 years? *American Journal of Mental Deficiency, 90,* 669–676.

Seltzer, G.B. (1985). Selected psychological processes and aging among older developmentally disabled persons. In M.P. Janicki & H.M. Wisniewski (Eds.), *Aging and developmental disabilities: Issues and approaches* (pp. 211–228). Baltimore: Paul H. Brookes Publishing Co.

Seltzer, G.B., Begun, A., Seltzer, M.M., & Krauss, M.W. (1991). Adults with men-

tal retardation and their aging mothers: Impacts of siblings. *Family Relations, 40,*
    310–317.
Seltzer, M.M., & Krauss, M.W. (1989). Aging parents with mentally retarded children:
    Family risk factors and sources of support. *American Journal on Mental Retardation,*
    94, 303–312.
Spitze, G., & Logan, J. (1990). Sons, daughters, and intergenerational social support.
    Journal of Marriage and the Family, 52, 420–430.
Springer, D., & Brubaker, T.H. (1984). *Family caregivers and dependent elderly: Mini-*
    mizing stress and maximizing independence. Beverly Hills, CA: Sage (in cooperation
    with the University of Michigan School of Social Work).
Stoneman, Z., Brody, G.H., Davis, C.H., Crapps, J.M., & Malone, M. (1991). Ascribed
    role relations between children with mental retardation and their younger siblings.
    American Journal on Mental Retardation, 95, 537–550.
Wilson, J., Blacher, J., & Baker, B.L. (1989). Siblings of severely handicapped children.
    Mental Retardation, 27, 167–173.
Zetlin, A. (1986). Mentally retarded adults and their siblings. *American Journal of Mental*
    Deficiency, 91, 217–225.

9

Leisure Participation and Life Satisfaction of Older Adults with Mental Retardation and Down Syndrome

Barbara A. Hawkins

> The most urgent task at hand is to build from a hundred cultures, one culture which does what no other culture has ever done before . . . gives a place to every human gift. (Mead, 1957)

People with developmental disabilities will gain access to and inclusion in the full range of leisure activities in later adulthood as a life span perspective in supporting them unfolds and assumes more importance. Leisure activities that promote opportunities for self-development and creative expression will be vitally important. Furthermore, professionals who work with persons with mental retardation will need to increase their understanding of leisure in later adulthood and identify key factors that influence participation in leisure-based activity.

Patterns of leisure activity are influenced by transitions from one life stage to another. These transitions are accompanied by changes in social roles, time perception and use, variations in personal resources, and the normative expectations held toward the life stage being entered (Cutler & Hendricks, 1990). Leisure for older adults with mental retardation is influenced greatly by the many ways in which society focuses its values and expectations. Western cul-

ture historically has been oriented toward youth, work, and diversionary leisure. These perspectives are likely to be revised as the demography, economy,
national political ideology, and social value systems change and affect individual
lifestyles and society.

The fact that people are living longer and will have many years of retirement will result in the need to reinterpret the meaning of leisure in later life. The
legitimization of retirement as a time in life when adults with mental retardation
can exercise the freedom to choose what they wish to do and how they will involve themselves meaningfully in society is a salient issue (Ekerdt, 1986). Accompanying the transition to a retirement status, many citizens with mental
retardation may want to anticipate making a personal choice to replace a job-
oriented social role with a leisure-oriented lifestyle. Leisure may encompass
diversion and relaxation, as well as pursuits that are highly creative and developmental (Gordon, Gaitz, & Scott, 1976). This view of leisure in retirement is at
the center of the challenge for older adults with mental retardation.

This chapter presents information about leisure participation, life satisfaction, and the functional developmental needs of older adults with mental retardation. Data from a study of older adults with mental retardation are presented for
the purpose of illustrating leisure participation and life satisfaction in later life.
The chapter concludes with some recommended directions for future research
in this area.

THE NATURE OF LEISURE

The nature of leisure has been described broadly in the literature from both historical and cultural perspectives. Ancient Greco-Roman tradition characterized
leisure as a state of being free and able to cultivate creativity and learning. One
who was engaged in leisure was not encumbered with the common labors of
society. Not everyone in society engaged in leisure; it was reserved for a chosen
few (e.g., Aristotle).

In more recent history, religious doctrine has been an influential factor.
The virtue of work dominated, while leisure was viewed as the "devil's workshop" (DeGrazia, 1962). During the twentieth century, a class theory of leisure
was proposed by Thorstein Veblen (1953) wherein conspicuous consumption
and engagement in self-indulgent pleasures were prevailing themes. As the
character of leisure moved away from relaxation, a consumer orientation dis-
tinctly emerged. Mass leisure activity and consumerism continue today as dominant themes that have pervaded the character of leisure in twenty-first century
western culture.

Contemporary leisure philosophers have wrestled with the relationship between past views and present cultural influences. Today's technocratic society
challenges the meaning and context of many of life's major domains (e.g., work,
education, play, love, leisure, and a sense of family, community, self, and human-

ity). Should leisure be reduced to only those activities that are engaged in for relaxation, recuperation, recreation, and diversion? Does leisure represent something more significant? Is it the complex expression of self through creative endeavors, educational growth, and personal development (Reisman, 1952)? From a socio-cultural viewpoint, is leisure largely dictated by the economic marketplace, cultural traditions, care system policies, or some combination of all these factors? Whatever the viewpoint, the meaning of leisure in modern cultures remains largely influenced by the preservation of personal *choice and control* over unobligated time.

Leisure as Increasingly Intensive Activity and Activity Participation

Gordon et al. (1976) have proposed a conceptual structure for leisure that builds upon past research, including that of Dumazedier (1967), Havighurst (1972, 1973) Reisman (1952), Mead (1957, 1960), and Anderson (1959). Their framework includes five objectives: relaxation, diversion, development, creativity, and sensual transcendence. These objectives are the "forms of personal expressivity that are increasing intensities of cognitive, emotional, and physical involvement" (Gordon et al., 1976, p. 314). Gordon et al. (1976) proposed that leisure "may therefore be conceptualized . . . as discretionary personal activity in which expressive meanings have primacy over instrumental themes . . ." (p. 311).

Very low intensity activities of expressive involvement are subsumed under the objective of relaxation and include: quiet resting, solitude, and sleeping. Medium-low-intensity, or diversionary-type activities, are pursuits that provide relief and a change of pace, such as light social conversation, passive hobbies, and passive entertainment (e. g., light reading, television viewing).

Leisure activities that meet a self-development objective are characterized as having a medium intensity of expressive involvement that results in increased involvement of the physical, mental, and emotional aspects of oneself. This type of leisure participation includes activities such as continuing education, singing, dancing, and art. In this context, advancing personal knowledge through continuing education is not necessarily related to an expected occupational application.

Activities that are a medium-high intensity of expressive involvement are those that are reflective of creativity. Included under this type of involvement are performances, serious discussion, or acts of altruism and nurturing. Finally, activities of a high intensity of expressive involvement reflect the "pursuit of sensual pleasure" (Gordon et al., 1976, p. 315) or sensual transcendence. Pursuits in this realm entail the fullest possible involvement of the senses. Concomitantly, the expectation is for the experience of intense gratification, joy, excitement, pleasure, and titillation. Examples of activities at this level include intense dancing, strong wit and humor, sex, and fervent religious experiences. Other leisure pursuits that provide great adventure or great challenge also are included in this level, for example, sky diving, rock rapelling, river rafting, and spiritual retreats. These experiences often are described as "peak experiences," or those that reflect the social values of the need for personal wholeness, feeling alive, truth, and a sense self-actualization.

These varying intensities of expressive involvement are useful in interpreting the ways in which leisure contributes to individual growth and development in adulthood. This framework also may be useful in understanding leisure in the lives of older adults with mental retardation, as seen in the study presented in this chapter.

A FUNCTIONAL DEVELOPMENTAL VIEW OF LATER ADULTHOOD

Developmental Models

Program interventions for people with mental retardation traditionally have used a child development model and, since the 1980s, a functional skills model with adolescents and young adults. The functional skills approach examines the skills that adolescents and young adults need to live and work in the community at large. However, older adults confront different life challenges. To date, a model that is age-appropriate and aging sensitive has not been well developed for persons with mental retardation (Hawkins & Kultgen, 1991).

Some professionals are beginning to describe a model for older adults with mental retardation that is adapted from the social gerontological literature (Havighurst, 1973; Hawkins & Kultgen, 1991). The *functional developmental model of adult development for persons with mental retardation* forms "a general working orientation, rather than a comprehensive set of interrelated propositions" (George, 1982, p. 23). It focuses on the following kinds of age-related issues: 1) personal adjustment to the aging process; 2) residential environments that promote skill maintenance and growth; 3) residential environments that support the individual to age in place; 4) awareness of depression and other psychiatric issues; 5) preparation for active retirement; 6) opportunities to deal with grief, death, and dying; and 7) the need to actively address health maintenance and health care. Leisure activities can be utilized in meeting the functional and developmental needs that characterize later life, thus enhancing the perception of life satisfaction by older adults with mental retardation.

Leisure Participation and Life Satisfaction

Professionals and careproviders can support leisure activity opportunities within the context of the *functional developmental model* by addressing the following specific areas: 1) retirement preparation, 2) leisure skill development, 3) maintenance and promotion of physical fitness and health, 4) development of friendship networks, 5) community inclusion, 6) enhancement of residential environments that foster social relationships, and 7) promoting the empowerment of individuals for self-advocacy and self-determination (Hawkins & Kultgen,

1991). Each of these areas can be addressed productively through leisure activity that promotes a sense of well-being and satisfaction.

Life satisfaction has been found to be related significantly to leisure activity in older adults (Lawton, Ross, & Fulcomer, 1986–1987; McGuire, 1979, 1984; Riddick & Daniel, 1984; Tinsley, Teaff, Colbs, & Kaufman, 1985). Furthermore, research has supported leisure activity as the leading factor contributing to perceptions of satisfaction in later life (Kelly, Steinkamp, & Kelly, 1986). It has been suggested that leisure along with other social factors (e.g., friendship, residence, and opportunities for community inclusion) contribute to psychological perceptions of life satisfaction among persons with mental retardation (Hutchison & Lord, 1979; Schalock, Keith, Hoffman, & Karan, 1989).

The relationship between quality of leisure activity and perceptions of life satisfaction in older adults with mental retardation, however, is not well understood. Several factors that might influence this relationship include: 1) the presence or absence of leisure skills, 2) the effects of aging-related changes and declines, 3) preconceived ideas of professionals and careproviders in regard to what older people with mental retardation *ought* to be doing, 4) the enablement or barriers created by the human services system, and 5) the assessment of individual interests and preferences as necessary information in understanding personal choice-making. Furthermore, the relationship between leisure activity and perceptions of life satisfaction has not been widely researched among older adults with mental retardation.

Leisure activities can make a significant contribution toward meeting individual functional and developmental needs of aging adults with mental retardation, as well as promoting life satisfaction. Leisure provides an opportunity to choose activities that meet the individual's preferences, interests, and particular functional or developmental needs. In this regard, leisure may be instrumental in the preservation of health, the promotion of happiness, the facilitation of perceptions of life satisfaction, and the achievement of a decent quality of life in later adulthood.

The next section of the chapter highlights selected results from a study of leisure interests, barriers to leisure, and life satisfaction for a sample of older adults with mental retardation. This kind of information will help professionals and careproviders to better support age-sensitive and age-appropriate lifestyles for these individuals.

A STUDY OF LEISURE AND LIFE SATISFACTION AMONG OLDER ADULTS WITH MENTAL RETARDATION

Movement through later adulthood typically brings changes in social roles, perceptions of free time, and preferences for activity participation to the extent that work begins to fade and there is an accompanying anticipation of increased leisure (McGuire, 1984). Although this anticipation tends to be felt commonly by people without mental disabilities, little is known about this process for older adults with mental retardation (Hawkins, 1991).

Research in gerontology has demonstrated a pattern of steady decline in leisure participation with age (Kelly et al., 1986), especially in what are called *balance* activities (Kelly, 1987). Balance activities are those activities in which participation tends to vary and change depending on life stage, temporary interests, and circumstances. *Core* activities, however, are those that remain central to an individual's leisure repertoire throughout adult life. Typical core activities in later-life include home-based and social interaction activities.

These possible changes in the pattern of leisure participation can be compounded by the presence of disability. The following are some concerns that may arise for older individuals with mental retardation:

1. Will there be opportunities to express choice in the pursuit of core leisure activities?
2. Will there be discretionary or free choice time?
3. Will older adults with mental retardation be aware of new options for activity involvement (e.g., balance activities), as well as the necessary resources with which to pursue these choices?
4. Will there be preparation for retirement with the skills necessary for a leisure-oriented lifestyle?
5. Will careproviders and human services professionals facilitate or impede later-life fulfillment that is associated with leisure participation for adults with mental retardation?

Participants

The leisure patterns, preferences, and barriers to participation of 128 older adults with mental retardation were investigated. The sample consisted of 64 individuals with Down syndrome ranging in age from 32 to 56 years ($M = 42$) and 64 individuals without Down syndrome ranging in age from 52 to 79 years ($M = 63$). While these two groups differed in their age range and etiology of mental disability, the level of support they required was the same, that is, less than the most significant amount. On average, the individuals in both groups required limited regular supervision or personal care (Hawkins, Eklund, & Martz, 1991). There were equal numbers of men and women in each group. Eighty-seven percent of the total sample lived in group homes or with family members, and the remaining 13% lived in other residential arrangements. A distinguishing characteristic between the two groups was residential arrangement distribution. For the group with Down syndrome, 61% were living with their parent(s) or another relative and 38% were living in group homes. The group without Down syndrome showed an opposite pattern of residential arrangement, with 51% living in group homes and 36% living with their parent(s) or another relative (Hawkins et al., 1991).

All of the participants were involved in a 3-year study of bio-psycho-social decline in adults with mental retardation at Indiana University (Hawkins et al., 1991). The results reported in this chapter are based upon data from Year 3 of the study. Individuals were recruited through state and local agency contacts using the following criteria:

1. Participants could not be living in a large institution for people with mental disabilities.
2. Participants had to be known to the service system and be receiving day program or other services.
3. Participants had to be able to respond to simple directions and questions.
4. Participants without Down syndrome had to be over the age of 50; participants with Down syndrome had to be over the age of 30.
5. Participants were categorized by gender, age group, and diagnostic group (with Down syndrome and without Down syndrome).

Methods

Formal instruments to assess leisure functioning of older adults with mental retardation are not abundant in the literature. Thus, the *Leisure Assessment Inventory* was used to probe 50 picture-cued leisure activities and 20 leisure constraints. The activities and constraints are presented in Figure 9.1 and Figure 9.2. Reliability and validity data for the *Inventory* are available in Hawkins, Eklund, and Martz (1991).

While numerous instruments for assessing life satisfaction have been developed for older adults without mental disabilities (cf. George & Bearon, 1980), only a few instruments exist for use with people who have mental retardation (Heal & Chadsey-Rusch, 1985; Landesman, 1986; Schalock et al., 1989). An even smaller number of survey instruments have been developed that specifically address the concerns of older adults with mental retardation (Hawkins, 1989). Thus, the *Life Satisfaction Scale for Aging Adults with Mental Retardation-Modified (LSS-M)* was developed to provide a measure of life satisfaction.

The *LSS-M* is a composition of the *Lifestyle Satisfaction Scale (LSS)* (Heal & Chadsey-Rusch, 1985) with added items that represent specific concerns of older adults to form the modified version. The original *LSS* contains subscales that assess: 1) friends and free time satisfaction, 2) satisfaction with services, 3) community satisfaction, and 4) general satisfaction. The additional questions address the following concerns: 1) work or retirement activity; 2) happiness and worry, including what people worry about (e.g., money, growing older, friends, death, and dying); and 3) self-perceived health status (Bradburn, 1969; Lawton, 1975; Wood, Wylie, & Sheafer, 1969). A more complete discussion of the reliability and validity of the instruments is available in Hawkins et al. (1991). Both instruments (*Leisure Assessment Inventory* and *LSS-M*) were administered in a structured interview in which care was taken to avoid difficult or emotionally

Traveling	Dancing
Singing	Sewing or weaving
Playing volleyball, basketball, or	Bicycling
baseball	Playing cards or chess or
Reading for pleasure	checkers
Camping or backpacking	Golfing
Watching television	Dating
Playing tennis	Snow skiing
Listening to the radio or record	Going to parties
player	Water skiing
Walking for pleasure	Doing things at a club or
Pottery making or painting	senior center
Gardening or taking care of plants	Picnicking or cooking
Going to art museums	outdoors
Going to the theater	Volunteering or helping
Taking classes	people
Jogging or running	Going to a concert
Relaxing or day dreaming	Going to a church or temple
Swimming	Playing shuffleboard
Playing a musical instrument	Talking on the telephone to
Fishing	friends
Shopping for pleasure	Riding horses
Working with tools	Visiting with friends or family
Watching a baseball or football game	Bowling
Taking pictures with a camera	Ice skating
Collecting things like stamps or	Cooking or baking for fun
shells	Exercising for fun or to be fit
Boating or canoeing	Taking care of pets
Dining out	Playing table tennis

Figure 9.1.   Leisure activities explored in the study.

laden language; avoid complex, abstract, or difficult concepts; maintain questions as short as possible; and structure questions to guard against acquiescence (Sigelman et al., 1983; Sudman & Bradburn, 1974). A private room at the day program site was used for the interviews.

Results

Three primary questions were asked about patterns of leisure participation. Additionally, a constraints scale was used to evaluate major barriers to participation (Hawkins et al., 1991). For the three primary questions, individuals were asked: 1) to indicate whether they were participating in 50 common leisure activities; 2) for those activities in which they were engaged, whether they preferred to increase participation or maintain it at the same level; and 3) for those activities in which they were *not* engaged, whether they were interested in initiating participation. With regard to activities that they indicated an interest in initiating, they were asked about 20 barriers to their participation. From this assess-

1. Do you *have* enough time to do these activities or do you *not have* enough time? If "not have," ask, Why don't you have enough time?
2. Do you *have* enough money to do these activities or do you *not have* enough money?
3. Are you *not afraid* of making a mistake when doing these activities or are you *afraid* of making a mistake?
4. Do you *have someone* to do these activities with or do you *not have someone*?
5. Do you *know how* to do these activities or do you *not know how*?
6. Would you do these activities with *anyone you know* or *only* with your friends?
7. Are you not too busy with *other* activities to do these activities or are you *too busy*? If "too busy," ask, What other activities are you too busy with?
8. Do you *have someone* to teach you how to do these activities or do you *not have someone* to teach you?
9. Do you feel you are *not too old* to learn these activities or are you *too old*?
10. Do you feel you are *not too sick* to do these activities or are you *too sick*?
11. Do you *have* transportation to these activities or do you *not have* transportation?
12. Would you *not feel* guilty or bad about doing these activities or would you *feel* guilty or bad?
13. Do you feel you would be *good* at these activities or do you feel you would *not be good*?
14. Are you *not afraid* of hurting yourself if you did these activities or are you *afraid* of hurting yourself.
15. Would your family or friends feel it was *okay* for you to do these activities or would they feel it was *not okay*?
16. Do you *have* enough energy to do these activities or do you *not have* enough energy?
17. Do *you* make the decision to do the activities or does *someone else* make the decision?
18. Do you *have* the equipment you need to do these activities or do you *not have* the equipment you need?
19. Do you *have* someplace to do these activities or do you *not have* someplace?
20. Are you *not afraid* that others would make fun of you if you did these activities or are you *afraid*?

Figure 9.2.   Leisure constraints explored in the study.

ment procedure, four indexes of leisure behavior were derived: 1) leisure activity participation (LAP), 2) leisure preferences for increasing participation (L-PREF), 3) leisure interest (L-INT), and 4) leisure constraint (L-CON).

Table 9.1 summarizes the means, standard deviations, and number of respondents for each index plus the overall measure of life satisfaction from the *LSS-M*. The results are organized by the two major groups of individuals, those

Table 9.1.   Means and standard deviations for activity indexes and life satisfaction scores

	$\bar{x}$	n	sd
With Down syndrome			
LSS-M	28.1	61	8.8
LAP	29.5	58	8.8
L-PREF	3.9	58	7.9
L-INT	9.6	58	6.1
L-CON	9.5	58	3.4
Without Down syndrome			
LSS-M	24.7	60	13.7
LAP	23.3	59	5.8
L-PREF	7.4	59	6.6
L-INT	13.7	59	8.9
L-CON	9.0	59	3.3

with Down syndrome and those without Down syndrome. (Missing cases have been deleted.)

Each of these variables was entered into an analysis of covariance for analyzing differences between the groups, using age as a covariate. Results of the analyses showed that the group with Down syndrome was not significantly different in life satisfaction compared with the group without syndrome. The covariate of age, however, was found to be significant in regard to life satisfaction. This finding suggests that all older individuals in this study were less satisfied with life.

For the index of leisure activity participation (LAP), there was no significant difference between the groups; however, the covariate of age was significant ($F = 27.23$, $p < .01$) in the negative direction. That is, the older the study participants were, the fewer the number of activities in which they were participating, regardless of whether they had Down syndrome or did not have Down syndrome. Age did not significantly affect indexes of preference (desire to increase or maintain the level of activity participation) and interest (desire to initiate new activity participation) in either group. However, the two groups did differ significantly from one another on these indexes. For leisure preference, the group with Down syndrome showed a significantly lower desire to increase involvement than the group without Down syndrome ($F = 5.91$, $p < .01$). For the index of leisure interest, participants with Down syndrome were again significantly lower in their interest in initiating involvement in new activities ($F = 7.37$, $p < .008$). The analysis that compared the two groups on perceived constraints resulted in no significant differences between the two groups, controlling for age.

Primary leisure participation patterns based on frequency of response to the 50 activities for each group were typical of the majority of adults with mental retardation. That is, they most commonly engaged in watching television or listening to the radio, visiting or calling friends, attending parties, going out to eat, shopping, some walking, and general relaxation. These activities tend to cluster in the relaxation or diversionary levels of intensity of expressive involvement according to the Gordon et al. (1976) typology and also constitute core activities across the life span. The most frequently cited activities in which individuals preferred to increase participation included going out to eat and socializing with friends by visiting or calling.

One prominent finding of the study was that a large number of individuals with Down syndrome did not indicate a desire to increase participation in any of the activities in which they were currently participating. This difference between the two groups represents an interesting topic for future research. There also was no similar or systematic pattern in the rank ordering of activities of interest between the two groups. In regard to constraints on leisure, both groups listed not knowing how to do the activity, not having the equipment, someone else making decisions about what they do, and the need for a friend to do the activity with as the most frequently encountered barriers to being able to try new activities.

The leisure indexes and life satisfaction measure were analyzed further for the purpose of exploring the relationship between leisure participation and life satisfaction. Multiple regression analyses were utilized to examine the potential of the indexes of leisure participation to explain individuals' perceived life satisfaction. These analyses were done separately for the group with Down syndrome and the group without Down syndrome. Table 9.2 presents the correlations for each leisure index with the life satisfaction measure.

For the group with Down syndrome, none of the indexes of leisure were found to be significant in explaining perceived life satisfaction. However, for the group without Down syndrome, two of the leisure indexes were found to be significant in explaining the variance in life satisfaction; these indexes were leisure activity participation (LAP), and leisure preference for increasing participation (L-PREF). The correlation between leisure participation and life satisfaction was positive ($r = .260$, $p < .05$); that is, the higher the level of activity participation, the higher the perceived life satisfaction. In contrast, there was a negative correlation between life satisfaction and leisure preference to increase

Table 9.2. Correlations between leisure activity participation indexes and life satisfaction measure

	LAP r	L-PREF r	L-INT r	L-CON r
With Down syndrome				
LSS-M	.114	−.152	.016	−.251
Without Down syndrome				
LSS-M	.260*	−.318**	−.238	−.187

*$p < .05$.
**$p < .01$.

participation ($r = -.318$, $p < .01$); that is, the lower the desire to increase participation, the higher the life satisfaction. When leisure activity participation was combined with preference to increase participation, 17% of the variance in life satisfaction was explained ($R^2 = .17$, $f = 5.87$, $p < .004$). Leisure interest and leisure constraint were not found to be significantly related to the life satisfaction measure in this study.

Discussion

While leisure participation has been presented as a factor that is important in contributing to perceived life satisfaction among older adults without mental disabilities (Lawton et al., 1986–1987; Riddick & Daniel, 1984; Tinsley et al., 1985), little is known about this area for older adults with mental retardation. The results of the study described in this chapter begin to shed some light on important functional and developmental concerns in this area.

The correlation between two of the leisure indexes and the life satisfaction measure confirms that leisure participation and life satisfaction are significantly related in later life. Specifically, in this study, leisure activity participation and leisure preference to increase participation among the group without Down syndrome were significantly related to perceived life satisfaction. For this group, the study results suggest that unfulfilled leisure preference to increase participation explains, in part, a lowered perceived life satisfaction in older adults with mental retardation (specifically, people without Down syndrome).

Age was shown to have a significant negative influence both on life satisfaction and on leisure activity participation in the group with Down syndrome and the group without Down syndrome; that is, older individuals had lower life satisfaction and were engaged in fewer leisure activities. When the two groups were compared with each other, however, they were not significantly different on either of these measures. Multiple regression analyses also revealed that, for the group without Down syndrome, activity participation was significant in explaining, in part, perceptions of life satisfaction. This finding is consistent with other research with older adults without mental disabilities (Kelly et al., 1986).

Controlling for age within each of the two groups revealed that older individuals were not significantly different from younger individuals on the measures of leisure preference or leisure interest. However, when the group with Down syndrome was compared with the group without Down syndrome, the group with Down syndrome had significantly lower desire to increase participation and significantly lower interest in initiating new activity participation. This pattern should be explored in future research in which other variables are examined. For example, research is needed on whether a difference in residential arrangement (e.g., the family home versus a group home) has a significant influence over degree of participation or in facilitating interest in new activities.

Based on previous gerontological research on leisure participation patterns across the life span (Kelly et al., 1986), the finding that, in both groups, overall, older individuals participated in fewer activities, was not unexpected. However, of some concern is the finding that the level of leisure preference for increasing participation in current activities and the level of interest in initiating new activities were significantly higher in the group without Down syndrome. These differences raise questions about possible unmet need for leisure participation of the individuals in the group without Down syndrome. Do these older persons have adequate opportunities to engage in familiar activities or to try new activities? These questions also suggest the need for further research, especially since this study has implications for retirement planning.

SUMMARY

In summary, the research agenda on leisure participation and life satisfaction for older adults with mental retardation, their families, and professionals is just beginning to emerge. Older adults with mental retardation need opportunities to receive preparation to make the transition from a work-oriented lifestyle to a retirement status wherein they have daily choices to pursue activities that promote their senses of involvement and well-being. Leisure skill building is a significant aspect of retirement preparation; thus, it is an important research area. Self-awareness, leisure awareness, attitudes, choice-making skills, social interaction, and leisure activity skills are easily assessed aspects of adult development and functioning. These are also functional areas that will benefit older adults in the maintenance of optimal health and well-being.

Future research on leisure participation and life satisfaction in older adults with mental retardation should include longitudinal designs to enable understanding of the impact of major life transitions (e.g., retirement) on the functional and developmental status of these individuals. Little is known about the role and importance of leisure in later-life satisfaction. Thus, as initiatives continue to mount in the development of retirement transition programs, sustained efforts to provide information about leisure interest, preferences, barriers to participation, and life satisfaction will enable progress to be made on a sound basis. With careful, empirically based planning, older adults with mental retardation will be supported to be fit, well, and involved in lifestyles that bring a sense of belonging and purpose in later life.

REFERENCES

Anderson, N. (1959). The use of time and energy. In J.E. Birren (Ed.), *Handbook of aging and the individual* (pp. 769–796). Chicago: University of Chicago Press.

Bradburn, N.M. (1969). *The structure of psychological well-being.* Chicago: Aldine.

Cutler, S.J., & Hendricks, J. (1990). Leisure and time use across the life course. In R.H. Binstock & L.K. George (Eds.), *Handbook of aging and the social sciences* (pp. 169–185). San Diego: Academic Press.

DeGrazia, S. (1962). *Of time, work and leisure.* New York: The Twentieth Century Fund.

Dumazedier, J. (1967). *Toward a society of leisure*. McClure, S.E. (Trans.). New York: Free Press.

Ekerdt, D.J. (1986). The busy ethic: Moral continuity between work and retirement. *The Gerontologist, 26*(3), 239–244.

George, L.K. (1982). Models of transition in middle and later life. *Annals of the American Academy of Political and Social Science, 464,* 22–37.

George, L.K., & Bearon, L.C. (1980). *Quality of life in older persons—Meaning and measurement.* New York: Human Sciences Press.

Gordon, C., Gaitz, C.M., & Scott, J. (1976). Leisure and lives: Personal expressivity across the life span. In R.H. Binstock & E. Shannas (Eds.), *Handbook on aging and the social sciences* (pp. 310–341). New York: Van Nostrand Reinhold.

Havighurst, R.J. (1972). Life style and leisure patterns: Their evolution through the life cycle. *International Course in Social Gerontology, Proceedings, 3,* 35–48.

Havighurst, R.J. (1973). Social rules, work, leisure, and education. In C. Eisdorfor & M.P. Lawton (Eds.), *The psychology of adult development and aging* (pp. 598–618). Washington, DC: American Psychological Association.

Hawkins, B. (1989). Life satisfaction, activity patterns and constraints on leisure: Measurement protocols for older adults with mental retardation. In L.H. McAvoy & D. Howard (Eds.), *Abstracts from the 1989 Symposium on Leisure Research* (p. 27). Alexandria, VA: National Recreation and Park Association.

Hawkins, B.A. (1991). An exploration of adaptive skills and leisure activity of older adults with mental retardation. *Therapeutic Recreation Journal, 17*(4), 9–27.

Hawkins, B.A., Eklund, S.J., & Martz, B. (1991). *Detection of decline in aging adults with developmental disabilities*. Cincinnati, OH: Rehabilitation Research and Training Center Consortium on Aging and Developmental Disabilities.

Hawkins, B.A., & Kultgen, P. (1991). *The challenge presented by an aging population.* Concept paper submitted to the Indiana Governor's Planning Council for People with Disabilities, Indianapolis. Indiana University, Institute for the study of Developmental Disabilities.

Heal, L.W., & Chadsey-Rusch, J. (1985). The Lifestyle Satisfaction Scale (LSS): Assessing individuals' satisfaction with residence, community setting and associated services. *Applied Research in Mental Retardation, 6,* 475–490.

Hutchison, P., & Lord, J. (1979). *Recreation integration: Issues and alternatives in leisure services and community involvement.* Ottawa, Ontario, Canada: Leisurability Publications, Inc.

Kelly, J.R. (1987). *Recreation trends: Toward the year 2000.* Champaign, IL: Management Learning Laboratories.

Kelly, J.R., Steinkamp, M.W., & Kelly, J. (1986). Later life leisure: How they play in Peoria. *The Gerontologist, 26*(5), 531–537.

Landesman, S. (1986). Quality of life and personal satisfaction: Definition and measurement issues. *Mental Retardation, 24,* 141–143.

Lawton, M.P. (1975). The Philadelphia Geriatric Center Morale Scale: A revision. *Journal of Gerontology, 30,* 59–85.

Lawton, M.P., Ross, M., & Fulcomer, M. (1986–1987). Objective and subjective uses of time by older people. *International Journal of Aging and Human Development, 24*(3), 171–187.

McGuire, F.A. (1979). *An exploratory study of leisure constraints in advanced adulthood.* Doctoral dissertation, University of Illinois-Champaign.

McGuire, F.A. (1984). A factor analytic study of leisure constraints in advanced adulthood. *Leisure Sciences, 6,* 313–326.

Mead, M. (1957). The pattern of leisure in contemporary American culture. *Annals, 313*, 11–15.

Mead, M. (1960). Work, leisure, and creativity, *Daedalus, 89*, 13–23.

Reisman, D. (1952). Some observations on changes in leisure activities. *The Antioch Review, 12*, 417–436.

Riddick, C.A., & Daniel, S.N. (1984). The relative contribution of leisure activities and other factors to the mental health of older women. *Journal of Leisure Research, 16*(2), 136–148.

Schalock, R.L., Keith, D.D., Hoffman, K., & Karan, O.C. (1989). Quality of life: Its measurement and use. *Mental Retardation, 27*, 25–31.

Sigelman, C.K., Schoenrock, C.J., Budd, E.C., Winer, J.L., Spanhel, C.L., Martin, P.W., Hronmas, S., & Bensberg, G.J. (1983). *Communicating with mentally retarded persons: Asking questions and getting answers.* Lubbock: Texas Tech University, Research and Training Center in Mental Retardation.

Sudman, S., & Bradburn, N.M. (1974). *Response effects in surveys: A review and synthesis.* Chicago: Aldine Publishing Company.

Tinsley, H.E.A., Teaff, J.D., Colbs, S.L., & Kaufman, N. (1985). A system of classifying leisure activities in terms of the psychological benefits of participation reported by older adults. *Journal of Gerontology, 40*(2), 172–178.

Veblen, T. (1953). *The theory of the leisure class.* New York: Mentor Books. (Original work published 1899)

Wood, V., Wylie, M.L., & Sheafer, B. (1969). An analysis of a short self-report measure of life satisfaction: Correlation with rater judgment. *Journal of Gerontology, 24*, 465–469.

10

Psychological Adjustment in Midlife for Persons with Mental Retardation

Gary B. Seltzer

Midlife is an important marker, a midpoint between birth and death. As such, it has developmental challenges associated with it, including coping with the reality of one's increasing morbidity and mortality (Gould, 1978). For many people, approaching or avoiding the midlife transition produces psychological struggle and stress. For others, it can be a time of personality growth and development (Levinson, Darrow, Klein, Levinson, & McKee, 1978; Vaillant, 1977).

Investigators have paid almost no attention to the normative developmental transitions experienced by the majority of adults with mental retardation in the middle age, post-World War II generation. This absence has been accompanied by a conspicuous lack of theory and research dedicated to understanding personality development in persons with mental retardation. The lack of a program of study of personality development in adults with mental retardation, including the "recurring, long-term aspects of behavior that characterize individual differences" (Cromwell, 1967, p. 67), persists in spite of the rapid proliferation of ideology (e.g., Taylor, Bogdan, & Racino, 1991; Wolfensberger, 1972) that promotes the acceptance of individual differences.

Much of the ideology of the 1970s and 1980s emphasized the environmental side of the nature–nurture developmental dichotomy. Opportunities for persons to live, work, recreate, and love in normative settings were emphasized (Baker, Seltzer, & Seltzer, 1977). Making socially normative opportunities available was assumed to benefit the development and life satisfaction of adults with mental retardation.

The intent to include persons with mental retardation in the community, minimizing their intellectual and social differences and maximizing their humanity, was an appropriate response to the stereotypical characterization of these persons in society. This stereotypical presentation of persons with mental retardation was paralleled in the personality and developmental literature. Persons with mental retardation were characterized, for example, as rigid, suggestible, and impulsive.

The extant research on personality and development was methodologically flawed by selection problems and by the traditional procedures used to assess personality (MacMillian, 1982). Rarely were adults selected as study participants, but inferences to all ages were drawn. Most personality assessment instruments, such as projective tests and self-report protocols, required considerable verbal ability. Actual limitations in verbal abilities were complicated further by the assumption that most persons with mental retardation could not speak for themselves. Against this backdrop of negative personality characterizations and methodological flaws, researchers ceased the study of adult development and personality development for persons with mental retardation. Thus, there remain many unanswered and provocative questions about adult development in midlife among persons with mental retardation. The failure to ask these questions may be misunderstood to mean that adults with mental retardation are not capable of normative developmental patterns.

Questions that might be addressed include: To what extent does personality development actually follow developmentally normative patterns among persons with mental retardation? How do these patterns relate to the assumption of adult social roles? Do these roles change as persons with mental retardation move through the adult life course? Controlling for cognitive ability, to what extent do personality characteristics mediate the psychosocial and other achievements of persons with mental retardation? How do role transitions and development vary with different environmental opportunities? Under what conditions, if any, do persons with mental retardation experience a midlife crisis?

Given the lack of knowledge about personality and adult development in persons with mental retardation, researchers can begin to address the questions above only by extrapolating from the burgeoning life span and adult development literatures (Baltes, Reese, & Nesselroade, 1988). Although there are methodological problems in extrapolating from one population to another (M. Seltzer, 1985), the purpose of this chapter is to do just that: to extrapolate from the generic adult developmental literature while examining developmental and personality patterns that may occur among persons with mental retardation in midlife.

This chapter offers a primarily theoretical presentation of developmental and personality challenges related to midlife and persons with mental retardation. There are few empirical studies; thus, developmental theories are used to organize and help interpret observations drawn from the literature on normative development in midlife. There are many sociodemographic, health, and cognitive variables that influence diversity among middle aged persons with mental retardation—too many to be included in this chapter. These limitations are reflected in the scope of the chapter and in the knowledge base from which this chapter crafts its investigation of midlife development and personality in persons with mental retardation.

In the first section of this chapter, the normative definition and nature of aging and its meaning for persons with mental retardation are examined. In the next two sections the major theories of adult development and midlife are examined, and the theoretical constructs are applied to midlife developmental issues for persons with mental retardation. The last section presents a schematic model that illustrates the relationships among antecedent conditions, developmental tasks, and expected developmental outcomes, and highlights dimensions of quality of life for middle-age persons with mental retardation.

THE NATURE AND MEANING OF AGING

Sometime around the age of 40, people realize that their lives are about half over. The childhood fantasies of wanting to accelerate time in order to grow up and have the privileges and power of adulthood become the opposite; now a primal wish is to arrest the flow of time and to stop the aging process. The desire to be immortal competes with the realities, meaning, and substance of aging, including physical changes, social changes, and psychological changes. Biologically, people are programmed to age. Physical ontogeny, the process of biological regulation that accounts for age-related changes, occurs among all people. However, as people age, they interact with their environment socially and psychologically, accumulating life histories and adapting to the changes that occur inside and outside of themselves. Physical and social environments, thus, affect the course of physical ontogeny. In fact, interindividual differences, that is, differences in patterns of change across individuals, increase as people age. The accumulated interactions among biological, social, and psychological factors result in greater diversity among people; the longer people live, the greater the differences among them (Neugarten & Neugarten, 1986).

It follows then, that in formulating theories about the aging process, researchers have stressed biological (Lochshin & Zakeri, 1990; Rossman, 1980); psychological (Bengston, Reedy & Gordon, 1985; G. Seltzer, 1985); and social (Adams, 1987; Lowy, 1980; Maddox, 1970) aging factors. Each of these perspectives is important. Together, they provide a holistic picture of the multifaceted nature of aging.

When years are used as the measure of aging, the *chronological and biological* aspects of aging are emphasized. The physiological changes that occur during midlife usually are less obvious than those that occur during childhood and old age. Nevertheless, there are recognizable signs of aging at midlife, such as decreased elasticity of the skin with the accompanying wrinkles, the need for reading glasses, the irregularity and eventual cessation of menstruation, the graying of hair and eventual balding, decreased muscle tone, a tendency toward increase in weight, and an increasing probability of morbidity and mortality related to chronic or acute diseases of the cardiovascular and musculoskeletal systems. These and other biological changes in the human body confront middle aged persons with the need to accommodate progressively their biological destiny or with the situation of remaining in conflict with it. For persons with mental retardation and a known organic etiology, it may be appropriate to place even more emphasis on the biological and chronological determinants of middle age, as there is evidence that their aging is atypical (see Adlin, chap. 2, this volume; Zigman, Seltzer, Adlin, & Silverman, 1991).

PERSPECTIVES ON AGING

Psychological aging refers to both age-related cognitive changes (Seltzer, 1985a) and the affective reactions one experiences related to the perception of and meaning one associates with the aging process. In this society, a society that generally devalues aging, adults are discouraged from feeling or looking their age. It is an insult to tell people that they look their age. Given this negative perception of aging, a statement such as, "I feel younger these days than I did 10 years ago," suggests that a person's chronological age is not impeding, and may even be enhancing, his or her psychological assessment of well-being. In fact, there are some developmental theorists who believe that people should welcome old age.

On the one hand, according to Gutmann (1987) *successful aging* occurs when one challenges the notion of adjustment to age-related losses and, instead, develops new abilities and seeks new challenges. On the other hand, when people feel much older than their chronolgoical age, they usually are despairing about the losses associated with aging, for example, losses of youth, intimacy, children at home, parents, or physical health.

People age biologically; at the same time, people can maintain and even improve their psychological and, correspondingly, their physical sense of well-being. Physically, successful aging is associated with, among other things, a healthy diet, regular exercise, and avoiding tobacco and heavy alcohol consumption (Perlmutter & Hall, 1992). Psychologically, being included socially, being autonomous, and having control over one's environment are greatly associated with successful aging. A number of investigators have studied the deleterious psychological effects and the corresponding physical deterioration that occur when people feel infantilized and unable to control their lives (Langer, 1989; Rodin, 1986; Rowe & Kahn, 1987). Given society's propensity for overprotecting and restricting the autonomy of persons with mental retardation, one wonders how and under what conditions successful aging occurs for them.

The ability to assess oneself relative to one's chronological age and to compare where one fits with where others fit along the age continuum requires a concrete operational level of cognitive ability. A person's cognitive ability to make this comparison can be assessed by the measure of one's attainment of the ability to perform classification skills. When a person has achieved this cognitive ability, he or she can group objects according to some dimension they share (e.g., age) (Piaget & Inhelder, 1969). Going to the next step, that is deriving psychological meaning from the comparison, may require an even higher level of cognitive ability, that is, the operational level of cognitive ability. Generally, persons with this ability also are able to think abstractly and symbolically and can therefore react psychologically to the symbolic meaning of the aging process (Seltzer, 1989). Most persons with mild and some with moderate mental retardation have the cognitive ability to assess themselves along the aging continuum (Lipe-Goodson & Goebel, 1983). In spite of this ability, often persons with mental retardation make reference to themselves as being much younger than their chronological age. When a person's cognitive ability to retain knowledge of his or her correct age is present, but the person, for reasons other than vanity, refers to himself or herself as younger, there is a need for investigation of the psychological correlates of the error. For persons with mental retardation, the relationship between being treated like a younger person (and perhaps living with few adult roles) and the error of conceiving of oneself as younger bears investigation.

In one of the only studies to ask older persons with mental retardation their perceptions of aging, Erickson, Krauss, and Seltzer (1989) found that participants were able to articulate a large number of codeable categories of statements that described their perceptions of aging. The categories of these statements included anticipated physical health changes; general acknowledgment of one's own aging; anticipated work-related changes; anticipated social life changes; associations with death, dying, or depression; and denial of aging. The investigators noted that statements in the last category included emphatic claims such as, "I not old yet," "Getting old doesn't mean anything," or "I haven't thought of that yet; I'm not looking forward to it." According to the investigators, another form of denial occurred when some participants perceived themselves as younger than they really were, as illustrated when one participant said, "I look 16, but I'm 52." Because participants were able to share so many concerns and aspirations related to their psychological and social well-being as they aged, the investigators concluded the study by recommending extensive research on the psychological and social adaptations to aging.

THE SOCIAL PROCESS OF AGING

Critical to understanding the *social process of aging* is the timing of social roles and events. Neugarten (1968b) has stressed the importance of attending to the social as well as the biological clock when studying the aging process. Her research suggests that personality changes in adulthood are a function of social definition and age-appropriate behavior together with biological aging. The types of social roles that people play and the timing of these roles in comparison to those played by peers shape and modify the adult personality. Specifically, Neugarten (1979) stated, "Leaving the parents' home, marriage, parenthood, occupational achievement, one's own children leaving home, the climacteric, grandparenthood, retirement—these are the normal turning points, the punctuation marks along the lifeline. They call forth changes in self-concept and identity but whether or not they produce crises depends on their timing" (p. 888). For Neugarten, adult development unfolds because certain social roles occur, but not necessarily according to a predictable chronological age. She has suggested that society has become increasingly diverse and that there is no longer a particular age when, for example, women marry, have children, or enter the labor force.

However, contextual theorists do attribute meaning to the way that social, historical, or other life events (e.g., having first child when married or single, divorcing) affect one's development and personality (Kogan, 1990). Although cultures vary, as do historical periods, in holding age-related life cycle expectations for their members, all people grow up expecting to experience specific events within specific time periods of their lives. The assumptive world, that is, everything people know or think they know about themselves (Parkes, 1971), is influenced by these expectations. When a person is off cycle, for example, when teenagers have children or grandparents care for their grandchildren, there is a higher probability that the person will feel out of sync with his or her peers. Being thrown off cycle by some event unexpectedly occurring or not occuring is likely to cause people to experience an intrapsychic crisis. In this theory of adult development, the social expectations or timing of events (Rossi, 1980) is the focal point in assessing normative development.

When the trajectory of events and transitions is influenced by an impairment, such as mental retardation, a person's life may not fulfill the expected social expectations, an outcome which is likely to have a negative effect on a person's sense of self. Furthermore, persons with mental retardation may not be engaged sufficiently in planning for expression of their assumptive selves (Mount, Beeman, & Ducharme, 1988). Research suggests that for persons who set long-term goals early in their adult years, even if they do not reach these goals, in midlife they are more likely to show self-control, independence, and psychological mindedness (Helson & Moane, 1987). It seems that enhancing midlife empowerment for persons with mental retardation should be brought about through a planning process in early adulthood that is mindful of the future social goals and objectives held by these individuals (Mount & Zwernik, 1988).

MIDLIFE AND DEVELOPMENTAL THEORY

Stage Theories of Development

Since the 1960s, developmental theorists and other social scientists have become interested in studying adult development and aging. Levinson et al. (1978) noted that, historically, the great figures in development, Freud (1964) and Piaget (1972), assumed that development was mostly complete by the end of adolescence. Jung (1968), a contemporary of Freud, was among the first to distinguish adult development in general, and specifically the first half of life from the second half. He described the first half as having two stages: childhood and youth. These stages are oriented primarily to adaptation and conformity to the *outer* world. During the second half of life the focus of development shifts from the outer world to the inner world, from an extroverted lifestyle to an introverted one. Jung's formulation stresses that the "afternoon of life" is not just an appendage to life's morning but has significance of its own.

Theories that conceive of adulthood as a sequence of stages point out midlife as one of those stages. The term "transition" implies that there is a change occurring. In life transitions specifically, there is movement from a relatively stable or quiescent period of personality development to another phase of life, one that is accompanied by new developmental tasks and social role expectations for adaptive behavior. A developmental task is a normative achievement expected of a person relative to his or her age, social class, ethnic background, and other pertinent demographic delimiters (Havighurst, 1972). The process of growth that unfolds during any one phase is related to the successful mastery of age-appropriate developmental tasks and social roles in all of the former phases of development. From this perspective, psychological development is conceived of as progressive change in one's adaptive behavior.

Stage theorists who study emotional, cognitive, or moral development assume that development is biologically programmed, an epigenetic unfolding that proceeds in an invariant, hierarchical sequence of stages. Theorists such as Freud (1964), Erikson (1982), Piaget (1972), and Kohlberg (1978) contended that growth and development occur as a function of resolution of specific challenges posed within each stage. Once the tasks of a stage are mastered, there may be a quiescent period followed by the transition to new developmental challenges. Thus, each stage is viewed as having unique content but being dependent upon the dynamic resolution of tasks from previously completed stages, and the complexity of the stages increases in a hierarchical fashion. These theories posit that the unfolding of increasingly complex stages is both biologically based and a function of the increasingly demanding role expectations in the social environment.

Theories of Stability in Development

Stage theories of development are not without their critics. McCrae and Costa (1990), after extensive empirical investigation, have concluded that personality does not change and develop through a hierarchical invariant sequence of increasingly complex and differentiated stages; instead, after the age of 30, it remains stable throughout adulthood. They argue that who an individual is remains the same, but as life goes on, what an individual experiences changes. They have identified five factors that they suggest account for all the traits identified in scientific theories of personality. Using the Baltimore Longitudinal Study of Aging data set, McCrae and Costa (1990) found that people scored similarly on these five factors over an adult lifetime. These are agreeableness, conscientiousness, neuroticism, extraversion, and openness to experience. They believe that it is important to study how enduring personalities affect the aging processes and shape the life course rather than predicting the personality changes that are a function of age, and the associated social, biological, psychological, and historical changes.

Later in this chapter, the work of Zigler and his colleagues is reviewed. They, too, suggest that there are identifiable personality structures found among many persons with mental retardation. These personality structures are seen as antecedent conditions that influence the experience of performing developmental tasks.

Pearlin (1980) stressed the dominant role of societal demands in contrast to that of age or stage. He suggested that there are many developmental patterns shaped by the "confluence of the social characteristics of adults, their standing in the social order, the problematic experiences to which they must adapt, the social contexts and situations in which they are embedded, and the coping resources with which they are equipped" (p. 177).

Interestingly, the McCrae and Costa trait theory of personality and the Pearlin social system view represent the two sides of a debate as to whether mental retardation is itself a trait, is a relatively stable characteristic that exists across a range of situations, or exists only to the extent that people persist in labeling other people as having mental retardation (Braginsky & Braginsky, 1971). On the one hand, Zigler and Hodapp (1986) argue that since intelligence is a relatively stable and continuous trait, someone with subnormal intellectual functioning has mental retardation, whether given this label or not. Mercer (1973), on the other hand, argues against the trait theory, saying, "A person may be mentally retarded in one system and not mentally retarded in another" (p. 31). This chapter suggests that in exploring midlife development for persons with mental retardation, both their level of mental retardation—or their intelligence trait—and the social role expectations are important. In fact, the following discussion of midlife development and mental retardation is based on these and other factors.

MENTAL RETARDATION, DEVELOPMENTAL THEORY, AND MIDLIFE

Social Roles and Environment

Developmental challenges and their associated tasks can be understood within the context of expectations related to the adult social roles in family, work, community, and leisure (Havighurst, 1973). The emphasis on role underscores the point that human behavior is socially patterned and environmentally stimulated (Perlman, 1968). During the 1970s and 1980s, many professionals in the field of mental retardation supported the ideology of normalization and deinstitutionalization in order to foster community inclusion and developmental growth of persons with mental retardation. Wolfensberger's (1972) exposition on normalization emphasized the "utilization of means which are as culturally normative as possible, in order to establish and/or maintain personal behaviors and characteristics which are as culturally normative as possible" (p. 28). Later, Wolfensberger (1983) became even more explicit about the value of social roles in that he substituted the term "social role valorization" for normalization, a change that underscores the importance of environmental opportunities for persons with mental retardation. Most of the research available to address the impact of environmental opportunities comes from comparisons of residential environments, particularly comparisons between institutional and community-based residential settings. Empirical findings suggest that environmental influences during adulthood do play a critical role in helping to stimulate the potential for growth and development among persons with mental retardation. Eyman and Widaman (1987) examined longitudinal changes in adaptive behavior in a group of adults with mental retardation who lived in either community-based or institutional settings. Life span improvements in adpatvie behavior were observed for persons with mild and moderate mental retardation and some with severe mental retardation who lived in community-based settings. For example, individuals with mild and moderate mental retardation who lived in community settings made considerable gains in intellectual abilities across the life span. In contrast, those who lived in institutions experienced decrements in intellectual abilities after age 21. These findings, though suggestive that environment influences adaptive behavior throughout the life cycle, need to be interpreted cautiously since selection and/or assignment of who was placed or remained in each kind of setting was not determined randomly. Thus, although there is evidence that developmental growth occurs in adulthood, it is not known to what extent this growth may be related to environmental changes, in this case, in residential environments.

Quality of Life

There are a few other large scale studies that document the adaptive behavior, cognitive, and mental health changes associated with adulthood. (See Zigman et al., 1991, for a review of this literature.) Generating suitable developmental norms for middle aged persons with mental retardation remains a challenge. The culturally normative transitions expected earlier in adulthood—the movement from school to the work world and, later in life, the movement from work to retirement—provide clearer milestones to guide assessment and support for developmental transitions in the lives of people with mental retardation than do transitions in midlife. In fact, some investigators have suggested that there is a tedium in life quality for some middle-age persons with mental retardation. According to this literature, once a person with mental retardation reaches midlife, less attention is paid to his or her developmental growth, social roles, and quality of life than was earlier. Koch (1986) noted that this lack of attention fosters the impression that after the age of 30 or 35 people with mental retardation have reached their potential, and little more can be done to promote growth. Koch pointed out that the consequences of this impression are "that advancing life is an experience where close relationships are few, and growing fewer, where daily activities, whether in the residential or vocational setting, are characterized by the sameness day by day and where leisure-time activities are limited to watching television, going on occasional shopping trips, or attending day programs in agencies . . . . The looking forward to which most of us have been acculturated seems to reveal nothing but a blank page for retarded persons entering middle life" (pp. 1–2). Similarly, in a review of the impact of deinstitutionalization on the lives of persons with mental retardation, Emerson (1985) concluded that persons with mental retardation who live in the community interact mainly with other people with disabilities and paid staff, experience loneliness as a considerable problem, continue to be excluded from the labor force, and experience minimal autonomy in their lives.

In contrast, the longitudinal studies of Edgerton and his colleagues (Edgerton, 1967; Edgerton & Bercovici, 1976; Edgerton, Bollinger, & Herr, 1984; Edgerton & Gaston, 1991) have shown an increased level of independence among study participants with mild mental retardation and reported an increasingly higher degree of life satisfaction during the 30 or more years that they spent in the community following deinstitutionalization. When Edgerton (1988) described the quality of life of the remaining participants, he suggested that it paralleled that of their neighbors of low income and little education. It is worth noting that, generally, participants in Edgerton's study had better cognitive and functional abilities than persons who have been deinstitutionalized subsequently. Additionally, many participants did not receive formal services from the mental retardation services system after deinstitutionalization. Edgerton et al. (1984) suggested that their participants, having survived without the aid of services of the developmental disabilities network, were more self-reliant. "There is something almost indomitable about these people. They truly believed that somehow they would manage. No doubt they forgot some of the debts that they owned to their benefactors, but they had few enough debts to agencies, and none at all to those funded to help mentally retarded persons" (pp. 350–351). Both the factors of higher functional level and remaining outside the mental retardation services system may be reasons for the better quality of life reported in Edgerton's study as compared with that reported in other studies. In addition, the number of Edgerton's participants fell from 48 to 15 between the 2 decades of observation, an attrition rate that may account for a select group of persons capable of remaining outside of the formal services system.

Receiving formal residential services does benefit the lives of some adults with mental retardation. Halpern, Close, and Nelson (1986) studied the impact of semi-independent living programs and found that the majority of persons living in these programs were well adjusted, with little evidence of movement into more restrictive settings or other serious problems. Data for this study were collected in 1981 and 1982. At that time the authors noted the mean age of their subjects to be 28. Nearly 80% of the sample was between the ages of 16 and 30. These investigators commented that a relatively important age segment of the group, persons who were middle age and older, was not being served by these semi-independent programs. Of course, in the early 1990s, the majority of persons who remain in the program are middle age, and one wonders how they have fared after 10 years in the community. How well have they become included socially in the community? Do they have more friends in their support network? These investigators did find that the major problems experienced by these residents of semi-independent programs were unemployment, underemployment, and too few leisure activities outside of the home. Both employment and leisure remain critical domains in improving community inclusion and developing an understanding of individual differences and characteristics that influence interactions with others (Hogg, 1991).

Investigative Difficulties

Although community inclusion has been a focus for program innovation and study, the effects of these programs on personality development and role fulfillment for middle age persons with mental retardation remain under investigation. Zigler and Balla (1982) noted the tendency among professionals in the field of mental retardation to overemphasize the importance of cognitive functioning to the exclusion of personality and motivational issues. Furthermore, Zigler and Balla pointed out that this exclusion continues in spite of the research evidence that suggests that community adjustment is more a function of personality factors and poor social adjustment than a function of intelligence.

It is difficult, however, to investigate developmental patterns, personality characteristics, and social role heterogeneity of persons with mental retardation. Some of this difficulty is related to the poor quality of life conditions that many persons with mental retardation have experienced, including marginal incomes, institutionalization, and surrogate social support systems. Poverty and institutionalization are extreme conditions that increase the risk of health, mental health, and other problems that negatively influence normative developmental trajectories. Thus, it is difficult to determine what in these individuals lives is due to these environmental conditions and what is related to individual characteristics.

Selections of study participants also is problematic because many adults with mental retardation are unknown to the services system (Jacobson, Sutton, & Janicki, 1985), and, therefore, population characteristics can only be estimated. In addition, it is estimated that as many as 40% of persons with mental retardation are unknown to the services system (Krauss, 1988). Their quality of life and adult social roles are not examined.

Social Support Networks

The limitation of social roles is evidenced most dramatically by those few studies that have looked at the social support systems of adults with mental retardation. Krauss and Erickson (1988) found smaller social support networks for persons living with their families in comparison with those living in community or institutional residences. National estimates are that more than 80% of U.S. citizens with mental retardation live with their families (Fujiura, Garza, & Braddock, 1990; Lakin, 1985). The vast majority of these persons may have much social contact with their family members but correspondingly limited social roles from which to develop a broad array of social supports and social inclusion. Krauss, Seltzer, and Goodman (1992) also found that although the adults living with their mothers tended to have large and active support networks, nearly three quarters of the networks were composed of family members, and almost half of the participants had no friends included in their networks. For 40% of those who had friends, the same friends were part of their mothers' social support networks. The mean age of these shared friends was 58.1, suggesting that these friends most likely were the mothers' friends whom the mothers perceived to be in a supportive relationship with their adult children with mental retardation. One must conclude from these data on social support networks that adults with mental retardation who live with their families are not developing friendships and supports typically found in the lives of individuals living on their own and fulfilling adult social and work-related roles. It seems that there is a restricted range of experiences available to middle-age persons with mental retardation, mostly those who live with their families. This conclusion requires some expansive thinking, which the following schematic model is presented to facilitate.

A SCHEMATIC MODEL OF MIDLIFE PSYCHOLOGICAL ADJUSTMENT

Figure 10.1 depicts six developmental tasks and their systemically related antecedent conditions and classes of outcomes. The outline for this model is derived from one designed by the author for studying psychological adjustment among older adults with developmental disabilities (G. Seltzer, 1985). As was true of that schematic model, this model is presented as a heuristic device. It depicts only some of the domains relevant to an understanding of the meaning of midlife for persons with mental retardation. In addition, the model is offered with the knowledge of its limitations imposed by the lack of empirical verification. Hopefully, as a schematic illustration of systemic relationships among developmental variables, it will serve as a guidepost for empirical studies and clinical interventions.

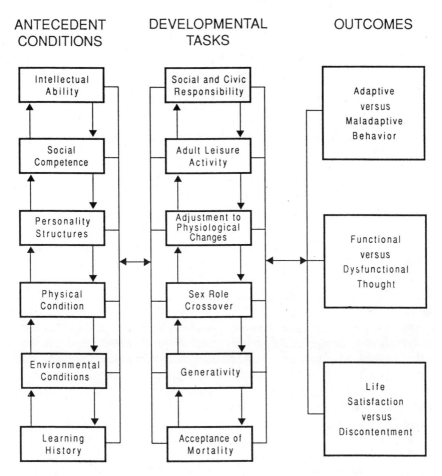

ANTECEDENT   DEVELOPMENTAL   OUTCOMES
CONDITIONS   TASKS

Figure 10.1. A schematic model of midlife psychological adjustment experienced by persons with developmental disabilities.

Antecedent Conditions

Antecedent conditions are viewed in this model as factors that influence experience and completion of midlife developmental tasks. The first of these antecedent conditions listed in Figure 10.1 is *intellectual ability*. As noted earlier, Eyman and his colleagues (Eyman & Arndt, 1982; Eyman, Borthwick, & Miller, 1981; Eyman & Widaman, 1987) have studied the relationship between intellectual abilities and adaptive behavior. It has been hypothesized that the expression of behavioral potential probably lies in the interaction between intellectual ability and *environmental conditions*, another antecedent condition listed in the figure. For example, Eyman and Widaman (1987) noted that when they controlled for level of mental retardation, adaptive behavior level varied according to residential status, another environmental antecedent condition.

The interaction effect described in the example above and those that result from other possible combinations of antecedent conditions are depicted in Figure 10.1 by the bi-directional and continuous flow of arrows among the boxes containing the six antecedent conditions. The research of Zigler and his colleagues (Zigler & Balla, 1972, 1982; Zigler & Butterfield, 1968; Zigler & Yando, 1972) is reviewed below to illustrate the relationships among all the antecedent conditions.

Zigler and Balla (1982) pointed out that the assessment of *intellectual ability* depends upon measuring: 1) formal cognitive abilities such as reasoning, memory, abstract ability, and speed of information processing; 2) the ability to acquire specific information to be used in problem-solving; and 3) a variety of personality factors including motivational style. Moving down Figure 10.1 from intellectual ability to the next antecedent condition, *social comptence*, it can be argued that a person's social competence is also influenced by formal intellectual abilities, knowledge of and previous experience in the situation (i.e., learning history), and *personality structures*. To illustrate, Zigler and Balla (1982) suggested that given some minimal intellectual level, the most important transition for people with mental retardation to achieve is the shift from dependence to independence. This transition toward social competence allows persons with mental retardation to become self-sustaining members of society. The extent to which this shift is likely to occur is influenced by *personality structures* (another antecedent condition) such as outerdirectedness, strong social approach and avoidance tendencies, and expectation of failure. Furthermore, Zigler and his colleagues (Balla, 1976; Balla & Zigler, 1975, 1982; Zigler, 1963; Zigler & Balla, 1972) have demonstrated that there is an increased probability that socially and intellectually debilitating personality structures and motivational styles will be expressed among persons with mental retardation with a history of social deprivation (which is itself a function of *environmental conditions* and *learning history*, two more antecedent conditions).

The body of research on the effect of environmental conditions on personality structures and intellectual ability illustrates well the impact of antecedent conditions on midlife development. Midlife adjustment patterns in persons with mental retardation who were reared in environmentally deprived settings would be different from patterns of those reared in enriched settings. The former group is more likely to seek social approval, that is, be externally directed, whereas the latter group will tend to be more internally directed. Among the implications of these findings is that when individuals with mental retardation are deinstitutionalized (usually before or during midlife) and then expected to make choices about their lives, some are likely to be directed more by external cues than by internal desires. Decision-making in midlife, or in adulthood in general, is a skill that needs to be developed over a long period of time in those who have disadvantaged social histories. The decision-making process relies upon an ability to trust one's internal desires rather than be swayed for the reinforcement of social approval.

In addition, Zigler and his colleagues (Zigler, Balla, & Hodapp, 1984) have argued for a "two-group approach" to understanding the development of persons with mental retardation, based on the presence or absence of a known organic etiology for the mental retardation. According to Zigler et al. (1984) the presence of a known abnormal *physical condition* (another antecedent condition) results in the expression of "two distributions of intelligence—one for those whose intelligence is accounted for by some interaction between hereditary and environmental components, the other for those whose intellectual apparatus has been physically damaged, thus altering the biological side of the formula" (p. 219). Zigler (1967) contended that persons with mental retardation of unknown organic etiology develop at a slower rate than persons without mental retardation. Thus, although there is a difference in rate and sometimes degree of developmental growth, the sequencing of stages is the same as in persons without mental retardation. In contrast, persons with a known organic etiology for their mental retardation show cognitive and behavioral patterns that are qualitatively different from those of both persons without mental retardation and persons with no known organic etiology for their mental retardation. (See Weisz, Yeates, & Zigler [1982]; Zigler [1969]; Zigler et al. [1984].) Data about premature aging, or precocious aging, and Down syndrome (e. g., Zigman et al., 1991) may be additional confirmation of Zigler's position that persons with known organic syndromes are not just delayed in their development but instead actually develop in atypical ways.

This section has examined one body of research that illustrates the interrelationships among the antecedent conditions delineated in Figure 10.1. These antecedent conditions set the stage for the unfolding of the developmental tasks described in the following section.

Developmental Tasks

Since the 1970s, it has become fashionable to expect that during midlife disruptive behaviors such as fighting with one's children and spouse and feeling dissatisfied with one's job, home life, and self are not pathological but rather a function of a "predictable crisis of adult life," the midlife crisis (Sheehy, 1976). The existence of this adult crisis has been supported by reputable scholars such as Gould (1972), Levinson et al. (1978), and Vaillant (1977), at least for the predominantly white, male, middle-class group that each of these investigators studied.

There are a few critics who note that the midlife crisis has been popularized beyond the boundaries of scientific foundation. Costa and McCrae (1980) studied midlife crisis in two large groups of men whose ages ranged from 33 to 79. They found no age differences on a measure of midlife characteristics; however, they did find a highly significant correlation between their midlife characteristics scale and a scale measuring neuroticism (the Eysenck N Scale [Eysenck, 1975]). These findings suggest that persons prone to crises are likely to experience them regardless of age. For this group of people, achieving quiescence and completion of developmental tasks may be intrapersonally difficult at any age.

As noted in the discussion of antecedent conditions, many people with mental retardation show crisis-like behavior as a consequence of what Szymanski and Crocker (1985) suggested are the most common personality features among these individuals: negative self-image and low self-esteem. Conflict between real and self-image and expected self-image, in addition to environmental constraints, may cause persons with mental retardation to experience considerable stress and anxiety, emotions that are likely to impede the successful completion of many developmental tasks. Similar to the findings of the Costa and McCrae (1980) study, it may be difficult to distinguish midlife crisis from a steady state of behavior that is prone to be disruptive because of negative self-image and limited environmental opportunities.

Giele (1980) also noted that some people experience growth through developmental tasks and stages while other people do not. She suggested that the critical discriminating variable between those who do and those who do not is the degree of social complexity people experience in their daily environments. Less change and variety is associated with less differentiation of experiences within stages and thus less opportunity to engage in developmental growth. The delineations of developmental tasks illustrated in Figure 10.1 and described below are offered in order to focus some attention on the types of environmental challenges that may be possible for middle-age persons with mental retardation. As was done for the description of antecedent conditions, the description of developmental tasks is presented in a systemic manner so that the interactions among the tasks are emphasized.

Generativity   The first developmental task listed in Figure 10.1 is *social and civic responsibility*. This task is closely associated with Erikson's (1982) formulation for the middle years of *generativity* versus stagnation. As a rule, persons with mental retardation rarely are offered and rarely initiate social and civic activities that are generative. According to Erikson, generativity is the psychosocial press on the adult to be committed to improving life conditions of future generations. Generativity reflects a desire to care about the people and things that one has produced. It is a developmental task intertwined with that of *acceptance of mortality*. Since a person will not live forever, he or she must make a contribution to society that likely will make a difference after the person dies. In Erikson's scheme, generativity is counterbalanced with the negative ego quality of stagnation. Stagnation occurs when a person falls into routines in which he or she no longer seek to learn and grow. There is a lack of interest expressed in daily activities, a disillusionment with life and self. In contrast, generativity extends the sense of self from the past into the future, anticipating meaningful accomplishments and contributions.

Unfortunately, activities such as those commonly engaged in by persons with mental retardation in sheltered workshops (e. g., putting elephant stickers on soap or plastic widgets in transparent plastic bags, year after year) may arrest or at least dull the drive toward generativity. Also *adult leisure activities* often are organized around the consensus of the group, either at the residence or workshop. Independent leisure activity rarely is encouraged so that individual creativity in art, graphics, music, theater, and other expressions of the inner self are cultivated and shared with others. Furthermore, for adults with mental retardation who do not have spouses or children, generativity at work could become very important. Persons without mental retardation often make a generative contribution by helping those junior to themselves in the mentor-protégé relationship. It is rare to find persons with mental retardation engaged in parenting or mentoring relationships. In contrast, citizen advocacy programs attempt to provide mentors for persons with mental retardation. The availability of this role often is successfully marketed to people without mental disabilities as one means of meeting their desire to fulfill *social and civic responsibilities*. Relationships important to both parties are formed in these types of volunteer programs (Stroud & Sutton, 1988). It may also be important, though, to offer similar peer or volunteer activities to persons with mental retardation, so they too can be the contributing citizens and thus achieve a higher level of self-efficacy.

Sex Role Crossover Another developmental task is that of *sex role crossover*. Adult developmental theorists such as Brim (1976), Gutmann (1977, 1987), and Neugarten (1968a) suggested that during the mid to late years of life, both men and women tend to exchange some of the traditionally held sex roles. Women tend to move toward greater instrumentality, integrating more autonomous and competitive qualities into their personalities, while men become more expressive, affiliative, sensitive, and sensual. These theorists see sex role crossover, or the movement toward androgyny, as an age-related, developmental task that is likely to occur during the stage of middle age. Levinson et al. (1978) suggested that sex role crossover promotes individuation, a process by which a person attains an integrated sense of internal control. Over time, developmental growth occurs as a function of the dialectic balance between increased differentiation of affective states such as those related to sex role crossover and, simultaneously, greater personality integration.

Giele (1980) also suggested that there is a "crossover motif" for both age and sex. She noted that there are new assumptions held about age and sex that are changing the conceptualization of adulthood. It is now considered healthy to combine masculine and feminine qualities (Bem, 1974). According to this perspective, there should be increasing similarities between men and women as they age. Levinson et al. (1978) added "age crossover" as yet another dimension

toward which adults move as they age. These authors write about the reconciliation between young adulthood and old age and suggest that a healthy resolution
of midlife issues depends on an intergenerational crossover. When that happens,
the self carries aspects of every generation.

There is some empirical evidence that there are different developmental
periods when men and women move closer or further away from androgyny.
Studies have found that men and women are least alike during adolescence and
young adulthood and become more alike toward the end of middle adulthood
(Huyck, 1990; Sinnott, 1986).

There may also be a biological basis for androgyny in middle adulthood,
particularly for women. Sheehy (1992) posited a hormonal explanation for sex
role crossover. Post-menopausal women no longer produce estrogen but still
produce testosterone, the male sex hormone. To the extent that this hormore
plays a role in behavior change in some women, its abundance may be associated
with the increase in behaviors that are associated with men. Men do not, at least
physically, experience menopause. Decrease in the male hormone testosterone
takes place very gradually with age, if at all, and the rate varies considerably
among men (Butler & Lewis, 1988).

This crossover motif for age and sex is difficult to project onto persons with
mental retardation. That very fact says a great deal. First, persons with mental
retardation too rarely are seen as sexual partners, of any sexual orientation, that
is, persons who are actively engaged in a long-term love relationship so that after
many years of sexual relationship, companionship, and cohabitation, they experience a crossover in their gender qualities. Most often, persons with mental
retardation live with their parents or in residential facilities, where opportunities to explore their age-appropriate sex roles are very limited. Participants
in the Krauss, Seltzer, and Goodman (1992) study had few friendships and particularly few age-appropriate friendships; thus, they were very unlikely to experience intimate relationships that over time would stimulate or support sex role
changes.

Investigating the experience of sex role crossover in development un-
covers a fundamental absence in the lives of persons with mental retardation. A
sex role is a theoretical construct that suggests that there are normative expectations and gender-related rules about social discourse that exist within a particular culture, ethnic group, or historical context (Spence, Deaux, & Helmreich,
1985). An individual develops a sex role identity through cultural, institutional,
and interpersonal experiences. A person's sex role identity refers to a set of
beliefs and values that the person holds in regard to his or her functional ability
as a man or a woman in many areas of psychosocial life including in family,
friendship, religion, community, work, and, as noted above, intimate relations
(Giele, 1988).

At least two problems emerge when the sex role construct is applied to
persons with mental retardation. First, the noted absence of role opportunities

diminishes their chances to receive feedback about themselves as masculine or feminine. They have little opportunity to discover their value or develop their beliefs about themselves as men and women. There is little opportunity for them to have functional sex roles to play in their communities. Second, and even more damaging, may be that they receive negative feedback about themselves as incapable of being masculine or feminine.

It is important, though sad, to acknowledge that there are realistic fears about persons with mental retardation being raped or otherwise sexually abused, and becoming victims of unwanted pregnancy. This vulnerability to criminals creates even more difficulty and, in some instances, makes it impossible for persons with mental retardation to express themselves as masculine, feminine, or androgynous individuals. Their right to live as sexual beings is jeopardized by social deviances. The hope among many who care deeply for their loved ones is for persons with mental retardation to remain asexual beings. The forced choice between safety and sexuality presents caregivers and persons with mental retardation with a serious dilemma.

Adjustment to Physiological Changes *Physiological changes* related to sexuality also present midlife challenges to persons with mental retardation, particularly women. For some women, the physical symptoms associated with menopause may manifest themselves in a variety of psychological expressions such as loss, confusion, and labile behavior. Women with mental retardation have difficulty understanding the biologically related etiology of these feelings. Some of these women who are cognitively egocentric may view the cessation of menstruation as occurring because of something bad in themselves or because of something bad that they have done. These disturbing misperceptions are not limited to occurring at menopause. In general, health problems can become severe in midlife. Mailick (1984) noted that midlife is a stage when life-threatening illnesses are considerably more prevalent than in preceding stages. Death rates jump dramatically. For those persons with mental retardation and a known organic etiology, the likelihood of morbidity and mortality is even greater. The cognitive deficits and limited life experiences characteristic of many persons with mental retardation blur the lines between the physiological cause of the changes and the psychological experience of these changes.

Acceptance of Mortality Developing an *acceptance of mortality* and physiological change are coterminous. At midlife there tends to be a change in time orientation so that time is anchored less by the date of birth and more by the number of years left to live. A number of theorists (e.g., Jacques, 1965; Levinson et al., 1978; Neugarten, 1968b) have argued that the personal confrontation with death and the shift in time orientation are the critical triggers of midlife transition. Little is known about the relationships among understanding the concept of death, cognitive ability, age, affect, and other sociodemographic variables for persons with mental retardation. There is a need to assess the extent to which these individuals understand that death is an irreversible, inevitable, universal, and biologically based phenomenon (Seltzer, 1989). In one of the only studies to investigate the ability of persons with mental retardation to understand the concept of death, Lipe-Goodson and Goebel (1983) found that age, and to a lesser extent IQ, were related to an understanding of the meaning of death. Specifically, older adults with mental retardation appeared to have a better understanding of death than younger persons with mental retardation. This finding is consistent with gerontological studies suggesting that as people age, seemingly, there is a better understanding and acceptance and a lower fear of death (Kalish, 1981). Among the explanations for these findings is that as a person ages, he or she accrues experiences and practices the rituals associated with death and dying. These experiences may break through some of the denial of death, leading to a better formulation of and attribution of personal meaning to the concept of death.

Midlife is a time when persons with mental retardation may gain first hand experience with death, since during this time many have aging parents who eventually will become ill and die. Too frequently, however, persons with mental retardation are not permitted to participate in the rituals of death and dying. In some instances, they are not allowed to attend funerals or visit loved ones in the hospital. These restricitons may make the *acceptance of mortality* more difficult, particularly since these individuals are likely to need more exposure to death-related rituals in order to construct meaning from their experiences.

For middle-age persons with mental retardation, just as important as accepting their parents' death, is the opportunity to engage in planning for how they will live after their parents' death, including where they will live and who their primary contact will be. These are but a few of the innumerable details that need to be worked out, and yet, studies conducted on parents' involvement in planning suggest that they select not to talk about it with their adult children with and without mental retardation (Heller & Factor, chap. 7, this volume; Heller & Factor, 1991; Seltzer, Krauss, & Heller, 1991). Even parents who have placed their adult children out of the home expect their adult children without mental retardation to take an increasingly active role in the future decision-making responsibility for their children with mental retardation, but they, too, tend not to discuss these expectations openly. (See Seltzer, Begun, Magen, & Luchterhand, chap. 8, this volume.) The lack of overt communication and planning in some families results in the crisis of a sibling assuming responsibility for the care of his or her brother or sister with mental retardation when a parent dies. The dynamics for all are very complicated; there is a lifetime accumulation of frustrations about the lack of control over one's destiny and perhaps the unspoken wish that the child with developmental disabilities would die first (Seltzer, 1992). These complicated family dynamics suggest that the midlife challenge of accepting mortality is an emotionally charged topic in a family system in which parents are old and their adult children are middle age.

Outcomes

The last column in Figure 10.1 shows the classes of developmental adjustment outcomes that are interrelated with the relationships between antecedent conditions and developmental tasks. Behavioral, cognitive, and affective domains are listed as outcomes. These outcomes may be assessed by scales that measure the extent to which and quality with which individuals adjust to, move through, and resolve developmental tasks. Schematically, the model suggests that how a person acts, thinks, and feels in midlife is affected by his or her ability to cope with developmental tasks and by the antecedent conditions that directly affect the experience of these developmental challenges.

There may be a relationship between quality of life as depicted by the outcomes of this model and the level of competence of the individual. Lawton and Simon (1968) hypothesized that as an individual's competence decreases, the proportion of behavior attributable to the environment increases, while the proportion of behavior attributable to personal characteristics decreases. Thus, individuals with severe or profound mental retardation or abilities waning due to age or debilitating illnesses are more apt to be controlled by environmental stimuli. This relationship between competence and environment is used by Lawton and Nahemow (1973), who theorized that developmental growth is best understood through assessment of the relationship between environmental demands and level of competence. Viewed through this framework applied to Figure 10.1, an individual is more likely to experience maladaptive behavioral, cognitive, and affective outcomes under conditions in which the environmental demands are too strong for his or her competence level, or the person's level of competence is higher than the level of stimulus provided by the environment. Thus, applying the Lawton and Nahemow theory to the structure and content of Figure 10.1 may provide a conceptual underpinning for assessing quality of life in middle age. The environmental and individual competence variables listed as antecedent conditions may interact systemically toward the goal of performing the developmental tasks listed. In turn, reaching these goals can be measured by scales such as those that assess maladaptive versus adaptive behaviors, dysfunctional thoughts, and life satisfaction. Outcomes completed then fit into some of the antecedent condition boxes for the next round of developmental task challenges, and the process continues iteratively.

Together, the outcomes determine the quality of a person's life. The concept of quality of life poses many definitional challenges. Landesman (1986) and Rosen (1986) noted that, although good quality of life is a concept and goal close to people's hearts, the field of mental retardation has relegated this goal to secondary status because the field has not established good definitional criteria and related outcome measures for it. Landesman's challenge to the field has been responded to by the American Association on Mental Retardation's publication of a monograph entitled *Quality of Life: Perspectives and Issues* (Schalock, 1990). This edited monograph moves the field closer to operational definitions of the concept; nevertheless, it remains subjectively defined. Rather than lamenting this subjective status, Borthwick-Duffy (1992) argued "to presume that we can generate group-derived criteria for evaluating a person's personal values, experiences, and feelings is almost an invasion of privacy. The only justification for engaging in this kind of study is to do so with the objective of improving quality of life as it is viewed by the individual" (p. 63). Through this model, good quality of life for middle-age persons with mental retardation is understood to occur because of prior conditions that influence the developmental experience, resulting in the individual's subjective assessment of thoughts, feelings, and behaviors.

SUMMARY AND CONCLUSIONS

Knowledge about adult development and mental retardation is quite limited. This limitation is related to the dearth of empirical or theoretical investigations of adult development in general, and development in middle-age persons in particular. Furthermore, there are only a few longitudinal studies of persons of different genders, races, and socio-economic strata, and taking into account other important demographic variables. An often voiced criticism of theories of adult development is that they were formulated on a white, middle class, and largely male population, and, therefore, may not be applicable to others in the general population. Certainly, caution should be exercised in generalizing from these limited theories when approaching persons with mental retardation.

Nevertheless, in this chapter a number of theoretical propositions about midlife development were presented. The differences and similarities were explored between theories that use a stage approach to development and those that find too few homogeneous developmental patterns to categorize development by stages. These theoretical propositions were then applied to a body of empirical studies and clinical observations of persons with mental retardation in order to explore the fit between the two. Last, a schematic model was presented to illustrate the interrelationships among antecedent conditions, developmental tasks, and adjustment outcomes.

Throughout this chapter, the need to be cautious about the application of theories that have no empirical referent has been noted. The fact that so little research has been conducted on the adult development of persons with mental retardation is telling. One reason for this void is that, historically, the emphasis in the field was placed on child development and the promotion of advocacy, education, and clinical services for children with mental retardation. Since the 1970s, however, professionals in the field of mental retardation have become increasingly attentive to quality of life issues for adults because of the influence of such concepts as normalization, the least restrictive environment, and community inclusion (Seltzer & Seltzer, 1985). Still, quality of life is a concept that is difficult to convert into meaningful operational terms. Life satisfaction, economic security, good residential arrangements, good health, and employment satisfaction are but a few of the variables included on most assessments claiming to measure a good quality of life. However, there remains some confusion as to which of these are the independent variables and which are the dependent variables. Because this chapter focused on psychological adjustment, the broad psychological outcomes related to behavior, cognition, and emotion were viewed as dependent variables. It is important to continue to ask persons with mental retardation about their developmental experiences and quality of life, thereby, hopefully, stimulating future research that improves the quality of their midlife development.

REFERENCES

Adams, R.G. (1987). Patterns of network change: A longitudinal study of friendships of elderly women. *Gerontologist, 27,* 222–227.

Baker, B.L., Seltzer, G.B., & Seltzer, M.M. (1977). *As close as possible: Community residences for retarded adults.* Boston: Little, Brown.

Balla, D. (1976). Relationship of institution size to quality of care: A review of the literature. *American Journal of Mental Deficiency, 81,* 117–124.

Balla, D., & Zigler, E. (1975). Preinstitutional social deprivation and responsiveness to social reinforcement in institutionalized retarded individuals: A 6-year follow-up study. *American Journal of Mental Deficiency, 80,* 228–230.

Balla, D., & Zigler, E. (1982). Impact of institutional experience on the behavior and development of retarded persons. In E. Zigler & D. Balla (Eds.), *Mental retardation: The developmental-difference controversy* (pp. 41–58). Hillsdale, NJ: Lawrence Erlbaum Associates.

Baltes, P.B., Reese, H.W., & Nesselroade, J.R. (1988). *Life-span developmental psychology: Introduction to research methods.* Hillsdale, NJ: Lawrence Erlbaum Associates.

Bem, S. (1974). The measurement of psychological androgyny. *Journal of Consulting and Clinical Psychology, 42,* 155–162.

Bengston, V.L., Reedy, M.N., & Gordon, C. (1985). Aging and self-conceptions: Personality processes and social contexts. In J.E. Birren & K.W. Schaie (Eds.), *Handbook of the psychology of aging* (2nd ed.) (pp. 544–593). New York: Van Nostrand Reinhold.

Borthwick-Duffy, S.A. (1992). Quality of life and quality of care in mental retardation. In L. Rowitz (Ed.), *Mental retardation in the year 2000* (pp. 52–66). New York: Springer-Verlag.

Braginsky, D.D., & Braginsky, B.M. (1971). *Hansels and Gretels: Studies of children in institutions for the mentally retarded.* New York: Holt, Rhinehart & Winston.

Brim, O.G. (1976). Theories of the male midlife crisis. *The Counseling Psychologist, 6,* 2–9.

Butler, R.N., & Lewis, M.I. (1988). *Love & sex after 60* (rev. ed.). New York: Harper & Row.

Costa, P.T., & McCrae, R.R. (1980). Still stable after all these years: Personality as key to some issues in adulthood and old age. In P.B. Baltes & O.G. Brim (Eds.), *Life-span development and behavior* (Vol. 3, pp. 65–102). New York: Academic Press.

Cromwell, R.L. (1967). Personality evaluation. In A.A. Baumeister (Ed.), *Mental retardation: Appraisal, education, and rehabilitation* (pp. 66–85). Chicago: Aldine.

Edgerton, R.B. (1967). *The cloak of competence: Stigma in the lives of the mentally retarded.* Berkeley: University of California Press.

Edgerton, R.B. (1988). Aging in the community—A matter of choice. *American Journal of Mental Deficiency, 92,* 331–335.

Edgerton, R.B., & Bercovici, S.M. (1976). The cloak of competence: Years later. *American Journal of Mental Deficiency, 80,* 485–497.

Edgerton, R.B., Bollinger, M., & Herr, B. (1984). The cloak of competence: After two decades. *American Journal of Mental Deficiency, 88,* 345–351.

Edgerton, R.B., & Gaston, M.A. (Eds.). (1991). *I've seen it all! Lives of older persons with mental retardation in the community.* Baltimore: Paul H. Brookes Publishing Co.

Emerson, E.B. (1985). Evaluating the impact of deinstitutionalization on the lives of mentally retarded people. *American Journal of Mental Deficiency, 90,* 277–288.

Erickson, M., Krauss, M.W., & Seltzer, M.M. (1989). Perception of old age among a sample of aging mentally retarded persons. *The Journal of Applied Gerontology, 8,* 251–260.

Erikson, E.H. (1982). *The life cycle completed: A review.* New York: Norton.

Eyman, R.K., & Arndt, S. (1982). Life-span development of institutionalized and community-based mentally retarded residents. *American Journal of Mental Deficiency, 86,* 342–350.

Eyman, R.K., Borthwick, S.A., & Miller, C. (1981). Trends in maladaptive behavior of mentally retarded persons placed in community and institutional settings. *American Journal of Mental Deficiency, 85,* 473–477.

Eyman, R.K., & Widaman, K.F. (1987). Life-span development of institutionalized and community-based mentally retarded persons, revisited. *American Journal of Mental Deficiency, 91,* 559–569.

Eysenck, H.J., & Eysenck, S.R.G. (1975). *Manual of the Eysenck Personality Questionnaire.* San Diego: EdITS.

Freud, S. (1964). *The complete psychological works of Sigmund Freud.* London: Hogarth Press.

Fujiura, G.T., Garza, J., & Braddock, D. (1990). *National survey of family support services in developmental disabilities.* Chicago: University of Illinois.

Giele, J.Z. (1980). Adulthood as transcendence of age and sex. In N.J. Smelser & E.H. Erikson (Eds.), *Themes of work and love in adulthood* (pp. 151–173). Cambridge, MA: Harvard University Press.

Giele, J.Z. (1988). Gender and sex roles. In N.J. Smelser (Ed.), *Handbook of sociology* (pp. 291–316). Newbury Park, CA: Sage Publications.

Gould, R.L. (1972). The phases of adult life: A study in developmental psychology. *American Journal of Psychiatry, 129,* 521–531.

Gould, R.L. (1978). *Transformations.* New York: Simon & Schuster.

Gutmann, D.L. (1977). The cross cultural perspective: Notes toward a comparative psychology of aging. In J.E. Birren & K.W. Schaie (Eds.), *Handbook of the psychology of aging* (pp. 302–326). New York: Van Nostrand Reinhold.

Gutmann, D.L. (1987). *Reclaimed powers.* New York: Basic Books.

Halpern, A.S., Close, D.W., & Nelson, D.J. (1986). *On my own: The impact of semi-independent living programs for adults with mental retardation.* Baltimore: Paul H. Brookes Publishing Co.

Havighurst, R.J. (1972). *Developmental tasks and education* (3rd ed.). New York: David McKay.

Havighurst, R.J. (1973). Social roles, work, leisure, and education. In C. Eisdorfer & M.P. Lawton (Eds.), *The psychology of adult development and aging* (pp. 598–618). Washington, DC: American Psychological Association.

Heller, T., & Factor, A. (1991). Permanency planning for adults with mental retardation living with family caregivers. *American Journal on Mental Retardation, 96,* 163–176.

Helson, R., & Moane, G. (1987). Personality change in women from college to midlife. *Journal of Personality and Social Psychology, 53,* 176–186.

Hogg, J. (1991). Social and community integration. In M.P. Janicki & M.M. Seltzer (Eds.), *Aging and developmental disabilities: Challenges for the 1990s* (pp. 25–51). Washington, DC: Special Interest Group on Aging, American Association on Mental Retardation.

Huyck, M.H. (1990). Gender differences in aging. In J.E. Birren & K.W. Schaie (Eds.), *Handbook of psychology and aging* (3rd ed.) (pp. 124–132). San Diego: Academic Press.

Jacobson, J.W., Sutton, M.S., & Janicki, M.P. (1985). Demography and characteristics of aging and aged mentally retarded persons. In M.P. Janicki & H.M. Wisniewski (Eds.), *Aging and developmental disabilities: Issues and approaches* (pp. 115–142). Baltimore: Paul H. Brookes Publishing Co.

Jacques, E. (1965). Death and the mid-life crisis. *International Journal of Psycho-Analysis, 46,* 502–514.

Jung, C.G. (1968). *The archetypes and the collective unconscious.* Princeton: Princeton University Press.

Kalish, R.A. (1981). *Death, grief, and caring relationships.* Monterey, CA: Brooks/Cole.

Koch, W.H. (1986). *Planning for an aging developmentally disabled population: Some considerations.* Unpublished manuscript, University of Wisconsin Center for Adult Development, Milwaukee.

Kogan, N. (1990). Personality and aging. In J.E. Birren & K.W. Schaie (Eds.). *Handbook of psychology and aging* (3rd ed.) (pp. 330–346). San Diego: Academic Press.

Kohlberg, L. (1978). Revisions in the theory and practice of moral development. *New Directions for Child Development, 2,* 83–87.

Krauss, M.W. (1988). Long-term care issues in mental retardation. In J. Kavanagh (Ed.), *Understanding mental retardation: Research accomplishments and new frontiers* (pp. 331–339). Baltimore: Paul H. Brookes Publishing Co.

Krauss, M.W., & Erickson, M. (1988). Informal support networks among aging persons with mental retardation: A pilot study. *Mental Retardation, 26,* 197–201.

Krauss, M.W., Seltzer, M.M., & Goodman, S.J. (1992). Social support networks of adults with mental retardation who live at home. *American Journal on Mental Retardation, 96,* 432–441.

Lakin, K.C. (1985). Service system and settings for mentally retarded people. In K.C. Lakin, B. Hill, & R. Bruininks (Eds.), *An analysis of Medicaid's intermediate care facility for the mentally retarded (ICF-MR) program.* Minneapolis: University of Minnesota.

Landesman, S. (1986). Quality of life and personal satisfaction: Definition and measurement issues. *Mental Retardation, 24,* 141–143.

Langer, E.J. (1989). *Mindfulness.* Reading, MA: Addison-Wesley.

Lawton, M.P., & Nahemow, L. (1973). Ecology and the aging process. In C. Eisdorfer & M.P. Lawton (Eds.), *The psychology of adult development and aging* (pp. 619–674). Washington, DC: American Psychological Association.

Lawton, M.P., & Simon, B.B. (1968). The ecology of social relationships in housing for the elderly. *The Gerontologist, 8,* 108–115.

Levinson, D.J., Darrow, C.N., Klein, E.B., Levinson, M.H., & McKee, B. (1978). *The seasons of man's life.* New York: Ballantine Books.

Lipe-Goodson, P.S., & Goebel, B.L. (1983). Perception of age and death in mentally retarded adults. *Mental Retardation, 21,* 68–75.

Lochshin, R.A., & Zakeri, Z.F. (1990). Programmed cell death: New thoughts and relevance to aging. *Journal of Gerontology: Biological Science, 45*, B145–150.

Lowy, L. (1980). *Social policies and programs on aging.* Lexington, MA: Lexington Books.

MacMillian, D.L. (1982). *Mental retardation in school and society* (2nd ed.). Boston: Little, Brown.

Maddox, G.L. (1970). Themes and issues in sociological theories of aging. *Human Development, 13,* 17–27.

Mailick, M.M. (1984). Lost opportunity: Terminal illness in middle age. In L.H. Suszycki, M. Abramson, E. Prichard, A.H. Kutscher, & D. Fisher (Eds.), *Social work and terminal care* (pp. 31–41). New York: Praeger.

McCrae, R.R., & Costa, P.T. (1990). *Personality in adulthood.* New York: Guilford Press.

Mercer, J. (1973). *Labeling the mentally retarded.* Berkeley: University of California Press.

Mount, B., Beeman, P., & Ducharme, G. (1988). *What are we learning about bridge-building?* Manchester, CT: Communitas.

Mount, B., & Zwernik, K. (1988). *It's never too early, it's never too late: A booklet about personal futures planning.* St. Paul: Metropolitan Council.

Neugarten, B.L. (1968a). Adult personality: Toward a psychology of the life cycle. In B.L. Neugarten (Ed.), *Middle age and aging* (pp. 137–147). Chicago: The University of Chicago Press.

Neugarten, B.L. (1968b). The awareness of middle age. In B.L. Neugarten (Ed.), *Middle age and aging* (pp. 93–98). Chicago: The University of Chicago Press.

Neugarten, B.L. (1979). Time, age and the life cycle. *American Journal of Psychiatry, 136,* 887–894.

Neugarten, B.L., & Neugarten, D.A. (1986). Age in the aging society. *Daedalus, 115,* 31–49.

Parkes, C.M. (1971). Psychosocial transitions: A field for study. *Social Science and Medicine, 5,* 101–115.

Pearlin, L.I. (1980). Life strains and psychological distress among adults. In N.J. Smelsor & E.H. Erikson (Eds.), *Themes of work and love in adulthood* (pp. 174–192). Cambridge: Harvard University Press.

Perlman, H.H. (1968). *Persona: Social roles and personality.* Chicago: University of Chicago Press.

Perlmutter, M., & Hall, E. (1992). *Adult development and aging* (2nd ed.). New York: John Wiley & Sons.

Piaget, J. (1972). Intellectual evolution from adolescence to adulthood. *Human Development, 15,* 1–12.

Piaget, J., & Inhelder, B. (1969). *The psychology of the child.* New York: Basic Books.

Rodin, J. (1986). Aging and health: The effects of the sense of control. *Science, 233,* 1271–1276.

Rosen, M. (1986). Quality of life for persons with mental retardation: A question of entitlement. *Mental Retardation, 24,* 365–366.

Rossi, A.S. (1980). Life-span theories and women's lives. *Journal of Women in Culture and Society, 6,* 4–32.

Rossman, I. (1980). Bodily changes with aging. In E.W. Busse & D.G. Blazer (Eds.), *Handbook of geriatric psychiatry* (pp. 125–146). New York: Van Nostrand Reinhold.

Rowe, J.W., & Kahn, R.L. (1987). Human aging: Usual and successful. *Science, 237,* 143–149.

Schalock, R.L. (Ed.). (1990). *Quality of life: Perspectives and issues.* Washington, DC: American Association on Mental Retardation.

Seltzer, G.B. (1985). Selected psychological processes and aging among older developmentally disabled persons. In M.P. Janicki & H.M. Wisniewski (Eds.), *Aging and de-*

velopmental disabilities: Issues and approaches (pp. 211–227). Baltimore: Paul H. Brookes Publishing Co.

Seltzer, G.B. (1989). A developmental approach to cognitive understanding of death and dying. In M.C. Howell, D.G. Gavin, G.A. Cabrera, & H.A. Beyer (Eds.), Serving the underserved: Caring for people who are both old and mentally retarded (pp. 331–337). Boston: Exceptional Parent Press.

Seltzer, G.B. (1992). Long-term planning for persons with mental retardation: Clinical concerns. Paper presented at the 116th annual meeting of the American Association on Mental Retardation, New Orleans.

Seltzer, M.M. (1985). Research in social aspects of aging and developmental disabilities. In M.P. Janicki & H.M. Wisniewski (Eds.), Aging and developmental disabilities: Issues and approaches (pp. 161–173). Baltimore: Paul H. Brookes Publishing Co.

Seltzer, M.M., Krauss, M.W., & Heller, T. (1991). Family caregiving over the life course. In M.P. Janicki & M.M. Seltzer (Eds.), Aging and developmental disabilities: Challenges for the 1990s (pp. 3–24). Washington, DC: Special Interest Group on Aging, American Association on Mental Retardation.

Seltzer, M.M., & Seltzer, G.B. (1985). The elderly mentally retarded: A group in need of service. The Journal of Gerontological Social Work, 8, 99–119.

Sheehy, G. (1976). Passages: Predictable crises of adult life. New York: Dutton.

Sheehy, G. (1992). The silent passage: Menopause. New York: Random House.

Sinnott, J.D. (1986). Sex roles and aging: Theory and research from a systems perspective. Contributions to human development (Vol. 15). New York: Karger.

Spence, J.T., Deaux, K., & Helmreich, R.L. (1985). Sex roles in contemporary American society. In G. Lindzey & E. Aronson (Eds.), Handbook of social psychology (Vol. 1, pp. 149–178). New York: Random House.

Stroud, M., & Sutton, E. (1988). Expanding options for older adults with developmental disabilities: A practical guide to achieving community access. Baltimore: Paul H. Brookes Publishing Co.

Szymanski, L.S., & Crocker, A.C. (1985). Mental retardation. In H.I. Kaplan & B.J. Sadock (Eds.), Comprehensive textbook psychiatry/IV (pp. 1635–1671). Baltimore: Williams & Wilkins.

Taylor, S.J., Bogdan, R., & Racino, J.A. (Eds.). (1991). Life in the community: Case studies of organizations supporting people with disabilities. Paul H. Brookes Publishing Co.

Vaillant, G.E. (1977). Adaptation to life. Boston: Little, Brown.

Weisz, J.R., Yeates, K.O., & Zigler, E. (1982). Piagetian evidence and the developmental-difference controversy. In E. Zigler & D. Balla (Eds.), Mental retardation: The developmental difference controversy (pp. 213–276). Hillsdale, NJ: Lawrence Erlbaum Associates.

Wisniewski, H.M., & Merz, G.S. (1985). Aging, Alzheimer's disease, and developmental disabilities. In M.P. Janicki & H.M. Wisniewski (Eds.), Aging and developmental disabilities: Issues and approaches (pp. 177–184). Baltimore: Paul H. Brookes Publishing Co.

Wolfensberger, W. (1972). The principle of normalization in human services. Toronto: National Institute on Mental Retardation.

Wolfensberger, W. (1983). Social role valorization: A proposed new term for the principle of normalization. Mental Retardation, 21, 234–239.

Zigler, E. (1963). Rigidity and social reinforcement effects in the performance of institutionalized and noninstitutionalized normal and retarded children. Journal of Personality, 31, 258–269.

Zigler, E. (1967). Familial mental retardation: A continuing dilemma. Science, 155, 292–298.

Zigler, E. (1969). Developmental versus difference theories of mental retardation and the problem of motivation. American Journal of Mental Deficiency, 73, 536–556.

Zigler, E., & Balla, D. (1972). Developmental course of responsiveness to social reinforcement in normal and institutionalized retarded children. *Developmental Psychology, 6,* 66–73.

Zigler, E., & Balla, D. (1982). Motivational and personality factors in the performance of the retarded. In E. Zigler & D. Balla (Eds.), *Mental retardation: The developmental-difference controversy* (pp. 9–26). Hillsdale, NJ: Lawrence Erlbaum Associates.

Zigler, E., Balla, D., & Hodapp, R. (1984). On the definition and classification of mental retardation. *American Journal of Mental Deficiency, 89,* 215–230.

Zigler, E., & Butterfield, E.C. (1968). Motivational aspects of changes in IQ test performance of culturally deprived nursery school children. *Child Development, 39,* 1–14.

Zigler, E., & Hodapp, R.M. (1986). *Understanding mental retardation.* New York: Cambridge University Press.

Zigler, E., & Yando, R. (1972). Outerdirectedness and imitative behavior of institutionalized and noninstitutionalized younger and older children. *Child Development, 43,* 413–425.

Zigman, W.B., Seltzer, G.S., Adlin, M., & Silverman, W.P. (1991). Physical, behavioral and mental health changes associated with aging. In M.P. Janicki & M.M. Seltzer, (Eds.), *Aging and developmental disabilities: Challenges for the 1990s* (pp. 52–75). Washington, DC: Special Interest Group on Aging, American Association on Mental Retardation.

III

COMMUNITY LIVING OPTIONS

Tamar Heller

The development of sufficient small-scale community living options is critical to maintaining older adults with developmental disabilities in the community, particularly since the option of care by their parents becomes less likely as their parents age. This section: 1) addresses the numerous federal and state funding resources that have made small-scale community living options possible, 2) describes a wide variety of model programs that have sought to develop more flexible programs for these individuals, and 3) reports on the results of national surveys of small-scale community living options. The chapters in this section provide a unique guide to the numerous funding streams and the varied possibilities that can be considered in developing community living options for older adults with developmental disabilities.

Despite the trend to more community services and the increase in the number of some exciting and creative model programs, the number of persons receiving services is drastically smaller than the number who are estimated to need the services. This section points clearly to the importance of increasing available funding for these services and increasing the flexibility of programs to enable these services to improve their ability to meet individual needs. Community support options must be more than brick and mortar; they must include an array of supports and services tailored to these needs. This requires programs that incorporate principles of individualization, links with natural support systems, and increased freedom for persons with developmental disabilities to make their own choices.

11

A National Survey of Community Living Options

Melton C. Martinson and James A. Stone

Studies and reports on residential trends and fiscal expenditures (Anderson, Lakin, Bruininks, & Hill, 1987; Braddock, Hemp, Fujiura, Bachelder, & Mitchell, 1989) indicate that state mental retardation/developmental disabilities (MR/DD) agencies are using smaller community living options for individuals with mental retardation and developmental disabilities. The 1980s saw increased funding allocations for community-based services compared with large, congregate settings. Since 1985 there has been a sharp increase in attention to the needs of older adults with developmental disabilities and the availability of age-appropriate programs and services resulting in improved life opportunities for people with disabilities (Cotten & Spirrison, 1986; Janicki & Wisniewski, 1985; Seltzer & Krauss, 1988). Gettings (1989) outlined four major policy goals for people with developmental disabilities:

1. Commitment to the home and community as the places to live
2. Raising the support level under Supplemental Security Income (SSI)
3. Providing affordable and decent housing for every American
4. Assuring civil rights

The policy changes reflected in federal legislation enacted by the 100th Congress provided new opportunities for older Americans with developmental disabilities. The Developmental Disabilities Act Amendments of 1987 (PL 100-146) established the welfare of older adults with developmental disabilities as a new priority. The Older Americans Act Amendments of 1987 (PL 100-175) contains a new definition of disability identical to the definition in PL 100-146, except for the words "must have occurred before the age of 22." The impact of these public policy initiatives has increased the opportunity for older adults with developmental disabilities to use the services offered by the generic aging network. Program priorities for older adults with developmental disabilities in the MR/DD services network are supported by provisions of PL 100-146. These policy changes and developing trends have created an opportunity to answer the question: What are appropriate community living options for older adults with developmental disabilities, and how can they be supported effectively?

GENERAL DESCRIPTION OF THE
NATIONAL SURVEY OF COMMUNITY LIVING OPTIONS

This chapter reports on a national survey of state agencies responsible for services to older adults (ages 60 and older) with mental retardation/developmental disabilities. It also describes a secondary data analysis of responses of state DD planning councils concerning council priorities and activities related to community living options. Computer searches of national databases also are reported on. The survey was conducted by the Interdisciplinary Human Development Institute-University Affiliated Program (IHDI-UAP), University of Kentucky. The purpose of this study was to identify effective small-scale community living options for older adults with developmental disabilities. State MR/DD agencies were surveyed for information on community living options and funding sources that these state agencies used in serving older adults with developmental disabilities. Questions concerned the types of support services available to older adults, innovative funding sources that had been used, and the use of interagency planning focused on the needs of older adults with developmental disabilities. The responses of state MR/DD agencies to the survey provided information on approximately 20,000 older adults with developmental disabilities. Of this group, 98.5% lived with nonrelatives, with the majority (63.7%) in congregate living units of four or more persons. In comparison, only 1.8% of older adults without developmental disabilities lived with nonrelatives in a community setting (United States Bureau of the Census, 1984).

Data from the secondary analysis of state developmental disabilities planning councils indicated that only eight of these councils had addressed community living options as a priority. None of this activity was specific to older adults with developmental disabilities.

Computer searches were conducted on six national databases. Data found indicated that there was minimal information available on older adults with developmental disabilities and small-scale community living options. This review provided insight into the types of information needed and the questions to ask in the survey of state MR/DD agencies.

SURVEY METHODOLOGIES

The IHDI-UAP Consortium on Aging and Developmental Disabilities research staff developed a survey instrument to gather information on three levels of long-term funding, community living options, support services, state mandates or regulations, efforts of interagency task force planning, and numbers of older adults served by the state MR/DD services system. A multi-directional approach was incorporated in the collection of information on small-scale community living options for older adults with developmental disabilities. The survey questions were reviewed by the University of Kentucky Survey Research Center, The University of Minnesota University Affiliated Program in Developmental Disabilities, and The University of Illinois at Chicago University Affiliated Program on Developmental Disabilities. The questions were directed to the state MR/DD agencies with a major focus on small-scale community living options (those with 15 persons or fewer).

A survey of 12 states was conducted from April through June of 1989. The survey was expanded in July of 1989 to include all 50 states and the District of Columbia. The follow-up procedures to assist the state agencies in completing the surveys included a second mailing to those states that had not returned the surveys before September 15, 1989 and telephone calls to those states that were unresponsive to the mailings.

The national survey was developed with the following definitions provided to the state MR/DD agencies:

- **Age category** The minimum age of the older adults with developmental disabilities is 60. This is the age of eligibility for services provided under the Older Americans Act (PL 100-175).
- **ICF/MR** The intermediate care facility for persons with mental retardation program is an optional service under the Medicaid program. It provides services to all age groups on a 24-hour basis, 7 days per week, in an establishment with permanent facilities, including residential beds for persons whose mental or physical conditions require developmental nursing services along with a planned program of active intervention. For this survey, ICF/MRs were facilities with 15 residents or fewer.
- **Group home** In this kind of residence staff provide care, supervision, and training for one to eight nonrelated people with developmental disabilities.
- **Supervised home or apartment** This kind of residence has semi-independent units or apartments with staff living in a separate unit in the same location. The residents may live alone or with roommates.
- **Adult foster care** In this arrangement a house or apartment is owned or rented by a family, with one to three persons with developmental disabilities living as surrogate family members.
- **Section 8 housing** This Housing and Urban Development (HUD) pro-

gram provides vouchers as payment for rental property. Payment is negotiated between the low-income tenant and the landlord.

- **Section 202 housing** This HUD program is for aging individuals and individuals with disabilities. It is open only to nonprofit agencies possessing tax exempt status from the Internal Revenue Service (IRS). The amount of rent may not exceed 30% of a tenant's income. Section 8 vouchers are automatically supplied to the Section 202 program by HUD.
- **Demonstration housing** This program is funded by the Administration on Aging to develop residential options for older individuals. Examples include accessory apartments, elderly congregate care, and echo housing. Echo housing is the temporary installation of a housing module for an older individual behind or beside an established home on a residential lot so that the family in the home can assist the older person. The module is removed when no longer needed.
- **Independent living** In this arrangement an individual lives without residential support or supervision.
- **Semi-independent living** In this arrangement an individual is in a residential setting with varying levels of assistance and supervision.
- **Personal care home** In this kind of residence staff provide assistance with dressing, bathing, or other personal care, but provide no formal training for the resident. The bed capacity is determined by state regulations.
- **Board-and-care home** This kind of residence provides sleeping rooms, all meals, and regular care or supervision for the residents. The level of assistance is less than that in skilled nursing care or in ICFs /MR.
- **Own home** An individual lives in her or his home or that of the immediate family or other relatives.
- **Shared home or apartment** An individual shares a house or apartment with one or more nonrelated people.
- **Other living options** These may include nursing homes and any other options not covered under the other definitions.

The options of independent living, semi-independent living, own home, shared home or apartment, board-and-care, personal care home, and others are not mutually exclusive. For example, independent living and own home could come together into one category, and the distinction between board and care and personal care may vary between states. However, the definitions above are used in other residential surveys and the state MR/DD agencies were familiar with these terms.

SUMMARY OF DATA ANALYSES

The IHDI-UAP questionnaire was returned by 47 states (94%) and the Office of Mental Retardation in Washington, D.C. Analysis of the data provided the following information:

1. There is a trend for state MR/DD agencies to use state funding rather than federal funding to support community living options for older adults with developmental disabilities. The states reported 13,007 older adults in community living options supported by state funds and 5,406 older adults in community living options supported by federal funds. This is a 2.4:1 ratio of state funding of community living options to federal funding of community living options. This finding applies to facilities with 15 people or fewer ages 60 or older.

2. Support services identified were those offered to the general adult population. For example, if networking and linking efforts had been accomplished between the state MR/DD agency and the state agency for aging, there was access to generic aging services.

3. Only five states (Alabama, Colorado, Connecticut, Nebraska, and Wyoming) reported information or knowledge of local funding of community living options programs for older adults with developmental disabilities.

4. Only three states (Florida, Massachusetts, and North Dakota) reported state regulations, statutes, or mandates for specific housing services or programs for older adults with developmental disabilities.

5. Massachusetts was the only state to report local regulations, statutes, or mandates to provide housing services or other programs to older adults with developmental disabilities.

6. Thirteen states reported interagency task force activities (Arizona, Connecticut, Delaware, Illinois, Maryland, Massachusetts, Mississippi, New York, North Carolina, Ohio, Rhode Island, Virginia, and Washington).

7. The state MR/DD agencies reported data by three discrete funding sources: federal, state, and local. States were the main funding source for community living options for older adults with developmental disabilities.

SUMMARY DATA ON FUNDING STREAMS

The survey requested funding information on small-scale community living options provided through federal, state, and local sources. Federal Funding for Community Living Options ICF/MR through the Medicaid program was the most frequently cited federal source of funding for community living options for older adults with developmental disabilities. Fifty-one and one half percent (2,794) of the older adults reported on were living in ICFs/MR. Foster care served 1,189 (21.9%) older adults, followed by the group home option for 1,008 (18.6%). The data regarding relative use of federally funded living options are presented in Table 11.1.

Board and care was the living option reported as used most frequently by the state MR/DD agencies. This state-based option served 3,522 (27.1%) of the older adults with developmental disabilities reported on in the survey. Group homes served 1,867 (14.3%), and personal care served 1,854 (14.2%) of these

Table 11.1. Specific community living options supported by federal funding

Option	%	n
ICF/MR	51.5	2794
Adult foster care	21.9	1189
Group home	18.6	1008
HUD options	4.4	237
Supervised home or apartment	3.6	198
Total	100.0	5426

older adults. The category of living option labeled "other" was reported for 2,480 (19.1%). The data reported on the small-scale family-size community living options of independent living, semi-independent living, own home, supervised home or apartment, and shared home or apartment reflected that these were the more recently developed options. The survey data indicated that 1,904 older adults (14.6%) were using the small-scale community living options. The data regarding relative use of state funded living options are presented in Table 11.2.

Examining the combination of all the living options available in the community without controlling for the funding source showed board and care as the living option used most frequently by older adults with developmental disabilities (19.3%). The group home option was used by 15.7%. ICFs/MR of 15 persons or fewer were reported as serving 15.1%. Adult foster care was reported for 14.0%. The option of "other" was used by 13.6% of the persons reported on. Personal care served 10.2%.

Controlling for funding from federal or state sources in examining use of different living options revealed that board and care and "other" living options accounted for use of 46.2% of the state funded options. The ICF/MR option accounted for 51.5% of the reported federally funded living options for older adults with developmental disabilities. The state agencies did not report use of

Table 11.2. Specific community living options supported by state funding

Option	%	n
Board and care	27.1	3522
Other	19.1	2480
Group home	14.3	1867
Personal care home	14.2	1854
Adult foster care	10.6	1380
Own home	4.7	619
Semi-independent living	4.3	564
Shared home or apartment	3.3	426
Independent living	2.3	295
Total	99.9	13007

or access to the Farm/Home Act (FmHA, PL 95-128, the Housing Act of 1949), Title V, Section 515 funding for low-income housing assistance administered by the Farmer's Home Administration, the United States Department of Agriculture, or the Administration on Aging (AoA) demonstration housing funds for community options for older adults with developmental disabilities.

Only Alabama, Florida, North Dakota, Oklahoma, Rhode Island, and South Carolina reported the number of persons using Title IV (of PL 93-383), Sections 7, 8, and 202 HUD funds. Title IV funding was used by 161 older adults and accounted for 5.6% of all federal funding of community living options.

When focusing on the small-scale community living options for three people or fewer, the survey identified five options (independent living, semi-independent living, own home, shared home or apartment, and adult foster care) that combined to make up 25.3% of the total reported community living options available to older adults with developmental disabilities in 1989.

The combined results of two national surveys (a 1987 survey by the University of Minnesota [Anderson et al., 1987] examining facilities for 16 persons or more and the present survey focusing on facilities that serve 15 people or fewer) provided information on the living options for approximately 29,870 older adults with mental retardation/developmental disabilities. Analyses of these data suggest a trend toward small-scale community living options as a viable choice for older adults with developmental disabilities.

The community living options (independent living, semi-independent living, own home, and shared home or apartment) reported in the IHDI-UAP survey data reflect this general trend. Older adults were reported to be living independently in 10 states, living semi-independently in 20 states, living in their own homes with agency support in 13 states, living in supervised apartments in seven states, and living in shared homes or apartments in seven states. Following is the report on states having the most inclusive living options:

- Independent living options:
    Arizona, California, Connecticut, Louisiana, Maryland, Massachusetts, Nebraska, North Dakota, South Carolina, and Washington
- Semi-independent living options:
    Alabama, Arizona, California, Delaware, District of Columbia, Illinois, Louisiana, Maryland, Michigan, Minnesota, Nebraska, New Mexico, New York, North Dakota, Ohio, South Carolina, South Dakota, Tennessee, Virginia, and Washington
- Living in own home:
    Arizona, District of Columbia, Delaware, Florida, Kentucky, Maryland, Massachusetts, Nebraska, North Dakota, Ohio, South Carolina, Texas, and Washington
- Supervised apartments:
    Arizona, Maryland, Mississippi, North Dakota, New York, Ohio, and South Dakota

- Shared home or apartment:
  Alabama, California, Illinois, Louisiana, Maryland, Mississippi, and Washington

These examples of small-scale community living options that provide living arrangements for three or fewer older adults with developmental disabilities meet the criteria for effectiveness of small-scale community living options responding to individual need, personal choice, and community inclusion for these individuals.

SECONDARY ANALYSES AND COMPUTER SEARCHES

The research effort of the IHDI-UAP survey included looking for existing models and examples of small-scale community living options for older adults with developmental disabilities beyond the state MR/DD agencies. Two resources were utilized: 1) secondary analyses through a survey completed by the Kentucky Developmental Disability Planning Council (KDDPC) examining residential initiatives for people with developmental disabilities, and 2) six national computer databases that were searched for information on older adults with developmental disabilities.

A secondary data analysis was conducted using information provided by the KDDPC. This information had been obtained through requests from state DD councils regarding efforts to develop community living options. The following 14 state planning councils responded to the request: Alabama, Arkansas, California, Connecticut, Florida, Georgia, Indiana, Massachusetts, Minnesota, Missouri, Ohio, Oklahoma, Virginia, and Wisconsin. Following are summaries of some information from this survey specific to community living but not focused directly on older adults with developmental disabilities.

California

The California DD Planning Council was funding a study on community residential needs and transportation options for people with developmental disabilities (1988). The report discussed the current arrangements, needs, barriers, and issues. The recurrent theme was the individuality of the person and the need for progressive options that would be based in the home of the person, rather than in congregate group homes or shared living arrangements with more than six residents. The data indicated that the out-of-home arrangement used for adults with developmental disabilities was basic congregate care in an environment providing 24-hour supervision. This was Medicaid funded under the Intermediate Care Facility/DD Habilitation (ICF/DD H) programs for 4–15 people.

Connecticut

The Connecticut DD Planning Council was supporting a non-profit housing cooperative agency and was planning to invest $162,000 from 1988 to 1990 to promote the development of housing cooperatives that would include services for people with disabilities. Further plans were to invest $25,000 a year beginning in 1990 with the Cooperative Fund of New England to make zero- or no-interest loans or grants to individuals with developmental disabilities moving from congregate living facilities to independent living cooperatives.

Georgia

The Georgia DD Council was designating community living as a planning goal rather than a service priority. The council actively pursued the McKinney Homeless Assistance Act and developed the Georgia Residential Finance Authority in conjunction with the Department of Human Resources (DHR) Residential Work Committee. The latter are major interdepartmental planning and program partnerships for residential housing and support services for people with disabilities in Georgia. Since 1988 they have accomplished the following:

1. Existing residential services sites have received a $150,000 allocation to meet energy conservation needs.
2. Three permanent housing grants for $980,000 have been made.
3. For transitional housing, $198,000 has been provided through the McKinney Homeless Assistance Act.
4. The DHR has joined in the development of a Group Home Ownership Program, which is a Community Provider Loaned Pool concept using municipal bonds.
5. Residential support services have been selected as the #12 priority for state appropriations.
6. The first edition of a newsletter called *Community Exchange*, which covers housing and residential support for agencies and individuals, has been published.

Minnesota

The Minnesota DD Planning Council had multiple support initiatives, including the *Guidebook to New Housing Options* from the Minnesota Department of Mental Retardation, to provide guidelines for individualizing service provision, providing community-based waivers, and obtaining an overview of the housing programs in the state that provided funding (e.g., Section 8 and Section 202 programs).

Ohio

The Ohio DD Planning Council funded a project in 1987 that resulted in the development of the Perry (County) Housing Association.

Virginia

The Virginia DD Planning Council confirmed development of the Virginia Housing Development Authority program, an initiative connected to the community independent living centers and referencing the first computerized clearinghouse for people with disabilities. Three hundred and twenty-two people were assisted through this program in 1988. There was $7.6 million available for joint programs between the Department of Mental Health/Mental Retardation/ Substance Abuse Services and the Housing Authority for 8% loans for individuals with disabilities. The program provided 5% housing loans for individual families and 4% loans for multi-family housing through nonprofit agencies.

Wisconsin

The Wisconsin DD Planning Council had just created a Housing Trust Fund to provide housing grants and loans to low-income households. As of August 1989, this was funded with $5.5 million of state funds.

Computer Database Searches

Computer searches of national databases were conducted for information on community living options for older adults with developmental disabilities. Efforts were made to access databases with information on aging, housing, and disabilities. Six different databases were accessed. As their information was made available and the computer searches were completed, the information reported for the study was narrowed to that addressing aging/older adults with developmental disabilities and community living/housing options. No information of consequence came from the searches specific to aging/older adults with developmental disabilities that had not been discovered already. Databases reviewed included the ERIC Database, the Iquest Database, the Ageline Database at the American Association for Retired Persons, the National Aeronautics and Space Administration/Technology Application Center (NASA/Tac) at the University of Kentucky, the National Institute on Disability and Rehabilitation Research Database, and the Community-Based Living Database. The overall review of data obtained revealed minimal information on community living options for older adults with mental retardation/developmental disabilities. These searches were useful in the development of the survey protocols sent to the state MR/DD agencies.

CONCLUSION

The data reported in this chapter indicate a trend toward smaller community living options for older adults with developmental disabilities. State agency resources supporting small-scale community living options were available in arrangements for three persons or fewer for 25.3% of the people reported on in the survey. Data obtained from the state MR/DD agencies indicate that the data systems maintained by many states commonly do not include information on older adults. A combination of the totals from the 1987 University of Minnesota survey of large facilities (16 persons or more) and the totals from the present research project, focusing on residences of 15 persons or fewer, provided information on approximately 30,000 older adults with mental retardation/developmental disabilities. If estimations of the number of older adults living beyond age 60 (300,000–1,000,000) during the 1980s are accurate (Janicki et al.), major national initiatives are necessary to identify and provide community living options for the great majority of older adults with developmental disabilities. In 1987 the Senate and House Select Committees on Aging held the congressional forum, "Legislative Agenda for an Aging Society: 1988 and Beyond." This forum provided a profile on America's aging citizens. Focusing on housing options for older adults in general, the information from the forum indicated that 75% of older adults live in urban areas. The residential mobility of this group was found to be low, with most remaining in the same home for 6–22 years. As of the 1980 census, there were 16.3 million older adults who were heads of households.

The forum also reported that, among older adults with disabilities who needed help with daily living activities, 40% lived with a spouse; 35.7% lived with their children; and of the 15% remaining, most lived with nonrelatives. Approximately 33% of these older adults with disabilities were poor. In contrast to this congressional forum information, responses to the IHDI-UAP survey indicated that 6.3% of the older adults with developmental disabilities lived in their own homes; 1.4% lived alone; and the rest lived in congregate settings.

Older adults with developmental disabilities should have the opportunity to participate in the communities in which they live, instead of being neglected into invisibility. To provide the opportunity for older adults to be involved in the decisions affecting their own lives, it will be necessary for policymakers, planners, and community program staff to understand the concepts of collaborative planning and values-based planning. The data from the IHDI-UAP national survey indicated that 13 states had made efforts toward interagency planning for meeting the residential needs of older adults with developmental disabilities. Such interagency planning and national collaborative efforts must be encouraged.

The focus of the IHDI-UAP was to provide models and examples of state responses to the need for development of options for older adults with developmental disabilities that reflect dignity and good quality of life. Continued analysis of the information provided from the national survey will suggest additional strategies for developing interagency planning models for obtaining long-term funding streams to support the family-size, small-scale community living options for older adults with developmental disabilities.

REFERENCES

Anderson, D.J., Lakin, K.C., Bruininks, R.H., & Hill, B.K. (1987). *A national study of residential and support services for elderly persons with mental retardation.* Minneapolis: University of Minnesota, Department of Educational Psychology.

Braddock, D., Hemp, R., Fujiura, G., Bachelder, L., & Mitchell, D. (1989). *Public expenditures for mental retardation and developmental disabilities in the United States: State profiles.* (Working paper, 3rd. ed.). Chicago: University Affiliated Program in Developmental Disabilities, University of Illinois-Chicago.

Cotten, P.D., & Spirrison, C.L. (1986). The elderly mentally retarded (developmentally disabled) population: A challenge for the service delivery system. In S.J. Brody & G.E. Ruff (Eds.), *Aging and rehabilitation: Advances in the state of the art* (pp. 159–187). New York: Springer.

Gettings, R. (1989). Barriers to and opportunities for cooperation between the aging and developmental disabilities service delivery systems. In E.F. Ansello & T. Rose (Eds.), *Aging and lifelong disabilities: Partnership for the twenty first century* (pp. 27–30). College Park: University of Maryland Center on Aging.

Janicki, M.P., & Wisniewski, H.M. (Eds.). (1985). *Aging and developmental disabilities: Issues and approaches.* Baltimore: Paul H. Brookes Publishing Co.

Seltzer, M.M., & Krauss, M.W. (1988). *Planning for the future: Meeting the needs of elderly developmentally disabled persons.* Boston: Boston University School of Social Work.

United States Bureau of the Census. (1984). Current Population Reports, Series P-23, No. 138. *Demographic and socioeconomic aspects of aging in the United States.* Washington, DC: United States Government Printing Office.

12

Federal Legislation and Long-Term Funding Streams that Support Community Living Options

Melton C. Martinson and James A. Stone

The Older Americans Act Amendments of 1987 (PL 100-175) designate age 60 as the minimum age for entitlement to the services it provides. There is no universal agreement about the minimum age at which people with developmental disabilities are considered old. Older adults and people with developmental disabilities shared a common fate until the 1980s, which was either to live at home or to move to an institution (older adults to nursing homes, people with developmental disabilities to institutions or developmental centers, nursing homes, or group homes). The vision since the 1980s has been for older adults with developmental disabilities to have choices. There is growing recognition that having a real home is as important to people with developmental disabilities as it is for everyone else. People with developmental disabilities who live in the community show greater independence and life satisfaction than their counterparts in institutions. As a result of this change in perspective, almost all states continue to reduce the number of people who live in institutions and increase the level of support to individuals and families to maintain them in their homes in the community.

Supported living can be provided in typical houses in typical neighbor-hoods. Studies (e.g., Seltzer & Krauss, 1987) have suggested that more than 60% of older adults with developmental disabilities currently are aging in place, with their parents, in two-generation geriatric families and are not receiving services provided by the mental retardation/developmental disabilities (MR/DD) services system.

A NEW VISION

The vision for older adults with developmental disabilities is focused on individuals. The individual approach to services in the community reflects a new and evolving way of thinking about where people live. The emphasis is on promoting desirable outcomes through individualized planning and management. The individualized planning process for community living and support includes the person for whom supports are needed, formal and informal support providers, and others interested in the welfare of the older adult with developmental disabilities. Service support goals and objectives are planned to reflect the older individual's needs based on her or his preferences and choices. For example, a community living goal would not be to "make a placement," but to design and manage a variety of settings and resources that will support the development of a real home and maintain the older adult there. The effort will be to use typical residential settings. Support can vary from minor to intensive: a daily telephone call or visit, a ramp, a bathlift, specialized training, periodic respite, or full-time paid careprovider or personal assistant services. The choice of supportive services depends on the needs of the older individual. Additional supports for older adults with developmental disabilities may reflect medical needs and include in-home health services, homemaker services, and arrangements for out-of-home medical services. The supports are critical, but should not dictate the desirable characteristics of a real home. Home for an older adult with developmental disabilities should mean emotional and material security and a place to invite friends and family (Ohio Department of Mental Retardation and Developmental Disabilities, 1990; Wieck, 1989). Supports and services also may be needed by frail, including medically fragile, older adults without developmental disabilities. The intensity and array of supports would be determined by the individual.

The Americans with Disabilities Act (PL 101-336, 1990) entitlements offer a new vision of individualized opportunities and options for older adults. This new vision could extend to later-life employment, opportunities to receive new government services, enhancing friendship and support networks by providing access to new communication services, and enabling travel in the community, across the state, or across the country with the necessary supports and accessibility. PL 101-336 provides clear and consistent enforceable civil rights protections to individuals with disabilities. These protections cover employment in the private sector, services by state and local governments, transportation and public accommodations, and telecommunications relay services. The impact of this legislation on older adults with disabilities will become known toward and into the 21st century.

CURRENT LEGISLATION AND FUNDING RESOURCES FOR SUPPORT SERVICES

There are a number of federal programs that provide support services or income to people with developmental disabilities, regardless of their age, while other support service programs are based on age eligibility. The following sections describe the major programs.

Supplemental Security Income (SSI)

Supplemental Security Income (Title XVI of PL 74-271, the Social Security Act of 1937 as Amended) is an income program for individuals in need who are aging or are blind or meet other federal disability criteria. This program provides monthly payments (based on amounts determined federally) that result in incomes well below the federal poverty level. The ability to earn more than $300 per month in employment is considered evidence that a person does not have a disability and therefore is ineligible.

Social Security Disability Insurance (SSDI)

Social Security Disability Insurance provides a benefit paid to individual workers who become disabled and have worked long enough to reach federal Social Security eligibility; it also pays benefits for their dependents, or the "adult disabled child" of retired, deceased, or "disabled workers" covered by Social Security (Title I, PL 74-271). SSDI benefits for disabled workers are considerably higher than those in the SSI program, averaging $530 per month in 1988. The average monthly benefit under the disabled adult child program was approximately $300 in 1988. Approximately 21.3% of the 43,035 SSDI beneficiaries added to the rolls in 1985 and identified as people with developmental disabilities qualified as disabled workers. Over 1 million people with developmental disabilities receive either SSI or SSDI. The level of support provided by PL 74-271 means impoverishment for people with disabilities and little likelihood of decent, affordable housing.

Food Stamps

The food stamp program (PL 95-113, the Food Stamp Act of 1977 as Amended) is federally funded and was designed to provide assistance with food purchases to individuals and families in need through monthly benefits established on the basis of family size and income level. Under federal law, the definition of family may include nonrelated groups of people with disabilities who are living together. The monthly allotment of food stamps provided through the program can be used to some extent at the discretion of the beneficiary; however, purchases are limited to specified food items and must be made with the stamps themselves, which identifies a person as a food stamp recipient.

Social Services Block Grant (SSBG)

The Social Services Block Grant (SSBG, also known as Title XX of PL 74-271) provides federal funds to the states and territories to support a wide range of social services, including child protective and foster care, homemaker and personal assistance, counseling, case management, home delivered meals, and socialization or recreation opportunities. If federal appropriation levels had kept pace with inflation, current funding would be $4.1 billion rather than $2.7 billion. Most states report that part of their SSBG allocation is used for services to people with disabilities. SSBG funds specifically identified by states as resources for services to people with developmental disabilities for FY 1988 totaled $207,082,206. All but $1,223,200 of this amount was expended for community rather than institution-based services (Braddock, Hemp, Fujiura, Bachelder, & Mitchell, 1989). The FY 1988 total is almost $46 million less than the $253,037,391 reported for FY 1981, the year the Title XX program was converted to a block grant.

Medicaid/Optional Services

A variety of Medicaid (Title XIX of PL 74-271) service categories can be used by states to finance supports to individuals. These include optional services such as personal care and mandatory services such as home health care. Federal regulations require that services covered by Medicaid be based on medical needs and include medical supervision. In FY 1987, 21 states included personal care as a discrete optional service. Medicaid funds are a significant resource to programs providing personal assistance services (Litvak, Simi, Zukas, & Heumann, 1987). Limits on service coverage (e.g., the maximum number of hours of service that may be provided per month or year) are set by the individual states.

Medicaid/Targeted Case Management

Many states use the Medicaid program to finance case management for people with disabilities who are eligible for Medicaid. As of July 1988, the targeted case management option had been added by nine states since it became an optional Medicaid service in 1986 (National Association of State Mental Retardation Programs Directors, 1988). Some states also finance case management services as a Medicaid administrative cost.

Medicare

The Medicare program (Title XVIII of PL 74-271) permits limited financing of individual supports; however, these are limited to health-related services, generally in connection with an episode of hospitalization for an acute illness. Medicare is an insurance program funded partially by the federal government and partially by individual contributions.

Technology-Related Assistance for Individuals with Disabilities

The Technology-Related Assistance for Individuals with Disabilities Act (PL 100-407, 1988) provides grants to the states to assist them in the development and implementation of consumer-responsive, statewide systems of technology-related assistance. The goal of the program is to promote the independence and productivity of people with disabilities by expanding the availability of the benefits of new technology in assistive devices. This is one area in which very little has been developed for older adults with or without developmental disabilities.

Older Americans Act Amendments

Title III of the Older Americans Act Amendments of 1987 (PL 100-175) funds a variety of support services to people ages 60 and older, including support provided at designated senior centers and support provided in the home. Services include counseling, home health care, recreation, transportation, home modifications for older adults with disabilities, meals, and information referral services. Federal grants are distributed to state agencies on aging on a formula basis to finance these services. Part D of Title III authorizes an additional allocation to states for in-home services to older adults with Alzheimer's disease or a related disorder, as well as supports to family members caring for these individuals. Approximately 8.6 million older individuals received support services funded by Title III grants in FY 1987; 2.8 million participated in the congregate meals program (sometimes located in senior centers, but also in congregate living facilities). Approximately 729,000 received meals in their home during that year. The most frequent source of care for people with developmental disabilities or older people has been the family or other informal careproviders. The majority of adults with developmental disabilities have been cared for by their families in the community, rather than by professional careproviders in formal, institutional settings. At the same time, estimates are that 70%–80% of the continuing care received by formerly independent and now frail, dependent older adults is provided by family members, unassisted and often unrecognized by the formal care network. Supporting and reinforcing the irreplaceable resource of family is central to the functioning of both the MR/DD and aging services systems.

FEDERAL LEGISLATION AND PROGRAMS
THAT SUPPORT COMMUNITY LIVING OPTIONS

The Housing Act of 1949 as Amended (PL 95-128) was the first basic housing law. It was enacted with the goal of providing affordable and decent housing for every American. However, in 1992 there is some question as to when the federal government will ever fully assist states in meeting this goal. With the problems in the programs through the Department of Housing and Urban Development and the cuts in housing programs during the 1980s, it seems unlikely that the original intent will ever be met. There is a severe national shortage of housing that is affordable for people with low incomes. Many people with developmental disabilities have incomes below the poverty level because they are dependent upon income support programs such as SSI or because their employment income is at or below the poverty level. Older adults with developmental disabilities living in rural areas often lack knowledge of their eligibility for SSI benefits. Illiteracy may contribute to this gap in access to services (Cotten, Britt, & Moreland, 1986; Stone, 1987).

In 1985 almost half (47.6%) of the households below the poverty line paid more than 70% of their monthly income for housing (Scallet, Needleman, Jaskulski, in press). An estimated half of the 4.5 million units of housing stock permanently removed between 1973 and 1983 were occupied by people with low incomes. Over 300,000 federally supported rental assistance units for low-income households will be eligible for withdrawal from the program over the next 5 years.

The combined factors of the shortage of affordable housing, increases in the overall poverty rate, the lack of community services, and the deinstitutionalization of people with mental illness and mental disabilities are primarily responsible for the significant increase in homelessness since the 1980s (Institute of Medicine, 1988). The goal of decent, affordable housing for every American seems extremely elusive as a reality in the 1990s.

The single largest federal program that funds housing for people with developmental disabilities is the Medicaid (Title XIX of PL 74-271) program, primarily through the Intermediate Care Facilities for People with Mental Retardation and Related Conditions (ICF/MR) program. Eighty-eight percent of the institutional "placements" in the current developmental disabilities residential services system are financed by the ICF/MR program. Only 25% of the community-based living arrangements are supported by the federal Medicaid program, including both the ICF/MR and Home and Community-Based Care Services Waiver (Lakin et al., 1989) ICF/MR expenditures in FY 1987 reached $5.6 billion, and nearly 75% of these expenditures went for care in large state institutions. The total population of state institutions for people with mental retardation and other developmental disabilities decreased from an average daily population of 194,650 in 1967, to 151,532 in 1977, to 94,696 in 1987 (Anderson, Lakin, Bruininks, & Hill, 1987). This indicates a trend away from the use of large institutions and toward expanded use of community living options.

Federal expenditures for people with developmental disabilities for institutional and facility-based services are much greater than those for community-based supports to individuals and families. In FY 1988, federal expenditures for the ICF/MR program and large institutions (not including nursing homes) were over $3 billion, almost four times greater than expenditures for community-based services and supports to individuals and families through the Social Services Block Grant program, expenditures for regular Medicaid services, and expenditures for services through the Medicaid Home and Community-Based Care Services Waiver (Braddock et al., 1989). The programs described in the following sections provide different methods of financing community living options for older adults with developmental disabilities. Tables 12.1–12.4 show information on federal legislation for programs that may be resources for older adults with developmental disabilities.

ICF/MR Program

The ICF/MR program is an optional service provided under the Medicaid program. It is now available in all states and the District of Columbia. Growth in the cost of the ICF/MR program is primarily responsible for the major increase in Medicaid funded, long-term care expenditures since 1982 (Department of Health and Human Services, 1988). ICFs/MR provide services for all age groups on a 24-hour basis, 7 days a week, in an establishment with permanent facilities, including beds for residents whose mental or physical conditions require developmental nursing services along with a planned program of active intervention. The facility provides special programs as indicated by individual care plans to maximize the person's mental, physical, and social development in accordance with the normalization principle. The last survey of large facilities (serving 16 people or more) in 1987 indicated less than 12,000 people over the age of 65 living in the ICF/MR facilities.

Home and Community-Based
(HCB) Care Services Waiver Program

The Home and Community-Based Care Services Waiver program (Title XIX of PL 74-271) was authorized in 1981 as an alternative approach to the use of Medicaid financing for long-term care in ICF/MR facilities and nursing homes. It is an optional program and requires federal approval of the waiver application. Initial waivers are for 3 years, with renewals approved for 5-year periods. People with developmental disabilities may be served through the waiver if they would otherwise require ICF/MR (or in some cases, nursing home) services funded by Medicaid, so long as Medicaid costs are less than would have been incurred without the waiver. The program has expanded rapidly, with 40 states now participating or applying. Expenditures for waivers serving people with developmental disabilities have grown from $2.2 million in FY 1982 to over $441 million in FY 1988 (Braddock et al., 1989).

The services most commonly covered by the HCB Care Services Waiver program include case management, residential services, habilitation, transportation, respite, homemaker, and adult day programs (Clinkscale & Ray, 1987). Waivers cannot be used to fund room and board costs. However, they can be

Table 12.1. Public laws assisting persons with developmental disabilities and/or older adults

Public law number	Statute or title of public law	Relation to support service needs of persons who are aging or have disabilities	Federal agency administering public law
PL 100-146	Developmental Disabilities Act Amendments of 1987	State planning councils have the opportunity to determine the priority areas and needs of the population with developmental disabilities.	Administration on Developmental Disabilities Department of Health and Human Services
PL 100-175	Older Americans Act Amendments of 1987	Housing was included as one of four priorities in 1975. The 1987 amendments include a definition of disability and severe disability. Area agencies on aging are now required to include older persons with disabilities in the plans.	Administration on Aging Department of Health and Human Services
PL 100-628	Stewart B. McKinney Homeless Assistance Act Amendments of 1988	Provides funding for 19 programs to assist homeless people and people who are "at risk of being" homeless. These programs include temporary and permanent housing, support services, and training.	Department of Housing and Urban Development
PL 100-407	Technology-Related Assistance for Individuals with Disabilities Act of 1988	The "Tech Act" provides a 3- to 5-year period to expand the use of assistive technology to provide new opportunities for employment, community living and recreation. Provides assistive devices and services to individuals through local organizations.	Department of Education
PL 90-284	Civil Rights Act of 1968	Provides equal rights to all individuals regardless of race or sex.	Department of Justice Office of Civil Rights

Table 12.2.   Public laws for the Social Security Act and Amendments

Public law number	Statute or title of public law	Relation to support service needs of persons who are aging or have disabilities	Federal agency administering public law
PL 74-271	Social Security Act of 1935 as amended Title I Social Security Disability Insurance (SSDI)	Provides benefits to workers who have contributed to the Social Security fund who become disabled before retirement age. Dependents of disabled workers are included as beneficiaries.	
	Title XVI Supplemental Security Income (SSI)	Provides direct cash payments to low-income aging people and to children and adults who are blind or have other disabilities and whose income and resources are below specified levels. SSI eligibility criteria also serve as eligibility criteria for other services and programs under the Social Security Act	
	Title XVIII Medicare	The national insurance program for people over the age of 65 and many persons with disabilities assists in meeting medical costs by providing hospital insurance protection and general medical protection.	
	Title XIX Medicaid	Provides financial assistance to states to pay for health care services to low-income individuals and families. The two subsidiary programs: Intermediate care facilities for people with mental retardation and the	Administration on Social Security

(continued)

Table 12.2. (continued)

Public law number	Statute or title of public law	Relation to support service needs of persons who are aging or have disabilities	Federal agency administering public law
		Home and Community-Based Care Services Waiver program are two of the major funding sources for residential and support services for people with mental retardation.	
	Title XX Social Services Block Grant	Provides federal funding to states to provide social services where needed.	

used to fund services provided within residential care programs, and to fund supports to individuals and families living at home. A study of seven HCB Care Services Waiver states found that six were using the waiver primarily as an adjunct to their residential services system. Among these six, the proportion of waiver beneficiaries in supervised residential settings ranged from 67% to 100% (Lakin et al., 1989). Room and board for HCB Care Services Waiver recipients in residential services programs generally are funded with income maintenance programs such as SSI, state SSI supplement programs, and SSDI.

Housing and Urban Development: Section 202

The Housing and Urban Development (HUD) Act of 1970 (PL 99-609) funding has been the most frequently used source of capital monies for construction or rehabilitation of housing for people with developmental disabilities (McIver, 1989). The allotment of funds set aside for older adults with disabilities comes from Section 202. Awards are made only to nonprofit agencies possessing tax exempt status from the Internal Revenue Service (IRS). The monies are given in the form of a loan which is repaid to HUD over a 40-year mortgage period at an interest rate pegged to the long-term average of federal borrowing. The operational monies needed to pay that mortgage and maintain the facility are derived from Section 8 (see the next section) subsidies. These are automatically supplied by HUD in a Section 202 project from tenant rent payments limited to no more than 30% of a tenant's income. Other funds, for example, state program monies or private resources, also may be used for this purpose.

Housing and Urban Development: Section 8

The Section 8 voucher program of the HUD Act, also known as the Modified Section 8 Existing Housing Certificate Program, provides payments to participating owners of rental housing stock. The primary difference between the

Table 12.3.   Public laws affecting support of older adults

Public law number	Statute or title of public law	Relation to support service needs of persons who are aging or have disabilities	Federal agency administering public law
PL 95-113	Food Stamp Act of 1977 as amended	Provides coupons issued by the Department of Agriculture to low-income and other households in need to purchase food or meals. Available to individuals in small community living arrangements for fewer than 16 persons.	United States Department of Agriculture Department of Health and Human Services
PL 93-112	Rehabilitation Act of 1973 Section 504	Prohibits any recipient of any federal funding from discriminating against a person with a disability solely because of the disability.	Department of Education Office of Vocational Rehabilitation
PL 100-203	Omnibus Budget Reconciliation Act of 1987; Nursing Home Reform Amendments	Provides for the reform of nursing facility admissions and on-going programs for individuals with mental illnesses, mental retardation, and developmental disabilities.	Department of Health and Human Services Health Care Finance Administration

Section 8 voucher program and the Section 202 rent subsidy program is that in the former the tenant contribution varies depending on the rent negotiated between the low-income tenant and landlord. Rents may exceed the official "fair market value," with the tenant paying the difference. Under the rent subsidy program, rents cannot exceed the federally determined fair market value for the type of housing and geographical area, and tenant payments are limited to 30% of their available income. The supply of Section 8 certificates in many areas is far less than the number of requests. Because low-income rental assistance is not an entitlement, subsidies are available only to the extent that federal funds are available.

Federal Housing Assistance in Rural Areas

The Farmers Home Administration of the Department of Agriculture administers federal housing assistance programs through Title V of PL 95-128. These

Table 12.4. Housing laws providing assistance and support

Public law number	Statute or title of public law	Relation to support service needs of persons who are aging or have disabilities	Federal agency administering public law
PL 73-479	National Housing Act of 1934 as amended Section 232	Provides federal mortgage insurance to assist sponsors to obtain financing for the development of nursing homes and ICFs. Amendments in 1978 allowed the development of additional facilities for the nonresidential care of people with disabilities who are able to live independently and require care during the day.	Department of Housing and Urban Development
PL 95-128	Housing Act of 1949 as amended, Title V, Section 515 Section 521	Provides loans for construction of low-income housing in rural areas. Provides rental assistance to low-income individuals and families in rural areas.	Department of Housing and Urban Development
PL 100-403	Fair Housing Act Amendments of 1988	Extends the principle of equal housing opportunity from Title VII of the Civil Rights Act of 1968 to people with disabilities.	Department of Housing and Urban Development Department of Justice
PL 99-609	Housing and Urban Development Act of 1970	Section 202 provides funding to nonprofit agencies possessing IRS tax exempt status for construction and rehabilitation of housing for people with developmental disabilities. Loans are repayable to HUD over 40 years. Section 8 vouchers are included.	Department of Housing and Urban Development

(continued)

Table 12.4.   (*continued*)

Public law number	Statute or title of public law	Relation to support service needs of persons who are aging or have disabilities	Federal agency administering public law
PL 93-383	Housing Act of 1937 as amended, Title IV	Authorized congregate housing services for people who are aging or have disabilities.	Department of Housing and Urban Development
	Section 8	Authorized direct payments to private homeowners or public housing agencies to provide housing for low-income families. Families are to contribute 30% of the adjusted family income for rent. Allows the individual to negotiate rent with the landlord and keep or pay the difference of the standard Section 8 rent.	
	Section 8 Housing Vouchers	Provides individuals with functional impairments the opportunity to remain substantially independent within their residence.	
	Section 7 Congregate Housing	Sponsorship of housing for people who are aging or have disabilities comes through public housing agencies or Section 202. Provides for social services and a full service meal program to frail tenants who are aging or have disabilities. Other services may include transportation, personal care, or housekeeping assistance.	

programs target low-income residents with disabilities living in rural areas. The Rural Rental Assistance Payments (Section 521) program provides rental subsidies through contracts with rural housing sponsors with the same goals, target populations, and eligibility requirements in relation to disabilities as the HUD Section 8 program. The Rural Housing for Persons Who Are Elderly or Have Handicaps (Section 515) program provides loans for the purchase, construction, improvement, or repair of rental or cooperative housing for rural area residents who are aging or have disabilities and is comparable to the HUD Section 202 program. Unlike the HUD Section 202 program, which may be used for the construction of ICF/MR facilities, these funds may not be used for nursing homes, special care facilities, or institutional-type dwellings. Survey data analysis indicated that this source of funding was not reported by any state (Martinson & Stone, 1990).

Two Congressional actions have provided opportunities to increase the rights of older adults with disabilities to have options. The Fair Housing Amendments of 1988 (PL 100-403) not only provide administrative procedures for handling complaints, but also provide specific protections regarding zoning. The Americans with Disabilities Act of 1990 (PL 101-336) provides civil rights protections in the private sector comparable to the Section 504 protections in the Rehabilitation Act of 1973 (PL 93-112) in federally financed programs.

McKinney Act: Assistance to People Who Are Homeless

A variety of federal programs were authorized by the Stewart B. McKinney Homeless Assistance Act Amendments of 1988 (PL 100-628). The act primarily provides federal grants to the states and Puerto Rico to assist them in meeting the current needs of homeless individuals and families, decreasing the number of homeless people, and preventing future homelessness. Special emphasis is to be placed on community living options for older adults, people with disabilities, families with children, Native Americans, and veterans. Stopgap programs include an emergency food and shelter program and grants for temporary shelter for people who are homeless. A Supportive Housing Demonstration Program, which is administered by HUD, funds transitional and permanent housing demonstration grants for the McKinney Act. These projects include supportive community living arrangements targeted to deinstitutionalized homeless individuals, homeless people with mental disabilities and other people with disabilities, and people with disabilities who are at risk of being homeless. This key phrase, "at risk of being homeless," makes these supportive options available to older adults with developmental disabilities. The options are described in the following sections.

Permanent Housing Program   The Permanent Housing Program provides permanent housing assistance in developing community-based, long-term housing and support services for projects serving no more than eight people with disabilities who are homeless or at risk of being homeless. States are eligible to apply for themselves or in cooperation with private nonprofit sponsors.

Supportive Housing Demonstration Program   The Supportive Housing Demonstration Program funds innovative approaches to providing short-term (18 months or less) supportive services to homeless persons who are capable of making the transition to independent living. It targets deinstitutionalized homeless persons, other homeless persons with mental disabilities, and homeless families with children. States, metropolitan cities, urban counties, public housing agencies, and private nonprofit agencies are eligible.

Adult Education for the Homeless   State education agencies may receive assistance through the Adult Education for the Homeless program to plan literacy training and basic skills remediation for adults who are homeless. State education agencies are eligible applicants.

Community Demonstration Projects for Alcohol and Drug Abuse Treatment   Community Demonstration Projects for Alcohol and Drug Abuse Treatment provide discretionary grants for demonstration projects that develop community-based alcohol and/or drug abuse treatment and rehabilitation services for individuals with alcohol or drug-related problems who are homeless or at imminent risk of becoming homeless. Community-based public and private nonprofit agencies are eligible applicants.

Community Mental Health Services Block Grant   The Community Mental Health Services Block Grant funds outreach services, case managment, mental health and substance abuse treatment, and supportive housing for homeless persons with mental illness and training for service providers. States are eligible.

Community Mental Health Services Demonstration Projects   Community Mental Health Services Demonstration Projects award discretionary grants to community-based demonstration projects for homeless adults with severe and long-term mental illness and homeless children and adolescents with severe emotional disturbances. State mental health authorities are eligible.

Emergency Community Services Homeless Assistance Grant   Emergency Community Services Homeless Assistance Grants are intended to increase and enhance existing local programs and services for people who are homeless, assist them in using these programs and services, and promote private sector assistance. States receiving Community Services Block Grants are eligible to pass funds down to the local community action agencies.

Emergency Shelter Grant Program   Under the Emergency Shelter Grant Program, buildings may be renovated, rehabilitated, or converted for use as emergency shelters for homeless people. Within limitations, funds may be used for essential services for homeless people and some operating costs. States, metropolitan cities, and urban counties are eligible based on the formula used for Community Development Block Grants.

Food Stamp Program for the Homeless   The Food Stamp Program for the Homeless allows people who are homeless increased access to food stamps by providing expedited service, excuses homeless people from monthly reporting of income changes, and excludes rent paid to maintain homeless people in hotels from countable income. It also permits families who are living with relatives to receive their own allotments. States have the option to receive federal matching funds to provide food stamp outreach to homeless people. Those eligible are homeless people.

Health Services for the Homeless   The Health Services for the Homeless program awards grants for health care delivery to homeless individuals, including primary care services, substance abuse treatment, and mental health care services. Local, private, nonprofit organizations and public entities are eligible.

Job Training for the Homeless Demonstration Program   The Job Training for the Homeless Demonstration Program provides funds for job training activities for homeless individuals, including remedial education, job search, job counseling, preparation training, and basic literacy instruction. States and local agencies, private nonprofit organizations, and private businesses are eligible.

Section 8 Moderate Rehabilitation Assistance for Single Room Occupancy (SRO) Dwellings   Rental assistance is available under the Section 8 Moderate Rehabilitation Assistance for Single Room Occupancy (SRO) Dwellings program for single room housing units for occupancy by homeless individuals. Public housing agencies are eligible.

Supplemental Assistance for Facilities To Assist the Homeless   Supplemental Assistance for Facilities To Assist the Homeless provides interest-free advances and grants to acquire, lease, convert, or rehabilitate existing facilities and to provide support services. Funds are available for comprehensive and innovative activities specifically designed to meet the needs of people who are homeless. States, metropolitan cities, urban counties, and nonprofit organizations are eligible.

In FY 1988, HUD awarded $3.6 million in grants to 41 projects nationwide to develop permanent housing for homeless people with disabilities. An additional $24.6 million appropriated for permanent housing grants was not expended due to a lack of applications meeting program requirements and was reallocated to the transitional housing grant program, as required by federal legislation. Fifteen million dollars for permanent housing grants, including grants for housing for people with disabilities who are homeless or at risk of being homeless, was available in FY 1989. However, $6 million were never allocated due to the small number of requests. While this illustrates the sometime underutilization of federal funds, small local agencies may not be willing to write grants or may not be experienced enough in grant writing to gain access to the larger funding resources. There are other resources and options for funding community living and support services to older adults. These are discussed in the following section.

LOCAL FUNDING POSSIBILITIES

The possibilities for local funding depend on the municipality and the agency seeking monies. In a municipality in Minnesota, for example, an agreement was reached between a local nonprofit organization and a municipal government for creative tax financing for an apartment complex for persons with disabilities (Wieck, 1989). Some townships have helped provide Community Development Block Grants for the purchase of land or the renovation of a building.

Options for local funding depend on the locale and the willingness of the township or city officials to work with organizations. Some funding sources (e.g., Community Development Block Grants) are threatened with reductions due to Gramm-Rudman-Hollings (PL 98-369, the Deficit Reduction Act of 1984) and federal budget cuts. A friendly relationship with an influential local official is always an asset when an agency is looking to a municipality for assistance. Additional funding sources in the community may include conventional mortgages, shared equity, trusts, and co-assignments of mortgages. Private investor financing may be available, and sources include individuals, corporations, foundations, and institutions. An agency should research and carefully develop its options in its own locale. The options described below are a few examples of the possibilities. Creative and imaginative financing are vital to a successful utilization of funding sources.

Syndication

Housing developed through syndication involves attracting investors to a project so they can provide the needed capital to build and operate a home. Since the 1970s, this financing method has been used to secure low-income housing, provide monies for needed renovations, develop group homes for individuals with developmental disabilities, and provide construction monies for living options for older adults, in addition to other activities. The basic process is for the nonprofit agency to approach a potential investor about syndicating a community living project. The investor then enters into a contract with the nonprofit agency to develop a syndication. The nonprofit agency and the syndicator develop an agreement that can then be sold to interested investors. The incentive for investors is the tax benefit they can realize by providing some capital for the syndicated community living program. These investors provide capital to the nonprofit agency in exchange for part or total ownership of the project. Over the course of 7–12 years, the investor is able to recoup his or her original investment and realize a substantial tax advantage. The group of investors typically owns the actual building, while the nonprofit organization retains ownership of the land.

Many of the syndication agreements worked out in the early 1970s supported low-income housing that needed renovation or major repairs that could not be covered with existing revenue sources. The tax benefits developed since that time have proved very beneficial. There are organizations around the country that serve as nonprofit syndicators. The National Housing Law Project of Berkeley, California leads annual seminars that provide instruction on this type of low-income housing financing, including detailing how a nonprofit agency can construct a deal to sell to investors. The way a syndication deal is constructed and the responsibilities of and benefits for the nonprofit organization must be defined clearly prior to an agreement with the assistance of a tax lawyer. Syndication is a viable option, though less so than it once was.

Fund-Raising

Ventures to raise capital through fund-raising efforts are a more labor-intensive means of providing necessary capital; nevertheless, it can be successful. The options for fund-raising are quite extensive; they can include, but are not limited to, corporate donations, fund-raising events, individual donations, and in-kind donations such as building supplies, furniture, land, and appliances. The means by which an agency does its fund-raising can lend credibility to the organization and amplify the cause they represent. Publicizing events and major donations can help to further the campaign and assist in its success. In Kentucky and other southeastern states, low-income housing has been provided by Habitat for Humanity. Members and volunteers join to build a house over a 24-hour period for a family who also commits to making payments for 20 years. The land and materials usually are donations to the organization, and payments are expected to assist with financially supporting the organization in the future. The family is expected to provide sweat equity in the form of a commitment of 200 hours of assistance in other home building projects.

Cooperatives, Condominiums, and Private Ownership

The rapid development of cooperative housing and condominiums has been a phenomenon all over the United States. The cost of such housing often has been far in excess of the income of most persons with disabilities. There are now a few organizations that are developing financial options by which a person with disabilities can own a cooperative apartment or condominium. Parent groups in Massachusetts, for example, have purchased condominiums with a planned transfer of ownership to their adult children with disabilities. An organization in New Hampshire specializes in developing housing that provides a maximum of community inclusion and financial solvency with a minimum commitment of financial resources. Creative administration and management of both finances and housing real estate can improve availability of condominiums, cooperatives, and other types of private housing to people with disabilities.

The Community Reinvestment Act

The local funding resource that has great potential, but has not had adequate publicity since it has been available, is the Community Reinvestment Act (CRA) of 1977 (PL 95-557), which is part of a series of pieces of federal legislation intended to address problems that certain groups in society have in obtaining credit. The CRA is part of the Housing and Community Development Act of 1977. The CRA premise is that banks and thrift institutions have an ongoing obligation to help meet the credit needs of the communities in which they operate. All financial institutions whether wholesale, retail, urban, or rural have an affirmative responsibility to be available to meet the credit needs of low- and moderate-income members of their communities as they would any of their other clients. CRA was slow in developing due to the public's ignorance of the meaning and existence of community reinvestment and Congress's inability to provide standards by which to measure a community's credit needs or a financial institution's efforts to satisfy those needs. According to the Senate Banking, Housing and Urban Affairs Committee, government, through tax revenues and public debt, cannot and should not provide more than a limited part of the capital required for local housing and economic development needs. Financial institutions must play the lead role. The local bank has the responsibility of defining the community it will serve. The regulation requires the bank to maintain: 1) a map of the local community, 2) a list of the specific types of credit the bank is prepared to extend to the community, and 3) a copy of the public notice of the regulation.

The regulatory agencies of the financial institutions, the Board of Governors of the Federal Reserve System, the Comptroller of the Currency, the Federal Deposit Insurance Corporation, and the Federal Home Loan Bank Board share in the authority to implement CRA. While there is substantial leeway in meeting the CRA responsibilities, some of the more effective components of meeting these responsibilities could include the following:

1. Increasing efforts to make loans to meet the credit needs of the community for home loans, home improvement loans, and small business loans
2. Making lines of credit available to nonprofit developers of low-income housing, including low-income, multi-family new construction and rehabilitation projects
3. Developing guidance and/or assistance to potential customers or actual customers regarding federal, state, and local assistance programs for housing and other similar community needs

The American Banking Association has offered successful models of CBA programs. These include multi-bank consortia making loan decisions on a common area of concern or need. The consortia have been involved in development of low- and moderate-income housing, in-house banking programs to train specialty staff to deliver services to low- and moderate-income groups, and development of private–public partnerships to address intercity and rural redevelopment problems. An example of this type of cooperative effort was the Boston Housing Partnership, which included multiple agencies involved in rehabilitating 1,800 homes and apartments in the Boston area.

CONCLUSION

The following sections discuss the four major conclusions that can be drawn from the review of federal legislation and long-term funding streams supporting community living options that has been presented in this chapter.

Availability of Community Living Options

There is a national crisis in the availability of affordable community living options, especially for people with the lowest incomes. The rapid growth in homelessness throughout the 1980s has affected many people with disabilities and their families. They are especially vulnerable because of their low-income status and, in some cases, because of discrimination and also other factors associated with the disability itself.

There are insufficient data on the numbers and characteristics of people with developmental disabilities in generic community living programs, such as low-income rental assistance programs. More information is needed on the people with developmental disabilities who are homeless, in nursing homes, and in board-and-care homes or personal care homes. There is a lack of data on residents with developmental disabilities in board-and-care facilities, and there are widespread difficulties in the monitoring of conditions in board-and-care units, especially those that are unlicensed.

Perspective/Attitude Shift

The approach to housing for people with developmental disabilities needs a paradigm shift from residential services that provide basic supervision and active intervention to supported community living options that provide individualized choices from an array of supports so that people are living in their own homes rather than being "placed" in residential care facilities. Group homes serving eight to 15 persons are being scaled down to serve four to six persons and, in some areas, even fewer persons.

The "not in my backyard" (NIMBY) syndrome continues to reduce opportunities for housing for people with developmental disabilities in some neighborhoods and communities. The Fair Housing Amendments of 1988 (PL 100-403), however, consider this situation discrimination, and, therefore, legal remedy is available.

There is widespread insensitivity among community members, as well as policymakers outside the field of developmental disabilities, to the overwhelming evidence that people who live in the community make much greater gains in independence, productivity, and inclusion than their counterparts in institutions. There is a comparable lack of knowledge and understanding about the proven ability of people with severe disabilities, people who depend on technology, and people with challenging behaviors to live in homes in the community and be included in neighborhoods with people who do not have visible disabilities.

Supports

The major issue is the relative lack of resources for support to individuals with developmental disabilities and their families despite the critical importance of supports to the promotion of independence, productivity, and community inclusion. There is an increasing number of people with functional limitations in their activities of daily living, especially among older adults, whose numbers also are growing. There is no corresponding rate of growth in the availability of support to individuals.

In provision of both individual and family supports, frequently there is a lack of involvement and focus on the consumer. Individual supports seldom are available to be directed by the person with developmental disabilities. Few individuals have available to them an array of supports from which to select a "package" of supports tailored specifically to their needs and preferences.

Reinforcement of the emphasis on consumer control in the Independent Living Program is still awaiting publication of the federal performance standards. Family supports tend to provide somewhat more flexibility, such as those available through a cash subsidy program. Overall, however, there is little family input in the design and monitoring of family support programs.

Federally financed supports to individuals and families tend to be tied to medical care needs because of their basis in health finance programs. For example, personal care services provided through the Medicaid program are defined as medically oriented tasks that have to do with a patient's physical requirements, that must be prescribed by a physician and supervised by a registered nurse, and that must be in accordance with the recipient's plan of treatment. Basic Medicare coverage reimburses only for services that are reasonable and necessary for the diagnosis and treatment of an illness or injury and excludes coverage of assistance in activities of daily living.

Almost none of the supports to individuals with developmental disabilities and their families are considered entitlements. Most federal funding that is available is at state or local option, including Medicaid waivers, Medicaid funding of optional services, and extension of Medicaid eligibility to children with disabilities who otherwise would be eligible only if they were institutionalized. Discretionary grants for demonstration programs and special projects, including special recreation program, ILCs, community support programs for people with serious mental illness, and the development of statewide systems to make assistive devices and services available, also are state or local options.

There are gaps reported across the nation in the availability of supports to individuals with developmental disabilities and their families living in rural areas, supports to consumers with the most severe disabilities, and supports that can be obtained in an emergency. Many ILCs restrict services to people with only certain kinds of disabilities. Over 40% do not serve people with mental retardation. Many older adults with developmental disabilities find it difficult

to obtain services through the programs funded through the Older Americans
Act Amendments because they are illiterate and, therefore, do not understand
the requirements of eligibility for benefits and services (Cotten et al., 1986;
Stone, 1987).

Funding

There is a need corresponding to those discussed above to shift resources from
institutional and facility-based care to individual and family supports that are
tailored to the needs and preferences of individuals with developmental disabilities. A related issued is the bias in many publicly supported programs toward
funding services in facilities, but not in homes and communities. Although
efforts to reduce this bias have led to the development of programs such as the
Medicaid Home and Community-Based Care Services Waiver and the Technology-Related Assistance Grants, these programs generally are at state option,
limited in availability, and funded at significantly lower levels than facility-based
services. This is especially the case for services that are nonmedical, such as
personal assistance to people with disabilities that enable them to live independently and maintain competitive employment.

Limited funding is available for home and community-based supports to
individuals with developmental disabilities and their families. Expenditures for
home supports consistently are much lower than those for facility-based care
despite the fact that these expenditures broaden the availability of services so
that they reach many more people than the relatively few served by facility-
based programs.

The Social Services Block Grant, which is a major source of funding for
supports to individuals with developmental disabilities and their families in many
states, has been significantly underfunded since the mid 1980s in comparison to
its original authorization levels. Current legislative proposals to increase federal
appropriation levels will provide only partial restoration. In this era of deficit
reduction, increased costs of existing facility-based services, such as those provided in large state institutions, frequently leave few resources for individual
and family support, which shows no regard for the relative cost-effectiveness
and significance in the promotion of independence, productivity, and community
inclusion of the latter.

The situation in which older adults with developmental disabilities, family
members, and service agencies and providers find themselves when attempting
to provide age-appropriate options that reflect individualized needs and preferences is complex and problematic. The information presented in this chapter
pertains to combinations of options based on both disability and age. The authors encourage the development of innovative efforts to provide access to
available resources and funding on an individual basis and in combinations of
options to assist older adults with developmental disabilities and their families
not only to live in their communities, but also to be involved in their communities.

REFERENCES

Anderson, D.J., Lakin, K.C., Bruininks, R.H., & Hill, B.K. (1987). *A national study of residential and support services for elderly persons with mental retardation.* Minneapolis: University of Minnesota, Department of Educational Psychology.

Braddock, D., Hemp, R., Fujiura, G., Bachelder, L., & Mitchell, D. (1989) *Public expenditures for mental retardation and developmental disabilities in the United States: State profiles.* (Working paper, 3rd ed.). Chicago: University Affiliated Program in Developmental Disabilities, University of Illinois at Chicago.

Clinkscale, R., & Ray, S. (1987). *Survey of Medicaid Home and Community-Based Care Waivers: FY 1986.* Medicaid Program Evaluation Working Paper No. 1.11. Columbia, MD: LaJolla Management Corporation.

Cotten, P.D., Britt, C.R., & Moreland, A. (1986). *State plans for providing services for the elderly Mississippian with mental handicaps; a coordinated plan.* Jackson: Mississippi Department of Mental Health.

Department of Health and Human Services. (1988). *Report from the working group on improving public policies and programs affecting persons with mental retardation and other developmental disabilities.* Washington, DC: Author.

Institute of Medicine. (1988). *Homelessness, health, and human needs.* Washington, DC: National Academy Press.

Lakin, K.C., Jaskulski, T., Hill, B.K., Bruininks, R.H.. Menke, J.M., White, C.C., & Wright, E.A. (1989). *Medicaid services for people with mental retardation and other related conditions.* (Report No. 27). Minneapolis: University of Minnesota, Minnesota University Affiliated Program, Center for Residential and Community Services.

Litvak, S., Simi, Zukas, H., & Heumann, J.E. (1987). *Attending to America: Personal assistance for independent living, a survey of attendant service programs in the United States for people of all ages with disabilities. Executive summary.* Berkeley: World Institute on Disability.

Martinson, M.C., & Stone, J.A. (1990). *Results of a national survey of state MR/DD agencies serving older persons with developmental disabilities.* Lexington: University of Kentucky, Interdisciplinary Human Development Institute.

McIver, D. (1989). *Developing housing for persons with disabilities: A guide to HUD's Section 202 program.* Austin: The Housing and Community Development Resource Center, Inc.

National Association of State Mental Retardation Program Directors. (1988). *Implications for services to persons with developmental disabilities.* Alexandria, VA: Author.

Ohio Department of Mental Retardation and Developmental Disabilities. (1990). *The supported living reference manual.* Columbus, OH: Author.

Scallet, L., Needleman, J., & Jaskulski, T. (1992). *Deinstitutionalization and homelessness.* Unpublished manuscript.

Seltzer, M.M., & Krauss, M.W. (1987). *Aging and mental retardation: Extending the continuum.* Washington, DC: Monographs of the American Association on Mental Retardation.

Stone, J.A. (1987, June). *Residential options for the elderly.* Presentation to the National Association of State Mental Retardation/Developmental Disabilities Directors, Los Angeles.

Wieck, C. (1989). *Critical issues of housing for individuals with developmental disabilities who are elderly.* Document prepared for the Interdisciplinary Human Development Institute-University Affiliated Program, University of Kentucky, Lexington. Unpublished manuscript.

13

Small-Scale Community Living Options Serving Three or Fewer Older Adults with Developmental Disabilities

Melton C. Martinson and James A. Stone

The most current approach to older adults with developmental disabilities is a focus on individualization. The individualized approach to services in the community reflects an evolving way of thinking about where people live and the services and programs they use. The emphasis is on promoting desirable outcomes through individualized planning and management. The goal is to design and manage a variety of settings and resources that will support older adults in environments that are much like real homes. Supports can be provided in typical houses in typical neighborhoods. Planning and providing such small-scale options are considered best practice in provision of community living options and support services to older adults with developmental disabilities.

Hauber, Rotegard, and Bruininks (1985) concluded that small-scale family type living options for older adults with developmental disabilities are increasing. They issued the warning: "Meaningful and lasting support for qualitative living alternatives will depend on a growing commitment to elderly disabled individuals and to a funding mechanism that ensures the success of such a commitment" (p. 349). Currently, a rapidly evolving approach to services focuses on individualized planning and flexibility that allows the person to make choices and exercise preferences.

To date there has been little research on small-scale community living options for people with developmental disabilities. The small-scale context in this chapter refers to settings for 15 individuals or fewer. The national surveys discussed in Chapters 11 and 12 did not cover this option (Anderson, Lakin, Bruininks, & Hill, 1987; Seltzer & Krauss, 1987). It was not until 1990 that a study on this option was undertaken by the Rehabilitation Research and Training Center (RRTC) Consortium on Aging and Developmental Disabilities (Martinson & Stone, 1990). The investigators represented The Interdisciplinary Human Development Institute at The University of Kentucky (UK). Data from this survey of state mental retardation/developmental disabilities (MR/DD) agencies indicated that 19,750 older adults were residing in small-scale homes. Such community living options appear to be relatively new to the developmental disabilities system. This chapter reports on the RRTC/UK national survey and addresses the merits and problems of different types of small-scale community living options.

METHOD

Selected variables of the national survey of state MR/DD agencies provided an opportunity to determine whether small-scale community living options were, in fact, available and whether there were specific efforts for older adults with developmental disabilities. In this investigation older adults with developmental disabilities were defined as ages 60 and older. Following are the variables the survey looked for in state MR/DD agency programs.

1. A minimum of 25% of the living options for three older adults or fewer
2. Support services available
3. Statutes or regulations for services to older adults with developmental disabilities
4. Interagency work groups or task forces with a focus on the needs of older adults with developmental disabilities

States that reported at least three of these variables were chosen for in-depth examination. These were Delaware, Maryland, Massachusetts, Ohio, Nebraska, New York, North Dakota, and South Carolina.

An 11-item open-ended questionnaire was developed for a telephone survey of the eight states selected. A preliminary call was made to each state's MR/DD division to affirm agreement to participate in the survey, to identify a contact person, and to determine the most convenient time to take the survey. Following are the survey questions:

1. Could you share how small-scale community living options for older persons started?
2. How long have these options been available?
3. Are there any plans to expand these options?
4. What types of support services/programs are available?
5. Are these support services individualized/age-related or part of the standard services offered to all clients?
6. What would you consider to be positive about the small-scale options?
7. Were there barriers or problems in the early stages of your program?
8. Do these barriers/problems exist today?
9. If you could start over today, would you do anything differently?
10. As far as the older person is concerned, does one have the opportunity to make choices in where they may live or whom they may live with?
11. Do you have additional information you would consider sharing or that the questions did not address concerning your agency's efforts to provide residential options to older persons? (Martinson & Stone, 1990, p. 38)

GENERAL INFORMATION FROM EACH STATE

Each state had a different name for its small-scale living options, and each state started its program at a different time. Delaware started its program in 1960 as foster care for adults in rural areas. Maryland has provided leisure homes for older adults since 1987. Massachusetts has used specialized home care with a focus on aging since 1986. Nebraska has provided small, supported settings since 1985. New York began specialized family care in 1937. North Dakota has provided individualized support homes for older adults since 1986. Ohio has provided supported living services since 1989. South Carolina has provided supervised living in community training homes at two levels for one to three persons and a matchup roommate/companion program for older adults with and without disabilities since 1988. Each state expressed an interest in expanding these living options to serve more older adults with developmental disabilities; however, expansion was based on availability of more funding.

Responses to the question about the positive elements of the small-scale community living options noted the flexibility of the options; individuals living in familiar settings, individualization; more natural and normal living through community participation; and living in a regular home or apartment with a family in which there is social involvement, a family-like atmosphere, more freedom, and the opportunity to make choices. The respondents gave particular weight to the benefits of a family-like atmosphere and the opportunity to be involved in social activities through informal support from careproviders and friends.

When asked if the older adults with developmental disabilities had the opportunity to make choices about where they lived or with whom, all states gave positive responses. The responses follow:

Definitely, with emergencies being the exception.

A person has some choices but not complete freedom.

Developing those abilities now; limits are in funding.

A person is provided with opportunities for visit(s) to the community living options before placement.

Yes, this is a key factor that allows choice.

Yes, older adults choose services and programs.

Yes, with an Individual Program Planning Team

Yes, limited by where they live at the time. (Martinson & Stone, 1990, p. 39)

These states have similarities and unique differences in their approaches to providing small-scale community living options concerning the level of supervision they offer and the types of additional support services available. A common theme in responses from all the states was that small-scale community living options need to be developed around the older adult's individual needs and preferences. Three states that illustrate the similarities and differences are Ohio, North Dakota, and Delaware. The following sections present summaries of the information supplied by each of these states.

OHIO'S SUPPORTED LIVING OPTION

Philosophy of the Supported Living Option

Of the eight states surveyed, Ohio was found to be the state with the most flexible program, the Supported Living Option, for providing living options to individuals with developmental disabilities. The Ohio Department of Mental Retardation and Developmental Disabilities' (ODMRDD) concept of supported living has this definition: "Supported living is a residential service system that provides the necessary supports that will enable an individual to live in settings of their choice. It seeks to provide an array of supervision, adaptive devices, and other interventions that will enable an individual to live in a setting of his or her choice" (Ohio Department of Mental Retardation and Developmental Disabilities, 1990, p. II-1). Supported living is not grounded in a concept of readiness or in a continuum of progressively less restrictive environments; rather, it seeks to match supports to an individual where he or she wants to be. The ODMRDD goals for supported living are:

1. People with mental retardation/developmental disabilities will have choices and opportunities regarding life decisions.
2. People with mental retardation/developmental disabilities will have the support that they need.

The objectives of supported living are:

1. An individual will be able to choose a home that is safe, secure, and permanent.
2. An individual will have the opportunity to make friends, visit in the community, and choose a roommate if desired.
3. An individual will be able to take risks in a supported manner, learn to handle daily problems, and be productive.
4. An individual will be able to rely on friends, advocates, relatives, and professionals for support.
5. As an individual is better able to handle challenges of daily living, she or he will be able to lessen reliance on supports.
6. An individual will be able to increase financial independence, including retaining personal resources.

The ODMRDD affirmed both in policy and practice that the individuals they serve are like all other human beings. Their philosophy was "a home is a home is a home." Homes should provide safe and secure environments. Activities in the homes of people with developmental disabilities should be similar to activities that occur in anyone else's home. The home atmosphere should be conducive to learning focused on activities that lead to higher levels of independence and community inclusion. "The challenge for each of us who play a part in the complex system of service delivery is to re-examine our definition of a home as it relates to those we serve" (Ohio Department of Mental Retardation and Developmental Disabilities, 1990, p. I-2). Supported living is designed to serve any person identified as eligible for services from ODMRDD. Persons must be determined to have moderate, severe, or profound disabilities as verified by the ODMRDD or the County Board of MR/DD, or a person must be a resident of a developmental center, or be eligible for admission into a developmental center. Supported living is designed to be flexible and accommodate new program strategies as they develop. An array of services includes the following types: vocational, leisure/recreation, domestic, respite, financial, advocacy, medical care, receivership, mobility, or community services. Supported living allows an individual to receive supports and services that will enable him or her to have choices. Available choices include a community linkage person, an independent skill development coach, chore services, transportation, medical supplies, a paid neighbor or roommate, delivered meals, appointment/errand assistance, adaptive devices and/or environmental modifications, rent, utilities, and home furnishings. Virtually anything that an individual needs to be successful in the setting of choice is available. The individual program is driven by the needs of the person.

Supported living funds cannot be used to supplant other funding sources for similar services. Case managers are expected to ensure that supported living funds are used only for goods and services that are not available to an individual from another funding source. Funding for supported living comes from the following array of sources: Personal Care Assistance, Medicaid Waiver, Rehabilitation Services, Medicaid, Generic Social Service, HUD Rental Subsidy, Case Management, ODMRDD, and the Food Stamp program.

How the Supported Living Option Works

The state of Ohio and the county boards developed a reasonable array of living options with supports at an affordable cost. Service plans are to be designed to maximize the combined use of state, local, and consumer resources. Generic or existing services are to be used whenever possible. Funds are to be provided directly to the individual to choose and maintain his or her own home. Systems are to be revised to allow the provision of funds directly to counties and agencies. The provision of safe and secure housing and care are to be ensured through certification, monitoring, and evaluation. Systems are to be developed to address an individualized service plan (ISP) that determines the amount, type, and frequency of services provided. This ISP is to be reviewed on a regular basis and changed as necessary. Assistance is to be provided to the individual in making informed choices. The Supported Living Option should ensure adequate support so that the possibility of harm to any individual is minimized. Living arrangements and necessary supports, that are identified in an ISP, should be developed or arranged. Support should include definite action by providers to assist the individual in initiating relationships.

Following is an example of a Supported Living Option arrangement offered for an individual with aging parents:

Debbie is currently living with her parents. They have cared for Debbie all of her 55 years. They have decided it is time for her to learn to live without their constant support since they will not always be able to care for her. They contacted the county board case manager to ask about living options available. The case manager knows Debbie has many strengths that would be valuable in supported living. Before the meeting to develop Debbie's support plan, her parents asked her if she had any friend she would like to live with. Debbie chose to live alone. At the planning team meeting it was noted that Debbie has good personal hygiene and housekeeping skills. She can get herself up in the morning with an alarm clock if someone sets it for her. She can cook simple meals but likes to heat frozen TV dinners in a microwave oven. She rides the county board bus to a workshop. She can talk on the telephone but has a hard time dialing numbers. She does not know how to use public transportation but would like to learn. Debbie has never managed her own money. Workshop earnings and other benefits total about $425.00 per month. Debbie's parents are willing to help with rent if necessary.

The planning team members believe they can help Debbie live alone in an apartment. Debbie and her parents think they would like to try this but are concerned about safety. It is suggested that she have a monitored security system with color coded buttons for emergencies. They think this is an acceptable solution. Everyone agrees that a selected provider will help Debbie with managing her money, shopping, learning to use public transportation, and learning to use the security system. Also, they will buy her an automatic dial telephone, a microwave oven, a security system, and an electric alarm clock with an automatic alarm setting. The agreed upon services are recorded in the ISP and anywhere else formal programs require a record.

NORTH DAKOTA'S INDIVIDUALIZED SUPPORTED LIVING ARRANGEMENT

The program model used in North Dakota provides only residential services, with room, board, and case management, for older adults with developmental disabilities, and funding does not follow the individual. This program model may be adapted for serving older adults with any disabilities. North Dakota began planning for the Individualized Supported Living Arrangement (ISLA) in 1986. The major programmatic concepts were: 1) normalizing individual's environments, 2) continuing to include individuals in their communities, and 3) developing individualized consumer-driven systems. The philosophy of ISLA encompasses the following concepts:

1. Whenever possible individuals should be trained in the environment of ultimate functioning.
2. Physical movement of individuals from one residential facility to another impairs their progress.
3. Systems, along with programs, should be individualized.

Previously, North Dakota had a residential service continuum demanding the transfer of skills from one living environment to another, requiring as many as five relocations to reach the most inclusive environment. Services through the ISLA are provided by private, nonprofit or private, for-profit corporations. These providers are licensed as Supported Living Arrangement programs. Those eligible for services live in the state developmental centers or are deemed eligible to receive services through the developmental disabilities system. The program design is defined by what is appropriate and cost-effective for the individual. Options are unlimited and may include active intervention, personal care, maintenance, live-in staff, paid neighbors, and paid companions. The ISLA is a residential program without other programs or services attached. Room and board and case management are the basic services.

Role of the Case Manager

The case manager functions are the key elements of the program and cover the following responsibilities:

1. Identify social needs of each individual.
2. Assist the team with the development of objectives to meet identified social needs.
3. Attend pre-admission and admission committee meetings.
4. Communicate admissions committee decisions to the referring agency.

5. Serve as an internal advocate by ensuring that the human and civil rights of the individual are not violated, and conduct internal investigations of abuse/neglect complaints.
6. Initiate and maintain ongoing communication with the parents/guardians of the individuals by providing written reports on progress or problems. Serve as contact person for the family/guardian. Arrange vacations and visits within established guidelines. Assist families with understanding of objectives, philosophies, requirements, plans, and so forth. Assist the family in the development of positive, meaningful ways to support the individual.
7. Facilitate community inclusion efforts by assisting with the development of individual community contact (e.g., with friends, or volunteers). Arrange for attendance at religious services. Arrange individualized, inclusive community recreational opportunities.
8. Establish trust with the individual, and encourage her or him to express concerns, needs, wants, likes, dislikes, and so forth.
9. Communicate the individual's emotional status to appropriate staff along with suggestions for possible improvement of services. Provide counseling for the individual when appropriate. Arrange for referral to more formal counseling or therapy if necessary.
10. Assist with efforts to obtain the benefits of federal, state, and private support programs (e.g., SSI, food stamps, railroad benefits).
11. Monitor the individual's progress toward objectives listed on the individualized program plan (IPP) by reviewing progress notes from day and residential programs. Note corrective actions if necessary, and consult with appropriate staff about the individual's needs or the necessity to reconvene the IPP team.

North Dakota recognizes the fact that new programs sometimes are more expensive at start up. However, the focus is on the duration of the learning experience for the individual and movement into less costly residential services.

Categories of Support Services

The Title XIX waiver (through PL 74-271, the Social Security Act of 1937 as Amended) provides support services in two categories—habilitation and personal care. Habilitation is active intervention that involves teaching the individual to do needed tasks. Personal care provides others to do tasks for the individual. Habilitation services may include: health care, medications, nutrition counseling, communication, and mobility/adaptive equipment; self-care, such as toileting, bathing, oral hygiene, dressing, and grooming; environmental support and safety, such as laundry chores, meal preparation and serving/cleanup, homemaker chores, adapting behavior to a home environment, attending to financial and personal affairs, and emergency exit; and community support, such as transportation, therapeutic recreation, and obtaining emergency services.

The major focus for persons receiving personal care service is maintenance, assistance, and/or supervision. Personal care services may include health care to ensure that the person receives medications and/or specialized treatment prescribed by a physician, and observing and reporting the effects of this medication and treatment; assisting the person with movement through the home, including positioning and transferring; and ensuring that specialized activities are provided, if necessary. Personal care services may ensure that meals comply with basic nutritional needs and special dietary requirements of the individual. Also, assisting individuals in communicating personal needs and assistance in maintaining prosthetic, orthotic, or adaptive equipment and using this equipment may be included. There is assistance in self care, environmental support and safety, and community support services that will assist the individual in using and benefiting from the resources available in the general community that may enhance the health, safety, welfare, and psycho-social development of the individual with developmental disabilities.

The personal care provider assists the individual with transportation to nonmedical activities. The IPP provides for transportation to appropriate community services, assistance for the individual in participating in therapeutic recreational activities designed to maintain psycho-social development, and obtaining emergency services.

The ISLA/Supportive Home Care is another option, designed to assist with services to children or adults living in the home of a relative. The relative is the primary caregiver, and the direct service staff assist this primary caregiver in providing the services. The primary caregiver is designated for the following reasons:

1. Some programs, for example, respite care, replace the primary caregiver. In situations like this, the ISLA/Supportive Home Care staff could assist the respite care worker.
2. The ISLA/Supportive Home Care staff do not assume direct responsibility for the individual.
3. If this program assumed primary caregiver responsibilities, parents might not qualify for other family support programs.

DELAWARE'S ADULT FAMILY LIVING OPTIONS

The program in Delaware falls between those of Ohio and North Dakota. The services are designed to provide community involvement and family-type residential options. However, funding is directed to the service providers, not to the individuals. The objectives of the Delaware Division of Mental Retardation (DMR) is to provide residential services and encourage community involvement for individuals with mental retardation. Community residential services options are group homes, neighborhood homes, supervised apartment living, and foster care.

The Foster Care Programs are: Adult Family Living Homes, Foster Training Homes, Intensive Foster Care Homes, and Respite Homes. These programs are designed to serve persons who no longer can live with their own families but are unable to live independently.

The Adult Family Living Program

Through the Adult Family Living Program, a private home is selected carefully to provide guidance and supervision for no more than three persons with mental retardation. The primary objective of the program is to offer older adults an opportunity to live in a family setting and to participate in community activities.

The provider emphasizes the adult's complete inclusion in the family and offers the opportunity for as many community experiences as possible. Each individual for which this arrangement is made attends a habilitation program Monday through Friday, which has been identified by the planning team as most appropriate based on the individual's needs. (Homes providing services to more than one adult also must be licensed by the Delaware Division of Public Health.)

The Foster Training Home Program

The Foster Training Home Program offers an individual the opportunity to live and participate in a family environment. In addition to the services provided in the Adult Family Living Program, the Foster Training Home Program includes a very important training component. The daily training provided to the person is determined by individual needs as identified by the interdisciplinary (ID) team and is in addition to any other training received in day habilitation programs. The individual program may include any or all of the following five categories: 1) adaptive skills, including drinking and eating, table manners, dressing, toileting, bathing, personal hygiene, and grooming; 2) community living skills, including health awareness, safety, use of the telephone, shopping, and eating in public; 3) basic communication, including nonverbal communication, verbal communication, and receptive language; 4) socialization, including social interaction and group behavior; and 5) domestic skills, including general cleaning, clothing care, and food preparation.

The Intensive Foster Care Program

A new program, the Intensive Foster Care Program, offers an individual with mental retardation the opportunity to live and participate in a family environment. The individuals in these programs have more intensive needs, either in the areas of self-help or in behavior modification, than those individuals involved in the Foster Training Home Program. The basic requirements for a Foster Care Provider include the desirable traits of patience, reliability, adaptability, understanding, warmth, open-mindedness, acceptance, maturity, and stability. Providers also must be Delaware residents, be at least 18 years old, and have a steady source of income other than the income received as a provider (one is not prohibited from working full time outside the home). Providers must not have a criminal record, may be single or married, must be physically able to provide continuity of care, and must have no active or contagious diseases (a negative test result is also required). Providers may not provide services to more than one state agency, no roomers or boarders may be living in the home, and all family members residing in the home must agree to participate in the Foster Care Program. Providers must be able to read, write, and keep records as assisted by the case manager; be able to provide competent adult supervision on a 24-hour basis; and make transportation available on a 24-hour basis. A telephone must be available, and providers must furnish character and employment references.

Basic Requirements for Provider Training

At least one adult member of the family must attend all required training sessions. These sessions cover the following: 1) an introduction to the field of mental retardation and overview of the division's philosophy, policies, procedures, and services; 2) individuals' rights; 3) behavior change and role of the behavior analysts; 4) individualized program plans and interdisciplinary teams; 5) home fire safety; 6) the DMR recordkeeping system; 7) health awareness and the role of the nurse consultant; 8) assistance with medication, including legal liabilities and responsibilities; and 9) the DMR placement process. Workshops and seminars will be held periodically to address areas of concern, enhance previously acquired skills, and offer instruction in methods of handling specific problem areas.

Other Support Services

Whenever a person with mental retardation is placed in a foster home, a case manager, behavior analyst, and a nurse consultant are assigned. The case manager is required to visit the home at least once monthly or more frequently if needed. The visits may or may not be announced beforehand. Other professionals are available for consultation according to individual need. These professionals offer support, guidance, monitoring of quality of care, coordination of services, encouragement for interaction with the family, and assistance in location of services. The case manager also is the liaison between the Foster Care provider and the DMR.

CONCLUSION

The examples of small-scale community living programs in Ohio, North Dakota, and Delaware were not developed specifically or exclusively for older adults with developmental disabilities but are available to all adults. The options available through these programs have been augmented by support services that are based on the needs of the individual. The Supported Living Option program available in Ohio empowers the individual so that she or he can select the programs and services needed with the assistance of a case manager and ISP. Funds are directed to the individual. The Individualized Supported Living Arrangment program available in North Dakota is specific to residential services. The individual receives services by either nonprofit or for-profit licensed programs. The two basic services are room and board and case management. Two categories of support services, habilitation and personal care, are provided. Delaware's Adult Family Living Options program has as its objective the provision of residential services for individuals who have mental retardation, with the opportunity to participate in the community. Foster Training Homes and Intensive Foster Care Programs, which are provided through the Delaware Adult Family Living Options program, also offer a family environment with more assistance based on the needs of the individual.

Flexible Funding

Funding availability and eligibility determined the way residential services were provided before the 1980s. Only since then has the concept of flexible funding been introduced, which permits funds to follow the individual in purchasing services. This is in keeping with the view that financing should "[be] tied to the person rather than programs, . . . be flexible, . . . use incentives to promote the use of least restrictive and most effective services, . . . reward good performance and not reward poor performance, . . . give providers incentives for good performance (preferred providers), . . . be linked to the choices made by individuals with disabilities, and be open and flexible enough to support these choices" (Minnesota Governor's Planning Council on Developmental Disability, 1987, p. 30).

The traditional long-term funding streams have been developed through federal programs and state initiatives. The amount of funding and assistance has eroded since 1980, especially for housing programs for moderate- and low-income individuals and families. New strategies are needed for access to both traditional and nontraditional funding streams to enhance the opportunities to initiate and develop options for older adults with developmental disabilities. The responses of the eight states surveyed indicate that services and options for older adults rely on the availability of adequate funding.

Benefits of Small-Scale Living Options

The benefits of providing small-scale living options have been realized by each of the eight states. They are listed below:

1. The flexibility of the options
2. Staying in familiar settings
3. Individualization
4. More natural and normalized lifestyles, allowing community participation

5. Living in regular homes or apartments with families
6. Social involvement
7. Family-like atmosphere
8. More freedom and the opportunity to make choices

As the numbers of older adults with developmental disabilities continue to grow and as the commitment to providing individualized services continues to strengthen, the future for community living options in the most inclusive setting may well be modeled after the programs in Ohio, North Dakota, and Delaware.

REFERENCES

Anderson, D.J., Lakin, K.C., Bruininks, R.H., & Hill, B.K. (1987). *A national study of residential and support services for elderly persons with mental retardation.* Minneapolis: University of Minnesota, Department of Educational Psychology.

Hauber, R.A., Rotegard, L.L., & Bruininks, R.H. Characteristics of residential services for older/elderly mentally retarded persons. In M.P. Janicki & H.M. Wisniewski (Eds.), *Aging and developmental disabilities: Issues and approaches* (pp. 327–350). Baltimore: Paul H. Brookes Publishing Co.

Martinson, M.C., & Stone, J.A. (1990). *Models for interagency planning for long-term funding of small-scale community living options for older persons with developmental disabilities.* Lexington: University of Kentucky, Interdisciplinary Human Development Institute.

Minnesota Governor's Planning Council on Developmental Disability. (1987). *A new way of thinking.* St. Paul, MN: Author.

Ohio Department of Mental Retardation and Developmental Disabilities. (1990). *The supported living reference manual.* Columbus: Author.

Seltzer, M.M., & Krauss, M.W. (1987). Aging and mental retardation: Extending the continuum. Washington, DC: *Monographs of the American Association of Mental Retardation.*

IV

Service Trends

Gary B. Seltzer

Only since the 1980s have personnel in the aging and developmental disabilities services systems recognized the need to cooperate, innovate, and develop a complex network of programs, services, and community supports for the ever-increasing number of older adults with developmental disabilities. Service models vary by size, composition (i.e., generic or specialized), geographic location, funding source, consumer involvement, level of disability, and ethnic or racial diversity.

This section presents an array of service trends that have been affected profoundly by philosophical and ideological perspectives. The overarching philosophical theme captured in this section is the inclusion of individuals with disabilities and their families on the management teams that plan and execute supports for a culturally and otherwise diverse group of older adults. Chapters in this section not only confront the difficulties in seeking full participation from individuals with developmental disabilities, but also illustrate many examples of successful, inclusive partnerships that have benefited all participants.

14

Cross Training within the Aging and Developmental Disabilities Services Systems

Phyllis Kultgen and Robert Rominger

As increasing numbers of persons with developmental disabilities grow old, needs for services, programs, and policies appropriate to later life development emerge. When it is recognized that for every older individual served by the developmental disabilities system today there will be three or four individuals enrolled 15 years from now (Janicki, 1990), the need for services, programs, and policies designed for older adults takes on a growing urgency. In earlier stages of life, service needs are met by utilization of knowledge and practice jointly derived from the field of developmental disabilities and discipline areas such as psychology, education, and adolescent and adult development. In a similar manner, gerontology informs the area of developmental disabilities to produce practices, programs, and policies appropriate to individuals as they age. In this chapter, the focus is on training modalities used to bring a gerontological perspective to habilitation planning for older adults. The assumption is made that both the aging and developmental disabilities services systems are involved in creating these modalities.

DEFINITION AND RATIONALE

There is some confusion about the meaning of the term "cross training," although that confusion usually can be traced to the context and setting in which training takes place. To clarify the meaning, a brief, but in no way complete, history of usage follows.

As early as 1976, the Administration on Developmental Disabilities awarded grants to several university affiliated programs (UAPs) for developmental disabilities to analyze needs for services among older individuals and to prepare and disseminate training materials targeting those needs (Rowitz, 1986). One of those programs, the University of Nebraska Project, was interdisciplinary in nature and involved a variety of agencies and service organizations. Segal (1978) and Daniels (1979) present the proceedings of several conferences and symposia devoted to the interdisciplinary issues that surround aging with a developmental disability.

The use of the term "cross training" to describe interdisciplinary and interagency efforts became common after the American Association of University Affiliated Programs Task Force on Aging issued its 1987 report. A full decade of commitment to the improvement of services for older adults with developmental disabilities was advocated therein (Davidson et al., 1987). UAP centers and gerontology centers were urged to incorporate into the aging curriculum didactic material and experiences relating to persons with developmental disabilities and to "mix UAP and gerontology trainees in a common setting" (p. 11). At the inservice level, that report urged better training of case managers and direct care staff as well as training planners, administrators, and program planners in both service delivery systems.

In 1989, the term "cross training" was linked to advocacy efforts. Inservice training of professionals and paraprofessionals in both systems as well as the public at large was seen as important to the elimination of stereotypes and other barriers to effective service delivery to older adults with lifelong disabilities (Ansello & Rose, 1989). "The search for solutions . . . [was understood to necessitate] a commitment to cross training and the development of a cross training plan that can accommodate different levels of knowledge and needs of diverse groups" (Davidson et al., 1987, pp. 35–36).

Based on the cited usage of the term and for purposes of the analyses and discussions presented in this chapter, the following definition is offered: *Cross training refers to instruction among persons representing the aging and developmental disabilities networks at the preservice and inservice levels in subject matter drawn from both fields. This interdisciplinary approach offers trainees exposure to the* unique knowledge and practice *content that creates the special area of aging and developmental disabilities.*

Cross training is needed because members of both service networks increasingly confront issues concerning older adults with developmental disabilities. They confront the fact that quality of life for older adults with developmental disabilities is enhanced by opportunities for community inclusion and by services available to all older adults. Successful community access and inclusion is dependent on service providers well versed in both the characteristics of older adults with developmental disabilities and the service networks through which quality of life is upgraded. In the following section the need for cross training is discussed from the point of view of each service system.

PERCEPTIONS OF THE SERVICE NETWORK

For members of the mental retardation/developmental disabilities services network, knowledge of age-related physical and psycho-social change is needed to understand how the special needs of individuals with developmental disabilities are affected by the aging process and how some of the general needs of these individuals can be served by the system of aging services. The special needs are those that stem from a lifelong developmental disability, and the general needs are those that stem from the aging process.

These considerations have several implications. First, a functional developmental model applicable to later life must be developed and disseminated to replace the vocational model used for younger adults (Kultgen, Hawkins, Eklund, & Rominger, 1990). Second, services offered by the aging system that apply to the needs of all older adults should be utilized, when appropriate, by older adults with developmental disabilities. A gerontological perspective applied to training should satisfy the implications drawn from the special and general needs of older adults with developmental disabilities.

Developmental Disabilities Service System

In a training needs survey of human services organizations in Indiana and eight rural states (Rominger, Mash, & Kultgen, 1990), need for training in the interdisciplinary area of aging and developmental disabilities was strongly endorsed by administrators, case workers, and direct care personnel, especially in a sample drawn from the mental retardation/developmental disabilities services system. (See Figure 14.1.) In an assessment of individual service needs, age-related physical changes and age-appropriate program planning were among the most highly rated training needs out of a list of 25 items. (See Table 14.1.)

Aging Services Network

Professionals and paraprofessionals from the aging services network are less likely to be aware of the numbers of and characteristics of individuals with disabilities who are growing old. Therefore, they require information regarding demographic characteristics of older adults with developmental disabilities and the scope of services they are likely to need. Moreover, familiarity with the structure and function of the developmental disabilities services system would

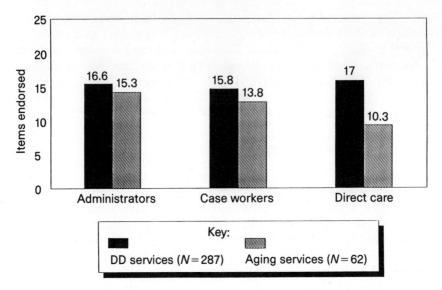

Figure 14.1.   Perceived need for training in aging and developmental disabilities across job levels.

greatly enhance the coordination of services. With respect to perceived training needs on the 1990 survey, the issues ranked highest by aging services were special medical concerns, managing life transitions, issues in mental retardation and mental illness, working with families, and in-home services. (See Table 14.2.) This ranking of issues appears to flow from expectations that case management for older adults with developmental disabilities will present a variety of unique challenges. Later in this chapter, in discussing the training needs survey more fully, the implications of some of the differences in perceived need and importance of training across job levels is considered.

In a prior survey (Kultgen, 1989) of all area agencies on aging in Indiana, each director was asked to review a list of 18 topics similar to the content listed on the 1990 survey questionnaire and rank them for use in case manager training sessions. They were also asked to discuss their own priorities regarding information about developmental disabilities and/or the mental retardation/developmental disabilities services system. Responses to both directives underscored a need for information regarding how to initiate interagency coordination around individuals eligible for services under provisions of both service systems. The four most requested topical areas were: issues in service coordination, population overview, mental health and mental retardation, and transitions and social adjustment.

In order to establish cooperative linkages across service networks, members of the aging services system must be encouraged to seek, or respond to overtures by, the mental retardation/developmental disabilities system of services. It is also essential that members of both service systems understand the

Table 14.1. Perceived need for training: Developmental disabilities topic area with percentages, frequencies, and rank order for service settings

	Developmental disabilities services			
	Yes	No	Unsure	Rank
Special medical concerns	80% 227	15% 43	5% 14	1
Assessing individual service needs	80% 227	14% 41	6% 17	1
Age-related physical changes	79% 224	14% 42	7% 19	3
Age-appropriate program planning	76% 216	18% 50	6% 18	4
Creative leisure activities	76% 215	17% 48	7% 20	5
Managing life transitions	74% 211	14% 38	12% 35	6
Day programs: rationale and options	74% 211	16% 47	10% 29	6
Inclusion in the community	73% 208	20% 57	7% 19	8
Retirement options	73% 207	17% 46	10% 29	9
Social support networks	73% 204	13% 36	14% 40	10
Counseling issues	75% 202	17% 49	8% 33	11
Working with families	70% 198	22% 62	8% 22	12
Issues in mental retardation and mental illness	69% 197	17% 46	14% 41	13
Preserving individual rights	70% 197	22% 61	8% 23	13
Developmental and normalization principles	68% 193	22% 62	10% 27	15
Interagency coordination	67% 186	20% 56	13% 37	16
Maintaining optimal health	64% 183	23% 64	13% 37	17
Residential options	63% 176	25% 69	13% 35	18
Legal and financial planning	62% 173	22% 62	16% 46	19
Pharmaceutical needs and medications	61% 171	27% 75	12% 36	20
Nutrition education	57% 161	32% 92	11% 31	21
Monitoring use of medications	56% 159	34% 95	10% 28	22
In-home services	56% 159	31% 87	13% 38	22
Case management	50% 141	35% 100	15% 42	24
Choosing a physician	30% 85	55% 156	15% 44	25

Table 14.2. Perceived need for training: Aging topic area with percentages, frequencies, and rank order for service settings

	Developmental disabilities services			
	Yes	No	Unsure	Rank
Special medical concerns	75% 47	16% 10	9% 6	1
Managing life transitions	71% 44	19% 12	10% 6	2
Issues in mental retardation and mental illness	68% 43	21% 13	11% 7	3
Working with families	68% 42	23% 14	9% 6	4
In-home services	66% 41	29% 18	5% 3	5
Age-related physical changes	63% 40	19% 12	18% 12	6
Maintaining optimal health	61% 37	31% 19	8% 5	7
Inclusion in the community	60% 37	31% 19	9% 6	7
Counseling issues	57% 35	30% 19	13% 8	9
Case management	58% 35	32% 19	10% 6	9
Assessing individual service needs	56% 34	34% 21	10% 6	11
Pharmaceutical needs and medications	55% 34	37% 23	8% 5	11
Social support networks	52% 33	37% 27	11% 7	13
Developmental and normalization principles	53% 32	28% 17	19% 12	14
Age-appropriate program planning	53% 32	31% 19	16% 10	14
Preserving individual rights	52% 32	38% 24	10% 6	14
Day programs: rationale and options	51% 31	34% 21	15% 9	17
Retirement options	51% 31	42% 26	7% 4	17
Monitoring use of medications	48% 30	45% 28	7% 4	19
Creative leisure activities	48% 30	42% 26	10% 6	19
Residential options	47% 29	40% 25	13% 8	21
Interagency coordination	48% 29	36% 22	16% 10	21
Legal and financial planning	44% 159	49% 95	7% 28	23
Nutrition education	41% 26	46% 29	13% 18	24
Choosing a physician	16% 10	69% 43	15% 9	25

mission and service domain of the other in order to serve older adults with life-long disabilities effectively.

APPROACHES TO CROSS TRAINING

Knowledge and practice in the interdisciplinary area of aging and developmental disabilities exist at both the systems impact level and the program implementation (individual impact) level. This fact suggests several model approaches to cross training. Those approaches, in turn, promote identifiable objectives. The approaches and the objectives of each approach are described in the next sections. It should be noted that these model approaches derive from the authors' extensive experience in preservice and inservice training and are consistent with findings from the two training needs surveys mentioned earlier in this chapter.

Systems Impact Level

At the systems impact level the general approach to cross training is characterized by *interaction among service professionals from the aging services network and the mental retardation/developmental disabilities services network*. Linkages between the two systems began informally in the early and mid 1980s in several states and were formalized at the federal level through the Older Americans Act Amendments of 1987 (PL 100-175) and the Memorandum of Understanding between the Administration on Aging (AoA) and the Administration on Developmental Disabilities (ADD) signed in 1989. These linkages promote two objectives: 1) service coordination in addressing the needs of older adults with developmental disabilities, and 2) inclusion of older adults with developmental disabilities in community-based, generic services such as senior centers, nutrition sites, and adult day care. One mechanism used to actualize these objectives is cross training among representatives of both service systems. This approach constitutes Model I, Interaction at the Systems Impact Level, and is subdivided into I.A and I.B according to whether training is directed primarily toward developmental disabilities services personnel or aging services personnel. (See Table 14.3.)

Keeping in mind the fact that the models discussed here are neither mutually exclusive nor exhaustive, Model I.A can be characterized as follows. Professionals representing the network of aging services address administrators and planners of programs for older adults with developmental disabilities about the services available to all persons over the age of 60 through aging services. This model was used effectively in Missouri during the mid 1980s (Kultgen & Rinck, 1988) to introduce administrators and case managers in the developmental disabilities system to area agency on aging services potentially available to individuals who were on those case managers' caseloads. In this example, area agency directors presented an overview of the area agency mission and structure. Trainer and trainee interaction centered around areas of cooperation between

Table 14.3. Approaches to cross training

Training model approach		Training objectives	Possible trainers	Potential trainees
I	System impact: Interagency interaction	1.1. Service coordination		
		1.2. Community inclusion		
I.A	Developmental disabilities services audience	(Emphasize Objective 1.1)	From state and regional divisions of aging	State and local planners for individuals with developmental disabilities
I.B	Aging services audience	(Emphasize Objective 1.2)	From state and regional offices of developmental disabilities, mental health, vocational rehabilitation	Program planners for all older adults
II	Individual/ program impact: Specialized training	2.1. Age-sensitive environments		
		2.2. Age-sensitive habilitation		
II.A	Developmental disabilities services audience	(Emphasize Objective 2.2)	Aging/developmental disabilities specialists	Planners, providers in developmental disabilities network
II.B	Aging services audience	(Emphasize Objective 2.1)	Aging/developmental disabilities specialists	Planners, providers in aging network

the two systems, for example, transportation and shared physical facilities, and the possibilities of community inclusion for individuals with developmental disabilities through participation in senior centers and nutrition sites.

In Model I.B, professionals representing the developmental disabilities system of services address members of the aging network about services provided to individuals through state offices of mental retardation and vocational rehabilitation and other public agencies. In Indiana this model proved to be an effective tool for informing members of the aging network about ways that interagency coordination can be effected. At issue was the challenge of responding appropriately to individuals with developmental disabilities eligible for services provided by the aging network (e.g., in-home services, home delivered meals, senior center programs) in addition to services from the developmental disabilities service system (e.g., job retraining through vocational rehabilitation, respite care, case management, and social skills training).

Program Impact Level

At the program impact level, the general approach to cross training is characterized as aging specialists alerting service providers to changes that accompany the aging process. Aging specialists are defined here as persons knowledgeable in the joint area of aging and developmental disabilities. Two objectives are realized from training at the program impact level: 1) the development of age-sensitive environments, and 2) the promotion of age-sensitive habilitation planning.

Although the content of the training is similar, two subdivisions emerge at the program impact level. As shown in Table 14.3, planners and providers in the developmental disabilities system make up one set of potential trainees, while planners and providers in the aging network of services make up a second group. Potential trainees within the developmental disabilities network in Indiana have, over several years, continued to request inservice information that will allow them to provide age-sensitive programming for individuals aging already and for an anticipated aging population. Although the Administration on Developmental Disabilities, as well as academics and planners in the discipline of developmental disabilities, have been aware of the need for interdisciplinary training in aging and developmental disabilities for well over a decade, not all providers share that awareness. Those who are directly experiencing an aging clientele are now eager to understand how the aging process affects adults with developmental disabilities. They also want to know how plans for successful transition into old age for participating individuals can be effected.

Persons knowledgeable in the joint area of aging and developmental disabilities are also needed at the program implementation level for inservice training to planners and providers in the aging system of services. Specific audiences here include, among others, nursing home staff and ombudsmen. Often the request from these audiences is for training that points out both differences and similarities among nursing home residents drawn from the general population and those who are older adults with developmental disabilities. In the approaches to cross training discussed above, professionals in each service system, along with aging/developmental disabilities specialists, have been identified as possible trainers. The distinction between systems impact level trainers (i.e., personnel from state and local agencies on aging and personnel from the developmental disabilities service system) and individual impact level trainers (i.e., specialists in the joint area of aging and developmental disabilities) has to do with practical limitations that may be found in potential trainers. That is, the competencies needed by one individual to train differing audiences (i.e., levels I.A, I.B, II.A, II.B) at the two major levels (system and program) may be unrealistic until selected individuals are specifically trained in this objective. Researchers at The University of Akron have developed a competency profile for potential aging specialists and a curriculum guide that will enable one individual to become competent in all facets of cross training. Following is a description of the role of the aging specialist as it relates to training:

> The specialist in Developmental Disabilities and Aging has the expertise and the knowledge to train others about this specialized population, its characteristics, needs, concerns and interests, as well as best practices in client motivation, behavior management and programming. Facts about aging and aging services are part of the content he/she transmits formally to the staff and volunteers within the agency. To the system of aging services the DD/Aging Specialist contributes information about client characteristics and the DD service system as a whole in cross-training events. In all these training efforts, the DD/Aging Specialist demonstrates his/her understanding of adult learning principles. (Sutton & Sterns, 1990, p. 3)

Preservice Level

University courses provide another avenue to the creation of aging specialists. Courses labeled interdisciplinary (aging and developmental disabilities) combine the system impact and the program impact levels identified above and address students (future and present) of both service systems. Aging with developmental disabilities, as a university offering, is a preservice approach to cross training and is characterized as: aging specialists addressing future and present professionals for both service systems simultaneously on issues concerning growing old with a developmental disability. This is a third model approach and combines the objectives of Models I and II and, as such, promotes service coordination, community inclusion, age-sensitive surroundings, and age-sensitive habilitation planning.

As actual university courses in aging and developmental disabilities emerge, they are taught by persons who combine the competencies identified by Sutton and Sterns (1990). This can mean one instructor as an aging/developmental disabilities specialist or several instructors whose educations and experience combine to bring the full knowledge required to cover issues ranging from the individual level to the systems level. One course, established at The University of Missouri in 1988, utilizes an instructor trained in both aging and developmental disabilities, a social gerontologist, and a legal expert. A similar course has been designed for Indiana University. Several other universities have courses in aging and developmental disabilities, for example, the University of Rochester and Miami University. Although no two courses are exactly alike, they are all examples of interdisciplinary training at the preservice level drawing students from a large number of disciplines.

Although students at the preservice level may not acquire the full range of competencies needed to become aging specialists, they can acquire knowledge that will take them several or many steps toward reaching that objective. Also, preservice training is an important consideration in sensitizing future professionals from a broad range of disciplines to the needs of older adults with developmental disabilities. Policy and planning, social work, nursing, occupational therapy, art and music training, recreation and leisure, and special education are among these disciplines. In the approaches to inservice training discussed above, emphasis has been placed on training members of each service system separately and on making distinctions between training levels (system impact or program implementation). At the preservice level these distinctions are unimportant. The objective of preservice training is the provision of educational opportunities that will enable students to become aging specialists with the background needed to instruct in a variety of settings. However, at the outreach (inservice) level members of the two service systems often have training preferences quite distinct from each other. That point is substantiated when the training needs survey, introduced earlier, is further elaborated on.

THE TRAINING NEEDS SURVEY

As indicated earlier in this chapter, cross training refers to instruction of persons representing both service systems in material drawn from the combined knowledge base of both fields. However, this does not mean that most members of the separate systems will want to tap into this joint body of knowledge at the same place or that they will always benefit from being part of common training audiences. It seems incumbent upon all trainers/aging developmental disabilities specialists, then, to assess training needs in such a way that the training preferences, which may vary within and between members of the major services systems for people with disabilities, become evident.

Gibson and Rabkin (1990) made such an attempt in the state of Washington. Results from a previous study conducted by the same researchers suggested that *health care training and education* was an area of immediate concern for service providers. In examining health care training needs specifically, the study found that providers of both aging and generic community-based services reported a need to know more about mental retardation. Providers of developmental disabilities services consistently reported lower levels of knowledge about various types of age-related change than did their aging and generic services counterparts. The topic, "changes in the central nervous system," was identified by the total sample group as the area in which they were least knowledgeable.

The training needs survey performed by researchers at Indiana University's Program on Aging/Developmental Disabilities from 1989–1990 assessed perceptions of training need in the area of aging and disability among providers of both aging and developmental disabilities services across a range of issues and domains. As noted earlier, differences in perception across job level categories were investigated. The survey effort also was an attempt to collect training needs data that could be generalized across states.

Method

Data were gathered using a survey instrument developed for the project. Twenty-five training areas were presented on the form (items listed in either Table 14.1 or Table 14.2). For each area the respondent was asked to provide ratings of need (Yes/No/Unsure), importance (High/Medium/Low), and immediacy (Right Now/Next Year/Long Range). The training areas included were based on content covered in *Aging and Developmental Disabilities: A Training Inservice Package* (Hawkins, Eklund, & Gaetani, 1989). An attempt was made to select a wide range of areas currently thought to be of importance in the provision of services to older adults with developmental disabilities. Information regarding such things as job status, previous training and education, and amount of experience in the field was also requested from each respondent.

The study sought respondents from both the developmental disabilities services and aging services networks. An emphasis was placed on surveying rural states and states that did not have a University Affiliated Program on Developmental Disabilities. Idaho, North Dakota, New Mexico, Oklahoma, Nevada, South Dakota, Wyoming, and Kentucky were selected as survey states. Additionally, the researchers were interested in assessing training need in their own state, Indiana. A total of 69 agencies were selected, and 1,386 survey forms were distributed. Three hundred and fifty-three surveys were returned, representing 49 agencies. Because of peculiarities in the sampling procedure (e.g., the availability of useful mailing lists and the avoidance of conflicts with other projects), most of the developmental disabilities services agencies were in Indiana, while most agencies on aging represented the other states named.

Results

Since partial findings regarding need for training in both service systems were presented earlier in this chapter, they will not be repeated here except to reemphasize two points:

1. In almost every topic area, need for training was more strongly endorsed by the developmental disabilities services data.
2. With the exception of the topic area, special medical concerns, priority needs were quite different between the two service sectors.

Regarding importance and immediacy of training, it was found that participants' rating of importance was highly correlated with their responses concerning immediacy. Because of this strong relationship, only data on importance are presented here. Understanding priorities among training needs affords trainers an opportunity to develop optimal learning experiences for trainees. Since responses were also analyzed by job level within service sectors, training priorities can be further refined. The overall results regarding priorities of training needs (importance) for both service sectors are presented below and are followed by a discussion of perceived need and perceived importance across job categories.

Perceived Importance of Training Needs Figure 14.2 presents graphs for the most important training areas as seen by providers of developmental disabilities services, with responses broken down by job level. Over all job categories, the four rated highest by developmental disabilities services providers are age-appropriate program planning (57%), day programs: rationale and options (54.9%), creative leisure activities (53.2%), and inclusion in the community (52.1%).

Figure 14.3 presents graphs of the four training areas most frequently rated as being of high importance by aging services providers, with responses again broken down by job level. The four topic areas most highly rated by aging services providers are in-home services (52.1%), assessing individual service needs (41.9%), issues in mental retardation and mental illness (40.0%), and working with families (39.2%).

Interestingly, the aging services list of areas receiving the highest ratings in importance appears to be oriented to individual services, whereas the developmental disabilities list emphasizes program development. The needs in one service domain can be seen as foundational concepts in the other. For example, knowledge of age-related needs and senior programs sought by persons within the developmental disabilities service system form the foundation of the aging network of services. In like manner, knowledge of individualized assessments and intervention planning, the essence of the developmental disabilities services system, is sought by representatives of the aging services network. This complementarity has implications for using experts from the respective service networks as resources for cooperative cross-discipline training activities and supports the Model I approach to cross training discussed earlier.

Perceived Need and Importance Across Job Categories Among aging services providers, the survey revealed a tendency for administrators to identify more training needs than direct providers. That is, upper administrators identified an average of 15 training needs out of a possible 25 as compared with 10 out of 25 identified at the direct care level. (See Figure 14.1.) In developmental disabilities services there was little difference in perceived training need across all three job levels. This difference in the findings regarding need may be a function of awareness of the aging/developmental disabilities population. For example, within the aging services network, some direct care respondents may as yet have no individuals with developmental disabilities at their service site, whereas administrators with overall supervisory authority over numerous sites are more likely to be aware of this group among older adults. In contrast, all personnel within the developmental disabilities services system are aware that those they serve are growing older.

As far as training importance is concerned, there were also differences between the two service networks in patterns of response across job levels.

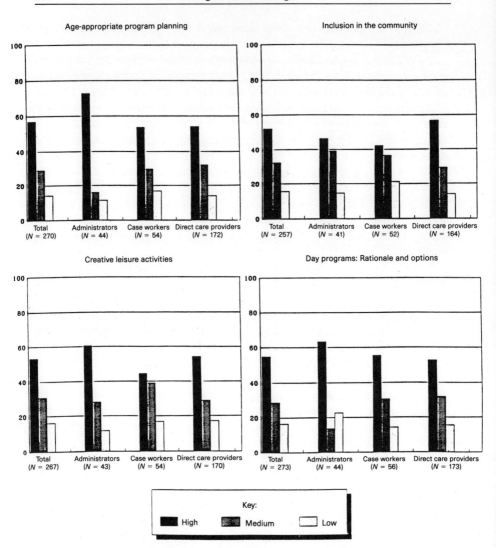

Figure 14.2. Importance of training needs: Content items rated by developmental disabilities services personnel as highest in importance, by percentage.

The aging service network showed slight differences across job levels, whereas the developmental disabilities service network did show some pronounced differences. (See Figure 14.4.) Here, direct care providers were significantly more likely than the middle-administrator and case worker groups to rate items as more important. Upper administrators' overall ratings fell between those of the other two groups differences. What this pattern most strongly suggests is that perceived importance of training is a function of job role related needs, particu-

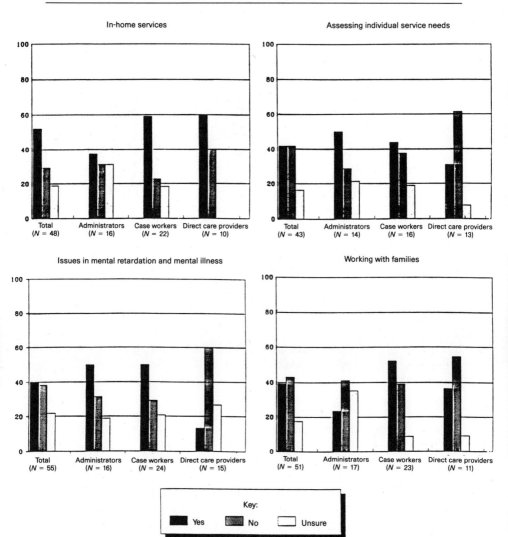

Figure 14.3.   Importance of training needs: Content items rated by aging services personnel as highest in importance, by percentage.

larly within the developmental disabilities service network. Items for which the difference in ratings is especially pronounced may help illustrate this point: managing use of medications; nutrition education; age-related physical changes; and managing life transitions. In all these cases importance ratings were higher for direct care providers than for either of the other groups. Another area of concern expressed more strongly by direct care providers than by the other two groups was the item, "developmental and normalization principles." It is possi-

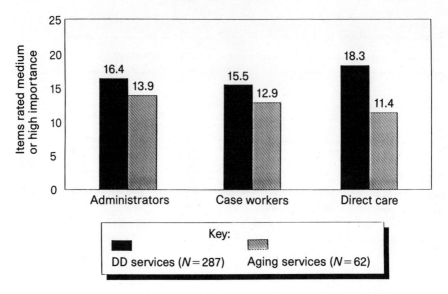

Figure 14.4.   Importance of training needs in aging and developmental disabilities across job levels.

ble that direct care providers simply may feel a lack of preparation for dealing with issues confronting older adults.

CONCLUSION

With the growth in the numbers of older adults with developmental disabilities has come a need for supportive training modalities to help professionals and paraprofessionals work more effectively on behalf of persons with developmental disabilities whose functional independence may be especially threatened by the physical, social, and psychological consequences of aging. This chapter has attempted to present useful approaches to cross training. Survey findings that illuminate both similarities and differences in perceptions of training need and importance for the two service networks that work with older adults with lifelong disabilities have been presented to support those approaches. The survey data suggest that both the aging services and developmental disabilities service networks are aware of the increase in numbers of these individuals and of the special needs that characterize them.

Both the training approaches outlined and the data on importance of training needs underscore the importance of sensitivity to each unique audience of training participants. Knowledge of trainees' preferences and job-relevant needs is fundamental to shaping training content and activities to create meaningful and worthwhile workshops. For some topic areas it can be expected that motivation for training will be universally high across service networks and job responsibility. When training involves these issues, and other issues fundamental to understanding the people being served, cross training with mixed audiences may offer an excellent opportunity for interagency interaction. However, the differences that exist from one network to the other and across job levels also must be acknowledged when cross training efforts are structured. It can be expected that most training issues in aging and developmental disabilities will be seen somewhat differently according to variations in job responsibilities, personal interests and background, and characteristics of a particular group of people being served. On the one hand, shaping the audience to the training where possible is advocated. That is, where training is targeted to a particular service setting, trainers should attempt to address a homogeneous training group. On the other hand, shaping the training to the audience is even more strongly advocated. Before inservice training is undertaken, it is very helpful to assess training preferences. Additionally, in the course of conducting training, it is important to be responsive to the dynamic of differences in training needs. Successful training in aging and developmental disabilities will begin with and maintain a sensitivity to trainee input.

REFERENCES

Ansello, E.F., & Rose, T. (1989). *Aging and lifelong disabilities: Partnership for the twenty-first century—The wingspread conference report.* The University of Maryland Center on Aging. Palm Springs: Elder Press.

Daniels, P.J. (1979). *Gerontological aspects of developmental disabilities. The state of the art.* Omaha: The University of Nebraska at Omaha Gerontology Program.

Davidson, P.W., Calkins, C.F., Harper, D., Hawkins, B.A., McClain, J.W., & Offner, R.B. (1987). *A decade of commitment to elderly persons with developmental disabilities.* Report submitted to the Administration on Developmental Disabilities, Office of Human Development Services, United States Department of Health and Human Services. Washington, DC: American Association of University Affiliated Programs.

Gibson, J.W., & Rabkin, J. (1990). *Aging and developmental disabilities: Service provider training needs in the area of health care* (Final Report). Seattle: University of Washington Child Development and Mental Retardation Center.

Hawkins, B.A., Eklund, S.J., & Gaetani, R.P. (Eds.). (1989). *Aging and developmental disabilities: A training in-service package.* Bloomington: Indiana University Institute for the Study of Developmental Disabilities, A University Affiliated Program.

Janicki, M. Quoted in Lewin, T. (1990, October 28). When the retarded grow old. *New York Times.*

Kultgen, P. (1989). [Survey of area agency directors: Training needs]. Unpublished raw data.

Kultgen, P., Hawkins, B.A., Eklund, S., & Rominger, R. (1990). *Training in aging and developmental disabilities: Critical audiences project.* Bloomington: Indiana University Institute for the Study of Developmental Disabilities, A University Affiliated Program.

Kultgen, P., & Rinck, C. (1988). *A composite approach to the service needs of the developmentally disabled elderly* (Final Report). Kansas City, MO: University of Missouri, The University of Missouri-Kansas City Institute for Human Development, University Affiliated Program for Developmental Disabilities.

Rominger, R., Mash, C., & Kultgen, P. (1990). *Planning for the 1990's: A survey of train-*

ing needs regarding older adults with developmental disabilities. Bloomington: Indiana University Institute for the Study of Developmental Disabilities, A University Affiliated Program.

Rowitz, L. (1986). *Survey of services used by the elderly retarded.* University of Illinois School of Public Health, Chicago.

Segal, R.M. (1978). Consultation conference on developmental disabilities and gerontology. *Conference proceeding.* Ann Arbor: University of Michigan, Institute for the Study of Mental Retardation and Related Disabilities.

Sutton, E., & Sterns, H.L. (1990). *Role of the specialist in developmental disabilities and aging: A competency-based profile.* Akron: The University of Akron, Rehabilitation Research and Training Center Consortium on Aging and Developmental Disabilities, National Institute on Disability and Rehabilitation Research, United States Department of Education.

15

Translating Policy into Practice

Alan R. Factor

Paralleling the increase in the numbers of older adults in the general population is the increase in the number of adults with developmental disabilities who are growing old. Advances in medical technologies and improvements in the quality of care are increasing their life expectancy. Their age-related needs have become more apparent to community service agencies as a result of the widespread deinstitutionalization initiatives, which started in the 1970s, and the emerging numbers of older adults with developmental disabilities who are coming to the attention of the service system as they outlive their parents.

The later-life needs of individuals with developmental disabilities are similar to those of the general older population. The following five key areas of concern have emerged (Factor, 1989; Janicki, Otis, Puccio, Rettig, & Jacobson, 1985; New York State Office on Mental Retardation and Developmental Disabilities, 1983; Segal, 1977):

1. The opportunity to retire from work or vocational training and to engage in meaningful community activities, or to continue working on a full-time or part-time basis
2. The option of aging in place through the availability of in-home support services to compensate for age-related physical and cognitive losses
3. Improved access to health care, including health monitoring and the promotion of wellness
4. Bolstering affective supports to help compensate for the loss of family and friends

5.   Outreach and assistance to families caring for an older relative with a developmental disability in the natural home

This chapter describes the efforts of 10 states to address the needs of older adults with developmental disabilities. These states were selected on the basis of their fiscal and program policies, which suggested that the needs of older adults with developmental disabilities were emerging as policy priorities at the state level. This chapter presents the program models funded by these 10 states' Fiscal Year (FY) 1988 community aging initiatives and discusses the factors leading to their development, including the nature of collaboration between their developmental disabilities and aging services systems. Last, future directions in addressing age-related needs are considered in the context of emerging trends within the disabilities and aging services systems. Data for this chapter were drawn from case studies of the factors contributing to these states' community services initiatives for older adults with developmental disabilities. This research was conducted by the author as part of the Rehabilitation Research and Training Center (RRTC) Consortium on Aging and Developmental Disabilities.

THE EVOLUTION OF SERVICES TO
OLDER ADULTS WITH DEVELOPMENTAL DISABILITIES

Innovative programs and services to meet the later-life needs of adults with developmental disabilities are a relatively recent phenomenon. A 1986 national survey of day and residential programs serving persons ages 55 and older with mental retardation identified 327 community-based and 202 institutional day and residential programs in operation as of January 1, 1985 (Seltzer & Krauss, 1987). The vast majority of these programs were established in the early to mid 1980s, with all but seven states reporting at least one initiative. Approximately one-half were pre-existing programs that were modified to meet the age-related needs of the individuals they were serving. States with age-specific day activities were more likely to have: 1) addressed aging issues in their state developmental disabilities services plan, 2) received funds from the state developmental disabilities planning council to fund special projects on aging, and 3) established special residential programs for older persons. States with specialized community-based residential programs for older adults were more likely to have a greater number of persons with developmental disabilities ages 55 and older, a greater number of community residential programs for all age groups, and a greater number of special day programs for older adults.

The Number of Older Adults
with Developmental Disabilities

While program initiatives to meet later-life needs are linked to the increasing numbers of older adults among states, exact numbers and future growth are difficult to estimate. Foremost, there is no consensus as to what chronological ages constitute valid markers of old age among adults with developmental disabilities. At present, there are limited clinical data documenting the effects of the aging process on people with lifelong disabilities. The variety of disabling conditions that can result in a developmental disability and their varying etiologies make it difficult to generalize about morbidity and mortality. A 1984 survey of the 3-year plans prepared by state developmental disabilities planning councils revealed states used such diverse ages as 50, 55, 62, and 65 to categorize their older adults (Janicki, Ackerman, & Jacobson, 1985). Increasingly, age 55 has been cited as the threshold for entry into "old age" for people with developmental disabilities. While this is an arbitrary benchmark, it reflects the lower life expectancy of people with Down syndrome and individuals with severe and profound mental retardation, who are likely to be more medically fragile (Zigman, Seltzer, Adlin, & Silverman, 1991).

Specific data also are lacking on the prevalence of mental retardation and other developmental disabilities for all age groups among the general population. Prevalence estimates have been confounded because the operational definitions of these conditions have become more rigorous over time, so that fewer older adults may meet the classification criteria. Consequently, estimates of the number of adults ages 55 and older with developmental disabilities according to the 1980 census have ranged from 195,680 (Jacobson, Sutton, & Janicki, 1985) to 472,440 (Seltzer & Krauss, 1987). The former figure is based upon an estimated prevalence rate of 0.4%, which reflects the proportion likely to be known to states' developmental disabilities service systems, while the latter figure corresponds to the estimated 1.0% prevalence rate for mental retardation within the general population. Applying the 0.4% prevalence rate to the 52.6 million Americans ages 55 and older reported in the 1990 census (United States Bureau of the Census, 1991) suggests that there are at least 210,000 older adults with lifelong disabilities, which is an 11% increase since 1980. The number of older persons with developmental disabilities could reach nearly 400,000 in the next 40 years, as the population of people ages 55 and older is projected to double by 2030 (Spencer, 1989). Regardless of their absolute numbers, almost half (42.6%) of the current numbers of older adults are estimated to be unknown to states' developmental disabilities services systems (Morton, 1988). These individuals will place an additional demand on the service system as their parents and siblings die or become too infirm to provide care. In Illinois for example, 3,300 adults with developmental disabilities ages 30 and older who are living with aging parents are projected to require another residential arrangement over the next 15 years (Heller & Factor, 1988).

Principles Guiding Service Delivery

Initiatives designed to meet older adults' age-specific needs have been driven by three principles, which have influenced the transition to community-based services and the nature of program development for persons with developmental disabilities: community inclusion, normalization, and active treatment. The widespread deinstitutionalization and community inclusion initiatives that began in the 1970s increased the numbers of older adults in the community and made their needs more apparent to community service providers. Nationwide, a total of 37 state-operated facilities serving people with developmental disabilities closed between 1970 and 1990, and an additional 16 closures are planned through 1995 (Illinois University Affiliated Program in Developmental Disabilities, 1991). Between 1977 and 1988, the aggregate institutional census for all 50 states and the District of Columbia decreased from 149,169 to 91,440 (Braddock, Hemp, Fujiura, Bachelder, & Mitchell, 1990). Community inclusion often is guided by the principle of normalization, a program philosophy that fosters life patterns for persons with developmental disabilities as close as possible to the norms of mainstream society. An emerging service paradigm is the move from community integration to community membership through the creation of individualized networks of informal and formal supports for people with developmental disabilities (Bradley & Knoll, 1990). Utilizing these generic resources to meet their needs within the community will enable individuals with disabilities truly to become an integral part of their communities.

The third program philosophy, active treatment, is the foundation for habilitative programming. Active treatment consists of the specialized training, treatment, and services an individual requires in order to develop the behaviors necessary to function with as much self-determination and independence as possible. In 1974, the Health Care Financing Administration (HCFA) established active treatment as a Condition of Participation for public and private intermediate care facilities for persons with mental retardation (ICFs/MR). Its intent was to help ensure that these facilities would provide more than just custodial care, and thus would meet the eligibility requirements for Medicaid reimbursement. In 1988, HCFA broadened the definition of active treatment beyond helping the individual to acquire behaviors that promote maximum independent functioning to include the prevention of skill regression and skill loss. This change helped legitimize the prospect of retirement for older adults with lifelong disabilities since it enabled service providers to shift the focus of day activities from developing new skills to maintaining existing skill levels, and to emphasize community living rather than vocational training.

SERVICE TRENDS AND THEIR
IMPLICATIONS FOR THE AGING SERVICES NETWORK

The Illinois University Affiliated Program (UAP) in Developmental Disabilities, as part of the RRTC Consortium on Aging and Developmental Disabilities, conducted detailed case studies of selected states that were addressing the needs of older adults with developmental disabilities to better understand the fiscal, program, and social policies influencing the development of services to older adults. States whose mental retardation/developmental disabilities (MR/DD) agencies had discrete community initiatives for aging services in FY 1988 were identified in conjunction with the Illinois UAP's third national study of public spending for mental retardation and developmental disabilities (Braddock et al., 1990). A discrete aging initiative within the MR/DD agency budget suggested a state-level policy commitment to address the needs of older adults with developmental disabilities. An activity was considered a discrete initiative if it attained either line item status in the state MR/DD agency's published budget or was identified in its internal planning or accounting system. These initiatives were gauged on an exploratory basis in terms of funding levels and individuals served. All funding associated with aging initiatives represented a subset of total community services spending within a state. Eleven states reporting discrete aging initiatives for FY 1988 were: Alabama, Connecticut, Kentucky, Maryland, Michigan, Mississippi, Montana, North Dakota, Ohio, Pennsylvania, and Washington.

To ensure that other states with aging policy initiatives were not overlooked, nominations were solicited from a panel of 14 nationally recognized experts in aging and developmental disabilities. All were knowledgeable resources regarding states' efforts in addressing the needs of older adults with developmental disabilities by virtue of their research or program development activities. New York was added according to the panel's recommendation because of its comprehensive planning activities and widespread local program development. The final case study sample consisted of New York plus nine of the 11 states reporting discrete aging initiatives: Connecticut, Kentucky, Maryland, Michigan, Mississippi, Montana, North Dakota, Ohio, and Washington. Alabama declined to participate because fiscal constraints resulted in program cutbacks affecting their aging initiative. Pennsylvania was excluded during the data collection stage when it became apparent that its aging initiative was not funded because of an unanticipated shortfall in state revenues.

Detailed case studies were undertaken for these 10 states to understand the factors shaping the development of their community aging initiatives for older persons with developmental disabilities. Information was obtained from telephone interviews with a network of key contacts identified in each state, including staff from the developmental disabilities planning council, the state agencies on aging and developmental disabilities, advocacy groups, service providers, and university affiliated programs in developmental disabilities. Community services agencies operating programs for older adults were also contacted for their programmatic data and their perspective on funding, program implementation, community inclusion, and coalition building between the aging and developmental disabilities networks. These data were supplemented with an analysis of state agency planning reports, state developmental disabilities planning council plans, states' 1990 reports to Congress, and other collateral materials containing information relevant to the development of a state's aging initiative. Data collection activities were designed to elicit a detailed description of aging initiative programs and services, including funding levels and sources and numbers served, the systemic changes, legislative action, litigation, executive branch decisions, advocacy activities and other significant factors contributing to program development; the nature of planning including collaboration between the aging and MR/DD services systems; and future directions for serving older adults with developmental disabilities.

The approaches used to select states and to collect data are subject to certain limitations. The sample was based upon fiscal and program policy indicators of state-level aging initiatives for FY 1988, and the case studies reflected states' activities through December, 1991. It is difficult to determine the degree to which apparent differences between states reflect idiosyncratic factors affecting the ability and willingness to provide information. A concerted effort was made to minimize these concerns and to maintain the study's credibility. A panel of national experts in aging and developmental disabilities helped ensure that other appropriate states were not excluded. Information was solicited from a broad range of constituency groups within each state to generate a comprehensive and nonbiased perspective. Respondents in each state were asked to review the case study narrative to verify the information provided and to reconcile any discrepancies.

CASE STUDY RESULTS

Program Models Funded by States' Discrete Aging Initiatives

Table 15.1 indicates that the community initiatives of these 10 states vary widely in terms of their fiscal effort. Total funding levels for FY 1988 aging initiatives ranged from $3.3 million in Connecticut to $33,034 in Kentucky. Six states reported substantial funding levels: Connecticut, New York, North Dakota, Montana, Ohio, and Washington. The 10 states' discrete community aging initiatives were directed primarily at funding retirement-oriented, day activities. Initiatives in Connecticut, Maryland, Michigan, New York Ohio, and Washington, supported only this kind of service models, while Montana's and North Dakota's initiatives also funded residential programs for older adults. Only two states, Mississippi and Kentucky, funded case management activities, and Mississippi also funded a residential program.

Retirement-Oriented Day Programs   The retirement-oriented day activities funded by these eight states' community aging initiatives share three common programmatic objectives: 1) the prevention of skill loss or skill regression as well as skill development; 2) an emphasis on enhancing community living, socialization, and leisure skills; and 3) participation in various natural community activities. States have operationalized plans for these objectives using a variety of service models that demonstrate flexibility and increased reliance on

Table 15.1. State MR/DD agencies reporting discrete community initiatives in aging for FY 1988

State	Expenditures	Initiative
Connecticut	$3,307,737	Opportunities for older adults serve 423 individuals age 55+ choosing to retire from employment, training programs, or other day services to community activities providing experiences to enhance or maintain skill competencies
North Dakota	$1,166,300	Eight-bed congregate care homes ($593,400) and adult day care retirement programs ($572,900) serving 109 older adults
New York	$ 985,000	Funding for the senior day program demonstration project based on the social model of adult day care at six sites
Ohio	$ 822,000	The $1,200 per capita state subsidy county boards received from the Ohio Department of Mental Retardation that was used to support retirement-oriented day program activities for 685 older individuals
Montana	$ 609,200	Retirement-oriented day programs for 86 older adults and four age-specialized eight-bed group homes serving 32 older adults
Michigan	$ 483,700	Retirement-oriented day activities funded through County Mental Health Boards and a DD Council-funded senior center integration demonstration project
Washington	$ 287,298	Retirement-oriented day activities emphasizing community inclusion for 172 older adults
Maryland	$ 140,877	Four retirement programs serving a total of 22 individuals—two programs operated by area agencies on aging, one by the State Office on Aging, and one by a private DD service provider
Mississippi	$ 45,882	Case management including health monitoring and evaluation for older adults residing in age-specific group homes in the community
Kentucky	$ 33,054	The Maysville component of the Kentucky Rural Elderly Project, which provides outreach, case management, and support services to older adults with mental retardation/developmental disabilities

generic community resources. For example, in Maryland and New York funds can flow directly from the state agencies on developmental disabilities to aging services providers who are serving older adults with developmental disabilities. Two of the four day programs funded by Maryland's FY 1988 day program initiative were operated by local area agencies on aging. The Maryland Developmental Disabilities Administration utilized day program and individual support services monies to directly fund each area agency on aging to serve a designated number of older adults with developmental disabilities at their local senior centers. Senior centers were able to use these funds for additional staff and any other extraordinary expenses they incurred in serving older adults with developmental disabilities. New York's Senior Day Program initiative was designed to serve older individuals with more intensive needs that cannot be met by participation in community senior center activities. It is based upon the social model of adult day care, which does not provide custodial care. Senior Day Programs can be operated by aging network services agencies, as well as developmental disabilities service providers (New York State Office of Mental Retardation and Developmental Disabilities, 1989). The Senior Day Program model was documented to be more cost effective than either traditional day treatment or day training programs because of its lower staffing ratio and greater use of volunteers (New York State Office of Mental Retardation and Developmental Disabilities, 1991). Several service models employ a one-on-one approach to include older adults into community activities. In Ohio, for example, the Senior Companion Program, developed by the University of Akron and with initial funding from the Joseph P. Kennedy, Jr. Foundation, recruited older adults without disabilities as volunteer companions who were matched with an older adult with developmental disabilities on the basis of their mutual interests. Retirement-oriented day activities in Montana and Connecticut facilitate community inclusion by employing a "supported retirement" approach based on the concept of supported employment. Retirement programs are designed around the individual's needs and interests, and staff assist in including these older adults into local senior centers and other community programs. Montana adopted this model because it has few older adults, and they are widely scattered. Retirement-oriented day programs in Washington and North Dakota are structured to enable individuals to spend more time at their residences and to participate in a variety of community activities. North Dakota's Adult Day Care service model for older adults is a nonvocational-oriented program which is funded as a service option under the state's Alternative Community Living Arrangement Services Program. Adult Day Care is generally run on site at Congregate Care Homes for older adults. The Adult Day Care rate structure facilitates community inclusion by covering costs for transportation and for an additional half-time staff person to escort older adults to community activities.

Residential Programs   The various residential services models funded by these states' discrete aging initiatives were age-specific settings designed to enable older adults with developmental disabilities to age in place. Staffing levels, supportive services, and programming are modified to address age-related changes in health, stamina, and cognitive status. For example, North Dakota's Congregate Care residences are eight-bed group homes for older adults with the unique feature of providing on-site Adult Day Care for residents. In Mississippi's residential program model, individuals have the opportunity of working full time or part time or being completely retired. Service components include recreation and leisure education activities, volunteer opportunities, ongoing monitoring and evaluation of health care needs, and maintenance of nutrition requirements. At one residence, a registered nurse serves as case manager and also monitors residents' health status and provides health education.

Case Management Kentucky was the only one of the 10 states whose discrete aging initiative funded outreach and case management specifically developed for older adults. The initiative funds the Maysville component of the Kentucky Rural Elderly Project, which serves a five-county rural area in northern Kentucky. The program was developed to assist older adults with developmental disabilities living in rural areas who are not likely to be known to the service system and are likely to become at risk because of age-related physical and cognitive decline and/or the loss of their family caregivers. Case managers are responsible for mobilizing a network of informal supports and generic community services to address older individuals' needs so they can remain in the community. Besides obtaining needed services, case managers also function as advocates and may even provide transportation and escort services if needed.

State Budgeting Practices

Only Connecticut, Montana, and North Dakota's community aging initiatives were largely indicative of each state's total fiscal effort directed toward the age-specific needs of older adults with developmental disabilities. Further budget analyses revealed that funding levels for several states' aging initiatives reflected their idiosyncratic budgeting practices and, therefore, were not indicative of total fiscal effort directed toward later-life needs. Ohio's initiative represented the $1,200 per capita general subsidy provided by the Department of Mental Retardation and Developmental Disabilities to county boards of mental retardation and developmental disabilities which had been allocated for the 685 older adults in retirement-oriented day programs. Consequently, these data underreported fiscal effort since they represented only a portion of total program costs. In Kentucky, Maryland, Michigan, Mississippi, and New York only certain service models or programs were tracked separately. For example, although the New York State Office of Mental Retardation and Developmental Disabilities (1988) reported that the number of programs providing residential, day, and support services for older adults increased from 35 to 121 between 1983 and 1987, the agency has not tracked these expenditures as a discrete aging initiative. Only the Senior Day Training Program, initially funded in 1989, was tracked separately as one of several demonstration projects implemented to establish effective and cost efficient day program models for adults who do not require intensive day services and for whom vocational services are not appropriate.

Kentucky's FY 1988 initiative represented the Division of Mental Retardation expenditures solely for the Maysville component of the Kentucky Rural Elderly Project. It did not include a group home for older adults funded by the Division of Mental Retardation that opened in 1986 nor projects funded by the state developmental disabilities planning council specifically to address later-life needs. The latter included a total of $50,000 annually for 1988–1991 to support replication of the Maysville project in three other areas of the state. In 1988, the Council also made three 1-year grants of up to $20,000 each supporting local programs providing futures planning for older parents of adults with developmental disabilities; staff training for paraprofessionals in nursing homes with residents with developmental disabilities; and Circles of Support for adults ages 40 and older, which establishes an informal support network to help individuals with developmental disabilities meet their needs. Maryland also funded other programs for older adults that were not being tracked separately. These include day programs for medically fragile older adults funded through Maryland's Administration on Medicaid, leisure homes for older adults who are retired from day programs, and age-specific support programs for older adults in the natural home and in foster care settings. Michigan's FY 1988 initiative supported retirement-oriented day activities funded through local community mental health boards and a senior center inclusion project funded by the Michigan Developmental Disabilities Council. In subsequent years, these expenditures were no longer tracked separately. Mississippi's aging initiative reflects only first-year grants from the Mississippi Bureau of Mental Retardation to fund new programs which subsequently are annualized within state mental retardation center community service budgets. In various years, Mississippi's discrete aging initiative has been used to implement alternative living arrangements for older adults, retirement-oriented day activities, a pre-retirement education program, case management, and training of staff in the aging and developmental disabilities service systems.

Factors Contributing to States' Aging Initiatives

The factors prompting these 10 states to address the later-life needs of adults with developmental disabilities were quite varied. Systemic changes which made the age-specific needs of older adults with developmental disabilities more apparent were a key factor contributing to the development of states' aging initiatives. Aging initiatives in Washington and Ohio were directly related to policy changes that restructured day services. In Ohio, older adults, community employment, and individuals with severe or profound mental retardation were the three specialized areas of program development recommended by a task force established to rewrite the rules governing the county boards of mental retardation and developmental disabilities in the early 1980s. County boards were required to provide retirement programs by a 1983 amendment to the Ohio Administrative Code which allowed older individuals the opportunity to retire from vocational training and work. In Washington, the age-specific programming needs of older adults became readily apparent as the developmental disabilities services system began a major transition in its day programming focus from social skills training to vocational training in 1981. Activity/developmental centers that provided prevocational training to adults of all ages were closed. Prevocational skills training was incorporated in the school curriculum, and living skills training became the responsibility of the schools and residential programs. As many adults as possible were put through the transition into sheltered workshops or supported employment. During this transition, service providers began to develop retirement alternatives for the large numbers of older adults for whom vocational training was not appropriate. Retirement-oriented day activities also met the needs of many older adults who were part of the Community Access Program (CAP) initiative, which emphasized linkages to generic community-based rather than facility-based programming. Washington implemented the CAP initiative in the early 1980s to facilitate the transition to community living for individuals recently discharged from state facilities and nursing homes.

Institutional closures in Connecticut, Montana and North Dakota increased the numbers of older adults receiving community services. For example, Montana's Boulder State School census was reduced from 800 to 200 residents between 1975 and 1990, and North Dakota reduced its total population in state facilities from 1,520 in 1982 to 250 by 1989. Closures in Connecticut and North Dakota resulted from class action suits filed in 1979 and 1981, respectively. Two subsequent issues in Connecticut also had an impact on older adults with developmental disabilities. Advocacy efforts by the Connecticut Association for Retarded Citizens resulted in 1987 legislation prohibiting the discharge of state facility residents into nursing homes. In 1989, an impending lawsuit by families seeking residential support for their older relatives with mental retardation living in the family home led the Department of Mental Retardation to attempt to balance the needs for expanded family supports and placement options with compliance with the Consent Decree.

The link between policy changes and the recognition of specific programming needs of older adults with developmental disabilities was less clear cut in New York, Maryland, Mississippi, Michigan, and Kentucky. Mississippi and Michigan incorporated the needs of older adults with developmental disabilities in statewide mandates to respond to the mental health needs of older persons. Mississippi's aging, mental health, and mental retardation networks jointly prepared a state plan for addressing the needs of older adults with mental health problems and mental retardation. The directors of Michigan's state agencies on aging and mental health mandated their joint planning body, the Michigan Mental Health and Aging Council, also to focus on the needs of older adults with developmental disabilities in response to the 1989 federal interagency agreement between the Administration on Aging and the Administration on Developmental Disabilities.

The experiences of New York, Maryland, and Kentucky, in particular, suggest that advocacy efforts by specific staff within the developmental disabilities services system were major catalysts in moving these states to address the unique needs of older adults. In 1987, the New York State Office of Mental Retardation and Developmental Disabilities established the Bureau of Aging Services, which is responsible for planning and coordinating activities related to services for older adults with developmental disabilities. Maryland revised its state code in 1988 to make retirement from traditional day programs a sanctioned option for older adults, designating a retired person as any individual age 60 or older who elects to withdraw from active participation in day habilitation services or sheltered or nonsheltered employment.

Collaboration Between States' Agencies on Aging and Mental Retardation/Developmental Disabilities Networks

The prevailing philosophies of community inclusion and normalization coupled with efforts to avoid creating a duplicate service system led states to establish linkages to the generic aging network. The Older Americans Act of 1965 (OAA) (PL 89-73), which is the only federal social services statute designed specifically for older adults, was primarily responsible for creating the current network of aging services and programs. The act's objectives are to promote the social, functional, and economic independence of older adults and to develop a variety of community services to meet these objectives. Funds are channeled into three priority areas: 1) social services, 2) senior centers, and 3) nutrition (congregate meal sites and home-delivered meals programs). One half of the social services budget of the OAA is allocated to three areas: 1) access services, such as Information and Referral, 2) transportation, and 3) outreach/in-home services such as home health care, friendly visiting, homemaker services, and legal services. These services are implemented through a national aging network composed of the Administration on Aging with 10 regional offices, 57 state agencies on aging, 672 area agencies on aging, over 15,000 Citizens Advisory Council members, over 15,000 congregate nutrition sites, and over 20,000 agencies providing home and community services (Quirk, 1991).

Interagency planning, joint training in aging and developmental disabilities, and funding to aging network service providers were the primary techniques the 10 states employed to establish and foster collaboration between their aging and developmental disabilities service systems. In several states, these activities began prior to federal efforts encouraging interagency collaboration at the state level that were contained in the 1987 amendments to the Older Americans Act (PL 100-175), in the Developmental Disabilities Assistance and Bill of Rights Act (PL 100-142), and in the 1989 Memorandum of Understanding between the Administration on Aging and the Administration on Developmental Disabilities. The dynamics these 10 states reported suggested that the nature and degree of collaboration between state aging and mental retardation/developmental disabilities networks were affected by: 1) advocacy efforts of staff within these two state agencies, 2) the degree of autonomy among local entities responsible for the planning and provision of mental retardation/developmental disabilities services, and 3) the availability of funding resources to support joint activities.

Although all 10 states reported having, at the very least, an informal interagency group working to identify the needs of older adults with developmental disabilities, the scopes of their activities varied markedly. For example, both Mississippi and New York convened interagency work groups specifically to prepare a formal plan for addressing the needs of older adults with developmental disabilities. New York State's report (New York State Office of Mental Retardation and Developmental Disabilities, 1983) presented a comprehensive review of the needs of older adults with developmental disabilities, which addressed philosophical, policy, and regulatory considerations and contained a detailed action plan for meeting these needs, which identified potential barriers that had to be overcome. Similarly, Mississippi's state plan (Cotten, Britt, & Moreland, 1986) was created from the findings of five task force groups created to address alternative living arrangements, day services, support services, training, and funding. Each task force was charged with identifying resources, services, and programs, and developing approaches for inclusion in generic services. A Conference on Elderly Handicapped Mississippians, which has since become an annual event, was convened in 1985 to sensitize task force members to the needs of older adults with developmental disabilities. Mississippi's state plan even contained a glossary of terms used in the fields of gerontology and developmental disabilities to help task force members understand the philosophies governing each service system and the network of programs and services each provided.

Concurrent with statewide planning efforts, several states also reported interagency planning at the regional level. In New York, coordinated planning between the state's local Developmental Disabilities Services Offices and local aging entities was an outgrowth of the 1983 needs assessment. It was reaffirmed by the 1990 Memorandum of Understanding between the State Office of Mental Retardation and Developmental Disabilities and the State Office for the Aging, which requests that the local offices of these agencies engage in joint planning and program ventures. In Ohio, interagency planning first occurred at the local level and provided the impetus for joint planning between the state agencies on aging and mental retardation/developmental disabilities. A 1986 Developmental Disabilities Planning Council grant funding statewide training in aging and developmental disabilities to both service networks led to the formation of local task forces involving the area agencies on aging and local MR/DD service providers in Akron, Athens, Cincinnati, and Columbus. Regional activities coupled with the efforts of the Ohio Interagency Training Network in Developmental Disabilities were instrumental in the Ohio Department of Mental Retardation and Developmental Disabilities establishing a statewide aging support group which meets semi-annually to provide technical assistance and support to local service providers in addressing the later-life needs of adults with developmental disabilities. Ongoing interagency planning at both the state and local levels also exists in Connecticut. A statewide planning committee headed by the Department of Mental Retardation and the Department of Aging was established in 1988, and in 1989 five regional Aging and Mental Retardation Planning

Committees were created to link Connecticut's five area agencies on aging with the six Department of Mental Retardation Regional Offices.

All 10 states also reported varying degrees of joint training activities in aging and developmental disabilities to address attitudinal and knowledge barriers to serving these older adults. Maryland's Partner's Project, which was funded by the Administration on Aging, provided training to over 600 professionals and paraprofessionals in the state's aging and developmental disabilities networks. The curriculum development and training sessions were a collaborative effort involving the University of Maryland Center on Aging, the Maryland State Office on Aging, and the Maryland Developmental Disabilities Administration.

Maryland and New York provide examples of allocating funds across service systems to invest the aging network in joint planning and service delivery. The Maryland Developmental Disabilities Administration funded two area agencies on aging to serve designated numbers of older adults with developmental disabilities at local senior centers. In New York ongoing fiscal support from the developmental disabilities services system has been a key mechanism for fostering interagency collaboration. The New York Developmental Disabilities Planning Council awarded a 3-year grant (1986–1989) to the State Office for the Aging to work with the Office of Mental Retardation and Developmental Disabilities. Their objective was to determine the feasibility and appropriateness of providing services for older persons with developmental disabilities through aging network programs. The first phase of this Aging and Developmental Disabilities Integration Feasibility Demonstration Project produced a report identifying the obstacles to including older adults in community aging programs and the strategies for overcoming them. The second phase funded and evaluated four local demonstration projects employing different approaches to including older adults with developmental disabilities in aging network services and programs. While these programs were successful in demonstrating that inclusion is feasible, they also identified a need for specialized programs for older individuals requiring more intensive services, which resulted in the Senior Day Program initiative.

Connecticut, Kentucky, Michigan, Montana, New York, and Ohio were among the 11 states nationwide that had formalized linkages between their aging and developmental disabilities services systems through interagency agreements as of January, 1992. The five states without special aging initiatives are California, Illinois, Massachusetts, Pennsylvania, and Virginia. In general, these agreements support joint efforts in planning for and providing services. While these agreements acknowledge the need for systemic involvement at the state level, their existence is by no means an indicator of actual collaboration. New York's Memorandum of Understanding is the most far reaching. Its specific provisions support collaboration at both the state and local levels and encourage joint program development. The agreement establishes an interagency services coordination committee, directs the two agencies to coordinate the funding of services and the sharing of case information across service systems, and designates the Office of Mental Retardation and Developmental Disabilities as responsible for the additional costs of serving older adults with developmental disabilities in aging network programs to the extent that resources are available.

Prioritizing Aging as a State-Level Policy Initiative

The FY 1988 expenditures these 10 states reported as discrete aging initiatives cannot be considered by themselves to indicate state policy commitment to addressing the needs of older adults with developmental disabilities. Program expenditures tracked in Kentucky, Maryland, Michigan, Mississippi, New York, and Ohio did not represent these states' total fiscal support but specific funding streams or programs that were earmarked because of idiosyncratic budgeting practices. Expenditures reported by Maryland, Mississippi, and New York underreported total funding allocated to specific programs for older adults with developmental disabilities. In terms of planning and interagency collaboration, Connecticut, Mississippi, and New York were among the more progressive states in prioritizing services to older adults with developmental disabilities as a policy initiative by the end of 1991. Their state mental retardation/developmental disabilities agencies all took the lead in formally identifying the needs of older adults as the basis for developing needed programs and services. Connecticut and New York also encouraged the formation of local planning groups, and Connecticut established formal guidelines for its statewide aging initiative, the Opportunities for Older Adults Program. From the outset, the New York State Office of Mental Retardation and Developmental Disabilities made funding available to the aging network to facilitate collaboration.

The 10 states' efforts to establish policy guiding the provision of services to older adults reinforces the effect a state's unique cultural, economic, and political factors have on the formulation of fiscal and program policy for persons with developmental disabilities. Formal planning at the state level was less prominent in Montana, North Dakota, Ohio, and Washington despite the fact that new residential and day activity program models for older adults evolved in the context of the major restructuring of these states' mental retardation/developmental disabilities services systems. Program implementation at the local level largely occurred without the benefit of any substantive state-level planning initiatives. Instead, these grassroots efforts were the catalyst for policy formulation at the state level. In Washington, attention to a statewide planning initiative involving the aging and developmental disabilities networks also has been eclipsed by the potential reorganization of the state's long-term care system. Montana, which is predominantly rural, reported a history of informal cooperation between service systems at the local level. Similarly, the longstanding informal working relationship between Mississippi's mental health/mental retardation and aging networks had reduced the need for a formal interagency agreement. In

Ohio and Kentucky, planning and program development traditionally have been vested in local entities responsible for administering developmental disabilities services. Ohio is organized into a network of county boards of mental retardation and developmental disabilities, and Kentucky has 14 Regional Boards, which are responsible for administering developmental disabilities, mental health, and substance abuse services. Among all 10 states, the advocacy efforts of individuals within the mental retardation/developmental disabilities and aging networks have been essential in prioritizing the needs of older adults with developmental disabilities as a policy issue.

CONCERNS FOR THE FUTURE

The experiences of the 10 states as well as the many other states that have begun to address the needs of older adults with developmental disabilities highlight several issues that need to be addressed in planning for and providing services. Policies guiding fiscal allocations and program development should be documented by sound data on the numbers of older individuals and their functional status. States must expand and improve their consumer information systems to develop more reliable data in order to facilitate planning for individuals with developmental disabilities of all ages. Few state mental retardation/ developmental disabilities services agencies had reliable data on the numbers and characteristics of the older adults they were serving or estimated the numbers of older adults who were not known to the service system but were likely to come forward when their families could no longer provide care.

States' policies for older adults with developmental disabilities will also be reflected in their response to the Omnibus Budget Reconciliation Act of 1987 (OBRA 87, PL 100-203), which mandates services for individuals with developmental disabilities who reside in generic nursing facilities. An analysis of 43 states' Alternative Disposition Plans submitted to the Health Care Financing Administration from December, 1988 through March, 1989 suggests that approximately 21,000 adults with mental retardation over the age of 65 reside in skilled nursing facilities in these states (Gettings, 1990). At present, there are no data on the numbers of older adults anticipated to make the transition to more appropriate residential settings in compliance with OBRA 87 or how states are addressing the program needs of those who relocate and the active treatment needs of residents who remain.

Planning for older adults with lifelong disabilities also must take into account differences in individual preferences as well as functional characteristics. The limited information currently available suggests that the attitudes and adjustment toward aging among older individuals with developmental disabilities are just as varied as that toward aging adults in general. For example, interviews conducted with 46 older adults ranging in age from 50 to 75 as part of Illinois' statewide needs assessment of older adults with developmental disabilities (Factor, 1989) revealed mixed sentiments about growing old. Although the majority associated growing old with poor health and reduced stamina, nearly one fourth were able to identify positive aspects such as wisdom and maturity and the economic benefits derived from age-related discounts. As in the general population, concerns about retirement centered around the loss of income when people stopped working, and most had few ideas as to how they would spend their increased free time. Virtually all (93%) looked forward to their earnings, and three quarters enjoyed the camaraderie of the workplace. Therefore, while older adults making the transition into retirement-oriented day activities creates openings in vocational programs for younger adults, older individuals should be able to make this later-life transition on the basis of an informed choice.

The varying needs and preferences of older adults with developmental disabilities also will be highlighted by the current self-advocacy movement, which is empowering individuals with developmental disabilities so they can have a greater voice in the decisions affecting their own lives. Concepts such as person-centered planning and circles of support actively involve the individual with a developmental disability in making choices about his or her future and encourage the use of resources beyond the traditional developmental disabilities service system to meet his or her needs. These service paradigms will help expand retirement and leisure options for older adults beyond community aging programs to a broader array of community activities. Developmental disabilities planning councils in Michigan and Connecticut awarded funds to foster involvement of older adults in age-inclusive community activities.

States' aging service systems are being looked upon to play an increasing role in meeting the needs of older adults with developmental disabilities at a time when the funding levels for the Older Americans Act services and programs have been declining. Between 1981 and 1991, while the number of persons ages 60 and older increased by 23% from 25.7 million to 31.6 million, the Older Americans Act budget decreased by 36% in constant dollars (Binstock, 1991). Two factors suggest that older adults with developmental disabilities will not be affected by any future policy changes resulting in the targeting of aging services and cost sharing by service users. Foremost, these individuals are among the priority groups designated to receive Older Americans Act services. Also, their relatively small numbers and varying needs and preferences are anticipated to have a minor impact on local aging network resources. Nonetheless, in light of the austere fiscal climate, the portability of funds or in-kind resources between states' mental retardation/developmental disabilities agencies and the aging network to cover additional costs associated with serving older adults with developmental disabilities and to support joint program development will be important in encouraging collaborations between these two service systems.

REFERENCES

Binstock, R. (1991). From the great society to the aging society: 25 years of the Older Americans Act. *Generations, 15*(3), 11–18.

Braddock, D., Hemp, R., Fujiura, G., Bachelder, L., & Mitchell, D. (1990). *The state of the states in developmental disabilities.* Baltimore: Paul H. Brookes Publishing Co.

Bradley, V.J., & Knoll, J. (1990). *Shifting paradigms in services to people with developmental disabilities.* Cambridge, MA: Human Services Research Institute.

Cotten, P.D., Britt, C.R., & Moreland, A. (1986). *Services for the elderly handicapped Mississippian: A coordinated plan.* Sanatorium, MS: Boswell Retardation Center, Mississippi Department of Mental Health.

Factor, A.R. (1989). *A statewide needs assessment of older persons with developmental disabilities in Illinois* (Public Policy Monograph Series No. 49). Chicago: University of Illinois at Chicago, Institute for the Study of Developmental Disabilities.

Gettings, R.M. (1990). *Eliminating inappropriate nursing home placements: An analysis of federal-state implementation of OBRA 87's PASARR requirements.* Alexandria, VA: National Association of State Mental Retardation Program Directors.

Heller, T., & Factor, A. (1988). *Development of a transition plan for older adults with developmental disabilities residing in the natural home* (Public Policy Monograph Series No. 37). Chicago: Illinois University Affiliated Program in Developmental Disabilities, University of Illinois at Chicago.

Illinois University Affiliated Program in Developmental Disabilities. (1991). [Closure data from the MR/DD Expenditures Data Base]. Unpublished raw data.

Jacobson, J.W., Sutton, M.S., & Janicki, M.P. (1985). Demography and characteristics of aging and aged mentally retarded persons. In M.P. Janicki & H.M. Wisniewski (Eds.), *Aging and developmental disabilities: Issues and approaches* (pp. 115–142). Baltimore: Paul H. Brookes Publishing Co.

Janicki, M.P., Ackerman, L., & Jacobson, J.W. (1985). State developmental disabilities/aging plans for an older developmental disabilities population. *Mental Retardation, 23,* 297–301.

Janicki, M.P., Otis, J.P., Puccio, P.S., Rettig, J.H., & Jacobson, J.W. (1985). Service needs among older developmentally disabled persons. In M.P. Janicki & H.M. Wisniewski (Eds.), *Aging and developmental disabilities: Issues and approaches* (pp. 289–304). Baltimore: Paul H. Brookes Publishing Co.

Morton, D. (1988). *Analysis of the fiscal impact of S. 1673 on Illinois* (Draft No. 2). Unpublished manuscript.

New York State Office of Mental Retardation and Developmental Disabilities. (1983). *Report of the committee on aging and developmental disabilities.* Albany: Author.

New York State Office of Mental Retardation and Developmental Disabilities. (1988). *Program resources directory for older persons with developmental disabilities.* Albany: Author.

New York State Office of Mental Retardation and Developmental Disabilities. (1989). *New directions for seniors: Senior Day Program demonstrations.* Albany: Author.

New York State Office of Mental Retardation and Developmental Disabilities. (1991). *Choices for the new generation: A follow-up report on New York's Senior Day Program demonstrations.* Albany: Author.

Quirk, D. (1991). The aging network: An agenda for the nineties and beyond. *Generations, 15*(3), 23–26.

Segal, R. (1977). Trends in services for the aged mentally retarded. *Mental Retardation, 15,* 25–27.

Seltzer, M.M., & Krauss, M.W. (1987). Aging and mental retardation: Extending the continuum. *Monographs of the American Society on Mental Retardation.* (No. 9).

Spencer, G. (1989). *Projections of the population of the United States by age, sex, and race, 1988 to 2080* (U.S. Bureau of the Census, Current Population Reports, Series P-25, No. 1018). Washington, DC: United States Government Printing Office.

United States Bureau of the Census. (1991). *Statistical abstract of the United States: 1991* (111th ed.). Washington, DC: United States Government Printing Office.

Zigman, W.B., Seltzer, G.B., Adlin, M., & Silverman, W.P. (1991). Physical, behavioral, and mental health changes associated with aging. In M.P. Janicki & M.M. Seltzer (Eds.), *Aging and developmental disabilities: Challenges for the 1990's (The proceedings of the Boston roundtable on research issues and applications in aging and developmental disabilities)* (pp. 52–75). Washington, DC: Special Interest Group on Aging, American Association on Mental Retardation.

16

Strategies that Close the Gap Between Research, Planning, and Self-Advocacy

Esther Lee Pederson, Marci Chaikin,
Dianne Koehler, Arthur Campbell, and
Maureen Arcand

Since the mid 1950s parents and other family members have had a leadership role in planning and service development in the field of mental retardation and developmental disabilities. In the 1990s consumer participation, empowerment, self-advocacy, and participatory action research are all concepts receiving much attention. Leadership opportunities are expanding to include both families and individuals with mental retardation/developmental disabilities. The purpose of this chapter is to explore with the reader strategies that can make these concepts meaningful and supportive of people with mental retardation/

Correspondence about this chapter should be directed to Esther Lee Pederson, M.Ed., RRTC Consortium on Aging and Developmental Disabilities, 3300 Elland Avenue, Cincinnati, Ohio 45229.

Special thanks go to Dianne Koehler for her enthusiasm and encouragement; to Arthur Campbell for his honesty; and to Maureen Arcand for her insights. Each of you and the other members of the RRTC Consortium on Aging and Developmental Disabilities Representative Participation Committee and the Cincinnati Advocacy Support Group have taught us daily that we can and should be partners for change. Thanks also go to Julie Ann Racino, at Community and Policy Studies, Syracuse, New York, for her assistance, support, and guidance in our attempts to produce a useful resource that clearly conveys the values and strategies of what we have learned so that others, if they choose, may also embrace them.

developmental disabilities being involved in the community. The community inclusion experiences of the Rehabilitation Research and Training Center (RRTC) Consortium on Aging and Developmental Disabilities and community advocacy and self-advocacy groups in Cincinnati, Ohio, provide the basis for discussion. Also, factors that have facilitated and/or hindered these research, planning, and decision-making processes are summarized. The last several pages of the chapter include the personal reflections of three self-advocates. In reading this chapter it is important to keep in mind that the information applies to all people involved in decision-making, not just people involved in the lives of individuals with mental retardation/developmental disabilities. References are made to people with mental retardation/developmental disabilities for the purpose of reinforcing the powerful and dynamic impact that their role is making on decision-making that affects their own lives.

One of the most common oversights in research and planning efforts has been not involving or enabling the involvement of individuals who will be the most affected by the outcomes, that is, people with disabilities and/or their family members. When reviewing the developmental disabilities and rehabilitation literature on consumer participation, participatory action research, self-advocacy and empowerment in policy and service planning, one can only conclude that it is not that consumer participation seldom works, but rather that it is seldom tried (Bradley & Knoll, 1990; Browning, Rhoades, & Crosson, 1980; Eddy, Cohen, Rinck, & Griggs, 1989; Graves, 1991; Pederson, Dick, & Riddle, 1991; Schalock, 1990; Valentine & Capponi, 1989). Members with mental retardation/developmental disabilities of the Cincinnati Advocacy Support Group[1] (1992) identified some specific reasons for their participation on boards and committees, saying: "I wanted to go and listen to what they said." "To help people with disabilities; to help make things better for them." "To give my view; to help the professionals to understand us better." "When I get involved, I want to be active and a leader; I want to do things." Committee/board members affiliated with these same individuals initially viewed the role of people with disabilities on committees/boards in a very similar manner. In essence their role was seen as adding a "new perspective to the committee's deliberations by helping the committee/board to focus and clarify its overall role."

Since 1988, the cornerstone of the operation of the RRTC Consortium on Aging and Developmental Disabilities at the University of Cincinnati and the local community advocacy organizations has been to achieve maximum consumer participation in all phases of programs and at all decision-making levels to ensure the relevance of the research, training, and planning activities and the utility of

[1]The Cincinnati Advocacy Support Group is a subgroup of United Services for the Handicapped II, an interagency group comprising 42 Cincinnati agencies that provide services to adults with disabilities. The purpose of the Advocacy Support Group is to support active participation of individuals with mental retardation/developmental disabilities on decision-making bodies. Members include people with mental retardation and others who are supporting them on committees or boards. The group is discussed in detail in the "Recruitment" section of this chapter.

program outcomes. These organizations, at the recommendation of individuals with disabilities and family members, are committed to having 30% of their memberships on all advisory boards, task forces, and committees made up of persons with mental retardation/developmental disabilities and/or their families. Of that 30%, at least two members are persons with mental retardation. Valentine and Capponi's (1989) review of the literature suggests "a variety of options, generally recommending a range from 25% to 50% or more consumer representation on boards" (p. 9). The intent is to ensure that more relevant research and planning questions will be considered; more relevant and acceptable intervention strategies designed; and better dissemination strategies employed. The outcome is a commitment from people with mental retardation/developmental disabilities and their families to promote use of the products and programs generated by the research and planning endeavors (Graves, 1991). However, participation by family members, and even more important, by persons with mental retardation/developmental disabilities themselves, has been difficult to achieve in the complex arena of research, training, and service planning. The extremes of tokenism and tedium have been pitfalls that have been difficult to avoid for many research and planning committees and agency boards.

This chapter discusses practical suggestions and raises issues for consideration when individuals with mental retardation/developmental disabilities are included as active participants on decision-making bodies. The role of family members is a secondary focus of this chapter, although their past and ongoing contributions are held in highest regard. The chapter builds upon the history and experiences of self-advocacy groups and how people with mental retardation/ developmental disabilities have joined family members and/or have stood on their own in leadership roles. Much emphasis is placed on the meaningful and active participation of persons with mental retardation and on a new research paradigm, participatory action research (PAR). Guidelines or implementation strategies are recommended as a working model or approach for replication.

Successful involvement of people with mental retardation/developmental disabilities must not only rely on knowing the implementation strategies, but also on the attitude and level of personal commitment of all researchers, planners, and committee members including the person with mental retardation/ developmental disabilities. Ideally, this commitment or belief that *all* people can make a contribution should be supported by *all* members of the group before the persons with mental retardation/developmental disabilities are even recruited. However, if this belief is not universal, this should not be a barrier to inclusion. The participation of people with mental retardation/developmental disabilities can effect change in members' personal levels of commitment. The chapter is divided into five sections addressing: 1) orientation and attitude, 2) recruitment strategies, 3) preparation and training, 4) participation strategies, and 5) dissemination and marketing. Throughout the chapter, factors that facilitate or hinder consumer participation are discussed. This chapter itself has been a collaboration of project staff, including persons with mental retardation/developmental disabilities.

ORIENTATION AND ATTITUDE: SUPPORTING PARTNERSHIPS

Is involvement of people with mental retardation/developmental disabilities in research and planning activities a good idea? For many, there is clearly no question as to the importance of enabling people with mental retardation/developmental disabilities and their family members to determine their own futures (Bradley & Bersani, 1990; Bradley & Knoll, 1990; O'Brien, 1987; Schalock, 1990; Worrell, 1988). There is, however, a question as to how they might best influence policy-makers, planners, researchers, and service providers in the process (Pederson et al., 1991). A critical issue arises when people with mental retardation/developmental disabilities are placed in situations in which true partnerships do not exist and they are vulnerable to negative consequences when they do speak up. The potential for this type of situation can become a barrier to involvement of people with mental retardation/developmental disabilities. A comfortable environment and willingness to share power must be provided to ensure active and meaningful participation. It must be acknowledged that people with mental retardation/developmental disabilities have not been reinforced for speaking out.

At a Consensus Conference on Principles of Family Research (National Conference on Self-Determination, 1989), it was concluded that researchers, families, and people with mental retardation/developmental disabilities must enter into a partnership related to the mission of research in order to lay the foundation for successful outcomes. Such a partnership must be based upon shared values and the belief that people with mental retardation/developmental disabilities, as well as family members, can participate and speak for themselves and that they are valuable contributors to the resolution of policy, research, and service issues (*Effective self-advocacy*, 1990; Graves, 1991; Lord, Schnarr, & Hutchison, 1987; Taylor, Biklen, & Knoll, 1987). It is important to acknowledge that the viewpoint and perspective of the person with mental retardation/developmental disabilities can be vital to researchers and planners in understanding why gaps might exist between research, service requirements, and the desires of people with mental retardation/developmental disabilities. In particular, the contribution that the older adults with mental retardation/developmental disabilities of today can make because of their historical perspective on services should be recognized. The challenge becomes even greater when a person with mental retardation/developmental disabilities is nonverbal, functionally noncommunicative, or verbalizes what she or he thinks is expected rather than what she or he actually feels (Lovett, 1985). However, those who cannot speak for themselves can make choices and exercise their will with appropriate supports. Such supports should be individualized and must be developed in consultation with the person who has mental retardation/developmental disabilities.

When people with mental retardation/developmental disabilities in the Cincinnati Advocacy Support Group (Chaikin, 1991) were asked to discuss their understanding of mutual help and support, they responded: "We help each other; sometimes it is hard to understand words I do not know." "If I could get someone to read what's happening before the meeting, then I could ask questions." "Talk about problems we are having and discuss them and try to solve them or make them better." "We remind each other about the meeting." "We learn from each other; everyone has different experiences." "People help me by reading information to me before the meeting" (p. 5). Initially, other board/committee members saw the participation of people with mental retardation/developmental disabilities solely in terms of a need to provide assistance to a person with mental retardation/developmental disabilities, for example, providing transportation, easy-to-read agendas, and easy-to-understand language. But as the level of involvement of the persons with mental retardation/developmental disabilities grew, they realized that actual mutual support and understanding were taking place. It included a "connectedness, a sense of inclusion and commitment" that could not result solely from environmental or external factors. It meant "respect, patience and acceptance . . . an equal partnership." Key factors that influence meaningful participation of people with mental retardation/developmental disabilities are discussed throughout this chapter and are summarized in Table 16.1. Recognition of these factors can guide all members of boards and committees in developing successful partnerships.

Involvement of People with Mental Retardation/Developmental Disabilities

The level and degree of involvement of persons who have mental retardation/developmental disabilities is questioned by many decision-making groups. On the one hand, there are strong sentiments that persons with mental retardation/developmental disabilities and their family members should be involved in research and decision-making that affects their lives. On the other hand, there is the view that some of these individuals are not capable of serving in leadership and advisory roles. There is particular opposition to their involvement with researchers and planners. Researchers and planners often view the issues they deal with as complex and sometimes difficult for other professionals in the field to understand. Therefore, they feel that expecting a person with mental retardation/developmental disabilities or a family member to understand the intent and design of such research is problematic (Pederson et al., 1991).

Clearly, including people with mental retardation/developmental disabilities as part of the decision-making process will take time, and there will be frustrations and setbacks. Acceptance and inclusion will not be accomplished over-

Table 16.1.   Factors for successful committee participation

Factors that facilitate involvement	Factors that hinder involvement
1. The desire and commitment of the person with mental retardation/developmental disabilities to be a contributing member of the committee	1. The negative attitudes of the committee members and the person with mental retardation/developmental disabilities that active participation will not work
2. The desire and commitment of the committee members to facilitate the person with mental retardation/developmental disabilities to be a contributing member of the committee	2. The work schedule of the person with mental retardation/developmental disabilities often limits his or her availability to attend meetings
3. Recognition that meaningful participation of a person with mental retardation/developmental disabilities in a committee is a process	3. A strong commitment by the person with mental retardation/developmental disabilities not to become involved in activities other than work because of fear of losing his or her job
4. Support and understanding by significant people (i.e., family, staff, employer) in the life of the person with mental retardation/developmental disabilities that they can serve as a member of a committee	4. The lack of financial support to provide needed supports, such as interpreters, a facilitator, travel expenses
5. The availability of fiscal resources to compensate the person with mental retardation/developmental disabilities for time away from work, transportation, adapting materials, and for the facilitator's time	5. The lack of time for the facilitator and the person with mental retardation/developmental disabilities to meet to prepare for meetings
6. The flexibility and openness of all members of the committee	6. Committee members' inability, or unwillingness, to speak in easy-to-understand words and to slow down meeting pace
7. Communication accessibility to all by adapting material as needed in multiple modes and formats	7. The expectations that only ONE person supports the person with mental retardation/developmental disabilities, not everyone
8. The recognition that a person with mental retardation/developmental disabilities has the ability and skills for speaking out	8. The ability and willingness of the committee members and facilitator to provide individual supports with the understanding that not all people require the same type of assistance
9. The gradual phase-in of opportunities for persons with mental retardation/developmental disabilities to accept more responsibility as members of the committee	9. Acceptance of the entry-level ability of the person with mental retardation/developmental disabilities on the committee
10. The provision of broadening experiences to nurture the presentation of varying points of view by all members	10. The lack of patience and creativity by all committee members to involve the person with mental retardation/developmental disabilities

(continued)

Table 16.1. (*continued*)

Factors that facilitate involvement	Factors that hinder involvement
11. The recognition that the person with mental retardation/developmental disabilities can contribute to the overall mission of the committee	11. The limited life experiences of the person with mental retardation/developmental disabilities
12. The opportunity for persons with mental retardation/developmental disabilities to assist with recruitment of new members with and without disabilities	12. The use of limited recruitment strategies for members with mental retardation/developmental disabilities
13. The use of people first language, which recognizes the individual first, his or her disability second; for example, Charles, who has mental retardation/developmental disabilities	13. The lack of awareness of people first language, which recognizes the individual first, his or her disability second

night, and some efforts will be more successful than others (Taylor et al., 1987). People with mental retardation/developmental disabilities, however, like everyone else, need to have a chance to make decisions, and their decisions should be respected. This participation will take time because active participation is a process. For this process, orientation is needed for all members of the committee, not just for the people with mental retardation/developmental disabilities and family members. This orientation should focus on the contributions that people with mental retardation/developmental disabilities can make and what those contributions can mean to everyone involved. The commitments to work together, to listen to each other, and to respect and support each other as equal partners must be made by all. The range of supports needed by individuals with mental retardation/developmental disabilities will vary according to the needs of those individuals and the needs of other group members. Examples of supports that might be needed by any committee members are: time to become acquainted; transportation; reimbursement for time off work; interpreters; travel expenses; adjustment of length and time of meetings; use of easy-to-read agendas and handouts; and use of easy-to-understand language in oral reporting. These issues must be addressed and understood during the group's orientation so that potential barriers to participation of persons with mental retardation/developmental disabilities can be removed immediately.

Participatory Action Research

Participatory action research (PAR) is a paradigm based upon the philosophy of participation and endorsed by the National Institute on Disability and Rehabilitation Research. PAR is an applied research model in which members of the community who have disabilities and their family members, along with professional researchers, work together to: define research problems, to develop appropriate ways for conducting the research, gather data, analyze outcomes, and disseminate results. In PAR, the researcher acts more as a coach for team building than as a disciplinary expert (Graves, 1991; Whyte, 1989). PAR is a paradigm that maximizes the participation of the consumer of the research (e.g., the person with a disability, family member, service provider) in designing policies and effecting outcomes (Graves, 1991). In PAR, the quality, rigor, and usefulness of the research endeavor is enhanced and strengthened by the partnership between the research community and the people with mental retardation/developmental disabilities and their families so that everyone benefits.

The involvement of consumers through active and ongoing participation with the research and dissemination programs' planning, implementation, and evaluation activities closes the gap between research and practice. It also perpetuates the RRTC's mission by making Consortium research findings and other advances in the field of aging and developmental disabilities available, accessible, and meaningful to those who are in the best position to effect improved lifestyles for older persons with mental retardation/developmental disabilities. The authors of this chapter believe that the PAR paradigm can be utilized in relation to planning as well as research. Following are examples of how to implement PAR with consumers through *real representation, relevant research, and real-life results.*

Real representation is accomplished when consumers are involved from planning to product development and dissemination through: 1) serving in leadership roles on advisory groups, 2) acting as full members of governing bodies, 3) serving as consultants for individual research and dissemination projects, 4) participating in evaluation strategies, and 5) providing training and technical assistance.

Relevant research is being conducted when consumers assist: 1) in curriculum and survey development, such as identifying specific questions to be asked and review of products prior to dissemination; 2) on translation teams that help to develop the format and content of products; 3) in new product development by proposing strategies for inclusion of people with mental retardation/developmental disabilities; 4) in testing products by being part of focus groups; and 5) in implementation of dissemination plans by mobilizing advocacy groups.

Real-life results can occur through meaningful involvement of consumers when their involvement is viewed as a process requiring a real investment of resources, time, and commitment through a variety of approaches such as: 1) consumers authoring publications; 2) consumers presenting at national, state, and local conferences; 3) consumers providing consultation to advocacy and professional organizations; 4) consumers experiencing personal growth; 5) consumers becoming empowered; and 6) professionals developing sensitivity to the desires and needs of individuals with mental retardation/developmental disabilities and their families.

Beyond Tokenism

If any committee or board member, including people with mental retardation/ developmental disabilities and other minority groups, are to be successful in a new role, then the committee or board must continually work to prevent the occurrence of tokenism by ensuring that everyone receives the resources and supports they need to participate (Browning et al., 1980). Tokenism must not be tolerated. Valentine and Capponi (1989) refer to tokenism both in terms of "the number of consumer representatives and the level of responsibility assigned" (p. 9). One way to prevent token representation is to provide for a minimum of two individuals with mental retardation/developmental disabilities to serve on a committee or board at the same time (Eddy, Cohen, & Rinck, 1989; *Effective self-advocacy*, 1990). Researchers and board members have noted that the mere presence of persons with mental retardation/developmental disabilities and their family members has served as a reminder of purpose and has promoted greater sensitivity toward issues (Eddy & Cohen, 1989). Meaningful participation, however, goes beyond mere presence. It requires a commitment and partnership of all working together. Tokenism will continue when a group fears placing decision-making control in the hands of people with disabilities. Committee members with mental retardation/developmental disabilities in Cincinnati summarized their participation saying: "We learn about self-advocacy; I give reports." "I listen and take in a lot. I put in my two cents worth." "If someone doesn't agree with me, I will argue with them, but still be friends; I don't back down." "I tell people things they may not know, and speak up if people say things that are wrong." Equal participation as perceived by other members often is measured by the level of consciousness raised that forced the group to focus on who the "primary constituency is for whom everyone is working."

The following sections discuss in more detail specific strategies to strengthen meaningful participation of people with mental retardation/developmental disabilities and their family members. PAR is an example of one vehicle of support for this new role.

RECRUITMENT STRATEGIES: MATCHING PARTNERS

The strategies used to recruit potential members are key to ensuring active and meaningful participation and partnerships. A campaign specifically conducted to recruit people with mental retardation/developmental disabilities takes time to execute well. The prerequisites of patience, understanding, and a true desire on behalf of the research and planning group to involve people with mental retardation/developmental disabilities is needed for the campaign to work (*Self-advocates and the ARC*, n.d.). It is essential that people not be recruited simply because they have a disability. Ideally, the candidate would be able to understand the concept of membership and committee responsibility before making the decision to join any group (Eddy, Cohen, Rinck, & Griggs, 1989; Pederson et al., 1991; Taylor et al., 1987). For some, actual attendance at meetings helps in making the decision to participate. Sometimes candidates who do not know the specific issues make excellent committee or board members because they do not have preconceived agendas. It is important, however, for recruitment to ensure a match between the needs of the group and the interests and expertise of the candidate (Eddy et al., 1989).

Before recruitment of any potential members begins, the committee or board must identify what types of life experiences or expertise it requires from its members. This will determine whether a match exists between the capabilities of the person and the mission of the group. An example of the importance of identifying this need is highlighted in the experience of Dianne Koehler, who has mental retardation and lives in Cincinnati. The Arc Hamilton County recruited Dianne to serve on its advocacy committee. She lives independently with informal supports and, therefore, had no experience with residential facilities. The other committee members also had no such experience. When an issue arose with a local Medicaid facility, this lack of exposure interfered with Dianne's and other committee members' ability and desire to advocate. As a remedy, committee members were provided opportunities to visit the facility. The opportunity to talk with the people who lived in the facility and the staff afforded Dianne and others the ability to advocate actively in connection with the issue in an informed manner. Limited life experiences of any candidate should not be a barrier to involvement. The group will need to recognize areas calling for ongoing education and training and provide opportunities to address them.

Because many people with mental retardation/developmental disabilities lack experience, the recruitment process must assure new candidates that they are not expected to know everything before they join the group, but that they must demonstrate a willingness to learn as they work with others. The group must then provide these new members with the opportunities to learn how it operates, what will be expected from them, and what the major issues are so that they can become contributing members. Members with mental retardation/ developmental disabilities in the Cincinnati Advocacy Support Group (1991) identified some characteristics of a good committee member: "Be ready with your questions and paperwork." "Don't interrupt." "Listen to other people's ideas." "Be on time." "Go by Robert's Rules of Order." "Use People First language." Other committee or board members quickly realized that these characteristics of a good member were valuable for them to keep in mind as well.

Finding Potential Members

Once the needed area(s) of expertise are identified, potential members must be sought out actively. Often it is easier to ask the same family members or advocates again and again to serve on committees, because working with the known rather than the unknown takes less time. Committee or board members are not always aware that there are many people with mental retardation/developmental disabilities who could speak out besides the more visible self-advocates they work with on a regular basis (Taylor et al., 1987). Reaching out and identifying new candidates does take time. Among the best recruiters may be people with mental retardation/developmental disabilities and/or family members who currently serve on committees or boards. They have experienced membership on committees or boards and frequently can be the best spokespeople to encourage new people to volunteer their time. If no one can be identified from the immediate network, service providers can be contacted. Maureen Arcand, a primary consumer in the Consortium on Aging and Developmental Disabilities, recommended that service providers be contacted to assist with recruitment because often they are the people who have the trust of and entree to people with mental retardation/developmental disabilities and their families. She added that service agencies would need to be educated about the role and function of the group so that they could adequately explain these aspects to the potential member with mental retardation/developmental disabilities and could assist the person in making an informed decision about membership.

In Cincinnati a unique recruitment process was initiated to identify new people with mental retardation/developmental disabilities who typically might not become involved in committees or boards. It was also a way to begin a support network for people who had limited experiences and skills; that network is the Advocacy Support Group. An easy-to-read letter and Personal Profile form (questionnaire) (shown in Appendix A at the end of this chapter) was disseminated to provider agencies serving people with mental retardation/developmental disabilities. These agencies shared the material with their clientele. Interested people who completed the questionnaire met with current group members to learn about the group in more detail and to have questions answered. Applicants then were invited to attend an Advocacy Support Group meeting to learn more about the various community committees and task forces with which they might become involved and to identify the types of individual supports, if any, they might need.

The Advocacy Support Group provides an orientation or training resource for all new candidates with mental retardation/developmental disabilities and their facilitators who serve in a support role if needed. Some people might choose never to advance beyond the small Advocacy Support Group, while others, as their skills and interest increase, become involved with larger groups or boards. The Advocacy Support Group provides interested agencies serving people who have mental retardation/developmental disabilities with technical assistance to better understand the role and function of a committee or board member with mental retardation/developmental disabilities. In addition, a resource pool of experienced committee members with mental retardation/developmental disabilities is created from which other community agencies and boards can recruit.

Responsibilities of Other Committee or Board Members

All too often, tokenism is the reality for people with mental retardation/developmental disabilities serving on committees or boards. Tedium, that is, an overwhelming feeling of all the extra work necessary to provide the appropriate supports for the person with mental retardation/developmental disabilities to be successful, may override the contribution that other members see the new committee or board member as able to make. Decision-making bodies must be committed and dedicated to active participation from the outset by relinquishing the power of decision-making to all members of the group, including people with mental retardation/developmental disabilities, in order for the participation process to be successful. When commitment is not unanimous, the key people, including the chair, staff, facilitator (if needed), and the person with mental retardation/developmental disabilities, at a minimum, must be committed to begin the process.

As noted earlier, one way to encourage active participation of members with mental retardation/developmental disabilities and prevent tokenism is to recruit more than one person with mental retardation/developmental disabilities. This way a more experienced person can go to meetings with a less experienced person, which builds leadership skills. If one person cannot attend, the other can represent the issues and keep the absent person up to date. Self-advocates feel more confident when they attend meetings with someone else, because they can support each other's active participation and discuss the issues before and after the meetings. Also, people with different types of disabilities and different life experiences can assist the group to gain a broader perspective about the research, policy, and service needs being considered by the group (*Effective self-advocacy*, 1990; Pederson et al., 1991; Taylor et al., 1987). In addition, there is much for people with mental retardation/developmental disabilities to gain by participating in decision-making about research, planning, and service issues. More self-esteem, leadership skills, and access to services that are more responsive to their needs and desires typically result.

Responsibilities of the Facilitator

All committee members need support, and people with mental retardation/developmental disabilities may need specific types of support at times throughout their term on a committee or board. Two types of facilitators or supporters could be utilized in developing the partnership between the committee or board and the individual with mental retardation/developmental disabilities. One type facilitates the role of the person with mental retardation/developmental disabilities on the committee or board; and the second facilitates the committee or board as a whole to involve the person with mental retardation/developmental disabilities. The role of a facilitator or supporter in helping people with mental retardation/developmental disabilities during the recruitment process or during their quest for an appointment to a committee or board could involve helping the person determine issues of interest, identifying committees or boards in the community, and assisting in carrying out the necessary steps to join the committee or board. The facilitator might, at times, be needed to work with a board to sell the concept of consumer participation. The committee or board needs to understand that when people with mental retardation/developmental disabilities are truly involved, everyone benefits. The first-hand guidance and life experiences of a person with mental retardation/developmental disabilities will assist a group in evaluating its purpose, programs, and services from the perspective of the people it serves.

Responsibilities of People with Mental Retardation/Developmental Disabilities

All potential members, including people with mental retardation/developmental disabilities, have some responsibility in the recruitment process. It is essential to determine whether involvement of individuals with mental retardation/developmental disabilities with an organization will be worthwhile for the individual. The potential member should screen the organization to find out, for example: what it actually does, whether, in fact, it truly helps people with disabilities, whether it is willing to change if it is not actually helping, whether it makes real decisions or is simply a rubber stamp, what kinds of decisions it makes, what is done about advice they give, and what the attitudes of other committee or board members are regarding the group role and contributions of people with mental retardation/developmental disabilities (*Effective self-advocacy*, 1990). Answers to the questions should provide a basis for an informed decision about the potential for partnership.

In a workshop presented at the North American People First Conference in Nashville in 1991, it was suggested that in order for persons with mental retardation/developmental disabilities to be considered as potential members of a decision-making group, it is important for them to be visible. Also, it was agreed that it would be helpful for them to be involved in a self-advocacy group, such as People First or Kentuckians Together. The importance of individuals with mental retardation/developmental disabilities knowing the process of appointment to a particular committee or board was identified. In addition, the responsibility that current committee or board members with mental retardation/developmental disabilities have to teach other individuals with mental retardation/developmental disabilities how to serve on committees or boards effectively and support new members throughout the process was stressed. Leaders with mental retardation/developmental disabilities generally have the following characteristics or should be willing to develop them in order to be successful advocates in a group: belief in the common vision of the group, motivation, being informed, being skilled, and having a strong willingness to speak up (World Institute on Disability and Minnesota Governor's Planning Council on Developmental Disabilities, 1991).

The recruitment and nomination process used for people with disabilities should be the same as that used for potential members without disabilities. It should also occur at the same time and afford the same terms of service and voting privileges as for other members. Gould (1990) supports this, saying, "This will ensure the identification of self advocates with experience and maturity to represent their peers" (p. 12). The partnership begins!

PREPARATION AND TRAINING: LEARNING TOGETHER

The key to training and preparation is that people with mental retardation/developmental disabilities must first believe that they can be effective in the role they have accepted and be willing to put the necessary time into learning how to become contributing members. With only a few leadership development programs preparing people with mental retardation/developmental disabilities for positions of leadership in local, state, and national organizations (World Institute on Disability and Minnesota Governor's Planning Council on Developmental Disabilities, 1991), one strategy for initial participation is membership on a task force rather than a full committee or board. Over time, supports can be built in, skills developed, and roles and responsibilities increased at the person's own pace rather than at the demands of the decision-making body. Maureen Arcand, a member of the RRTC Consortium on Aging and Developmental Disabilities who is from Wisconsin, noted:

> The part of the partnership that defines the needed supports becomes a transition or bridge to close the gap between the person with MR/DD's past experiences and the experiences he/she will acquire as a committee/board member. This transition process should be done on a one-to-one basis which eases the person away from a dependency on the agency that has brought them this far, and begins to help them understand the mission of the new decision-making body within which they will be working. The transition needs to be done in simple language and geared to the level of understanding of the person. It needs to include an explanation of who the people are they will be meeting with and what will be expected. The final step should be matching the person with MR/DD with a buddy or facilitator. Possibly someone already on the committee could serve in this role which would include meeting with the person with MR/DD before the meeting starts, and making a commitment to sit near the person and providing them with whatever support they might desire to understand their role and responsibilities. (personal communication, September, 1991)

Successful Strategies

The Arc Hamilton County followed a strategy similar to that just described when it recruited Dianne Koehler to serve on its advocacy committee. In the spring of 1991, after 2 years of serving on the committee, she was nominated to The Arc

Hamilton County board. The process proved to be successful for all involved. Dianne was able to learn how to participate in meetings and to develop a supportive relationship with committee members, some of whom were also on the board. At the same time, the committee members who were on the board learned to provide the support necessary for Dianne's active participation and were able to model this support for the rest of the board members.

Another strategy to consider when the decision-making body meets for an intensive period of time (e.g., semi-annually) is the approach utilized by the RRTC Consortium on Aging and Developmental Disabilities with its consumer representatives. These representatives have expressed the feeling that the term "consumer" implies power and choice as well as a specific community membership. However, there is some feeling on their part that the term has also developed certain negative connotations, suggesting that they are being used rather than contributing. The term also infers a sense of a group rather than a person in their view. Therefore, these members of the RRTC Consortium Coordinating Council choose not to be called consumers; they choose to be called "representative participants" instead. When the representative participants of the RRTC's Consortium Coordinating Council expressed a need for more information in preparation for the intensive 2-day meetings, pre-meetings were established. These pre-meetings serve as a time for briefings on agenda items scheduled for the upcoming meeting so that questions can be asked and answered in advance. Other Consortium members occasionally attend the meetings for clarification of issues in which they have been closely involved. Pre-meetings help each representative participant to feel more secure about items on which he or she will be expected to vote. The pre-meeting group, called the Representative Participation Committee, has become a standing committee of the Consortium Coordinating Council. Most important, the Consortium Coordinating Council refers research and training issues related to participation of people with mental retardation/developmental disabilities and their families to the Representative Participation Committee for discussion and recommendation. The latest action has been to partner Representative Participation Committee members with Consortium researchers and staff to provide another opportunity for clarification of agenda items and discussion during meeting breaks, if needed. This informal networking and preparation helps the representative participants to be involved meaningfully.

Once people with mental retardation/developmental disabilities are appointed to committees or boards, it is essential to recognize that meaningful participation by individuals with mental retardation/developmental disabilities and their family members does not occur instantly, and it must be encouraged and welcomed when it does occur (Pederson et al., 1991). There are steps that members of committees or boards can take to prepare for the inclusion of the new members; these are: a willingness to change their language so that it is understandable to the entire group; a willingness to slow down the pace of the meeting and adjust the timing of the agenda, if needed; a willingness to take time to come to know the person with mental retardation/developmental disabilities; a belief on the part of all committee members that people with mental retardation/developmental disabilities can make essential contributions to the mission of the group; and a willingness on the part of the chair to bring the person with mental retardation/developmental disabilities into committee activities and discussions (Cincinnati Advocacy Support Group, 1991).

Attitude, Knowledge, and Skill Training Competencies

It is essential that all committee members, including facilitators/supporters, and especially the individuals with mental retardation/developmental disabilities be committed to meaningful participation. The Cincinnati Advocacy Support Group identified specific training competencies for each of these groups of members, which are summarized in Table 16.2. The competencies have been grouped according to: 1) attitudinal competencies, 2) specific knowledge competencies, and 3) specific skill competencies. These competencies were identified as those that would encourage improved interactive skills of committee or board members, both with and without disabilities. These competencies can serve as a guide for committee or board members to use as they strive to achieve membership and meaningful participation of individuals with mental retardation/developmental disabilities. Similar types of competencies would be needed for a staff facilitator working with the committees or boards.

As the roles of people with mental retardation/developmental disabilities grow, the knowledge and skills required of them increase. People with mental retardation/developmental disabilities and their families have expressed concern that they are unaccustomed to being asked for input into policy, planning, and service activities (*Effective self-advocacy*, 1990). Initially, they were afraid or hesitant to offer an opinion, and even more hesitant to criticize an opinion expressed by a professional, and certainly hesitant to criticize a research hypothesis. Arthur Campbell, a member of the RRTC Consortium on Aging and Developmental Disabilities, reminds us, "People with MR/DD and their families are often afraid to provide input because, in the past, raising a question resulted in services being taken away rather than improved or increased" (personal communication, September 1991). Being a representative participant on a committee or board can be a very difficult task. The intent of participation is to have an impact on the activities and decisions of a particular group. This is not realized simply through membership in a group. Rather, people with mental retardation/developmental disabilities must possess the skills to advocate effectively and negotiate when necessary. This can be very difficult for a person who has not been prepared to do it. In an effort to remedy this problem, the participants at the National Conference on Self-Determination, in Washington, D.C. in 1989, recommended, "Persons with disabilities [should] be provided formal classes in self-assertion" (*National Conference on Self-Determination*, 1989, p. 9). People with mental retardation/developmental disabilities cannot serve as agents for

Table 16.2.   Attitude, knowledge, and skill training competencies

	Target audiences		
Competency area	Committee or board members without mental retardation/ developmental disabilities	Facilitators	Committee or board members with mental retardation/ developmental disabilities
Attitude	Belief that people with mental retardation/ developmental disabilities *can* participate on a committee Understanding of the self-advocacy movement Belief in the importance and benefits of having people with mental retardation/developmental disabilities on the committee Belief that supports should be individualized and developed in consultation with people with mental retardation/ developmental disabilities Belief that supporting people with mental retardation/ developmental disabilities is a process that takes commitment, time, and creativity	Belief in the same philosophy and values of any committee member Understanding of the importance of not making assumptions about people's capabilities Accepting the person with mental retardation/ developmental disabilities as a person	Belief that people with mental retardation/ developmental disabilities *can* serve in leadership roles

(*continued*)

Table 16.2.   (continued)

Competency area	Target audiences		
	Committee or board members without mental retardation/developmental disabilities	Facilitators	Committee or board members with mental retardation/developmental disabilities
Knowledge	Recognition of barriers to involvement of people with mental retardation/developmental disabilities on committees and knowledge of strategies to overcome those barriers	Recognition of how to be sensitive to the feelings of a person with mental retardation/developmental disabilities	Willingness to put in the time necessary to learn how to become an active and contributing committee member
	Understanding of the role of the facilitator as a supporter to the person with mental retardation/developmental disabilities	Recognition of the importance of empowering the person with mental retardation/developmental disabilities with leadership skills	Understanding of their role as a committee member
	Knowledge of strategies to orient new committee members with mental retardation/developmental disabilities	Understanding of how to match their interest and skills with those of the person they will be supporting	Understanding the purpose of the committee and the meeting
	Knowledge and understanding of the role and responsibilities of all committee members with or without a disability	Awareness of the importance of being responsive, flexible, and creative in working with people with mental retardation/developmental disabilities	Understanding the rules, both formal, for meetings (i.e., Robert's Rules of Order),and informal (e.g., how to make motions and vote)
		Knowing when and where to go for supports for them to be a better facilitator	Recognition of personal needs and how to get the help when they need it
			Knowledge of laws that affect people with mental retardation/developmental disabilities and the particular group they are representing (e.g., the Americans with Disabilities Act)

(continued)

Table 16.2.   (*continued*)

Competency area	Committee or board members without mental retardation/ developmental disabilities	Facilitators	Committee or board members with mental retardation/ developmental disabilities
		Target audiences	
			Understanding how to screen organizations to determine if they can work with the committee
Skill	Ability to recruit members with mental retardation/developmentmental disabilities Ability to make needed adaptations including making information accessible to people who have difficulty reading, by use of large type, pictures, and audiotapes Application of strategies to facilitate and support active participation of a person with mental retardation/ developmental disabilities: encouraging opportunities for them to speak out; making sure members understand how to vote and what they are voting on; listening to what people say; avoiding making assumptions;	Ability to break down ideas into steps that are understandable Ability to fade supports in and out Ability to solve problems Ability to respect another's opinion/or choice even when there might be disagreement Ability to be a good role model for other committee members Ability to help the person with mental retardation/developmental disabilities and the committee deal with termination, transition, and change Ability to keep information confidential Ability to plan his or her time so as not to become overwhelmed with the role of being a facilitator	Ability to speak in public Ability to dress for the meeting and maintain good personal hygiene Ability to prepare and plan ahead for a meeting (from understanding paperwork to transportation to and from meetings) Ability to follow an agenda Application of interpersonal skills such as eye contact, not interrupting others, and knowing when to speak Ability to be assertive and express his or her own opinion Ability to handle conflict and confidential information Ability to negotiate and to understand that the committee might not always accept their opinion

(*continued*)

Table 16.2. (*continued*)

Competency area	Target audiences		
	Committee or board members without mental retardation/ developmental disabilities	Facilitators	Committee or board members with mental retardation/ developmental disabilities
	arranging rooms to allow all committee members to see each other; greeting each committee member upon arrival; making introductions; use of name tags and table name plates	Ability to come to know the person they will be supporting to determine the best way to support them	Ability to sit and attend for some length of time Ability to tell when it is time for business and when it is time to be social
	Use of people first language		
	Use of words that are understandable to the entire group		
	Ability to serve as role models for persons with mental retardation/developmental disabilities		

change unless their personal growth and skills are nurtured through educational opportunities that develop leadership and self-advocacy skills.

Negotiation Skills

Information on conflict management and negotiation skills is voluminous in this society today. All of these resources do not, however, make it any easier to teach these skills to a person with mental retardation/developmental disabilities. Conflict management and negotiation principles are central to successful representative participation on committees or boards, but learning these skills takes time and opportunities to apply them. They are important skills because immediate agreement on issues often is the exception rather than the rule, and individual views need to be expressed and understood for consensus to be realized. People First, a national self-advocacy movement, encourages its members to face problems and face conflict or disagreement head on. Remembering the following helps members to better understand problem-solving skills: 1) every group has its ups and downs, 2) problems do not just go away on their own, 3) part of self-advocacy is solving problems, 4) group members must sit down as a group and talk about any problems the group is having and invite suggestions for solving the problems, and 5) group members must identify different aspects of problems and the different ways to solve the problems (Worrell, 1988). Conflict among members has proved to be an area where discussion and modeling appropriate responses become valuable strategies in teaching conflict management and negotiation skills (Eddy, Cohen, & Rinck, 1989).

The American Association of Retired Persons (Cohen, 1982) developed a resource to teach board member roles and responsibilities, including negotiating skills. Another excellent resource is an adapted guide, *How to Work With the System . . . and Win* (Gibbons & Osborne, 1981), for people with mental retardation/developmental disabilities. An example of learning how to deal with conflict occurred for Dianne Koehler while serving on the board of The Arc Hamilton County. The issue before the board was to identify a tag line to go with the new name, The Arc Hamilton County. She did not want the label "mental retardation" to be included in the tag line and presented her view. After many attempts to persuade members, a vote was taken and the majority of members wanted the inclusion of "mental retardation." She voiced her opinion once again and reminded everyone how much this label hurt her. She then contemplated quitting her position on the board. After much discussion with staff and friends, she decided that she would remain on the board and continue to advocate and express her views. She was able to understand that change does not happen overnight and that she had a responsibility to continue to educate the other members. This was a growing experience for Dianne. In the past when she was confronted with conflict, her response was to leave the situation, permanently, if possible. Through a great deal of support and new information, she learned to confront a situation.

Training and preparation take time and commitment from both other board members and members with mental retardation/developmental disabilities. It must be remembered that meaningful participation is a process. By learning together with other members and developing a true working partnership, active and meaningful participation can be realized for people with mental retardation/developmental disabilities on committees or boards.

PARTICIPATION STRATEGIES: WORKING TOGETHER

How can other committee members assist, not manipulate? How can other committee members enable, not complicate? How can other committee members include, not exclude? How can people with mental retardation/developmental disabilities and their co-committee members work together to create an environment that encourages participation? To begin with, the social, environmental, and policy factors that support everyone's understanding of what occurs in meetings and what is being talked about must be explored. At the foundation of meaningful involvement is social acceptance. When people with mental retardation/developmental disabilities and co-members have appropriate interactions, there is an increased likelihood that people with mental retardation/developmental disabilities will be accepted as contributing and valued members.

Logistics often become the major determinant of participation by the persons with mental retardation/developmental disabilities. Examples of environmental and logistical factors are the availability of transportation to and from the meetings, the willingness of the person's employer to grant leave time or the other committee members' willingness to meet at times that permit the person with mental retardation/developmental disabilities to attend, and the ability and willingness of staff and/or other members to provide whatever supports are needed (Eddy, Cohen, Rinck, & Griggs, 1989). Policy factors that have increased representative participation include the advent of the consumer/self-advocacy movement, federal legislation and mandates, and professional interest in involving people with mental retardation/developmental disabilities in their own life decisions (Browning et al., 1980).

Also, research, particularly applied research, has become more and more a collaborative endeavor based upon the mutual respect, trust, benefits, and acceptance of the role of persons with mental retardation/developmental disabilities and researchers in its design, implementation, and dissemination (Graves, 1991). Maureen Arcand, a member of the RRTC Consortium on Aging and Developmental Disabilities, believes, "Written policy statements on the involvement of people with MR/DD and their families give them confidence and credibility for membership and participation" (personal communication, September 1991).

Philosophical Issues

There is not complete agreement among people with mental retardation/developmental disabilities, their family members, and others about making financial investments for the participation of people with mental retardation/developmental disabilities. In these times of tight budgets, limited fiscal resources can become yet another barrier to participation of people with mental retardation/developmental disabilities (Valentine & Capponi, 1989). Financial support might include payment for an experienced person to provide technical assistance and/or training when needed and ensuring that members with mental retardation/developmental disabilities do not lose money because of their membership in the group by, for example, incurring transportation expenses, or taking time away from work. People with mental retardation/developmental disabilities who are employed often are payed by the hour and have no benefits. Therefore time spent at meetings results in loss of income. For people with limited incomes this becomes a disincentive for participation. To avoid this problem meetings could be held at times when people with mental retardation/developmental disabilities are free to attend them and can travel to them. It is also important to make adaptations in order to ease participation of persons with mental retardation/developmental disabilities, if needed, as discussed in the "Preparation and Training: Learning Together" section of this chapter.

Members of the RRTC Consortium on Aging and Developmental Disabilities have not resolved these philosophical issues surrounding financial investments and their effects on participation. The membership continues to have mixed points of view. Some feel that members with mental retardation/developmental disabilities, when payed for their time at meetings, no longer serve as advisors to the project, but as paid staff. Therefore, a conflict of interest may result. Members of the Cincinnati Advocacy Support Group object to paying representative participants because they feel it is stigmatizing and makes them different. The same problems discussed here also apply to potential committee members who do not have a disability and who are not given time away from work.

Measuring Progress

How do all committee members, including the people with mental retardation/developmental disabilities, know if their role is making a difference or a contribution? One way to make an assessment is evaluating the competencies gained by individuals with mental retardation/developmental disabilities. Figure 16.1 lists outcome indicators for people with mental retardation/developmental disabilities to use to evaluate their own personal skill development and impact on the committee or board operation. This instrument also can be used as a tool to determine ongoing training needs. Periodic use of the instrument can assist those with mental retardation/developmental disabilities in recognizing the progress they have made and in identifying skill areas in which they need to improve.

An instrument has also been developed to measure the effect of having persons with mental retardation/developmental disabilities serve on a committee or board. This instrument, Self-Evaluation for Committee or Board Members and Researchers (Oldendick, 1992), appears in Appendix B at the end of this chapter. Providing a close look at the positive and negative effects of having persons with mental retardation/developmental disabilities serve on decision-making bodies will assist the group in making future participation of this type more effective and meaningful. As discussed earlier, the social, environmental, and policy factors that make participation successful must be examined routinely to determine whether the group process is meeting its goals and mission effectively. This instrument can assist the group in measuring that effectiveness, while at the same time heightening their awareness of the progress

Self-evaluation questions for persons with mental retardation/developmental disabilities (HOW AM I DOING?)

Outcome indicators	Yes	No
1. I know what an agenda is and can follow it during the meeting.		
2. I know what the purpose and goals of the group are.		
3. I know what the rules of the group are and follow them.		
4. I know what minutes are.		
5. I can explain the main ideas of the meeting.		
6. I can get to and from meetings.		
7. I can name the people in the group.		
8. I know what my role is in the group.		
9. If I am given something to do, I do it.		
10. If I do not understand something I ask questions.		
11. If members talk to me they look at me.		
12. Members talk to me before and after meetings.		
13. Members use people first language.		
14. I get the help I need so I can understand.		
15. I am treated fairly by other members.		
16. I speak out on issues discussed at meetings.		
17. I respect other members' opinions.		
18. I understand how to vote and make a motion.		

(continued)

Figure 16.1.   Outcome indicators for committee or board members with mental retardation/developmental disabilities to use for self-evaluation.

Figure 16.2. (*continued*)

Outcome indicators	Yes	No
19. When I vote I know what I am voting on.		
20. I talk with members in between meetings.		
21. The group has made changes because of something I said.		
22. I like going to meetings.		
23. I am prepared for meetings.		
24. I bring my packet with me to meetings.		
25. I give suggestions on how to solve problems.		

or lack of progress they have made in meeting their commitment to involve people with mental retardation/developmental disabilities on their decision-making body.

Participatory Action Research as a Vehicle for Change

The authors have applied participatory action research to both research and planning initiatives. In PAR it is not sufficient for researchers and planners simply to be *consumer responsive*. Rather, they must reflect *true partnership with consumers* in all phases of the research or planning process. If the strategies for participation, as discussed in this chapter, are utilized, it will be difficult to give merely lip service to representative participation. Through these strategies, research and planning can become a "collaborative endeavor based upon mutual respect, trust, benefits and acceptance of each individual's responsibilities" (*Report on consensus conference on principles of family research*, 1989, p. 9). PAR is one vehicle for change that does not define a specific strategy for research or planning, but, instead, defines an attitude toward the development of research and planning. The involvement of people with mental retardation/developmental disabilities in the traditional advisory role in which individuals (consumers) give blessings to proposals and products is inadequate to meet the requirements of PAR (Lottman, 1991). Therefore, PAR results from people with disabilities and researchers or planners working together as equal partners, from the formation of the research question or identification of the service problem to the strategic dissemination of products and support of outcomes. The techniques for orientation, recruitment, preparation, participation, and dissemination are all applicable through the paradigm of PAR.

DISSEMINATION AND MARKETING
STRATEGIES: ROLE OF PARTNERSHIPS

When people with mental retardation/developmental disabilities and their families participate in the development of research and planning initiatives and review the outcomes, they can be provided with more meaningful and accurate information regarding rehabilitation information and services. This information empowers them to direct questions to service providers, planners, and policymakers regarding program content and service direction and to advocate for the development of formal and/or informal supports in communities where none may presently exist. Immediate implementation of research findings usually is directly related to the care with which the transfer of findings to program activity is planned. If dissemination strategies are addressed as a high priority for the research program, then implementation could be more immediate. Administrators need time to prepare budgets, realign staff, or effect policy change that adoption of findings or outcomes may entail (Engstrom, 1975).

It is important that the knowledge and level of understanding gained through research and planning be translated into an easy-to-use format for broad based dissemination. In essence, the results of research and planning must be marketed in different ways (Engstrom, 1975) in order for research findings and products to affect those intended successfully. In a presentation to project directors of the National Institute on Disability and Rehabilitation Research, Deborah Roody (1991) suggested that researchers and planners ask five basic questions up-front regarding dissemination of their research findings; they are: 1) On whom would you like to have this impact? 2) What knowledge do they have now about your work? 3) What do you need to do to increase their knowledge? 4) What do you need to do to develop their interest to "higher levels"? 5) How can you mastermind the use of this knowledge by your target populations? Roody challenged researchers and planners to expand the concept of dissemination to involve more than publication of results in scholarly journals with the belief that these publications eventually will find their way to the service and consumer sector. Participation of people with mental retardation/developmental disabilities assists researchers and planners in responding to the questions early in the planning process.

People with mental retardation/developmental disabilities and their families have been involved with the RRTC Consortium on Aging and Developmental Disabilities from the planning of the research program to the development and dissemination of products. They have done this by serving in leadership roles, developing policy, and providing training and technical assistance. Specifically, persons with mental retardation/developmental disabilities and their families have assisted the Consortium in curriculum and survey development by identifying specific content and questions to be asked and reviewing products prior to dissemination. A translation team composed of an individual with mental retardation/developmental disabilities and a family member has helped develop the content of new products, organize them into easy-to-use formats appropriate for specific audiences, and develop marketing strategies. Representative participants can assist in testing products by being members of focus groups and by mobilizing advocacy groups to implement dissemination plans. Meaningful participation of people with mental retardation/developmental disabilities in the dissemination process is a major investment of resources, time, and commitment. A variety of approaches may be considered. For example, persons with mental retardation/developmental disabilities may author publications, present at conferences, or provide technical assistance to other advocacy and professional organizations. Through these approaches, people with mental retardation/developmental disabilities experience personal growth and become empowered, while professionals develop a sensitivity to individual and family needs.

Another dissemination and marketing issue to be considered is the importance of ethnic and cultural characteristics of personal identity and individuality. The existence of mental retardation/developmental disabilities does not compromise this sense of cultural belongingness, and research findings clearly indicate that the existence of mental retardation/developmental disabilities does not culturally "homogenize" people with mental retardation/developmental disabilities. Researchers and planners must be aware of this empirical fact, and their products should demonstrate a sensitivity to cultural diversity (Kuehn & Imm-Thomas, chap. 17, this volume; Lottman, 1991).

CLOSING THE GAP BETWEEN RESEARCH, PLANNING, AND SELF-ADVOCACY: EMPOWERING EACH OTHER

Key factors that influence active participation of people with mental retardation/ developmental disabilities have been discussed throughout this chapter. These factors can guide committees or boards in developing successful partnerships. In addition, it must be remembered that people with mental retardation/ developmental disabilities bring to committees and boards their own personal values and skills. They are not always sophisticated in the way they present their contributions, but they do convey true feelings and reactions for researchers and planners to consider as they work together to close the gap between research, planning, and the desires of people with mental retardation/ developmental disabilities. Participatory Action Research, particularly in connection with applied research, also should do much to ensure that the research is relevant and meaningful to persons with MR/DD and their families.

The following section presents the personal reflections of three people with mental retardation/developmental disabilities who have had extensive experience on committees and boards. In the efforts to ensure active participation, it is important that their voices be heard. Only then can partnerships that truly empower everyone concerned be built.

People with Mental Retardation/Developmental Disabilities Serving on Committees and Boards Sharing Their Personal Experiences

Being part of the community . . . means being known as an individual, a unique person, and not as a label, a ward of the state, a client of an agency or the recipient of another altruistic act.
—Bogdan and Taylor, 1987, p. 210

These thoughts summarize the fundamental belief of the authors of this chapter. They also serve as one of the major principles of community inclusion that have guided the development of this chapter. Meaningful participation and involvement of people with mental retardation/developmental disabilities is a *partnership* and a *process*. Concepts and strategies that support this participation were discussed thoroughly by Factor in Chapter 15. The following sections describe lessons that people with mental retardation/developmental disabilities have learned by serving on committees or boards and issues they consider important. Their personal reflections highlight their true experiences as members of a variety of committees and boards, as well as involvement as representative participants of the RRTC Consortium on Aging and Developmental Disabilities and as members of the Cincinnati Advocacy Support Group. Not all of these experiences have been positive, but they have all resulted in lessons learned that can be utilized to improve the working relationship between members of committees or boards and individuals with mental retardation/developmental disabilities. The personal experiences presented in the following sections will assist the reader to better understand how successful collaborative partnerships work as they strive to close the gap between research and planning and the desires of people with mental retardation/developmental disabilities. Each author has written her or his own thoughts with minimal editorial assistance.

DIANNE'S REFLECTIONS

Dianne Koehler is 39 years old and has mental retardation. She lives alone in her apartment and uses public transportation to go around town. Since 1988 she has been working actively in the community developing her personal advocacy and leadership skills. She is a board member of The Arc Hamilton County and serves on its Advocacy Committee. Also, she is vice president of People First of Hamilton County, serves on the Advocacy Support Group of United Services for the Handicapped II, and is a member of Ohio Public Images. Following is her story about how she became involved on committees and boards.

I met a staff from The Arc Hamilton County 3 years ago. We went to Columbus to get more money for people in group homes. We had pictures on sticks. We also wrote letters to the governor asking for more money. After this, the staff asked me if I wanted to join the advocacy committee of The Arc Hamilton County. I felt strange and afraid because I didn't know anyone on the advocacy committee or what they were talking about. I was afraid, but I said yes I will become a member of the advocacy committee.

In the beginning I was afraid of the advocacy committee. I didn't know anybody or what they were doing. I didn't know if anyone would help me. As time went on, we started to do some things together to help me understand things better, like color coding the paper, picture agendas, and the staff went over the information before the meeting. A staff person took the time to help me understand what was going on. This helped me understand the information we were talking about. In the meetings sometimes we talked about things I didn't know anything about. One time we talked about a nursing home. The staff took me there and I talked to a staff person there who explained things to me about what they were doing. I saw the people out in the living and dining rooms sitting there talking and screaming. One man was getting upset. The people who lived there were not doing anything, just sitting there. It hurt me. I now know how it feels to be in a group home or in a place where people who have disabilities live. This helped me understand better when we talked about it at meetings because I saw it on the inside. I saw what all goes on, so when we talked about it, I just try to picture what it looked like. Before I visited I thought it was some kind of nursing home for older people who had disabilities, but I didn't know if they were sick or what kind of disabilities they had or what their problems were.

I have been on the advocacy committee for 2½ years now. I think the other members of the advocacy committee feel real good about me. They take the time to explain things to me or change a word around, or, if I have any questions, I can call them up on the telephone and ask. In the beginning people didn't listen to me, but I guess it took a long time for them to understand me and I have had to take time to get them to understand. Also, if they say something I don't understand, I speak out and ask them what they said.

I need support constantly on the advocacy committee. I need someone who is willing to take the time out of his or her schedule to explain what is going on and who will color code the paper so I can follow what it is being talked about. If there is a word I don't understand, I need them to explain it to me, to sit down and tell me in a different way so I know what they are talking about. I get help from the committee members, staff, and chairperson. The staff member who has been helping me is leaving the committee. I feel good about it, in a way, because it will change things around for me since I have had the same staff for 2½ years. Not having that staff person take the time with me is going to be a change for me because I'm used to getting help. Knowing that the staff person won't have the time to help me makes me feel good and bad because I don't know if anyone else is going to help me. But I do know the advocacy committee members will take the time to help me.

A couple of months ago, I received a phone call from the director of The Arc Hamilton County, and he asked me if I wanted to become a board member of The Arc Hamilton and I said yes. Then we went to lunch, and he told me what my role and duties will be as a board member, what his role and duties are, and we talked about what kind of help I will need on the board. He also took some notes down as to what help I need. Now I am on The Arc Hamilton County board. In the beginning I felt strange and afraid because I did not know if there would be support there or help. Being on the advocacy committee first let me get to know all the people on the committee. Because of working on the advocacy committee, I now understand a little bit more about the board and how it works. Half of the people on the advocacy committee are on the board, and I know they will support me.

When I joined the board, I didn't know if the director would take the time to help me, and I didn't know if he understood how I felt about being on the board and having a disability and how it would affect the board members. One day I talked with the director and told him that there has to be support there all the time. If the support is not there all the time, then I don't know what is going on. I don't know the information we're talking about.

It helped to talk to him. He is changing the words around and slowing down a little bit. There is another problem to work out. The problem is somebody on the advocacy committee (and the board) either has to take the time to go over the information with me or I'm lost and I don't know what is going on. That hasn't happened. I have to go back and talk to the director again. I already did this twice. I guess I have to make myself a little bit more clearer or change my story around. After being on the board for about four meetings, I think they are taking the time to listen to me now. I feel good about it because I know they are changing words and slowing down. If I don't understand what the director is talking about, he will change his words around or tell me in a different way so I can understand.

If someone with mental retardation/developmental disabilities asked me what they would have to do on a board, I would tell them that they would have to know what we're talking about because there is a lot more information talked about on the board than there is on the committee. We talk about money, professional things, staff doing their thing, and changes that are happening in the community. All the information is a lot to remember. We have to know what the director's duties and roles are because you get his report too. His report is a little more difficult than the staff report. You have to know what he is talking about. You get the advocacy committee report and you have to know what they are talking about. You get the People First report. I help fill in what we're doing and what's going on with People First. There is more information than the advocacy committee. Being on a board is not easy; you have hard times and difficult times. Sometimes you get frustrated if things don't go the way you want them to go.

If a board is thinking of bringing on a person with a disability, they need to know how to help them by supporting them and being willing to take time with them. If the time and support is not there, then the person with a disability will not know what is being talking about. If the board cannot provide any support at all, it is out of the question to have a person with a disability on the board. I would leave the advocacy committee or board if I did not have support. I want to be an active member, and to do that I need help.

Being on The Arc Hamilton County board helps me to know what we are all doing at The Arc Hamilton County, what kind of problems we have been in, what the staff people are doing on their jobs, and how we can understand staff roles better. On the advocacy committee we talk more about the disabilities. This helps me understand me as a person with a disability better. I tell people in the community to label candy, pencils, fruit but do not label people. I just wish people would stop looking at me funny and see me as a person, as Dianne, and for the things that I can do.

ARTHUR'S REFLECTIONS

Arthur Campbell, Jr. is 49 years old and has cerebral palsy. He has lived in his own apartment since 1983 with supports from a personal care attendant 20 hours per week. Because of his impairment he uses a linguistic board, which has letters and numbers on it, to spell words in order to communicate. He has been an advocate in the field of disability for 10 years. He is currently serving, or has served, on the following boards/committees: Center for Accessible Living, Kentucky Developmental Disabilities Planning Council, Kentucky State Protection and Advocacy Advisory Board, Interdisciplinary Human Development Institute Advisory Board, RRTC Consortium Coordinating Council, and Kentuckians Together. He is currently writing his autobiography for publication and has been approached about the book being used in a documentary and a movie. Following are his words.

I am what the vast majority of the disability community and the service systems call a consumer. I am called a consumer because I need special or adaptive services for me to live in the community independently. I was born in 1944 at my parents' home in the eastern Kentucky mountains. I was born with what the doctors now call spastic cerebral palsy. I have a very severe speech impairment, use a wheelchair to get around, and have very limited use of my hands.

Despite these many disabilities, I am quite healthy, both physically and mentally, and I am quite capable of directing my daily activities and my own affairs.

Back when I was born, our society believed that if a baby was born with such severe disabilities as mine, the parents should institutionalize him or her forever. In fact, the doctors told my parents to institutionalize me. Also, when I was growing up, our society did not believe in educating their young children with disabilities. So I never had a chance to get a formal education. However, I have taught myself to read and write. When I was 15, I enrolled in a ministry school 1 night per week. I went there for the next 20 years.

I lived with my parents until I was 39 years old, then about 9 years ago, I decided to force my parents to put me in a state institution. The main reason why I did this was that my parents were getting to be elderly and in very poor health. Neither I nor my family knew anything about any programs and services for people with severe disabilities. Up until I moved out on my own and got involved in the disability movement, I had always heard and thought that people with severe disabilities had to live with either their parents or relatives for the rest of their life, or live in a state institution. I decided to go to bed and not eat, drink, or get out of my bed again until they put me in an institution, or else I would lie there and die. Mom finally said that I had lost my mind and she asked my oldest sister and her husband to take her and me to the hospital.

They took me to the University of Louisville and put me in the psychiatric unit for 10 days of observation. After about 8 days, my doctor decided I was mentally all right, so she started to call different agencies to see what was out there for a person like myself. She told me about the Center for Accessible Living, an independent living center. The next day I met with a staff person from the center, and she told me that if I would work with her, she could get me into an accessible apartment. I get assistance through a program called Personal Care Attendant. These attendants do what my limbs cannot do for me, like dressing, preparing my food, and housekeeping.

Before I moved out on my own, I didn't know that there was a disability movement in the world. In fact, I had never been around another person with a disability. So when I first started to go around and work with people with disabilities, I felt uncomfortable, strange, and out of place. But after I worked with these people, I realized that they were no different from any group that makes up our society. After I worked with them on many different types of disability issues, I came to have love for my disabled brothers and sisters. But much more than love, I have come to have respect for my disabled brothers and sisters, and I cannot pay another person any higher honor than to give them my respect. As a matter of fact, I have decided to dedicate the rest of my life as a civil rights worker in the disability field.

To me, professionals are in their positions to empower the consumer to learn how to run programs. Before now, professionals did all of the planning that affected every aspect of the lives of people with disabilities. You might resent me for saying this, but think of it this way. We see professionals' jobs now as educators and trainers of the disabled population. Your job now is to train the disabled community to advocate for itself, for their brothers and sisters who are not able to speak for themselves.

It would be easy to get in an agency on their board of directors and keep my mouth shut and just vote the way the able-bodied board members vote. They usually vote the way the director of that agency wants them to vote. If I did this, they would probably ask me out for two or three rounds of drinks and even pay for this poor cripple board member's drinks. Then I would become one of the "good old boys."

Most organizations that serve people with disabilities have boards that are made up of able-bodied board members with two or three TINY TIMS, TOKEN DISABLED PERSONS to make them look good in the disability community. In the real activist disability movement, we have a saying about most disabled people who are on disability boards and in high places in government agencies. We call most of these disabled people Tiny Tims. Remember in the story, *A Christmas Carol*, one of Bob Cratchet's children was disabled? But in this story, this disabled person was portrayed as a poor, poor little crippled fellow who hobbled around all day every day singing, "Tomorrow, tomorrow, tomorrow, everything will be all right tomorrow." No matter what or how society treated him, he thought that he had to have a sick grin on his face and be what society expected of him. He thought that he had to play the role of the poor little crippled fellow. This is what we in the real disability movement think of most disabled people who are in high government and on these disability boards.

What I am trying to say here is not meant in a mean spirited way. Most of these Tiny Tims really believe that they are sincerely serving their disabled brothers and sisters. But they succumb to the back room mentality. They are appointed to some high agency, or appointed to a high position on a government board that is supposed to serve the disabled population. Before long, these high society officials are slapping this disabled person on the back and telling them, "You and I are doing great things for your people, but in the next meeting I want or need you to vote this way or that way." Realize what pressure this disabled board member is under. Especially when we disabled people feel inferior to our able-bodied peers and crave for people to accept us as their equals.

Some people ask me why don't I sit on boards and be a nice little cripple and do what I can without making waves and trouble for myself. But I will not be a token on these boards to make them look good. I had difficulty making the other board members realize what they were doing so I often went away from the meetings feeling frustrated and depressed.

I became involved with the RRTC Consortium on Aging and Developmental Disabilities by accident. But this committee has been a highlight of my committee work. In fact, it is one of the reasons that I am still in disabilities work, because I have seen these committee members grow in their understanding of disability issues. I have seen people with mental retardation/developmental disabilities and persons without disabilities work together for long hours and both sides come to realize that only by working together can we accomplish our goals and many objectives. Because of this, it has made a believer out of me that people with disabilities and without can work together. I am listened to and I get involved. They sometimes have to wait a long time for me to tell them what I think—and it is not always what they want to hear. But they do wait, and for this I have come to appreciate each committee member.

MAUREEN'S REFLECTIONS

Maureen Arcand is 63 years old and has cerebral palsy. She has six children and started a new career with the Access to Independence in 1984 on her 55th birthday. Her multitude of experiences over the last 25 years have culminated most recently in her election to serve as a County Commissioner. Following are her words.

My involvement on boards stretches from being a low-income representative on a Community Action Board of Directors to being an elected representative on a county board. It includes the boards of two nonprofit agencies, three city citizen boards, and the organizing and chairing of a neighborhood association and a welfare rights organization. This is over a period of 25 years. Each opportunity has allowed me to represent a group of people who could not, or would not, speak for themselves. That is what always "fires my engines" and keeps me on track.

I have always been an active member, often a chair, and never a token. I credit that to the first group of people I ever worked with—other low-income parents who wanted our kids to have something to do, and were willing to work for it. They put their confidence in me to lead them. They showed me that confidence, and people have been doing so ever since. The fruits of our efforts, a community center, celebrated its 25th anniversary recently.

It was that group that sent me to represent them on the broader Community Action Board where I came into contact with people from business and government. Because the organization was dedicated to the needs of low-income people, I learned to speak up, but I also learned to pay attention and follow process and meeting procedures. I learned to stop people if they were speaking in terms I didn't understand, and they respected me for it. I learned to listen, because people like to be listened to.

These are the things I learned that I took with me into other settings, including paying jobs. I worked as a staff person to a board and got a feel for the other side of the equation. As a committee or board member, I respect staff and, as a staff person, I have great respect for the role of a board of directors.

The knowledge that I could speak for others, that I could listen to others' ideas, that I knew process and procedure, and that I was wanted made me respond to the invitation to represent Wisconsin on the RRTC Consortium on Aging and Developmental Disabilities. The rest of this reflection is on that experience, which has been enhanced by my past experience and has added to my satisfaction of knowing that I have made a difference. It is less important to me that others understand my contribution than it is for me to build on that sense of satisfaction.

It should be noted that Consortium activities were underway when I replaced Wisconsin's first consumer representative. As a person with a disability, seeing the interest of all these people in the problems of aging and developmental disabilities was a gratifying and reassuring experience. The fact that they spoke of people and asked how best to involve more consumers in their decision-making went a long way toward reassuring me that I was not there as a token.

As a person with previous experience being part of decision-making bodies, I probably experienced less fear in my first Consortium meeting than someone with less experience. The realization of the magnitude of the subjects being studied and the professionalism of the staff people involved with the research projects could certainly prove intimidating to some people. However, it was those very people, almost without exception, who listened to consumers and showed that they valued the input.

As the years have passed, I have returned to Consortium meetings and been part of committee conference calls. I have seen new consumers welcomed. It has been a delight to see people exhibit the patience it takes to understand a person with a severe speech impediment or to wait for a person with mental retardation to relate to the issue and make a point. The addition of more parents as secondary consumers has given a much better perspective on who can benefit from the research results.

There may be a few gaps we haven't bridged, but in general we continue to move forward and to understand better and better that people with disabilities have an important decision-making role in the projects. Past experience tells me that as professionals and individuals with disabilities face problems and solve them, we will continue to grow in our ability to work together. Our respect for each other, the foundation for any working relationship, comes from seeing how people conduct themselves in stressful situations.

My greatest satisfactions have come from working with others to deal with conflict, distrust, and turf protection. These are the things that prevent people from working together, and can destroy an organization very quickly. Sharing this knowledge has become my purpose on the Consortium. We are a diverse group of people, but we have one concern—the quality of life of people with mental retardation/developmental disabilities as they age. This provides the incentive we need to accomplish the kinds of the things we have done in the past on behalf of people who were reluctant to speak for themselves until we provided a voice for them.

CONCLUSION: LEADING TOGETHER

By listening closely to people's stories and experiences, the reader can learn from what individuals with disabilities consider important and relevant as research and planning activities are conducted. For leadership voices of people with disabilities to be heard, everyone involved needs to have a strong commitment to the following basic values: 1) recognition that the beliefs, attitudes, and flexibility of all committee members in supporting people in leadership roles will influence their success as leaders; 2) recognition that meaningful participation and involvement is a partnership and a process; 3) recognition that individualized adaptations and accommodations must be provided; and 4) recognition that a person has the ability, desire, and skills to speak out.

It is not sufficient simply to be *consumer responsive*. Rather, a *true partnership with consumers* in all phases of the research and planning process is essential. If the values, principles, and strategies discussed in this chapter are considered, partnerships that truly empower everyone concerned can be built to assist people with disabilities to have a powerful and dynamic impact on decision-making that affects their own lives.

REFERENCES

Bogdan, R., & Taylor, S.J. (1987). Conclusion: The next wave. In S.J. Taylor, D. Biklen, & J. Knoll (Eds.), *Community integration for people with severe disabilities* (pp. 209–213). New York: Teachers College Press.

Bradley, V.J., & Bersani, H.A. (Eds.). (1990). *Quality assurance for individuals with developmental disabilities: It's everybody's business*. Baltimore: Paul H. Brookes Publishing Co.

Bradley, V.J., & Knoll, J. (1990). *Shifting paradigms in services to people with developmental disabilities*. Cambridge, MA: Human Services Research Institute.

Browning, P., Rhoades, C., & Crosson, A. (1980). *Advancing your citizenship: Essays on consumer involvement of the handicapped*. Eugene: Rehabilitation Research and Training Center in Mental Retardation.

Chaikin, M. (1992, March). Cincinnati project promotes leadership. *A/DDvantage Newsletter*, p. 5.

Cincinnati Advocacy Support Group. (1991, August). Cincinnati Focus Group Discussion. Cincinnati: University Affiliated Cincinnati Center for Developmental Disorders.

Cohen, R.A. (1982). *Representing the consumer: Strategies for effective board participation*. Washington, DC: American Association of Retired Persons.

Eddy, B.A., & Cohen, G.J. (1989). *Consumer roles in society*. Kansas City, MO: University of Missouri-Kansas City.

Eddy, B.A., Cohen, G.J., & Rinck, C. (1989). *How to be an effective board member*. Kansas City, MO: University of Missouri-Kansas City.

Eddy, B.A., Cohen, G.J., Rinck, C., & Griggs, P. (1989). *How to be an effective board member: A manual for facilitators.* Kansas City, MO: University of Missouri-Kansas City.

Effective self-advocacy: Empowering people with disabilities to speak for themselves. (1990). Minneapolis: Rehabilitation Research and Training Center on Community Living.

Engstrom, G.A. (1975). Research and research utilization—A many faceted approach. *Rehabilitation Counseling Bulletin, 19*(2), 357–364.

Gibbons, B.N., & Osborne, J. (1981). *How to work with the system . . . and win.* Lawrence: University of Kansas.

Gould, M. (1990, February). Self-advocates as board members: Guidelines and strategies for implementation by human service organizations: *The Association for Persons with Severe Handicaps Newsletter,* p. 12.

Graves, W.T. (1991, May). *Participatory action research: A new paradigm for disability and rehabilitation research.* Paper presented at the annual conference of the National Association of Rehabilitation Research and Training Centers, Washington, DC.

Lord, J., Schnarr, A., & Hutchison, P. (1987). The voice of the people: Qualitative research and the needs of consumers. *Canadian Journal of Community Mental Health, 6*(2), 25–36.

Lottman, T.J. (1991). *Emerging trends on aging and developmental disabilities: A planning paper.* Cincinnati, OH: Rehabilitation Research and Training Center Consortium on Aging and Developmental Disabilities.

Lovett, H. (1985). *Cognitive counseling & persons with special needs: Adapting behavioral approaches to social contexts.* Westport, CT: Praeger.

National conference on self-determination. (1989). Minneapolis: Institute on Community Integration.

O'Brien, J. (1987). A guide to life-style planning: Using The Activities Catalog to integrate services and natural support systems. In B. Wilcox & G.T. Bellamy, *A comprehensive guide to The Activities Catalog: An alternative curriculum for youth and adults with severe disabilities* (pp. 175–189). Baltimore: Paul H. Brookes Publishing Co.

Oldendick, R. (1992). *Evaluation for committee/board members and researchers.* Cincinnati: Rehabilitation Research and Training Center Consortium on Aging and Developmental Disabilities.

Pederson, E.L., Dick, E., & Riddle, B. (1991, May). *Consumers at work on research advisory boards.* Paper presented at Solidarity '91, Columbus, OH.

Report on consensus conference on principles of family research. (1989). Lawrence, KS: Beach Center on Families and Disability.

Rhoades, C., & Browning, P. (n.d.). *Self-advocacy for people with developmental disabilities.* Santa Monica: James Stanfield & Co.

Roody, D. (1991, October). *Knowledge, dissemination and utilization.* Paper presented at the National Institute on Disability and Rehabilitation Research Project Director's meeting, Washington, DC.

Schalock, R.L. (Ed.). (1990). *Quality of life: Perspectives and issues.* Washington, DC: American Association on Mental Retardation.

Self-advocates and the ARC: Guidelines for membership recruitment and involvement. (n.d.). Arlington, TX: Arc-United States.

Valentine, M.B., & Capponi, P. (1989). Mental health consumer participation on boards and committees: Barriers and strategies. *Canada's Mental Health, June,* 8–12.

Whyte, W.F. (1989). Advancing scientific knowledge through participatory action research. *Sociological Forum, 4*(3), 367–385.

World Institute on Disability and Minnesota Governor's Planning Council on Developmental Disabilities. (1991). *Partners in policymaking manual.* Oakland: Author.

Worrell, B. (1988). *People First: Leadership training manual.* Downsview, Ontario: National People First Project.

Appendix A

Rehabilitation Research and Training Center (RRTC)
Consortium Coordinating Council

The RRTC Consortium Coordinating Council is a group of people who help researchers ask questions and obtain answers about supports and services for older adults with mental retardation. We meet to make sure there are choices of services for older adults with mental retardation and developmental disabilities. We also work together to tell other people about what we learned.

   We are looking for people with mental retardation to be a part of this group. If you would like to join, we would like to know a little about your life and interests, so please fill out this form. It is called a personal profile. It will help us come to know you better. Essie Pederson will call you when she gets your personal profile to talk about ways to become involved.

PERSONAL PROFILE

NAME _____

ADDRESS _____

CITY _____ STATE _____ ZIP _____

TELEPHONE _____ DATE _____

DATE OF BIRTH _____

MY HOME

WHERE DO YOU LIVE NOW?

	YES	NO
I LIVE IN MY OWN HOUSE OR APARTMENT.	___	___
I LIVE WITH MY FAMILY.	___	___
I LIVE IN A GROUP HOME.	___	___
I LIVE IN AN APARTMENT WITH STAFF.	___	___
I LIVE IN A HOME WITH A FOSTER FAMILY.	___	___
I LIVE IN A NURSING HOME.	___	___
I LIVE IN AN INSTITUTION.	___	___
HAVE YOU LIVED ANYWHERE ELSE?	___	___

IF YES, WHERE DID YOU LIVE?

_____

	YES	NO
I USED TO LIVE IN MY OWN HOUSE OR APARTMENT.	___	___
I USED TO LIVE WITH MY FAMILY.	___	___
I USED TO LIVE IN A GROUP HOME.	___	___
I USED TO LIVE IN AN APARTMENT WITH STAFF.	___	___
I USED TO LIVE IN A HOME WITH A FOSTER FAMILY.	___	___
I USED TO LIVE IN A NURSING HOME.	___	___
I USED TO LIVE IN AN INSTITUTION.	___	___

WHAT DO YOU LIKE ABOUT WHERE YOU LIVE NOW?

_____

_____

_____

WOULD YOU LIKE TO LIVE SOMEWHERE ELSE? WHY?

_____

_____

_____

_____

MY JOB, OR WHAT I DO DURING THE DAY

WHAT DO YOU DO DURING THE DAY?

	YES	NO
I GO TO SCHOOL.	——	——
I WORK AT A JOB.	——	——
I VOLUNTEER MY TIME.	——	——
I ATTEND A SENIOR CENTER.	——	——
I AM RETIRED AND STAY HOME.	——	——
I STAY HOME.	——	——

DO YOU LIKE WHAT YOU DO DURING THE DAY? WHY OR WHY NOT?

_____

_____

_____

_____

_____

WOULD YOU RATHER DO SOMETHING ELSE DURING THE DAY? LIKE WHAT?

_____

_____

_____

_____

_____

WHAT I DO FOR FUN

WHAT DO YOU LIKE TO DO FOR FUN OR WHEN YOU HAVE FREE TIME?

	YES	NO
I LIKE TO PLAY SPORTS.	____	____
I LIKE TO LISTEN TO MUSIC.	____	____
I LIKE TO SING OR PLAY AN INSTRUMENT.	____	____
I LIKE TO VISIT WITH FRIENDS/FAMILY.	____	____
I LIKE TO WATCH TELEVISION.	____	____
I LIKE TO TAKE CLASSES.	____	____
I LIKE TO GO SHOPPING.	____	____
I LIKE TO DO ARTS AND CRAFTS.	____	____
I LIKE TO TAKE WALKS.	____	____
I LIKE TO EXERCISE.	____	____
I LIKE TO DO OTHER THINGS.	____	____

LIST OTHER ACTIVITIES _____

WHEN YOU WANT TO HAVE FUN, DO YOU LIKE TO DO IT BY YOUR-SELF OR WITH OTHER PEOPLE?

	YES	NO
I LIKE DOING THINGS ALONE.	____	____
I LIKE DOING THINGS WITH OTHER PEOPLE.	____	____

ARE THERE THINGS YOU WOULD LIKE TO DO FOR FUN, BUT YOU DON'T? WHY DON'T YOU DO THEM?

_____

_____

_____

HOW I GET PLACES

HOW DO YOU GET TO SCHOOL, WORK, OR OTHER PLACES?

	YES	NO
I USE THE REGULAR BUS.	___	___
I USE THE YELLOW SCHOOL BUS.	___	___
I USE A SPECIAL VAN.	___	___
MY FAMILY DRIVES ME.	___	___
I DRIVE MYSELF.	___	___
STAFF DRIVES ME.	___	___

WHAT DO YOU DO IF YOU WANT TO GO SOMEPLACE?

_____

_____

_____

_____

_____

ARE THERE PLACES YOU WOULD LIKE TO GO TO, BUT CAN'T BE-
CAUSE YOU HAVE NO WAY TO GET THERE? WHY CAN'T YOU GET
THERE?

_____

_____

_____

_____

_____

JOINING THE GROUP

DO YOU LET PEOPLE KNOW WHAT YOU NEED? YES _____ NO _____

WOULD YOU LIKE TO TELL OTHERS ABOUT YOUR IDEAS?
YES _____ NO _____

WOULD YOU LIKE TO GO TO MEETINGS WITH OTHER PEOPLE WHO CARE ABOUT HELPING PEOPLE WITH MENTAL RETARDATION?
YES _____ NO _____

CAN YOU GO TO A MEETING ON WEDNESDAY MORNINGS FROM 9:00 TO 11:00 EACH MONTH? YES _____ NO _____

IF YOU WOULD LIKE TO GO TO MEETINGS, WOULD YOU NEED HELP?
YES _____ NO _____

IF YES, WHAT KIND OF HELP WOULD YOU NEED?

	YES	NO
I NEED HELP GETTING TO THE MEETING.	_____	_____
I NEED HELP READING PAPERS.	_____	_____
I NEED HELP TALKING AT MEETINGS.	_____	_____
I NEED HELP UNDERSTANDING WHAT PEOPLE SAY.	_____	_____
I NEED HELP GETTING AROUND THE MEETING PLACE.	_____	_____
I NEED HELP TAKING MEDICINE.	_____	_____
I DON'T KNOW IF I NEED HELP.	_____	_____

I NEED OTHER SUPPORTS. (PLEASE LIST.) _____

_____

_____

WHY WOULD YOU LIKE TO JOIN THIS GROUP?

_____

_____

_____

_____

_____

LEADING A GROUP

HAVE YOU EVER BEEN A LEADER, OR IN CHARGE OF A GROUP?
YES _____   NO _____

HAVE YOU EVER TALKED TO A GROUP? YES _____   NO _____

WHAT GROUPS DO YOU BELONG TO?

_____

_____

_____

_____

_____

THANK YOU FOR TELLING US ABOUT YOURSELF AND FILLING OUT
THIS PERSONAL PROFILE. PLEASE RETURN THIS FORM AS SOON AS
POSSIBLE TO:

ESSIE PEDERSON
RRTC CONSORTIUM ON AGING AND DEVELOPMENTAL DISABILITIES
3300 ELLAND AVENUE
CINCINNATI, OHIO 45229
(513) 559-4639

Appendix B

Self-Evaluation for Committee or
Board Members and Researchers

The purpose of this evaluation is, in part, to measure the effect of having a person with mental retardation/developmental disabilities serve on the committee/board. The results of this survey will be used to identify both the positive and negative effects of this participation. In order to make future participation of this type more effective, it is important that you provide your personal reactions to these items, not how you think other committee or board members might feel or what you think the correct answers should be. Please check the one item that best describes your reaction.

1. In general, participation in committee or board meetings by the person with mental retardation/developmental disabilities has been:

_____ Much greater than that of other members
_____ Somewhat greater than that of other members
_____ About the same as that of other members
_____ Somewhat less than that of other members
_____ Much less than that of other members

2. In general, the issues a person with mental retardation/developmental disabilities raises during committee/board meetings are:

_____ Much more important than those of other members
_____ Somewhat more important than those of other members
_____ About the same importance as those of other members
_____ Somewhat less important than those of other members
_____ Much less important than those of other members

3. When the person with mental retardation/developmental disabilities speaks, generally I:

_____ Pay much more attention than when other members speak
_____ Pay somewhat more attention
_____ Pay about the same amount of attention
_____ Pay somewhat less attention
_____ Pay much less attention than when other members speak

4. Before or after meetings, generally I talk with the person with mental retardation/developmental disabilities:

_____ Much more than I do with other members
_____ Somewhat more than I do with other members
_____ About the same as I do with other members
_____ Somewhat less than I do with other members
_____ Much less than I do with other members

5. The board encourages the member with mental retardation/developmental disabilities to call another committee or board member between meetings if he or she has a question or would like to discuss some issue.

_____ Strongly agree
_____ Agree somewhat
_____ Unsure
_____ Somewhat disagree
_____ Strongly disagree

6. The person with mental retardation/developmental disabilities is receiving the help he or she needs from *other board members* in order to be an active participant in the committee or board.

_____ Strongly agree
_____ Agree somewhat
_____ Unsure
_____ Somewhat disagree
_____ Strongly disagree

7. The person with mental retardation/developmental disabilities is receiving the help he or she needs from *staff* in order to be an active participant in the committee or board.

_____ Strongly agree
_____ Agree somewhat
_____ Unsure
_____ Somewhat disagree
_____ Strongly disagree

8. In terms of helping the committee or board to carry out its overall mission (e.g., dealing with issues facing people with mental retardation/ developmental disabilities, fundraising, legislative issues), the effect of having a person with mental retardation/developmental disabilities on the board has been:

_____ Very positive
_____ Somewhat positive
_____ Neither positive nor negative
_____ Somewhat negative
_____ Very negative

9. Having a person with mental retardation/developmental disabilities on the committee or board has changed the activities of the board:

_____ A great deal
_____ Somewhat
_____ Only slightly
_____ Not at all

10. In general, the opinions of the person with mental retardation/developmental disabilities are given:

_____ Much more consideration than those of other members
_____ Somewhat more consideration than those of other members
_____ About the same consideration as those of other members
_____ Somewhat less consideration than those of other members
_____ Much less consideration than those of other members

11. Having a person with mental retardation/developmental disabilities on the committee or board sometimes requires the pace of the meetings to be slowed. During the past year, do you feel that this has been:

_____ A major problem
_____ A minor problem
_____ Not a problem

12. To what extent have you had to change the way you discuss issues and present materials at committee or board meetings in order to make sure they are clear to the person with mental retardation/developmental disabilities?

_____ A great deal
_____ Somewhat
_____ Only slightly
_____ Not at all

13. Which of the following statements comes closer to your point of view:

_____ The use of people first language is critical to changing the way in which people with mental retardation/developmental disabilities are perceived.

_____ The use of people first language is largely symbolic and sometimes diverts attention from more important issues facing people with mental retardation/developmental disabilities.

14. To what extent has having a person with mental retardation/developmental disabilities on the committee or board helped you to learn about the problems and desires of people with mental retardation/developmental disabilities?

_____ A great deal
_____ Somewhat
_____ Only slightly
_____ Not at all

15. Given the other responsibilities, providing the support that the person with mental retardation/developmental disabilities needs to be an effective committee or board member should be:

_____ One of the most important responsibilities of the staff
_____ A very important responsibility of the staff
_____ A somewhat important responsibility of the staff
_____ A not too important responsibility of the staff
_____ Not at all an important responsibility of the staff

16. During my experiences on this committee or board during the past year, my attitude about representation of people with mental retardation/developmental disabilities on the committee:

_____ Has been positive, and has become even more positive
_____ Has been positive, and has remained about the same
_____ Has been positive, but has become more negative
_____ Has been neutral, and has become even more positive
_____ Has been neutral, and has remained about the same
_____ Has been neutral, but has become more negative
_____ Has been negative, and has become even more positive
_____ Has been negative, and has remained about the same
_____ Has been negative, but has become more negative

17. In the past year, how many times has the committee or board member with mental retardation/developmental disabilities called you to ask a question or to discuss some issue?

_____ More than 10 times
_____ More than five times
_____ Less than five times
_____ One time
_____ Not at all

18. The committee or board currently consists of ___ members. In order for the committee to carry out its mission most effectively, how many of the persons who serve on the board do you feel should be people with mental retardation/developmental disabilities?

_____ More than three people
_____ Three people
_____ Two people
_____ One person
_____ None

19. List the most positive aspects of having a person with mental retardation/ developmental disabilities on the committee or board.

_____

_____

20. List the most negative aspects of having a person with mental retardation/ developmental disabilities on the committee or board.

_____

_____

21. What change(s) could be made in order to make participation on the committee or board by people with mental retardation/developmental disabilities work more effectively?

_____

_____

22. Are there any additional comments you would like to make?

_____

_____

THANK YOU VERY MUCH FOR YOUR ASSISTANCE.

17

A Multicultural Context

Mariellen Laucht Kuehn and Pamela Imm-Thomas

There have been very few studies of health and/or aging issues among people from different racial and/or ethnic minority groups in the United States since 1980. At present, there is little research or training designed to give professionals the knowledge and skills needed to provide specialized services to people with developmental disabilities from diverse racial/ethnic groups.

Since the 1974 publication of Victor Fuch's classic book, *Who Shall Live?*, there have been numerous economic, political, and social analyses of the utilization and effectiveness of health services. These analyses tend to focus on the lack of available services, the inability of consumers to obtain services, the high cost of medical care, and other barriers to the effective delivery of health care. Based on what is known from these analyses about the health care delivery system in the United States, it has been possible to do a systematic review of the studies that have been reported on minorities, health, and aging. The findings from this review provide useful information for expanding and improving services to people with developmental disabilities.

This chapter presents an overview of the demographic changes in the United States relative to minorities and aging, population estimates of the number of older adults with developmental disabilities from some racial/ethnic minority groups, and the service delivery issues that can be expected to affect older minority adults with developmental disabilities.

Throughout this chapter the term "racial/ethnic minority groups" is used as a generic reference for United States citizens who are not part of the non-

Work on this chapter was funded in part by Grant #90DD0149 through the Administration on Developmental Disabilities, United States Department of Health and Human Services.

Hispanic White majority racial group. There is little consensus on terminology or definitions for people from diverse races, ethnicities, or cultures at this time. The term "race" generally is used to refer to large groups of people with more or less distinctive physical characteristics, such as skin color. The term "ethnicity" is used primarily to refer to groups of people with similar national or cultural characteristics, such as Chinese-Americans, or Mexican-Americans. While ethnicity is the preferred descriptor for population groups, many of the references cited in this chapter have used only racial categorizations, and much of the available census data are based on race rather than ethnicity. Some of the specific population terms used in this chapter are neither racial nor ethnic descriptors but are categorizations that have been developed by demographers and statisticians. The term "Hispanic," for example, which was developed by the United States Bureau of the Census, is not an inclusive descriptor for any particular segment of society. It subsumes Black people and White people who are part of the Mexican, Cuban, Latin American, Puerto Rican and some other American ethnic groups. Finally, the term "minority," as used here, refers to racial/ethnic groups which, as a whole, have an unequal and unrepresentative share of the resources in United States society. The term minority refers, then, strictly to the social standing of a group, not its size.

DEMOGRAPHICS

Few people in the United States are unaware of the significant demographic shifts that are occurring within the United States as a result of the rapid growth rate among people of color. An analysis of the 1990 census data by Braddock (1991) indicated that, since 1980, the Asian-American population grew most rapidly (107.8%) among the racial/ethnic minority groups. The Hispanic population grew by 53%; the Black population by 13.2%, and the American Indian population by 37.9%. The non-Hispanic White population increased by only 6%. In absolute terms, between 1980 and 1990, the Asian-American population increased by 3,773,223. The Hispanic population increased by 7,745,059, which is more than double the 3,491,000 increase among Black people. The American Indian population increased by 538,834. From 1980 to 1990, 17 of the 50 states experienced significant growth rates among one or more of the four main racial/ethnic minority groups. (See Table 17.1.) Six states have experienced a rapid growth rate among two racial minority groups. New Hampshire and Florida had rapid population increases among three of the four racial/ethnic minority groups. According to Copeland (1988), from 1990 to 2000, racial/ethnic minority populations in the United States are expected to grow seven times faster than the non-Hispanic White population, and by the year 2000 it is anticipated that one third of the population in this country will be other than non-Hispanic White.

At the same time that the demographics for racial/ethnic minority groups are changing in the United States, the median age of the population also is shift-

Table 17.1. States experiencing rapid population growth 1980–1990 (percentage growth rates)

State	Blacks	Spanish Origin	American Indians	Asians
Alabama			117.7	
Alaska	60.4			
District of Columbia		81.7		
Florida		83.5	88.7	171.9
Georgia			75.3	209.9
Hawaii	60.0		84.2	
Maryland		92.5		
Massachusetts		103.9		189.7
Minnesota	79.1			193.5
Nevada		130.4		
New Hampshire	80.0	88.9		219.0
Rhode Island		128.8		245.6
South Dakota	62.9			
Tennessee			96.7	
Vermont	95.1		72.4	
Washington		78.8		
Wisconsin				195.0

Adapted from Braddock (1991).

ing. It is predicted that by 2000 there will be a marked increase in the number of people over the age of 45 and a marked decrease in the number of people under the age of 35, as indicated by Bruininks (1991). In 1987, people ages 65 and over numbered 29.8 million and represented 12.3% of the United States population. The fastest growing segment of this older population is among the Black population and is expected to increase by 40% (from 2.5 to 3.5 million) between 1988 and 2000. Between 1985 and 2030, the older Hispanic population is expected to grow by 530%, the older African-American population by 265%, and the older non-Hispanic White population by 97% (Harper & Alexander, 1990).

The number of people in the United States with developmental disabilities who are ages 60 and over is not known. However, it is generally accepted that the increase in the proportion of the general population that is ages 60 and over will be mirrored by similar patterns in the population of older persons with developmental disabilities (Janicki & Wisniewski, 1985). Jacobson, Sutton, and Janicki (1985) have estimated the number of people ages 55 and over with mental retardation at 196,000 or 0.396% of the total United States population. Using the same methods to project, they estimated the number of people ages 60 and over with developmental disabilities at approximately 150,000. These statistics can be used to derive a prevalence rate of .303% for people ages 60 and over with developmental disabilities. Since there is no national data system to track people with developmental disabilities, estimates of prevalence, such as the .0396 prevalence rate established by Jacobson et al. are developed from statistics gathered by state agencies for mental retardation and/or developmental disabilities. Most of these data sets do not include information on race or ethnicity. Those that do tend to group people into White and non-White categories only.

The data generated by state agencies is restricted to the number of older adults with developmental disabilities who have been served, and there is some evidence to suggest that the health care services system is not meeting the needs of racial/ethnic minority groups. Bowe (1983) and Wagner (1988, cited in McClain, 1990) have indicated that only 400,000 of the 2.3 million African-Americans with disabilities are receiving health or social services. Consequently, it is extremely difficult to use databases maintained by state agencies to estimate the number of people in different racial/ethnic minority populations with developmental disabilities regardless of age. Any attempt to develop population estimates of the number of people with developmental disabilities for racial/ethnic minority groups will be further confounded by the fact that health status statistics for these populations vary significantly.

POPULATION ESTIMATES OF RACIAL/ETHNIC
MINORITY OLDER ADULTS WITH DEVELOPMENTAL DISABILITIES

The population estimates presented in this chapter are based upon the assumption that the .303% rate is valid for racial/ethnic minority populations if the racial mortality crossover phenomenon and low birth weight rates are taken into consideration. It is generally accepted that there is a racial mortality crossover phenomenon such that the life expectancy for Black people and for American Indians is lower than for non-Hispanic White people at the early ages of life and higher at advanced ages (Harper, 1990; Wing, Manton, Stallard, Hames, & Tyroler, 1985). This racial mortality crossover phenomenon may be ascribed to the higher incidence and prevalence of infant mortality and deaths related to chronic diseases and injury among the Black and American Indian populations. Conceivably, only the more healthy and virile people are able to survive the impact of poverty, racial discrimination, differentials in health care, and other inequities throughout their younger years. Those who do survive may be stronger and more able to cope with the aging process. This assumption is supported by the fact that there is no crossover phenomenon among the Asian-American population, which has the lowest infant death rate in the United States, ranging from 4.0 to 6.5 deaths per 1,000 live births. The comparative infant mortality rate for the non-Hispanic White population is 10.4 (United States Department of Health and Human Services, 1991).

Low birth weight places children at risk for developmental disabilities. However, any population estimates based upon the number of children born with a low birth weight would be skewed if the infant mortality rates were high. For example, 12.9% of Black children have a low birth weight as compared to the United States national average of 6.9% (United States Department of Health and Human Services, 1991). This suggests a higher number of Black children with developmental disabilities and, consequently, a prevalence rate higher than .303% of older adults with developmental disabilities. However, the presence of the racial mortality crossover phenomenon, indicative of the higher mortality rates at the younger ages, suggests that the number of older African-Americans with developmental disabilities will be lower than the .303 prevalence rate.

Among American Indians, who, according to the United States Census include Eskimos and Aleuts, the low birth weight rate of 6.2% (United States Department of Health and Human Services, 1991) suggests a prevalence rate equivalent to .303%. However, the neonatal risk of death for American Indian infants with birth weights greater than 4,000 grams has been reported as 2.6 times greater than that of the White population, as indicated by Vanlandingham, Buehler, Hogue, and Strauss (1988). Most likely children and young adults with developmental disabilities are highly represented in this higher mortality rate. Also, the presence of the racial mortality crossover phenomenon among the American Indian populations suggests that the number of older adults with developmental disabilities among this racial group will be lower than the .303% prevalence rate.

Among Asian-Americans, the percentage of infants born in 1987 with a low birth weight ranged from 5.0% among Chinese-Americans to 6.6% among Hawaiians to 7.3% among Pilipino-Americans. Given the absence of the racial mortality crossover phenomenon among the Asian-American population and a low birth weight rate similar to that of the national average, it is anticipated that their prevalence rate of older adults with developmental disabilities will approximate .303% of the population.

If these assumptions are correct, population estimates can be derived from the 1990 United States census data (United States Department of Commerce, 1992). As indicated in Table 17.2:

- The number of older Black people who have developmental disabilities is estimated to be less than 90,797.
- The number of older American Indians who have developmental disabilities is estimated to be less than 5,936.
- The number of Asian-Americans who have developmental disabilities is estimated to approximate 22,039.

No conclusions can be drawn for the Hispanic population, for whom there are insufficient data on infant mortality and for whom the crossover phenomenon was observed only minimally by Schoen and Nelson (1981) among males with Spanish surnames. The inconclusive evidence of the racial mortality crossover phenomenon among the Hispanic population is most likely attributable to

Table 17.2. Population estimates of elder racial/ethnic minorities with developmental disabilities, based on 1990 census data

Racial/ethnic minority group	Incidence rate	United States population	Estimated elders with developmental disabilities
American Indians[a]	> .303	1,959,234	> 5,936
Asians[b]	.303	7,273,662	22,039
Blacks	> .303	29,986,080	>90,858
Hispanics	Unknown	22,354,059	Unknown

Adapted from United States Department of Commerce (1992).
[a]Includes Eskimos and Aleuts.
[b]Includes Pacific Islanders.

the fact that this is a highly heterogeneous population. For example, the median age of Mexican-Americans is 23.5, whereas the median age of Cuban-Americans is 35.8. Such factors as fertility rates, age structure, social class, and the geographic distributions of the various racial and ethnic groups subsumed under the Hispanic category significantly affect correlates of infant mortality and longevity. Unfortunately, statistics are not available for the major ethnic groups that are subsumed under the Hispanic category. This lack of data makes it impossible to determine the absence or presence of the racial mortality crossover phenomenon or the prevalence of low birth weight, by specific racial/ethnic minority groupings.

SERVICE ISSUES

Conclusions about the effectiveness of service delivery to older adults with developmental disabilities who are members of a racial/ethnic minority population cannot be extrapolated from the issues that are critical to the delivery of services across the life span. These include the issues of *availability, access, affordability, accommodation, and cultural appropriateness.*

Availability

Penchansky and Thomas (1981) have defined availability as the relationship between the volume of specific services (supply) and the consumer's need for services (demand). Approximately 40% of aging adults with developmental disabilities are known to be receiving services from state mental retardation or developmental disability services agencies (Krauss, 1986). Evidence from studies has suggested that the people with developmental disabilities who are served outside of the established services system live either independently or with their families; as this group ages, their service needs will increase substantially (Seltzer, 1985; Seltzer & Krauss, 1989). Whether the increased need for services will result in an increased demand for services across all population groups is not known. Most racial/ethnic minority groups are more dependent upon informal family and community supports than the general population. For example, a National Indian Council on Aging report (1981, cited in Manson & Callaway, 1990) indicated that 40% of the elder tribal members surveyed were assisted by extended family with one or more activities of daily living. In a discussion of diversity in family caregivers for Black elders, Barresi (1990) reported on the importance of informal supports from family, friends, and neighbors.

Despite efforts since 1980 to promote deinstitutionalization, the majority of older adults with developmental disabilities may still be located in nursing homes and residential facilities. The trends in nursing home utilization among specific racial/ethnic minority groups cannot be determined since the nursing home surveys of 1974, 1977, and 1985 each used different classification systems for the various racial/ethnic groups. However, it is known that the Asian/Pacific Island-American, African-American, Hispanic, and American Indian populations are proportionately underrepresented in nursing homes, with the rate of nursing home residence being 40%–80% of that of the White population (American Association of Retired Persons, 1987). American Indian communities are continuing to develop their own tribal nursing homes. According to Manson and Callaway (1990), there are 10 reservation nursing homes. These homes often are considered extensions of family care and expressions of the esteem and respect that the community has for its elder tribal members.

In a review of the studies conducted on differential utilization of nursing homes by racial/ethnic minority groups, Yeo (1990) noted that cultural roles and expectations of family and community members appear to increase the acceptability and the reality of intergenerational dependence while reducing the acceptability and the need for nursing home placement. She predicted that the aging of the racial/ethnic minority populations, the assimilation of these groups, increased familiarity with the services system, and the continuing immigration of older adults will result in an expanded use of nursing homes by ethnic elders in the future. One as yet unstudied question is whether nursing homes, when viewed as extensions of the community, will become an acceptable place of residence for people with developmental disabilities who are members of racial/ethnic minority groups, as they have been historically for the non-Hispanic White population.

Access

The issues of access and availability are closely related in that both affect the ability of people to utilize services. Access, as defined by Penchansky and Thomas (1981), is the relationship between the location of the needed services and the consumer's ability to reach those services. Even if services are available for older adults with disabilities, the location of those services often makes them inaccessible.

The inability of older adults to gain access to services is a major issue for people of all racial/ethnic groups, particularly those living in rural areas. About

52% of the older American Indian population lives in rural areas where health care services are more limited than in urban areas. Due to a lack of transportation, limited mobility outside of the home, and a lack of home care, most of these older American Indians do not receive adequate health care (Cuellar, 1990a; Edwards & Egbert-Edwards, 1990). Kuehn, Ladinsky, and Levine (1983) stated that difficulty with transportation is also a hindrance for older Asian-Americans, particularly for the Southeast Asian refugees living in rural settings. Even in urban areas, the ability of consumers and their family members to gain access to health care facilities can be a major concern. In a study conducted by Chee and Kane (1983), the location of the health facility was found to be an important consideration for 90% of Black respondents because family members frequently used public transportation to visit. Without financial assistance or supplemental supports to assist with the problems of limited mobility and transportation, most older Americans with or without a disability and regardless of location will have difficulty gaining access to services.

Affordability

Among the racial/ethnic minority groups in this country, the reality of economic poverty has a strong influence upon the affordability of services. Economic poverty is higher among racial/ethnic minority groups than it is among the non-Hispanic White population. As reported by the Indian Health Service (1989), about 28.2% of American Indians live below the poverty level, as compared with 12.4% for all other races. Among people ages 65 and over, the percentage of White people below the poverty level is 10.1%; for Black people, 33.9%; and for Hispanics, 27.4% (United States Department of Health and Human Services, 1990).

A 1982 National Long-Term Care Survey found that 53% of older Black people with functional impairments and their families had an annual family income of $3,000–$7,000 (Macken, 1986). Many Asian-Americans also live in economic conditions that limit their ability to obtain health care services. For example, Kim (1990) indicated that the Issei (first generation Japanese) who were sent to concentration camps during World War II continue to experience economic deprivation today. In 1979, 14.5% of the older Asian-Americans ages 65 and older had income levels below the poverty line (Morioka-Douglas & Yeo, 1990). According to Kwong (1988) and Forman, Lu, Leung, and Ponce (1990), the myth of the "model minority" or "healthy minority" denies the extreme variation of health and economic conditions among subpopulations.

The ability of people, regardless of race or ethnicity, to afford health care services is largely dependent upon their ability to obtain health care insurance, either through public or private insurers. Economic poverty limits one's ability to purchase health care insurance, and a significant number of people are not eligible for Medicare or other public benefits. In 1986, only 53.9% of the Black population ages 65 and older had Medicare, other public health insurance coverage, and/or private health insurance (United States Department of Health and Human Services, 1990). Neighbors and Jackson (1986), reporting on a cross-sectional study of the National Survey of Black Americans conducted among 12,107 male and female participants, ascribed the high rate of uninsured people among Black people ages 55–64, to poverty, unemployment, and ineligibility for Medicare. For Hispanics, particularly Mexican-Americans and Puerto Rican-Americans, the types of jobs they tend to acquire, usually low-paying manual labor jobs, often do not provide health insurance coverage or sufficient Social Security benefits. Therefore, they do not have the resources to obtain the needed health care services after retirement (Cuellar, 1990b). According to Rhoades (1990), among American Indians and Alaska Natives, about 80% are eligible for services from the Indian Health Service. The health care that is not available from the Indian Health Service is purchased from private providers through contracts that generally are limited to those services needed to preserve life, vision, or limb.

Accommodation

Accommodation refers to the climate within an agency and the methods used to show respect and concern for the consumers. It includes consideration of the working schedule of consumers, office decor, the style and format of the intake procedures, racial/ethnic minority professionals on the staff, the ability of staff to communicate in languages other than English, and the continuity of the services that are provided.

Failure to consider accommodation factors could result in older minority adults not utilizing health services. For example, Morioka-Douglas and Yeo (1990), reporting on a study of Asian-American, Black, and Hispanic older adults conducted in 1979 by Gutmann, suggested that the lack of bilingual staff or interpreters may be a critical barrier to service utilization. The findings indicated that logistical difficulties, a lack of understanding of procedures, and a lack of proficiency with the English language were significant barriers to the utilization of health care benefits.

Lacayo (1980), in a study of older Hispanics, reported that 76%–94% of the older Hispanics surveyed spoke Spanish most of the time. This inclination to speak Spanish, whether or not they are capable of speaking English, makes it difficult to communicate medical needs in English and understand medical regimens prescribed in English. However, the use of translators may not be the solution for the Hispanic population, as their presence may hinder the establishment of a close doctor–patient relationship (Espino, 1990). Translators appear to be inadequate for addressing the language needs of older Asian immigrants as well. Sakauye (1990) explained that the paraphrasing done by translators often leads to confusion and miscommunication. Furthermore, this racial group may distrust the translator and not communicate important and necessary medical information.

The importance of specific accommodation factors vary from one racial/ethnic minority group to another. The critical issues for each of the racial/ethnic groups being served need to be addressed. For example, continuity of care is an important concern of the Black population, as discussed by Richardson (1990). Dissatisfaction with services often is related to the lack of continuity of care from a primary physician. Continuity of care is defined differently for the Hispanic population. It includes such factors as making appointments, arranging transportation, assisting with financial arrangements, or scheduling follow-up appointments after a referral (COSSMHO—The National Coalition of Hispanic Health and Human Services Organizations, 1988). Another important accommodation factor for the Black population appears to be that of staff composition. An integrated staff, or more specifically, a largely Black staff, was found to be important for Black nursing home residents in a survey conducted by Weinstock and Bennett in 1968 (Yeo, 1990).

The attention to cultural factors as part of the environmental climate of health care settings, appears to be an important consideration for some racial/ethnic minority groups. However, the extent to which these factors influence a consumer's desire to utilize health care services varies from population to population. For American Indians, social and cultural factors have been identified as the most important reason for not utilizing nursing home services (Moss & Halamandaris, 1977). Problems resulting from the relocation of older American Indians into health care institutions can include depression as a result of the loss of language, family, and cultural and religious activities (Edwards & Egbert-Edwards, 1990). Brenes Jette and Remien (1988), in a study of the importance of cultural factors in an Hispanic nursing home, determined that language and the recognition of ethnic values were important considerations.

In a study of 181 Black, Chinese-American, and Puerto Rican-American nursing home residents, Chinese-Americans were the least likely to support the importance of celebrating cultural holidays, having ethnic art and music, or having staff taught about their culture (Morrison, 1983). However, Chee and Kane (1983) conducted a survey of patients and family members in a predominantly Japanese-American nursing home and a predominantly Black nursing home and found that ethnic food, ethnic programs, and staff and residents of the same ethnic background were considered more important by the Japanese-Americans than by the Black people. As these studies demonstrate, it is important to understand the differences among and within racial/ethnic minority groups. All racial groups are extremely heterogeneous and their attitudes and values will vary depending upon factors including their degree of assimilation and geographical location.

Cultural Appropriateness

Cultural appropriateness is defined as the awareness, knowledge, understanding, acceptance, and valuing of diverse racial/ethnic groups. The development of cultural acceptance can be expected to be a lifelong endeavor. It begins with an awareness that not all people are the same. Values, religious beliefs, assumptions about the causality of disease, and attitudes about the use of medical technology and prescription medicines can vary greatly among different racial/ethnic minority populations. These differences will influence the manner in which different groups gain access to and utilize services.

It is important to recognize the link between cultural appropriateness, the use of services, and the establishment of trust. When people have a lack of trust, or feel distrust, they will not use health services. Distrust often is related to a lack of cultural appropriateness. Displays of discrimination and racial bias among health care providers can be expected to evoke feelings of distrust and decrease the likelihood of access to the needed services.

Distrust of the health care system has been identified as a major barrier to Hispanics seeking health care (COSSMHO—The National Coalition of Hispanic Health and Human Services Organizations, 1988). This distrust results from repeated negative experiences with institutional policies that display insensitivity to important values of Hispanic communities and from cultural and social class stereotyping. Older Hispanics have reported fewer hospitalizations than the majority of older adults in the United States, and fear or distrust of hospitals was the major reason given for underutilization (Lacayo, 1980).

True (1985) suggested that, for many Asian-Americans, a lack of trust arises from a fear of jeopardizing their immigration status or because of past discriminatory acts such as relocation. Older Pilipino-Americans also are less likely to utilize services, in part, because of their distrust of American institutions and, in part, because of their feelings of personal shame related to the absence of social approval and acceptance (Kim, 1990). Dancy (1977) discussed the issues affecting the Black population and stated that there often is an extreme lack of trust toward institutions because of continued racial prejudice, discrimination, and segregation. For this reason, African-American consumers may be more receptive and communicative with African-American professional staff. However, there is no guarantee of culturally appropriate behavior from a member of one's own race or any other (Cross, 1988).

The establishment of trust, then, is an all-important factor in providing care to a culturally diverse population. Trust is a difficult concept to define, and there is no real consensus of definition. For the purposes of this chapter, trust is defined as feelings of confidence in a care provider inspired by the care-provider's concern for the general well-being of the consumer. A trusting relationship will rely on the care provider's ability to provide culturally appropriate care, which will emphasize respect, understanding, and acceptance of the differences and similarities among and within racial/ethnic groups.

The initiation of a trusting relationship begins with the first encounter. With most racial/ethnic minorities, it is usually important to use surnames rather than first names, as is the general custom in health care settings in the United States. Many older Vietnamese refugees prefer the use of their surname with a small head bow as a greeting. It is important to note that Vietnamese women, when married, retain their own surnames. Older Mexican-Americans also are to be addressed by their surnames as an indication of respect.

For Hispanics an ongoing trusting relationship will be dependent upon the ability of the health care provider to demonstrate "personalismo." Personalismo requires the provider of services to work at building a caring, interpersonal relationship with the consumer. Trust, respect, pride, and dignity are key concepts for establishing personalismo. This personalized attention helps to develop a trusting relationship and to avoid an uncaring institutional service image. Other important values to Hispanics seeking health care include "familismo" and "presentismo." Familismo relates to the importance of the family's needs over the individual's needs and emphasizes cooperation over competition. Presentismo emphasizes the present time. More value is given to the present than to the past or future. Cuellar (1990b) indicated that this value of presentismo may delay an individual from seeking health care.

Other trust-building factors include methods of interaction and contact. African-Americans often want the opportunity to express their opinions and feelings and to have a leisurely visit with the careprovider (Hikoyeda & Grudzen, 1991). Some racial/ethnic minority populations do not find it appropriate for care providers to touch them, or they have particular rules about touching. For example, Pilipino-American women may not be touched in the presence of others, and a female care provider may not be involved in changing the clothing of an older male. Eye contact also is related to trust and differs among racial/ethnic minority groups. Llorens (1988) explains that, for Pilipino-Americans, treachery is suspected if the provider looks down at the floor, and for Korean-Americans, eye contact should be avoided because it may be considered rude. In general, providers need to use nonverbal forms of communication with caution. For example, Asian-Americans should never be asked to move from one place to another with the wave of a forefinger, as this is a derogatory act that connotes disrespect and has a negative sexual meaning.

For Asian-Americans, the best physician is probably the one who is least intrusive with the body according to Muecke (1983). Many Southeast Asian refugees consider X rays, lab tests, blood pressure readings, temperature checks, and other diagnostic procedures as a sign that the physician does not know what he or she is doing, rather than accepted techniques for diagnosing the health problem (Ladinsky & Kuehn, 1983). Many Southeast Asian refugees feel that they are especially sensitive to Western drugs. This may, in fact, be true. In a review of the literature, Tien (1984) found that Asian-Americans may require lower dosages and display more side effects with low to medium dosages.

Some racial/ethnic minority groups use folk medicines, traditional herbal medicines, and/or traditional ceremonies and practices to treat health problems. American Indians may use Indian medicine, which is a cultural approach to health that focuses on the entire person rather than only the illness or disease (Garrett, 1990). Specialists, such as spiritual shamans or herbalists, may be consulted for medicines made of herbs or roots or for healing ceremonies. Also, Morrison and Gresson (1990) explained how older African-Americans may use folk medicines before seeking the services of health care professionals.

The use of folk medicine is dependent in part upon the belief about the cause of the illness. If the illness is considered natural, a medicine man, herbalist, or root doctor may be used. If the illness is attributed to unnatural causes, a voodoo doctor, conjurer, or faith healer may be called upon (Dennis, 1979, cited in Morrison & Gresson, 1990). To create an atmosphere of comfort for the consumer, the physician and other professional staff could try to incorporate folk remedies with prescribed medications. At the minimum, care providers should inquire about other drugs or traditional medicines being used, as some may have dangerous side effects when combined with Western prescription medications. Discussions of nontraditional treatments and the suspected cause of the illness (from the consumer's perspective) may help to build trust and so strengthen the relationship between the provider and the consumer.

The style of decision-making is another key element in the establishment of a trusting relationship and differs among racial/ethnic minority groups. As indicated by the National Indian Council on Aging (1981), American Indians value self-determination, which includes the active participation of American Indian tribes in the development and implementation of services. This value was incorporated into PL 93-638, the 1975 Indian Self-Determination and Education Act, which mandates the staff of the Indian Health Service to involve tribes in the administration and operation of programs, including health service programs. Among older Asian-Americans, the needs of the family and the opinions of certain family members are important components of the decision-making process. The inclusion of the family in the decision-making process is important also for older Hispanics. The family is a source of support that can greatly influence the delivery of services.

CONCLUSION

For the racial/ethnic minority populations in the United States, the availability, accessibility, affordability, accommodation, and cultural appropriateness of services are critical factors that affect the way services are utilized across the life span. Most important of all is the cultural appropriateness of services. No one professional can be expected to know, understand, accept, and value all of the beliefs and traditions of the multiple racial and ethnic minority groups among the citizenry of the United States. However, it is important for professionals to acquire some relevant knowledge and present a caring, responsive, and respectful attitude in their relationships with consumers and with colleagues.

REFERENCES

American Association of Retired Persons Minority Affairs Initiative. (1987). *A portrait of older minorities*. Washington, DC: American Association of Retired Persons.

Barresi, C.M. (1990). Diversity in Black family caregiving: Implications for geriatric education. In M.S. Harper (Ed.), *Minority aging: Essential curricula content for selected health and allied health professions* (pp. 297–312). Health Resources and Services Administration, United States Department of Health and Human Services. DHHS Publication No. HRS (P-DV-90-4). Washington, DC: United States Government Printing Office.

Bowe, F. (1983). *Black adults with disabilities—A statistical report drawn from Census Bureau data*. Washington, DC: The President's Committee on Employment of the Handicapped.

Braddock, D. (1991). *Technical note to census data*. Chicago: Illinois University Affiliated Program.

Brenes Jette, C.C., & Remien, R. (1988). Hispanic geriatric residents in a long-term care setting. *Journal of Applied Gerontology, 7,* 350–365.

Bruininks, R.H. (1991). Presidential Address 1991. Mental retardation: New realities, new challenges. *Mental Retardation, 29*(5), 239–251.

Chee, P., & Kane, R. (1983). Cultural factors affecting nursing home care for minorities: A study of Black-American and Japanese-American groups. *Journal of the American Geriatrics Society, 31*(2), 109–112.

Copeland, L. (1988). Valuing workplace diversity. *Personnel Administrator, November,* 38–40.

COSSMHO—The National Coalition of Hispanic Health and Human Services Organizations. (1988). *Delivering preventive health care to Hispanics: A manual for providers*. Washington, DC: Author.

Cross, T.L. (1988). Services to minority populations: Cultural competence continuum. *Focal Point, 3,* 1–4.

Cuellar, J. (1990a). *Aging and health: American Indian/Alaska Native*. Stanford: Stanford Geriatric Education Center.

Cuellar, J. (1990b). *Aging and health: Hispanic American elders*. Stanford: Stanford Geriatric Education Center.

Dancy, J. (1977). *The black elderly: A guide for practitioners*. Ann Arbor: University of Michigan Press.

Edwards, E.D., & Egbert-Edwards, M. (1990). Family care and the Native American elderly. In M.S. Harper (Ed.), *Minority aging: Essential curricula content for selected health and allied health professions* (pp. 145–164). Health Resources and Services Administration, United States Department of Health and Human Services. DHHS Publication No. HRS (P-DV-90-4). Washington, DC: United States Government Printing Office.

Espino, D.V. (1990). Mexican-American elderly: Problems in evaluation, diagnosis, and treatment. In M.S. Harper (Ed.), *Minority aging: Essential curricula content for selected health and allied health professions* (pp. 453–462). Health Resources and Services Administration, United States Department of Health and Human Services.

DHHS Publication No. HRS (P-DV-90-4). Washington, DC: United States Government Printing Office.

Forman, M., Lu, M.C., Leung, M., & Ponce, N. Asian American Health Forum Inc., Washington, DC. (1990). *Dispelling the myth of a healthy minority: Policy papers.* (Available from the Wisconsin Department of Health and Human Services.) Unpublished manuscript.

Fuchs, V. (1974). *Who shall live? Health, economics and social choice.* New York: Basic Books.

Garrett, J.T. (1990). Indian health: Values, beliefs, and practices. In M.S. Harper (Ed.), *Minority aging: Essential curricula content for selected health and allied health professions* (pp. 179–192). Health Resources and Services Administration, United States Department of Health and Human Services. DHHS Publication No. HRS (P-DV-90-4). Washington, DC: United States Government Printing Office.

Harper, M.S. (1990). Introduction. In M.S. Harper (Ed.), *Minority aging: Essential curricula content for selected health and allied health professions* (pp. 3–22). Health Resources and Services Administration, United States Department of Health and Human Services. DHHS Publication No. HRS (P-DV-90-4). Washington, DC: United States Government Printing Office.

Harper, M.S., & Alexander, C.D. (1990). Profile of the Black elderly. In M.S. Harper (Ed.), *Minority aging: Essential curricula content for selected health and allied health professions* (pp. 193–222). Health Resources and Services Administration, United States Department of Health and Human Services. DHHS Publication No. HRS (P-DV-90-4). Washington, DC: United States Government Printing Office.

Hikoyeda, N., & Grudzen, M. (1991). *Traditional and non-traditional medication use among ethnic elders: Selected proceedings of conference held April 28, 1989, San Jose, CA.* Stanford, CA: Stanford Geriatric Education Center.

Indian Health Service. (1989). *Trends in Indian health.* Washington, DC: United States Department of Health and Human Services, Division of Program Statistics, Indian Health Service.

Jacobson, J.W., Sutton, M.S., & Janicki, M.P. (1985). Demography and characteristics of aging and aged mentally retarded persons. In M.P. Janicki & H.M. Wisniewski (Eds.), *Aging and developmental disabilities: Issues and approaches* (pp. 115–142). Baltimore: Paul H. Brookes Publishing Co.

Janicki, M.P., & Wisniewski, H.M. (1985). Some comments on growing older and being developmentally disabled. In M.P. Janicki & H.M. Wisniewski (Eds.), *Aging and developmental disabilities: Issues and approaches* (pp. 1–5). Baltimore: Paul H. Brookes Publishing Co.

Kim, P.K.H. (1990). Asian-American families and the elderly. In M.S. Harper (Ed.), *Minority aging: Essential curricula content for selected health and allied health professions* (pp. 349–364). Health Resources and Services Administration, United States Department of Health and Human Services. DHHS Publication No. HRS (P-DV-90-4). Washington, DC: United States Government Printing Office.

Krauss, M.W. (1986). *Long-term care issues in mental retardation.* Bethesda, MD: Author.

Kuehn, M., Ladinsky, J., & Levine, R. (1983). *Cross-cultural aspects of rural health care: Indochinese culture.* Madison: Authors. Unpublished paper.

Kwong, P. (1988). *The new Chinatown.* Toronto: Collins Publishers.

Lacayo, C.G. (1980). *A national study to assess the service of the Hispanic elderly.* Los Angeles: Association Nacional Pro Personas Mayores.

Ladinsky, J.L., & Kuehn, M.L. (1983). *Good health—Good life: A Southeast Asian refugee's guide to the United States health care system.* Madison: Wisconsin Department of

Health and Social Services, Division of Health, Bureau of Community Health and Prevention, Wisconsin Refugee Health Program.

Llorens, L.A. (1988). *Health care for ethnic elders: The cultural context: Proceedings of conference held on September 22, 1988 at Stanford University.* Stanford: Stanford Geriatric Education Center.

Macken, C.L. (1986). A profile of functionally impaired elderly persons living in the community. *Health Care Financing Review, 7*(4), 33–49.

Manson, S.M., & Callaway, D.G. (1990). Health and aging among American Indians: Issues and challenges for the geriatric sciences. In M.S. Harper (Ed.), *Minority aging: Essential curricula content for selected health and allied health professions* (pp. 63–120). Health Resources and Services Administration, United States Department of Health and Human Services. DHHS Publication No. HRS (P-DV-90-4). Washington, DC: United States Government Printing Office.

McClain, J.W. (1990). *The recruitment and retention of minority trainees in University Affiliated Programs—African-Americans.* M.L. Kuehn (Series Ed.). Madison: University of Wisconsin-Madison.

Morioka-Douglas, N., & Yeo, G. (1990). *Aging and health: Asian/Pacific Island American elders.* Stanford: Stanford Geriatric Education Center.

Morrison, B.J. (1983). Sociocultural dimensions: Nursing homes and the minority aged. *Journal of Gerontological Social Work, 5,* 127–145.

Morrison, B.J., & Gresson, A.D. (1990). Curriculum content pertaining to the Black elderly for selected health care professions. In M.S. Harper (Ed.), *Minority aging: Essential curricula content for selected health and allied health professions* (pp. 223–268). Health Resources and Services Administration, United States Department of Health and Human Services. DHHS Publication No. HRS (P-DV-90-4). Washington, DC: United States Government Printing Office.

Moss, F.E., & Halamandaris, V.J. (1977). *Too old, too sick, too bad.* Germantown: Aspen Systems.

Muecke, M.A. (1983). Caring for Southeast Asian refugee patients in the USA. *American Journal of Public Health, 73*(4), 431–438.

National Indian Council on Aging. (1981). *American Indian elderly: A national profile.* Albuquerque: Author.

Neighbors, H.W., & Jackson, J.S. (1986). Uninsured risk groups in national survey of black Americans. *Journal of the National Medical Association, 78*(10), 979–983.

Penchansky, R., & Thomas, W. (1981). The concept of access: Definition and relationship to consumer satisfaction. *Medical Care, 19*(2), 127–140.

Rhoades, E.R. (1990). Profile of American Indians and Alaska Natives. In M.S. Harper (Ed.), *Minority aging: Essential curricula content for selected health and allied health professions* (pp. 45–62). Health Resources and Services Administration, United States Department of Health and Human Services. DHHS Publication No. HRS (P-DV-90-4). Washington, DC: United States Government Printing Office.

Richardson, J. (1990). *Aging and health: Black American elders.* Stanford: Stanford Geriatric Education Center.

Sakauye, K. (1990). Differential diagnosis, medication, treatment, and outcomes: Asian-American elderly. In M.S. Harper (Ed.), *Minority aging: Essential curricula content for selected health and allied health professions* (pp. 331–340). Health Resources and Services Administration, United States Department of Health and Human Services. DHHS Publication No. HRS (P-DV-90-4). Washington, DC: United States Government Printing Office.

Schoen, R., & Nelson, V.F. (1981). Mortality by cause among Spanish-surnamed Californians, 1969–1971. *Social Science Quarterly, 62,* 259–274.

Seltzer, M.M. (1985). Informal supports for aging mentally retarded persons. *American Journal of Mental Deficiency, 90,* 259–265.

Seltzer, M.M., & Krauss, M.W. (1989). Aging parents with mentally retarded children: Family risk factors and sources of support. *American Journal of Mental Retardation, 94,* 303–312.

Tien, J.L. (1984). Do Asians need less medication? *Journal of Psychosocial Nursing, 22,* 19–22.

True, R.H. (1985). Health care service delivery in Asian American communities. *Report of the Secretary's Task Force on Black and minority health. Volume II: Cross-cutting issues in minority health.* Rockville, MD: United States Department of Health and Human Services.

United States Department of Commerce. (1992). *1990 census of population and housing: Summary population housing characteristics, United States 1990.* Economics and Statistics Administration, Bureau of the Census. Publication CPH-1-1. Washington, DC: United States Government Printing Office.

United States Department of Health and Human Services. (1990). *Health status of the disadvantaged: Chartbook 1990.* Health Resources and Services Administration, Public Health Service, Bureau of Health Professions, Division of Disadvantaged Assistance. DHHS Publication No. (HRSA) HRS-P-DV; 90-1. Washington, DC: United States Government Printing Office.

United States Department of Health and Human Services. (1991). *Health status of minorities and low-income groups* (3rd ed.). Health Resources and Services Administration, Public Health Service, Bureau of Health Professions, Division of Disadvantaged Assistance. DHHS Publication No. 017-000-00257-1. Washington, DC: United States Government Printing Office.

Vanlandingham, M.J., Buehler, J.W., Hogue, C. J., & Strauss, L.T. (1988). Birthweight-specific infant mortality for Native Americans compared with Whites, six states, 1980. *American Journal of Public Health, 78*(5), 499–503.

Wagner, J. (1988). *Handicapped Americans report.* Washington, DC: Plus Publications, Inc.

Wing, S., Manton, K.G., Stallard, E., Hames, C.G., & Tyroler, H.A. (1985). The black/white mortality crossover: Investigation in a community-based study. *Journal of Gerontology, 40*(1), 78–84.

Yeo, G. (1990). *Ethnicity and nursing homes: Review and suggested components for culturally sensitive care.* Stanford: Stanford Geriatric Education Center.

Appendix

The Research and Training Consortium Process

Esther Lee Pederson

This appendix describes a consortium process model for research, training, and/or service program development to meet the psychosocial needs of older adults with developmental disabilities. Research consortium models are not new but have often limited themselves to extended research through increasing the group of participants and/or replication of research across multiple sites (Roush & Teitelman, 1990). The Rehabilitation Research and Training Center (RRTC) Consortium on Aging and Developmental Disabilities represents a response to the seven diverse priorities presented by the National Institute on Disability and Rehabilitation Research (NIDRR) in late 1987. These ranged from policy analysis to detection of age-related change. Mutual interest in issues of aging and developmental disabilities among faculty of seven universities, and their willingness to collaborate in order to expand the existing knowledge base, was the foundation on which this Consortium was built. A commitment of resources and expertise was required that, joined together, could respond to the NIDRR's equally broad research, training, and dissemination agenda.

There is evidence that organizational development principles can facilitate the successful operation of a Consortium (Judson, 1990). Many of the RRTC experiences reported here follow such principles. French and Bell (1973) define organizational development as "a planned, systematic process in which applied behavioral science principles and practices are introduced into an ongoing organization" [such as the Consortium] "in order to effect improvement and produce greater organizational competence and effectiveness" (p. 3). This chapter discusses the consortium process model and its related organizational development aspects as applied by the RRTC Consortium on Aging and Developmental Disabilities.

HISTORICAL BACKGROUND

Estimates indicate that within the United States there may be more than 150,000 persons over the age of 60 who have mental retardation and/or other developmental disabilities (Jacobson, Sutton, & Janicki, 1985). Predictions are that this number will approach 600,000 within 40 years. The consortium process created the opportunity to develop service models and recommend policy at a time when the numbers of these persons were still relatively small and making manageable demands on the service delivery system. There was ample time to develop constructive policy as opposed to emergency services for older adults with developmental disabilities. The system of community services for the general population of older persons, already in place, provided opportunities for training and program collaboration. As it moved into a developing field, it was the intent of the newly formed RRTC Consortium to gather reliable data, to design meaningful methods, and to field test service and training models. Their mandate from the NIDRR was to confront the challenge of community inclusion for older persons with developmental disabilities, with a particular emphasis on those with mental retardation and Down syndrome.

In pursuing this overarching goal and addressing the seven priority areas presented by the NIDRR, the consortium divided its work into four areas: 1) fiscal and program policy analysis, 2) collaborative training in aging and mental retardation/developmental disabilities (MR/DD) services, 3) detection of age-related change, and 4) transition reactions and support services.

Nine research projects were undertaken initially, leading, in years 4 and 5 of consortium operations, to a multi-site, integrated research and training program. Results of these efforts are presented throughout in this volume. Suffice it to say that the breadth and depth of this undertaking necessitated significant coordination and the development or application of organizational methods that ensured successful outcomes. This chapter is devoted to a full discussion of the consortium process as it evolved over a 5-year period.

CONSUMER INVOLVEMENT

From the inception of the research and training program, the RRTC Consortium endorsed the importance of consumer involvement as a means of ensuring the relevance of project activities and the utility of project outcomes. The principle of consumer involvment was reinforced in a new way by the NIDRR when, in 1991, it announced its commitment to participatory action research (PAR). PAR is an applied research model in which members of the community with disabilities and their family members work closely with professional researchers. (See chap. 16, this volume.) Together they define research problems, develop appropriate ways for conducting the research, gather data, analyze outcomes, and disseminate results. The director of the NIDRR stated that it is no longer sufficient for research programs merely to be consumer responsive. Rather, they are to reflect true partnerships with consumers in all phases of the research endeavor. Therefore, the consortium process expanded the participation of persons with developmental disabilities and their families during all phases and at all levels of program development. Figure A.1 presents a schematic diagram of the 5-year program. It illustrates the diversity of the research projects, consumer involvement, outcomes, and their convergence toward the integrated research and training program.

The consortium did not adopt the more traditional approach of operation, that is, knowing how to do something before actually doing it (French & Bell, 1973). Instead, it has operated under the deficiency model of "doing it" before "learning how to." The model represents an ambitious yet realistic plan for substantially increasing the knowledge base about older adults with developmental disabilities and for disseminating planning and programming strategies intended to have an impact on the quality of life for these individuals.

MISSION AND SHARED VALUES

Once the RRTC was funded and began operation, the first order of business was formalization of statements of mission and shared values (see p. xxiii) by the Consortium members. These have guided its research and training program throughout the years. All members of the Consortium agreed that an endorsed mission statement was essential to the operation of this RRTC. As formally adopted, the mission statement was built upon values to which each of the seven universities was committed prior to this venture. Interests of the consumer members were also fully incorporated. The statement identified as a critical need the establishment of a national resource to increase knowledge and skills of older adults with developmental disabilities, their family members, planners, providers, and students. The enhancement of the quality of life of older adults with developmental disabilities by ensuring that Consortium research and its application met the needs of these individuals and their families was viewed as paramount.

THE CONSORTIUM PROCESS

A consortium is an association of two or more groups and, as such, requires that certain functions be implemented to facilitate accomplishment of its overall goal (Roush & Teitelmann, 1990). Toward this end, a Project Management Center

(PMC) was created consisting of staff from the University Affiliated Cincinnati Center for Developmental Disorders and The University of Akron. The PMC's principal role and responsibilities were to: 1) provide fiscal and programmatic management; 2) maintain effective liaison with NIDRR; 3) maintain linkages with other RRTCs, University Affiliated Programs, and other national networks and programs involved with research, training, and service delivery in the fields of aging and developmental disabilities; 4) maintain the identity of the consortium as a national resource in the fields of aging and developmental disabilities; and 5) ensure effective coordination and communication among consortium participants.

The PMC reports to the Consortium Coordinating Council (CCC). The CCC has served as the principal governing body of the Consortium and was responsible for overall policy and program in accordance with the stated mission and in compliance with the cooperative agreement established with the NIDRR. The CCC gives approval to all policy and planning activities of the Consortium. In addition, it ensures interrelationships among research, training, and related initiatives. The Council also regularly reviews and assesses accrued research results. Membership of the CCC includes the project director, project co-director, the Consortium coordinator, research coordinator, training coordinator, a principal investigator from each university site, and a consumer representative from each state advisory group. The National Dissemination Advisory Group, described below, also is represented. All but the coordinators are voting members in matters of policy, research, and training activity. The CCC maintains six standing committees: Executive, Research, Training and Dissemination, the Representative Participation Committee, the National Dissemination Advisory Group, and the Editorial Review Committee. (The specific roles of these six standing committees in addition to the roles of the Ad Hoc Committee and the State Advisory Groups are described in Figure A.2.)

Organization and Management

At the outset, the Consortium addressed the typical issues identified by French and Bell (1973) for the organizational development processes: "(a) getting acquainted; (b) learning about each other's expertise; (c) clarifying roles; (d) achieving identification with and acceptance of program goals; (e) determining how each member fits into and contributes to the research and training program; and (f) exploring the nature of the interdependencies of the consortium members" (p. 6). The function of the PMC was viewed as facilitating the evolution of the Consortium from a cooperative effort in the development of the original proposal, to the coordinated research projects of the first 3 years, to the integrated research and training program of the 4th and 5th years. Fulfilling these start-up and ongoing functions necessitated six specific activities and responsibilities for maintaining coordination and accountability: 1) information sharing, 2) coordinated planning, 3) coordinated implementation of research and training priorities, 4) integrated research and training, 5) consumer involve-

CONCENTRATION AREA / RFP PRIORITIES ( )	PROJECTS	METHODS	CONSUMER PARTICIPATION	INTEGRATED RESEARCH & TRAINING PROGRAM	PROJECTED OUTCOMES
FISCAL AND PROGRAM POLICY ANALYSIS	National Data Base Reflecting Fiscal and Program Policy — Illinois	NATIONAL SURVEY & TECHNICAL ASSISTANCE	STATE ADVISORY GROUPS	STATE-OF-THE-ART RESEARCH STUDY: IMPROVING THE FUNCTIONING OF OLDER PERSONS WITH DD (PRIORITY VII)	PLANNERS' EFFECTIVENESS
ANALYSIS OF EXISTING SERVICES (I)	Analysis of Policy Issues in the Delivery of Community-Based Services — Minnesota			• Fiscal/Program Data Base • Technical Reports • Technical Assistance Teams • University Training	Direction for Future Research; Reliable Fiscal/Program Data Base for Planning; Recommendations for Policy Directions; Technical Assistance for Networking with Generic Aging Service
SMALL-SCALE LIVING ARRANGEMENTS (IV)	Interagency Funding Models for Family-Size Small-Scale Nonrestrictive Community Living Options for Older Persons with DD — Kentucky				
DETECTION OF DECLINE (II)	Behavioral Capabilities Assessment and Intervention for Older Persons with DD — Ohio (Cin); Detection of Decline in Older Adults with DD — Indiana	APPLIED RESEARCH AND TRAINING			PROVIDERS' EFFICIENCY — Prevention Strategies for Coping with Relocation; Directions for Rehabilitation Training; Models for Alternative Community Living Arrangements; Strategies for Detecting Decline
TRANSITION REACTIONS AND SUPPORT SERVICES	Residential Transitions for Older Adults with DD: Facilitating Family and Resident Adjustment — Illinois	MODEL DEVELOPMENT AND NEEDS ASSESSMENT		NATIONAL DISSEMINATION	
REACTION TO TRANSITIONS (III)	Investigation of need for Retirement Education for Older Persons with DD and Development of Appropriate Materials — Ohio (Akron)	CONSULTATION & TRAINING	NATIONAL DISSEMINATION ADVISORY GROUP	• Consumer/Family Education • National Newsletter • Planner/Provider Consultation • Technical Assistance Teams	CONSUMERS' QUALITY OF LIFE — Increased Internal and External Family Supports; Preparation for Life Changes; Increased Community Housing Options; Improved Community Integration through Accessibility to Generic Services
RESPITE AND SUPPORT SERVICES (V)	Stress, Health, and Social Support for Families and Caregivers — Wisconsin				
COLLABORATIVE TRAINING IN AGING AND MR/DD / GENERIC AGING AND DD COLLABORATION (VI)	Expanding & Disseminating Knowledge about Older Persons with DD: Strategies for Networking Among Service Systems — Ohio (Cin & Akron)				

CONSORTIUM COORDINATING COUNCIL

Figure A.1. The 5-year Consortium research and training program. (Created by Thomas J. Lottman [1987, revised 1989]. University Affiliated Cincinnati Center for Developmental Disorders.)

ment, and 6) product dissemination. Figure A.3 presents the varying levels of time intensity for these six major activities over the 5 years of the project. Ultimately, each of these coordination activities became an integral component of the ongoing operation.

The PMC was responsible for ongoing accountability while supporting creativity among the collaborating principal investigators. For the PMC, this meant a variety of tasks related to internal and external coordination, visibility, and role clarification. Performance quality, data collection, and fiscal management were major management concerns. Specific strategies were operationalized, including developing *operational policies and procedures, establishing coordination through system linkages,* and *promotional strategies.* Each of these strategies is discussed further below.

Operational Policies and Procedures

The development of *operational policies and procedures* to facilitate consortium coordination among the participating sites was accomplished through the various communication processes described below. The challenge in this area was to keep everyone informed and to promote opportunities for ongoing discussion and recognition of everyone's contribution.

Paperwork System Subcontracts, progress reports, database systems, and evaluation procedures were standardized with each of the seven universities and consultant staff.

Communication Technology Information technology facilitated communication among sites through facsimile machines, computer modems, conference calls, and diskettes. Regular conference calls among universities for simultaneous, quick exchange of information supported an ongoing flow of information and reduced the need for more frequent in-person meetings, thus eliminating their associated fiscal and time commitment.

Collective, In-Person Meetings Ongoing in-person meetings were very important, especially as a means of including people with developmental disabilities and their family members. The Consortium met in-person four times each year during the first 3 years of the project, and twice annually in the 4th and 5th years.

Operational Policies and Procedures Consistency among sites was very important; therefore, standardization was established regarding the population nomenclature and definitions. Policies and procedures were put in place regarding protection of research participants, outcome measures, replication, decision-making, and reporting procedures. Formal statements were found useful concerning the role of the clearinghouse, the newsletter mission, support for other aging and developmental disabilities initiatives, editorial review, and jurisdiction of the six standing committees. These were compiled into a *Policies and Procedures Manual* (Lottman, 1992). Implementation of some of these policies and procedures in the Consortium universities proved challenging at times

REHABILITATION RESEARCH AND TRAINING CENTER CONSORTIUM ON AGING AND DEVELOPMENTAL DISABILITIES SIX STANDING COMMITTEES, AD HOC COMMITTEES, AND STATE ADVISORY GROUPS

EXECUTIVE COMMITTEE

The Consortium Coordinating Council (CCC) established and maintained a standing Executive Committee of five people who acted in lieu of the CCC in day-to-day policy and procedure decisions that normally would be referred to the CCC. Members consisted of two principal investigators (PI), two Representative Participation Committee (RPC) members, and one Project Management Center (PMC) staff member. Terms were for 1 year.

RESEARCH COMMITTEE

The CCC established and maintained a standing Research Committee consisting of the research coordinator, principal investigators or a desig-nated representative from each site, a minimum of one RPC representa-tive, and others as deemed necessary by the committee. The PMC pro-vided staff support to the committee. The responsibilities of the committee included:

- Developing annual plans for a research program for CCC approval that is consistent with the RRTC mission and the cooperative agreement with NIDRR
- Effectively coordinating research projects among Consortium sites

TRAINING AND DISSEMINATION COMMITTEE

The CCC established and maintained a standing Training and Dissem-ination (T&D) Committee consisting of the T&D Coordinator, director of the clearinghouse, editor of the newsletter, principal investigators from each training project site, a minimum of one RPC representative, and oth-ers as deemed necessary by the committee. The PMC provided staff sup-port to the committee. The responsibilities of the committee included:

- Developing annual plans for a training and dissemination program for CCC approval that is consistent with the RRTC mission and the coop-erative agreement with NIDRR
- Effectively coordinating training and dissemination projects among Consortium sites

(continued)

Figure A.2.   Roles of the six Consortium standing committees, the Ad Hoc Committees, and the State Advisory Groups.

Figure A.2.. *(continued)*

REPRESENTATIVE PARTICIPATION COMMITTEE

The CCC established and maintained a standing Representative Participation Committee consisting of all CCC members who have a disability or who are family members of persons with a disability, the Consortium Coordinator, and others as deemed necessary by the committee. The PMC provided staff support to the committee. The responsibilities of the committee included:

- Developing plans for CCC approval to maximize consumer involvement and effective participation in all phases and at all levels of Consortium activities
- Recommending supplemental funding sources to support consumer involvement and leadership in the Consortium

NATIONAL DISSEMINATION ADVISORY GROUP

The CCC estabished and maintained a National Dissemination Advisory Group consisting of recognized authorities and representative participants from the fields of aging, rehabilitation, and MR/DD, and others as deemed necessary by the committee. The committee met at least once annually and its responsibilities included:

- Advising on effective channels for dissemination activities to serve the regional and national needs of the fields of rehabilitation, aging, and developmental disabilities
- Assisting with the identification of appropriate target populations for national training and dissemination of RRTC findings
- Assisting with the development of strategies to identify and utilize effectively a national resource network
- Assisting with other RRTC activities consistent with interest and availability, for example, mailing lists, the Clearinghouse, marketing, and so forth

EDITORIAL REVIEW COMMITTEE

In order to ensure that the products of the RRTC Consortium on Aging and Developmental Disabilities were of the highest quality and that they were consistent with the values and objectives of the Consortium mission statement, an Editorial Review Committee was established. The committee was composed of the director of the clearinghouse (chair), two principal investigators (to rotate according to the content to be reviewed) and two representative participants of the CCC serving staggered 2-year terms, and others as deemed necessary. The responsibilities of the committee included reviewing Consortium products that had NOT undergone an external refereed review or an internal formal university review in order to ensure product quality, people first language, and consistency with Consortium objectives.

(continued)

Figure A.2.. *(continued)*

AD HOC COMMITTEES

The CCC established and provided terms of reference for ad hoc committees as it deemed necessary to accomplish specific Consortium activities. The committees reported as directed to the CCC.

STATE ADVISORY GROUPS

As a provision of the subcontract with the PMC, principal investigators ensured that Consortium participating states established and maintained a State Advisory Group (SAG) that met and reported to the CCC at least twice annually. Policies and procedures affecting the operation of these SAGs were as follows:

- The SAGs consisted of primary and secondary consumers, and representatives from appropriate state agencies.
- A minimum of 30% of SAG membership consisted of persons with developmental disabilities and/or their families, with at least two persons with mental retardation.
- Where appropriate, a consumer member served as co-chair of the SAG.
- Each SAG appointed a representative participant to the CCC.
- The roles of each SAG evolved individually to meet the need of participatory sites; however, each maintained the following responsibilities:

  Advising members at each Consortium site as to whether their project research, planning, implementation, evaluation, and dissemination activities were relevant to the state's needs in the rehabilitation field

  Ensuring the project's utility to consumers and their families, direct service providers, and planning bodies and finding ways to improve both physical and service accessibility for consumers and families

  Assisting at each Consortium site with the identification of appropriate target populations and content for training and dissemination of research findings to ensure its appropriateness and applicability for people who will use the service (consumers) and those who will apply it (providers and planners)

- The annual evaluation process for each SAG included mailing a letter to SAG members signed by both the principal investigators and RPC members outlining a list of questions to be discussed at the next meeting of the SAG. At the meeting, the questions were to be discussed and answered with a group response. The responses were to be forwarded to the research coordinator for analysis by the end of each calendar year.

because introducing change or a different approach into an established program sometimes is difficult. The time required to reach consensus on areas such as nomenclature (e.g., the universal use of a single term to describe the group being studied) was not easy to resolve, nor was the question of age cutoff to define older adults. It was a very time-consuming process. Additionally, a process eventually was developed so that decisions could be made in an equitable, yet timely, manner. The establishment of an executive committee of the Consortium comprising the Consortium coordinator, two consumer representatives, and two principal investigators solved this problem; this committee was formally established by the coordinating council during its 3rd year.

Coordination through System Linkages

The establishment of *effective coordination through system linkages* with the funding source and other national organizations was an ever-increasing activity.

Ongoing Liaison   Meetings and correspondence were conducted with NIDRR. Annual meetings with the director and staff of NIDRR were attended for gathering information on NIDRR priorities and sharing status and direction of Consortium activities. During these meetings there was also an opportunity to contribute ideas and direction to NIDRR activities as a whole.

Monitoring   Telephone calls with the NIDRR Project Officer were made at least monthly for project monitoring. Different aspects of the Consortium program were highlighted so that each university site had an opportunity to interact with the Project Officer. Soon to be effective is an interactive computerized monitoring system called the Rehabilitation Information System.

Reports   Submission of required fiscal and programmatic reports to NIDRR occurred on a comprehensive and regular basis. Each university assumed responsibility for specific sections. These reports were submitted to the project officer and grants officer for review and comment.

Collaboration   Collaboration was initiated with national associations (i.e., National Association of Rehabilitation Research and Training Centers, American Association of University Affiliated Programs, National Association for Rehabilitation Information Center, American Association on Mental Retardation) to maximize coordination of all events and activities in the field of aging and developmental disabilities. This proved to be significant. Strategies used included convening Consortium meetings during annual meetings of these associations to decrease travel costs while effectively increasing Consortium visibility and dissemination capabilities to these organizations.

Promotional Strategies

The development of *promotional strategies* to establish the Consortium as a national resource took place immediately upon formation of the new RRTC. Critical strategies included printing a brochure describing the Consortium, its universities, and its research and training program.

The Clearinghouse on Aging and Developmental Disabilities   This information Clearinghouse serves as a major resource to persons with mental retardation and developmental disabilities, their families, researchers, and practitioners.

The A/DDvantage Newsletter   *The A/DDvantage Newsletter* is a quarterly publication that has served as a key vehicle to raise awareness of issues, disseminate findings of the Consortium, share state-of-the-art information, highlight legislative developments, feature training events, and promote the work of the Consortium.

Conferences   The Consortium held its initial meeting and was officially part of the first international conference on aging and developmental disabilities in October of 1988, which was entitled "Best Practices." All principal investigators involved in The Consortium were represented at this event as keynote speakers or session chairpersons. A major international training event in April of 1993, entitled "Sharing Solutions Through Partnerships in Aging and Developmental Disabilities," crowned the Consortium's 5-year program highlighting research and training findings.

Presentations   Principal investigators, Consortium staff, and consumer representatives have presented at national conferences and professional meetings in the fields of aging, developmental disabilities, and rehabilitation. For example, the Consortium coordinator and a member of the CCC, who has mental retardation, presented a leadership seminar for adults with Down syndrome and a separate session for family members at the National Down Syndrome Congress annual meeting in Atlanta in 1992. Approximately 434 presentations and workshops on aging and developmental disabilities were reported by principal investigators and staff by the end of the 4th year.

Recognizable Logo   Letterhead, brochure, newsletter, and exhibit materials have carried the unique Consortium logo so that the general public can identify the Consortium.

THE RESEARCH, TRAINING, AND DISSEMINATION PROGRAM

The RRTC Consortium on Aging and Developmental Disabilities has been at the forefront of an embryonic, yet rapidly developing, field of inquiry as it has generated a research and training program that addresses needs of older adults with developmental disabilities, families, researchers, planners, and service providers. This is the basis on which the 5-year research and training program was envisioned. The program started with a diverse agenda of nine research projects that were to be conducted during the first 3 years. These were organized into four areas of concentration: 1) fiscal and program policy analysis, 2) detection of age-related change, 3) transition reactions and family support, and 4) collaborative training. (See Figure A.1.) These initiatives provided, in large part, a basis for the 4th and 5th year research efforts, which were directed into

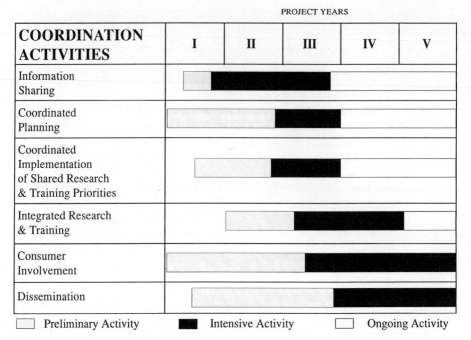

COORDINATION ACTIVITIES	I	II	III	IV	V
Information Sharing					
Coordinated Planning					
Coordinated Implementation of Shared Research & Training Priorities					
Integrated Research & Training					
Consumer Involvement					
Dissemination					

☐ Preliminary Activity   ■ Intensive Activity   ☐ Ongoing Activity

Figure A.3. Timeline for coordination of Consortium activities.

an integrated applied intervention study. This latest research effort has focused on the development of person-centered planning, training, and decision-making for older persons with developmental disabilities, their families, and staff. The effect of this intervention on the individual's participation and perceived life satisfaction in his or her individualized service plan were addressed. Also, during this 2-year period, Consortium researchers conducted a national survey of state case management agencies to determine the factors enabling and/or constraining the implementation of person-centered planning.

First year Consortium activities can be characterized as reflecting a period of cooperation and familiarization. The Consortium process model was developing as it was being implemented. Innovation distinguished the developing research and the training program. Expertise and resources were concentrated on the planned research and training activities. The specific activities of the universities were sufficiently diverse to ensure coverage of the identified priorities, yet sufficiently interrelated to allow short-term coordination and long-term integration. The geographic placement of the universities, although in contiguous mid-western states, was broad enough to provide wide dissemination of results. Specific capabilities bound together the cooperative spirit of these universities. Their past experience in addressing the needs of older adults with

developmental disabilities, their history of regional coordination and collaboration, and their proven ability to network with aging, developmental disabilities, and rehabilitation services, gave strength to the early years of process
development.

Integrated Research Program

In planning the integrated research program for the 4th and 5th years, a thema-
tic issue emerged from research discussions and from consumer input during
the first 3 years of operation. A model for person-centered planning and empowerment that would require training for persons with developmental disabilities and their careproviders was needed. This issue became the focus of the
integrated applied research and training program. The training intervention
study that evolved considered a number of issues. The first issue entailed the
determination of appropriate training content and the development of curricula.
What do older adults with developmental disabilities and their advocates want or
need to know about aging, retirement, and so forth? A study of this nature also
considered training process techniques that could effectively empower older
adults with developmental disabilities so they could develop or express preferences, maximize opportunities, and exercise choices. The person-centered
planning model developed for this investigation was intended to replace more
traditional practices for older adults with developmental disabilities, as well as
for the families and service system staff. The integrated research program addresses the validity of person-centered planning for older adults with developmental disabilities and examines the feasibility of such planning strategies within
the existing services system. To address this second focus, the Consortium
completed a complementary study to determine the policy and systemic factors
affecting the actual implementation of person-centered planning for later-life
transitions. Figure A.4 illustrates the integrated research and training program.

Training and Dissemination Program

The national training and dissemination program makes consortium research
findings and other advances in the field available, accessible, and meaningful to
those in the best position to effect improved community inclusion of older persons with developmental disabilities. A 24-member National Dissemination Advisory Group (NDAG), which has met annually to facilitate realization of this
objective, represents major consumer associations, as well as service and professional organizations in the fields of aging, rehabilitation, mental retardation/
developmental disabilities, and other information dissemination systems. Specific activities of the NDAG have included providing guidance on the newsletter,
clearinghouse, national conferences, and strategies for active consumer involvement. The NDAG also has reviewed training products developed at Consortium
sites. Strategies to accomplish the dissemination function include dissemination
at local, state, regional, and national levels; multiple information networks; mul-

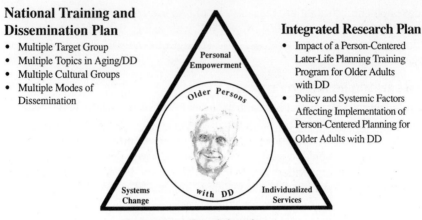

National Training and Dissemination Plan

- Multiple Target Group
- Multiple Topics in Aging/DD
- Multiple Cultural Groups
- Multiple Modes of Dissemination

Integrated Research Plan

- Impact of a Person-Centered Later-Life Planning Training Program for Older Adults with DD
- Policy and Systemic Factors Affecting Implementation of Person-Centered Planning for Older Adults with DD

Consumer Participation

- Consumer Empowerment Strategies
- Consumer Involvement in Planning

Figure A.4. The Consortium's integrated research and training program. (Drawing of "Ken" by Annette Orrock. Reprinted by permission from Stiehl, R., & Schmall, V. [1989]. *Creating a community program for seniors with developmental disabilities.* Salem, Oregon: Garten Foundation, p. 48.)

tiple systems dissemination (the fields of aging, rehabilitation, mental retardation/developmental disabilities); and multiple target dissemination (e.g., to planners, providers, consumers).

Dissemination activities have included the development of population-specific, culturally sensitive educational packages, and the identification of appropriate dissemination strategies. Three educational packages addressing a variety of issues have been produced. Each targets a specific population: older adults with developmental disabilities, their families, and administrators. The educational packages were developed in user-friendly formats and tested to determine the need for additional versions that would ensure cultural diversity in each package. The development process featured the involvement of persons with developmental disabilities, their families, and/or representatives from target populations. Their input in the planning of research activities, review of results, and suggestions for final product marketing have ensured consumer relevance throughout all phases of product development. Similar packages are targeted for legislators. The general public and professional/paraprofessional service providers were part of the 5th year dissemination activities.

Thus, in this 5-year program, the research activities proceeded from a relatively small knowledge base to concrete products that facilitate the application of this knowledge in person-centered planning for older adults with developmental disabilities and their families. These activities have impact at the individual level through personal empowerment of older persons with developmental disabilities and their families. They also reach the provider agency level through a focus on individualized services, and the systemic level through significant changes in policies and procedures for service planning and delivery.

CONSUMER INVOLVEMENT

The Consortium, from its inception, has been strongly influenced by consumer participation in all phases of the research and training program. In the process, innovative strategies have been developed for eliciting the meaningful and active participation of persons with mental retardation/developmental disabilities as key resources in project planning, implementation, and dissemination. Consumer representatives working with the Consortium expressed the view that the term "consumer" implies power and choice, as well as a specific community membership. There was some feeling, however, that the term "consumer" has developed certain negative connotations. Consequently, the consumer members of the Consortium chose not to be called consumers, but rather, *representative participants.*

After a policy was developed by all principal investigators and representative participants, the degree and level of involvement by the latter significantly improved. (See Figure A.2.) The policy supported active involvement by persons with developmental disabilities and their families in all phases and at all levels of the Consortium activities. The policy states that a minimum of 30% of state advisory group memberships be made up of persons with developmental disabilities and/or their families. The policy also states that at least two of the 30% are to be persons with mental retardation. These groups have proved vital to the successful operation of the consortium model.

It became evident, however, that having people with developmental disabilities and their family members on committees or advisory groups did not automatically result in real participation. Their willingness to expose and expand on their thoughts and preferences required nurturing and a different forum than originally envisioned. Direct input from consumers was initially obtained through three formal mechanisms: 1) the state advisory groups, 2) the consortium coordinating council, and 3) a national dissemination advisory group. Both the CCC and the NDAG were discussed previously. Subsequently, other informal and formal networks, such as the Representative Participation Committee, were identified and strengthened to further the outcomes of Consortium research and dissemination activities. (Involvement of consumers in research programs is disucssed in detail in Pederson, Chaikin, Koehler, Campbell, & Arcand chap. 15, this volume.)

State Advisory Groups

Each of the six participating states in the Consortium organized a State Advisory Group during the 1st quarter of the 1st project year. Membership included principal investigators and invited representatives from appropriate state agencies in the fields of aging, developmental disabilities, and rehabilitation, as well as individuals with developmental disabilities and/or their families and advocates. These groups met a minimum of two times annually to advise Consortium researchers about the relevance of their work to ensure its applicability and utility by consumers, providers, and planners. In addition, each state advisory group appointed a representative participant to the CCC to report directions, findings, and activities from their respective state advisory group.

Representative Participation Committee

Individuals with developmental disabilities and their families were unaccustomed to being asked to help plan the direction of future research and training. Initially, they were hesitant to offer an opinion and even more hesitant to criticize an approach or research hypothesis. Representative participants stated that, in the past, raising questions often resulted in services being taken away rather than improved or increased. Therefore, early in the evolution of Consortium process, trust was established, not only between the researcher and the PMC, but also between the representative participants and the researchers. At the beginning of the process, much time was spent building the relationship between the principal investigators and the PMC, with development of the representative participants' relationship with the group being secondary. However, in 1990, the CCC established a separate committee of the Consortium specifically to focus on desires, needs, issues, questions, and concerns of consumers. The Representative Participation Committee was charged with recommending strategies to increase the membership of consumers with mental retardation on state advisory groups and optimize consumer participation during all phases and at all levels of Consortium activities. The role and activities of primary consumers with other disabilities, as well as family members, were also addressed.

It became the policy of the Consortium that, when a standing committee met at a time and place where members of the Representative Participation Committee were already present, then a designated representative of the latter would participate as a member of the former with full rights and privileges. This policy used limited fiscal resources to support the involvement of people with disabilities and their family members. As a result, they became increasingly incorporated into the consortium process.

UNIQUE ASPECTS OF THE RRTC CONSORTIUM

As approaches to research and training are developed and tested by researchers, those that best meet needs and accomplish objectives will be given priority. When researchers select a consortium process model to complete their research, the following considerations are appropriate:

- The consortium process, when utilized in newly emerging fields, such as aging and developmental disabilities, can effectively address the state-of-the-art need through state-of-the-art research and training activities by bringing together special talents that may be present across multiple sites and disciplines. The particular consortium process model used by the RRTC Consortium on Aging and Developmental Disabilities differs from other models where recruitment of large pools of research participants is a paramount issue. The RRTC model evolved specifically to meet a *common* research agenda.
- The process can incorporate what has been learned at one site into the overall endeavors of the Consortium.
- A consortium need not operate with all of its members addressing the same research question. In the RRTC, all Consortium members share their individual research outcomes and serve as consultants to one another to accomplish the overall goal of the Consortium.
- This Consortium allowed the opportunity for involvement of a large number of consumers at all levels and in all phases of its process. The intention was to increase the empirical knowledge base and ensure its utility to consumers, planning bodies, and direct service providers.
- The voluntary endorsement of the consortium process by each of the universities facilitates the evolutionary process of a consortium model.

Question of Feasibility: Challenges and Limitations

While a consortium approach to applied research was selected as the preferred model to operate this RRTC, there remain significant questions about whether such a model is practical. These are questions about research effectiveness and efficiency through the operation of a consortium of seven universities. A considerable amount of the PMC's time has been dedicated to facilitating this process and evaluating progress. Annually, an internal evaluation that examined the research program, the training program, and the overall effectiveness of the consortium process was conducted with the principal investigators and all six state advisory groups. Elements covered in the evaluation were the level of consumer participation and the effectiveness of information transfer within and between consortium sites. Factors identified as challenges and/or limitations by these groups and observations of the PMC are presented below for consideration and guidance as other researchers contemplate a similar model.

Challenges of the Consortium Model

The RRTC Consortium model represents an ongoing process of learning how to operate effectively. The following list of challenges reflects not only activities or outcome challenges, but also attitudinal and philosophical challenges that each member of the Consortium has had to meet in order for the whole to move forward. (See Table A.1.)

Table A.1. Strategies that strengthened the Consortium model

Strategies that built compatibility, commitment, and trust	Strategies that accomplished understanding and stability	Strategies that supported diverse and complementary contributions
Development of a policy committing 30% consumer involvement and participation whenever feasible	Implementation of a schedule of ongoing in-person meetings	Promoting the self-selection of research areas by principal investigators to build upon their personal interests and strengths
Involvement of all members of the Consortium with decision-making and the formation of future plans	Convening of regularly scheduled conference calls covering agenda items requiring approval. This decreased the need for more expensive in-person meetings	Promoting utilization of the clearinghouse and newsletter as resources for information and training
Establishing a statement of shared values	Fostering individual member support of the consortium model	Integrated research program incorporated a paradigm of person-centered planning that strived to integrate research results from the first 3 years, while allowing for the development of targeted instruments
Agreement on population definition, description, and nomenclature	Cultivating a climate of respect and understanding of each member's strengths and style of operation	
Implementation of an Editorial Review Policy	Developing and implementing standardized reporting procedures	Joint presentations of research findings to professional and advocacy organizations by principal investigators, consumers, and project staff
Convening special committees chaired by an elected principal investigator or consumer representative rather than by the Project Management Center	Promoting in-kind contributions from each university to strengthen their commitment to the consortium process	
	Support for the continuation of individual projects through application for additional grants	

- Development of a spectrum of research and training projects that reflected the Consortium's broad mandate as conveyed in the NIDRR priorities
- Coordination of disparate project areas into a training and research program with the potential to move from theory development to practical application within a 5-year plan
- Agreement of all members of the Consortium on an evolutionary goal and process for research and training to increase community inclusion
- Adoption of a consensus or decision-making model with mechanisms to facilitate group cohesion

- Adoption of an evaluation or quality assurance model with specific measurement criteria
- Recognition of the Consortium as an ongoing process or "gate of entry" for this type of research rather than a short-lived endeavor
- Translation of research into meaningful applications for target groups that have the most to gain from its acquired knowledge (e.g., consumers, policy-makers, and service providers)
- Development and implementation of strategies involving primary consumers with mental retardation in the operation of the consortium
- Division of the allocated sum of money among the seven universities that resulted in less than optimal funding to each university

Lessons Learned from the Consortium Model

Lessons learned that influenced the progress of the Consortium fall into three categories: 1) organizational considerations, 2) role clarification, and 3) fiscal considerations. (See Table A.2.) Organizational development experts point out that close examination of the organizational culture of groups on a regular basis determines what is workable, what should be modified, and what should be eliminated (French & Bell, 1973). The Consortium, throughout its operation, did just that. The "doing it" before "learning how to" model was challenging for all members of the Consortium, but the lessons learned from it might assist others as they apply this consortium process model.

Organizational Considerations and Role Clarification The simultaneous discussion of these considerations is required because of their integral relationship to the consortium process. The consortium process strengthened its organizational structure by: 1) establishing a process based upon compatibility, commitment, and trust; 2) confirming ownership of the process by all members through understanding and stability; and 3) measuring the impact of the process through specific outcomes that supported the diverse and complimentary contributions of the membership of the Consortium. The roles of three key groups are significant in analyzing this process: 1) *consumers*, as they strive for a more assertive and recognized role in the organization of the Consortium; 2) *principal investigators*, as they attempt to reconcile the maintenance of their individual integrity within the collective goals of the consortium process; and 3) the *Project Management Center*, as it accomplishes its oversight functions with NIDRR, while at the same time promoting a democratic process within the consortium. Roush and Teitelman (1990) stated that it is not uncommon for networking endeavors to be "initially fraught with conflicts, but that it is this type of exposure that can eventually foster true integration and collaboration" (p. 53). This statement is descriptive of the experiences of the Consortium as it evolved.

Over time, as the processes of consortium operation fell into place, several lessons were learned: 1) size of the Consortium and backgrounds of the principal

Table A.2.   Lessons learned from the consortium model

Organizational considerations	Role clarification	Fiscal considerations
The number of participating sites in a consortium needs to be well thought out. Developing and building a level of trust and respect among and between research sites in a timely and equitable manner proved difficult with seven sites.	Principal investigators, at times, felt that academic freedom was threatened because of guidelines and policies developed to ensure quality control measures for products and materials developed.	The annual level funding from NIDRR, in conjunction with an initial 18% cut on the program's budget, drastically affected the Consortium sites' ability to complete their research activities and continue to meet the cost of living increases.
In striving to keep everyone *equally* informed, much information must be disseminated by the Project Management Center (PMC). Some Consortium sites considered this overwhelming.	Not all Consortium members were supportive of the integrated research model even though it was a part of the program from the inception and was agreed to by individual universities.	Lack of standardized fiscal and research policies and procedures among participating universities caused the fiscal and programmatic subcontracts to be an administrative challenge.
Time must be allowed for members to have ownership in the process rather than to feel imposed upon by the process. Feelings expressed by the consortium members that the PMC was too rigid, even dictatorial at times, encouraged change in the methods of communication and decision-making.	Not all Consortium members were receptive to involving consumers in all levels and all phases of the Consortium activities, even though it was a part of the program from the inception.	Changes in NIDRR Project and Grants Officers hindered liaison with the funding source in understanding programmatic and fiscal challenges, and obtaining approval for changes.
Collective and individual identity of the membership was important. Once the existing resources of the Consortium were centralized and integrated, while at the same time each individual site's hard work was preserved, relationships between and among sites improved.	Some of the researchers were more comfortable with traditional research approaches rather than the integrated consortium model. Time had to be allocated for all points of view and discussion on a regular basis to allow for this transition in thinking to occur.	Collaboration with other federally funded aging/developmental disabilities programs to centralize the information dissemination resource base in the area of aging and developmental disabilities was limited, which increased dissemination costs.
	The relative imbalance of MR/DD over gerontology backgrounds of principal investigators slowed true disciplinary integration and networking.	The limitation of fiscal resources prevented other interested universities within the geographic area to join the consortium effort.

(continued)

Table A.2. (*continued*)

Organizational considerations	Role clarification	Fiscal considerations
The task and time demands associated with planning processes were magnified by the fiscal and programmatic constraints placed on the consortium. This situation had to be monitored closely to ensure the development demands of the integrated research program were reasonable.	Consumer participation was slowed down because of the need to identify appropriate and meaningful roles for consumers with mental retardation in the operation of the Consortium.	Because of level funding, supports for consumer participation were restricted. Needed supports included attendant care, interpreters, travel expenses, and reimbursement for time off work.
Recognition of the collective Consortium efforts as well as the individual site efforts was important. Individual projects raised questions about the validity of an integrated intervention study and expressed anxiety about what might have been a premature termination of promising research activities. This integration process was very time consuming but did create a forum for active consumer input.	Some professionals with a research orientation initially had difficulty relating to the training and dissemination activities, while others wished to be more involved with the research and training activities.	The new federal requirements for fiscal auditing increased the challenges of subcontract with each of the universities by the PMC.
The research designs of the individual sites were of good quality, but each site was not always able to identify the number of research participants needed to complete the study.		

investigators must be considered, 2) shared values and operational policies and procedures must be identified, and 3) the involvement of all members in decision-making and planning is essential. The number of participating sites in a consortium needs to be thought out in advance. Developing and building a level of trust and respect among members at different research sites in a timely and equitable manner proved challenging with seven sites. Seven sites were chosen for this model because of the seven priorities issued by NIDRR. A smaller number of sites might be considered in future endeavors.

As fiscal and programmatic restraints were placed on the Consortium by NIDRR, its ability to meet the internal demands of planning and coordinating the research and training program required creativity and flexibility. There was an imbalance in the backgrounds of the principal investigators, with many more representing the field of developmental disabilities, and only a few representing gerontology. This slowed the process of interdisciplinary integration and networking. The membership agreed to a statement of shared values, operating policies, and procedures, which included strategies about how and when to include people with developmental disabilities and their family members. Such consensus was basic to an ongoing process. The philosophy and implementation of PAR were facilitated once these values, policies, and procedures were adopted. A final, yet highly important, lesson learned was that all members of the Consortium needed to be involved in decision-making and the formation of future plans. Procedures to support this involvement proved vital to the success of the Consortium's operation.

Establishing ownership and clear roles required time and patience. It was essential for members to experience ownership in the process, rather than feel imposed upon by the process. For example, feelings expressed by the Consortium members that the PMC was too rigid, even dictatorial at times, interfered with the process of establishing ownership. Changes in the methods of communication and decision-making used by the group had to be made before the sense of ownership could evolve. The sense of ownership also meant recognition of the collective and individual identity of the membership, which meant reconciliation of individual program identity and autonomy within the larger coordinated research program. This reconciliation process was very time-consuming while, at the same time, it created a forum for active and comfortable representative participant input. Another factor that strengthened the sense of ownership was the promotion of research areas that were self-selected based upon the personal interests and strengths of the principal investigators. This cultivated a climate of respect and understanding of members' strengths and styles of operation. To perpetuate this climate, whenever special committees were convened, they were chaired by an elected principal investigator or representative participant rather than by the PMC. The management center, however, provided staff support to all committees.

Planned evolution toward greater integration of the research program was easy to accept in theory early in the process. However, it became more difficult to implement in practice because it meant the sacrifice of individual project resources. Compromises had to be made, both fiscally and programmatically. Trust and respect had to be well-established for this transition to occur. Also, as the principal investigators moved from the more familiar roles of project designers and implementors to a less familiar role of working with consumers in the process, understanding, respect, and trust had to be firmly established. The true challenge, however, was involvement of representative participants with mental retardation and developmental disabilities. The sense of ownership of the process by this group grew more slowly than for other members, but it did occur. Last, the PMC had to learn to trust and believe in the democratic process, while at the same time meeting the oversight responsibilities as the primary fiscal agent. The balance of decision-making and accountability among the PMC, principal investigators, and representative participants had to be resolved before functional partnerships could be realized.

Outcomes of the process were influenced by the fact that some of the researchers were more comfortable with traditional approaches rather than the integrated consortium model. Time had to be allocated for expression of all points of view and discussion on a regular basis in order to allow for a transition in thinking to occur. Another outcome was that some of the research principal investigators initially had difficulty relating to training and dissemination activities required because NIDRR preferred to be more involved with the research activities. The balancing of interests and roles among the membership supported a diverse and complementary outcome representative of the entire group.

Fiscal Considerations The annual funding for the Consortium drastically affected its ability to complete original research activities and objectives. Also, because of level funding, supports for representative participants were restricted. Supports affected were: attendant care, interpreters, travel expenses, and reimbursement for time off work. This limitation necessitated the leveraging of resources which, while positive in principle, in practical application tended to jeopardize the individual site. The pursuit of supplemental grants to support ongoing research and training needs was necessary but compromised with the day-to-day implementation of the research and training program.

The diverse research priorities identified by NIDRR absorbed most of the available fiscal resources. This meant that other needs, such as rehabilitation training of students and consumer involvement, were not supported at the level needed to meet intended goals adequately. The limitations in fiscal resources also prevented other interested universities within the geographic area from joining the Consortium effort. A new requirement for fiscal auditing increased the challenge of a subcontractual arrangement between the PMC and each of the universities by adding an additional cost. Another fiscal challenge was the lack of standardized fiscal and research policies and procedures among the participating universities. Promoting in-kind contributions from each university to strengthen their commitment to the Consortium was important. This helped solidify the key component of ownership. Finally, collaboration with other federally funded initiatives in aging and developmental disabilities would have been useful in centralizing the information dissemination base in the area of aging and developmental disabilities. Unfortunately, this did not occur as extensively as hoped.

A review of the literature on cooperative agreements and other networking strategies, such as consortia, reveals that these arrangements historically are varied and diverse. However, several basic factors necessary to ensure success are cited, the first and most fundamental being that *each member's participation be voluntary* (Roush & Teitelman, 1990). Second, the *goal of the collaboration must be common to all participating groups* (Grupe, 1971). Third, through their collaboration, *the universities should expect to realize mutual gain and benefit* (Blyler, Brown, Drasnin, & Zalon, 1987). These principles contributed to the successful operation of this RRTC Consortium process model in its policy development, organizational development, and its research and training program development.

SUMMARY

As an increasing number of persons with developmental disabilities grow old, it is critical to maintain a specific RRTC on Aging and Developmental Disabilities that can advance the knowledge base and translate research into practical applications that improve quality of life. The RRTC Consortium on Aging and Developmental Disabilities provides one example of a process to meet the research and training challenges for these individuals. The Consortium has been dedicated to minimizing duplication and maximizing scarce resources in an organized and meaningful manner. Although the consortium process can be fraught with challenges, it has been found by many to be a profoundly worthwhile endeavor (Roush & Teitelman, 1990).

The consortium process model described here (see Tables A.1 and A.2) has emerged in response to a need to create a Rehabilitation Research and Training Center addressing the community inclusion of older adults with mental retardation/developmental disabilities. The resources and expertise needed to meet this goal were not available at any one university, so a consortium of universities was formed. Specific lessons learned in this endeavor and their relationship to organizational development principles were ever present in the experience of developing this RRTC Consortium of seven universities.

In addition to its achievements in research and training, this cooperative endeavor also has emphasized a participatory action approach involving consumer representatives at every level and every stage of development. In its own way, the RRTC Consortium stands as a unique prototype that others may find effective in the development of research and training.

REFERENCES

Blyler, J., Brown, J., Drasnis, S., & Zalon, M. (1987). An educator's consortium. *Nursing Outlook, 35*(1), 38.
French, W.L., & Bell, C.H. (1973). *Organizational development: Behavioral science interventions for organization improvement.* Englewood Cliffs, NJ: Prentice-Hall.

Grupe, F. (1971). Founding consortia: Idea and reality. *Journal of Higher Education, 42,* 747–762.

Jacobson, J.W., Sutton, M.S., & Janicki, M.P. (1985). Demography and characteristics of aging and aged mentally retarded persons. In M.P. Janicki & H.M. Wisniewski, (Eds.), *Aging and developmental disabilities: Issues and approaches* (pp. 115–142). Baltimore: Paul H. Brookes Publishing Co.

Judson, A.S. (1990). *Making strategy happen: Transforming plans into reality.* Cambridge, MA: Basil Blackwell, Inc.

Lottman, T. (1992). *Policies and procedures manual.* Cincinnati: University of Cincinnati, Rehabilitation Research and Training Center Consortium on Aging and Developmental Disabilities.

Roush, R.E., & Teitelman, J.L. (1990). The necessity of networking by geriatric education centers: Rationale, methods, and recommendations. *Gerontology and Gerontology Education, 10*(4), 49–61.

Stiehl, R., & Schmall, V. (1989). *Creating a community program for seniors with developmental disabilities.* Salem, Oregon: Garten Foundation.

INDEX

Page numbers followed by an "f" or a "t" indicate figures or tables, respectively.